The Old Farmer's Almanac

CALCULATED ON A NEW AND IMPROVED PLAN FOR THE YEAR OF OUR LORD

2008

BEING LEAP YEAR AND (UNTIL JULY 4) 232ND YEAR OF AMERICAN INDEPENDENCE

Fitted for Boston and the New England states, with special corrections and calculations to answer for all the United States.

Containing, besides the large number of Astronomical Calculations and the Farmer's Calendar for every month in the year, a variety of

NEW, USEFUL, & ENTERTAINING MATTER.

Established in 1792 by Robert B. Thomas

Time is the most valuable thing a man can spend.

–Theophrastus, Greek philosopher (c. 372–c. 287 B.C.)

Cover T.M. registered in U.S. Patent Office

Copyright © 2007 by Yankee Publishing Incorporated
ISSN 0078-4516

Library of Congress
Card No. 56-29681

Original wood engraving by Randy Miller

THE OLD FARMER'S ALMANAC • DUBLIN, NH 03444 • 603-563-8111 • ALMANAC.COM

Contents

THE OLD FARMER'S ALMANAC • 2008

178

90

46

214

204

tastes&trends 2008

The fads, fashions, and farsighted ideas that define our life and times.

by Stacey Kusterbeck

Around the House

HOMES ARE GETTING GREENER

Today's home owners are serious about cutting energy costs and avoiding the health risks of chemicals used in building products. According to a survey taken by the American Institute of Architects, 90% of those surveyed would pay $5,000 more for an energy-efficient house that protects Earth. "We will see a dramatic and rapid transition to buildings that use a lot less energy and are healthier for their occupants," says Alex Wilson of Brattleboro, Vermont–based Building Green.

STYLE MAKERS

Indoors, we'll see:

- home elevators as status symbols
- industrial-looking concrete counters
- stylish men's urinals that prevent odors and splashing and flush automatically
  - cork, recycled glass, and bamboo floors
    - "serviced" condominiums with hotel-style amenities—concierges, maids, and room service from gourmet restaurants
- electric bills that report power usage by device

Outdoors, we'll see:

- the "quarry" look in backyards, with natural rock and concrete-stamped ground that resembles stone and audio emanating from rock-shaped speakers. "Full-size trees and bushy plants will make people think that they're in an outdoor prehistoric oasis, but with modern conveniences," says R. Brandon Johnson, host of HGTV's *Get Out, Way Out.*
  - camp-style fire pits, with outdoor plasma TV screens
  - tumbled and distressed cobblestones that say "aged"

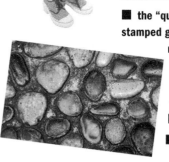

(continued)

■ outdoor air-conditioning units that look like almost-six-foot-tall table lamps without shades and are able to lower temperatures by 15°F in a 250-square-foot area.

NOT JUST SMART

Future homes will earn their keep. "The home of the future won't just sit there. It will be a hardworking place," says *Fortune* senior editor Cait Murphy. We'll see:

■ toilet seats that measure body fat, take body temperature, and analyze urine samples

■ homes that produce their own energy and treat their own waste

■ windows that change size and walls between patios and living rooms that open or close depending on humidity, sunlight, and rain

Responsive homes, built from many interconnected elements, will . . .

■ change shape and still be structurally sound

■ shrink in winter to reduce heating costs

■ shake snow off the roof

■ regulate heat and airflow with adjustable roofs and windows

How the Garden Grows

HARVEST THAT H₂O!

Cost-conscious gardeners are looking to use less water, and experts say that the best way to conserve is cost-free "water harvesting." "Contour the ground so that the water that falls on the roofline gets directed to plants instead of running off the property," says Scott Millard, owner of Ironwood Press, a Tucson, Arizona–based publisher of gardening books.

TREE-SAVING SIDEWALKS

To save trees, more than 60 U.S. cities have installed rubber sidewalks made from recycled tires. The rubber doesn't constrict tree roots like concrete slabs do, so root systems don't pull up and crack sidewalks. The rubber sidewalks last twice as long as concrete and also are easier on human joints.

GRASS, BE GONE

More than 70 Canadian municipalities have passed laws restricting pesticides used purely for cosmetic purposes—e.g., on lawns.

In drought-stricken southern Nevada, local water authorities are paying home owners to remove

PEOPLE ARE TALKING ABOUT . . .

■ **Wollemi pine, an endangered tree native to Australia** that dates to the dinosaur age. Fewer than 100 full-grown trees remain Down Under, but seedlings are selling like hotcakes at about $99 each. The hardy Wollemis thrive in many climates and stand 80-plus feet tall when mature, with up to 100 trunks.

–Cambridge 2000

lawns, and some are switching to artificial grass. This means no more mowing, but "you must sweep or vacuum the surface to remove debris," says Andrew McNitt, a turf specialist at Pennsylvania State University.

GROWING INTERESTS

■ **full-grown plants,** for instant impact. "Buyers today are looking to decorate their patios—now!" says Jimmy Turner, director of horticultural research for the Dallas Arboretum.

■ **motorized log splitters** that can be wheeled to a stack of wood

■ **a greater variety of containers** that are lightweight, weather-resistant, and self-watering

■ **decorative containers:** "It's just not your mom's old terra-cotta pots anymore. You can get containers now in all kinds of materials and colors, and even make your own," says Turner.

■ **vegetables anywhere:** in containers, mixed into annual beds or perennial borders, and in unexpected colors—e.g., orange eggplant and purple carrots

■ **ethnic-recipe herbs,** such as cilantro and Thai basil

■ **new varieties of wildflowers,** such as black-eyed Susan and echinacea

■ **tropical plants with knockout foliage and flowers—especially bananas, cannas, tropical hibiscus, ginger, and passionflowers.** "More gardeners want to grow a plant they have seen while traveling to warmer locations," says Susan Jellinek, horticulturist at Thompson & Morgan Seedsmen.

Signs of the Times

NORTHERN EXPOSURE

Older folks in a few tiny towns in Saskatchewan are taking on a surprising new role—as nude calendar pinups. Some appear knitting, skiing, and swimming, but others pose in political protest. Residents of Leader bared nearly all to call attention to a run-down highway.

LOST PLANETS

Shelburne, Massachusetts–based glassblower Josh Simpson has been hiding thousands of golf ball–size glass globes, or planets, around the world since 2000. Some will likely lie undetected for centuries, but others are hidden in plain sight. Some locations: Mexico's Chichén Itzá ruins, the New York Stock Exchange, and a train trestle in Bloomington, Indiana. "These are gifts for someone separated from me by distance, origin, culture, or by the biggest thing—a huge gulf in time," he says. (To hide one, go to www.megaplanet.com).

PEOPLE ARE TALKING ABOUT . . .

- ■ "outing" neighbors, coworkers, and strangers on Web sites, for transgressions such as parking outside the lines, yakking loudly on cell phones, and failing to clean up after their dogs

- ■ the "Virtual Family Dinner" system that will allow people in far-flung locations to eat together, using cameras, microphones, and speakers to see and hear one another

The Way We Look

FREE TO BE

Watch for some of fashion's "sacred cows" to moo-ve over. "There are no more rigid rules," says Leatrice Eiseman, executive director of the Pantone Color Institute. Some of her creative combos . . .

- ■ **Red and pink:** "At one time you never combined those two, but pink is an under-

- garments that heat our extremities, monitor blood pressure, power laptops, and convert sunlight into electricity
- GPS-equipped attire
- clothing with built-in insect repellents
- "welded" fabrics with no visible seams

tone of red, so it's just logical." Aim for a similar tone: If your red is a "blue" red, then pair with a pink in the same color family.

■ **Brown and black:** "This was another no-no. But brown, which can be anything from camel to tan to chocolate, can be quite beautiful when put against black," she says.

■ **Stripes and polka dots.** Think patchwork quilt: "The key is color—and the same holds true with clothing." A subtly striped suit, solid shirt, and dotted tie will work for men, but there must be a color connection.

■ **Silver and gold.** Wear an item with both metals. "This gives you the ability to wear any other jewelry."

WOMEN WANT . . .

■ **fashions impacted by world news.** "Clothing and accessories are becoming more in tune to the environment and politics, both in color palette and utility," says Sasha Iglehart, *Glamour*'s deputy fashion director. Look for biodegradable clothing and "street warrior" looks with tough, practical fabrics like khaki and denim.

■ **new *au naturel:*** socks and scarves made from corn-based yarn and clothing made of plant sugars, bamboo, and crab shells.

■ **handbags as large as luggage**

■ **antitheft handbags, to stop pickpockets.** A scanner, similar to a door's security entry system, opens the bag's lock.

■ **exaggerated looks:** big sleeves, wide pants, and overwhelming accessories

MEN ARE MOVING TOWARD . . .

■ **soft, plush coats made from angora, fur, and cashmere.** "This creates a personal retreat from the stress-filled world," says Stephen Watson, fashion director for *Men's Vogue.*

■ **"childlike" colors:** pale yellow, baby blue, and pink. "These colors subconsciously calm the mind," says Watson.

(continued)

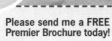

"'Acceptable' colors in menswear will be increasing in number, pastels not being so out of the ordinary."

- **uncomplicated garments:** no zippers, buttons, or laces
- **custom-made bags and shoes**
- **dress clothes that double as activewear:** suits made from stretchy fabrics, sports jackets with collars that can be flipped up while hiking or biking, and dress shoes with a sneaker tread

PEOPLE ARE TALKING ABOUT . . .

- dogs with minimal grooming needs
- mineral oil rubs, facials, and manicures for pot-bellied pigs; sorry, no mud packs.

PUPPY LOVE

Instead of bouquets, brides are carrying pup-

pies or kittens, and canines are serving as ring bearers, suitably attired: Tiaras, top hats, and tuxedos are available in formalwear shops for four-footed friends.

Pet-iculars

TINY DOGGIES GET THEIR DUE

Totable pets are all the rage. The big news from the American Kennel Club's top ten breed list is very little: The Yorkshire terrier jumped to number two, overtaking golden retrievers (the Labrador retriever is still number one). Other small (less-than-20-pound) winners: Yorkie, beagle, dachshund, and miniature schnauzer.

PETS (AND OWNERS), BEHAVE!

Owners of pampered pooches have a growing problem: Some of these dogs are spoiled rotten. "Folks who travel with their pets know that, in order to be welcome in hotels and cafes, Fido had better have some manners," says Lisa Peterson, American Kennel Club spokesperson. The best ways to teach your pet to behave: early socialization and obedience training.

On the Farm

FUTURE FARMERS

Over 95% of young farmers and ranchers surveyed hope that their children will

ESSIAC®

From Rene M. Caisse, RN
Original Herbal Formula
Trusted Worldwide Since 1922

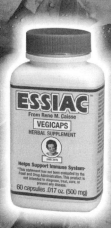

Powder Formula   Extract Formula   Vegicap Formula

Helps Support Immune System*

* THIS STATEMENT HAS NOT BEEN EVALUATED BY THE FOOD AND DRUG ADMINISTRATION. THIS PRODUCT IS NOT INTENDED TO DIAGNOSE, TREAT, CURE, OR PREVENT ANY DISEASE.

- Premium Quality Herbs
- c G.M.P. compliance
- Used in Canada and exported worldwide

Herbal Supplement

BEWARE OF COUNTERFEITS

Essiac® Canada International
P.O. Box 23155, Ottawa, Ont., Canada K2A 4E2
Tel.: (613) 729-9111 • Fax: (613) 729-9555
e-mail: maloney@essiac-canada.com

follow in their footsteps. "Producers are optimistic about the future of agriculture; otherwise, they wouldn't see a place for their children in farming and ranching," says the American Farm Bureau Federation's Bob Stallman.

FUTURE FARMS

A $5 million "seed vault" will open soon on Norway's Spitsbergen island. Its precious contents—millions of seeds—offer backup protection for the world's crop diversity. Because the "bank" is located north of the Arctic Circle in permafrost, the seeds won't be destroyed if the power goes out. Even considering global warming, computer models indicate that Spitsbergen will continue to be one of the coldest places on Earth.

GROWING BUSINESSES

A grassroots culinary effort is under way at a Grange in Dartmouth, Massachusetts. There, growers use commercial ovens and cookware to prepare their produce to sell. "A farmer could sell tomatoes for $1 a pound, but turning the tomatoes into a $5 jar of salsa is what today's farmers need to do to sustain their farms," says kitchen manager Becky Turner.

A NATION OF NEIGHBORS

More farmers are using online "farm forums" to compare notes. The two hottest topics: machinery and crop prices. Fifty-one percent of U.S. farms now have Internet access, according to the U.S. Department of Agriculture. "The information age has finally arrived in the countryside," says Mack Strickland, an agriculture professor at Purdue University.

(c o n t i n u e d)

PEOPLE ARE TALKING ABOUT . . .

- a new cattle-feed supplement that boosts the percentage of unsaturated fatty acids in cow's milk, giving us healthier whole milk, tastier cheese, and more spreadable butter

- Chinese "space potatoes": Bred from seeds that mutated while aboard a spacecraft, they're purple, slightly sweet, and said to be hearty and nutritious.

- manure from hog farms being converted into electricity

LOCATION = LIFE SPAN

Location plays a big role in longevity, according to a study from the Harvard University School of Public Health. Shared ancestry, dietary customs, and local industry are among the positive factors. At opposite ends in the life-expectancy spectrum would be an Asian woman living in Bergen County, New Jersey (91 years) and a Native American man in South Dakota (58 years).

BIOFUELS BOOST

With ethanol production expected to reach 12 billion gallons in 2008, the demand for corn will increase to 5 billion bushels per year. The rising prices of corn and soybeans are a boon to farmers and rural towns: The construction and plant management fields are sparking new job growth. Midwestern "Corn Belt" towns have been the first to benefit, but the use of cellulose ethanol (made from leafy plant material) may involve others. "This could open it up to other crops, and potentially, other geographies," says Joe Cornely, Ohio Farm Bureau spokesperson.

The Picture of Health

WALK FOR A BIGGER BRAIN

A stroll can increase the size of your brain, says a new study. Researchers compared the brain size of 60 people before and after six months of walking 45 minutes a day, three times a week. Regardless of age, "a relatively modest amount of exercise can produce increases in brain efficiency and brain volume as well as improvements in memory, attention, and decision making," says study author Arthur Kramer, a professor at the University of Illinois.

BETTER BEDSIDE MANNER?

Doctors may be nicer in the future, thanks to a first-of-its-kind medical course to explore the neurobiology of empathy, or how our bodies respond to compassion. "There is a huge concern about how many patients who expect compassionate exchanges are disappointed," says Helen Riess, M.D., assistant clinical professor of psychiatry at Harvard Medical School, where the course is offered.

(continued)

60 LBS OF TOMATOES FROM ONE TREE PLANT

Huge Yields Summer Through Fall

- **No Trimming**
- **No Pruning**
- **No Caging**

Constantly Harvesting All Season Treat It Like Any Fruit Tree!

LESS THAN 1¢ FOR ONE LARGE TOMATO!

Imagine! Now you can have large, red, juicy tomatoes up to 60 pounds each year. So why settle for a few short weeks of tomatoes every year? Not to mention the back-breaking time it takes to plant them. Our tomato harvesting tree yields garden fresh succulent tomatoes so abundant they seem to grow as quickly as you pick them. There's plenty of these delicious, plump, tomatoes to go around for family and friends. Frankly, it's the best-tasting tomato you will ever eat. It looks like a fruit tree and bears bushel after bushel of mouth watering flavor - up to 7 months or simply grow year round indoors and enjoy its sheer beauty. Grows to a full 8 ft. high or you can simply trim this exotic, beautiful tree to any size. Best of all, there is no pruning, no caging, no trimming and no special care. We ship well-rooted plants, not seeds.

Juicy & Delicious Zooms To 8 ft. Tall

You save on your grocery bills while enjoying these delectable tomatoes. They're simply fabulous in your salads, sandwiches, and spaghetti sauce. Even eating these yummy tomatoes by themselves is a real treat. There's nothing like the taste of fresh, home-grown tomatoes. These are huge tomatoes, some up to 2 lbs. All plants are guaranteed to arrive in perfect condition. So simply step back and watch your tree quickly zoom to the full height desired and supply you with yummy garden fresh tomatoes. Ideal for yard, garden, or patio. Shipped at proper planting time.

HARVEST FARMS, INC., Dept. HF97
P.O. Box 2254, Abingdon, VA 24212
30 Day Money Back Guarantee

❏ One Tomato Tree only $5.99
    plus $2.00 shipping and handling
❏ Two Tomato Trees only $10.99
    plus $3.00 shipping and handling
❏ Three Tomato Trees only $14.99
    plus $4.00 shipping and handling

Name _____

Address _____

City _____ State ____ Zip _____

2008   THE OLD FARMER'S ALMANAC   17

- home sellers offering buyers a 24-hour sleepover "test drive" before they commit

- the "simplicity" movement: "More Fun, Less Stuff" and "More of What Matters"

A PENNY SAVED . . . Youngsters are being taught the value of a dollar with tools ranging from piggy banks to video games. "We pass values of religion, love of country, and family to our children. We need to do the same with money values," says Jason Alderman, director of Practical Money Skills for Life.

Money Matters

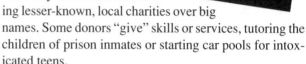

GIVING TIME, NOT MONEY

In ten years, the number of U.S. nonprofits is up 75%, to over 1 million (half are tiny, with budgets under $25,000)—evidence that many Americans are choosing lesser-known, local charities over big names. Some donors "give" skills or services, tutoring the children of prison inmates or starting car pools for intoxicated teens.

MORE DEBT THAN EVER

Canadian families now have an average net worth of $148,350, up 23% from 1999, but their total debt grew almost 38% in the same period, to $44,500 per family. "There has been a huge watershed shift from earlier attitudes that debt is a social stigma. For this generation, credit is seen as an entitlement," says Robert Manning, Ph.D., a consumer finance expert and author of *Credit Card Nation.* Expect to see "serial bankruptcies," with people in their 20s, 30s, and 40s going broke.

Hot Collectibles

WHERE INTEREST IS RISING

- early-20th-century teddy bears that were made in the U.S.A.

- 1970s furniture: simple, modern-looking sofas, coffee tables, and lamps

- memorabilia from ocean liners of the 1890s to 1950s: boarding cards, menus, flatware, ashtrays, lighters, and ice buckets

- automobile maps bought at gas stations during the 1930s and '40s

- department store displays, vintage advertising signs, and original packaging

- stamps, coins, and comic books in mint condition

(continued)

A MILITARY SURGE

Knickknacks, sweetheart pins, and correspondence from American GIs during World War II are hot. Daphne, Alabama–based arms and militaria expert Christopher Mitchell advises:

- Start looking close to home. There may be old medals, American dress uniforms, or even German helmets or daggers, in a relative's attic, hope chest, or basement.

- Buy from reputable dealers. "They began faking German stuff the day the war ended," Mitchell says.

- Buy the very best you can afford. Instead of buying three belts for $15 each, buy one in wonderful condition for $45.

YOU CAN'T GIVE THIS AWAY

- **Beanie Babies:** "Prices have gone down to next to zero," says Philip Weiss, an Oceanside, New York–based appraiser.

- **Victorian furniture:** The lace-and-doilies look is past passé for all but the most practical purposes.

- **Ohio art pottery and Depression-era glass:** Reproductions and a glut of supply on the Web melted this market.

- **limited-edition items:** "People want something unique," says Tim Luke, a Stuart, Florida–based appraiser.

Science & Technology

TRAFFIC BUSTERS

MIT's Smart Cities team has a solution for traffic congestion: Small, electrically charged cars with folding chassis. The wheels turn 360 degrees—ideal for urban streets. Likely cities to get them first: New York, San Francisco, Chicago, and Boston.

OUT OF THIS WORLD

A meteorite that crashed in northwest Canada may bear evidence of extraterrestrial life. It contains tiny bubbles that may have held the universe's earliest life forms. "Where they come from, we don't know," says cosmic minerologist Michael Zolensky, "but they're not from around here."

TOO HOT FOR COMFORT

Global temperatures will increase between 3.2° and 7.1°F in this century, says a report from the Intergovernmental Panel on Climate Change. Meanwhile, English businessman Sir Richard Branson is sponsoring the Virgin Earth Challenge: The first person who figures out how to remove billions of tons of greenhouse gases from the atmosphere might win a $25 million prize. Climate scientists and environmentalists will evaluate submissions.

(continued)

A Most Unusual Gift of Love

THE POEM READS:

"Across the years I will walk with you—
in deep, green forests; on shores of sand:
and when our time on earth is through,
in heaven, too, you will have my hand."

Dear Reader,

The drawing you see above is called *The Promise*. It is completely composed of dots of ink. After writing the poem, I worked with a quill pen and placed thousands of these dots, one at a time, to create this gift in honor of my youngest brother and his wife.

Now, I have decided to offer *The Promise* to those who share and value its sentiment. Each litho is numbered and signed by hand and precisely captures the detail of the drawing. As a wedding, anniversary or Christmas gift or simply as a standard for your own home, I believe you will find it most appropriate.

Measuring 14" by 16", it is available either fully framed in a subtle copper tone with hand-cut mats of pewter and rust at $110, or in the mats alone at $95. Please add $14.50 for insured shipping and packaging. Your satisfaction is completely guaranteed.

My best wishes are with you.

The Art of Robert Sexton, 491 Greenwich St. (at Grant), San Francisco, CA 94133

MASTERCARD and VISA orders welcome. Please send card name, card number, address and expiration date, or phone (415) 989-1630 between noon-8 P.M. EST. Checks are also accepted. *Please allow 3 weeks for delivery.*

The Promise is featured with many other recent works in my book, *Journeys of the Human Heart.*
It, too, is available from the address above at $12.95 per copy postpaid. Please visit my Web site at

www.robertsexton.com

LUNAR LIVING

Astronauts will be living on the Moon within 20 years. "The initial stays will last up to seven days. Later, after an outpost is built, astronauts will stay for months," says NASA spokesperson Michael Braukus. Entrepreneurs aren't wasting any time: One British couple claims to have made £4 million (about $7.8 million) selling land on the Moon.

PEOPLE ARE TALKING ABOUT . . .

■ one-woman companies, growing at twice the rate of the national average. One market-savvy mom's idea: pacifiers that snap shut when tossed to the ground.

■ "workplace negativity" (aka gossip): It costs companies $3 billion a year, says the U.S. Department of Labor.

Work and Play Time

RUDENESS OUT, KINDNESS IN

Bossy, backstabbing behavior is out. My-way-or-the-highway leaders will be replaced by bosses who give smiles, compliments, and, occasionally, homemade cookies. "The business world is ready for a 'nice' makeover," says Linda Kaplan Thaler, coauthor of *The Power of Nice*.

YOU CAN IN THE YUKON

More than 100 Yukoners make their living in the music business, generating $8.3 million annually, says a report from Music Yukon, an organization that offers business training for musicians. It's surprising, given the "limited audiences, infrastructure, and relative isolation," says Laurel Parry, who handles arts funding for the territory. She credits a "do-it-yourself" mentality, good public funding, and the inspiration of nature.

INFORMATION OVERLOAD

According to a forecast put together for the media industry, in 2007, the average American spent . . .

■ poker, as an alternative to video games for socializing teens: Educators say that it also helps with math skills.

■ 1,555 hours watching television

■ 974 hours listening to the radio

■ 195 hours using the Internet

■ 175 hours reading daily newspapers

■ 122 hours reading magazines

■ 106 hours reading books

■ 86 hours playing video games

These activities take place just about anywhere, and

New England style

*C*ountry Carpenters introduces Early New England Homes.

Our 1750s style cape home building system boasts beautiful timbered ceilings, a center chimney, wide board floors and many custom, handmade features. This home reflects all the charm of early New England life with the convenience and efficiency of a new home. Our model is open Monday-Friday, 8-4:30 and Saturdays, 9-3.

Come see how the timeless traditions of an Early New England Home can improve your lifestyle today!

Early New England HOMES™
by country carpenters, inc.

26 West Street (Route 85) Bolton, CT 860.643.1148
www.EarlyNewEnglandHomes.com

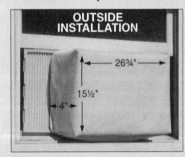
often one or more are undertaken simultaneously.

COMING SOON:

▨ TVs controlled with gestures and voice commands

▨ phones hidden in earrings or worn as tiny patches near the ear, or used as train tickets or front door keys

ALREADY HERE:

▨ "dry-land" dogsled racing on grass, due to unreliable snow cover

▨ videographers who document a child's year for well-to-do families

▨ people and companies (even IBM) "living" in a virtual, online world, such as at www.secondlife.com

GET OUT!

Regional campaigns are under way in 22 cities, and the National Wildlife Federation has launched a "Green Hour" program to get kids out-of-doors for at least one hour a day. Their ideas: a nature walk, putting up a bird feeder, going camping, or bug hunting. ▢▢

Stacey Kusterbeck, a trendy and frequent contributor to *The Old Farmer's Almanac,* writes about popular culture from her home in New York State.

SO WHAT ELSE IS NEW?
For more statistics, data, and colorful details about our life and times, go to
Almanac.com/extras.

Your bed should **relieve** your pain, not add to it

The DeluxeBed
by Tempur-Pedic™

Imagine a place of healing where the pain that comes along with how we live just goes away. And what if you could go there tonight... *and every night.*

At Tempur-Pedic,® *we believe* your bed should relieve your pain, not add to it.

Other beds, made of *metal springs,* create hundreds of pressure points that *push against your body* all night. But, our unique Swedish TEMPUR® material is designed to take the pressure away.

We invite you to learn more about our science... and experience our soul.

✚ **TEMPUR**-PEDIC

welcome to bed™

Call for your Night-time Renewal Kit with FREE In-Home Tryout Certificate

888-702-8557

Or visit us at **www.tempurpedic.com**

Home & Garden Resource

Gardening

Little Giants

I t is easy to grow plenty of produce

in a pint-size garden or proper container by making efficient use of every inch. Intensive gardening techniques have been used for centuries by many cultures to compensate for limitations of climate, water, labor, and arable land. Today, tiny vegetable plots are common, and we can employ those same practical ideas to get the most from a small space. Combine these concepts with petite plants, and your harvest promises to be bountiful.

1. RAISE YOUR BEDS

Forget about growing plants in single file in long, parallel rows separated by broad paths. You can grow up to 10 times the amount of produce in the same space by raising your beds. Raised beds allow you to concentrate your energy in a small area—working, watering, weeding, and fertilizing as economically as possible. Also, by utilizing season-extending devices such as cold frames, cloches, row covers, and plastic tunnels, you can make the most of the entire growing season.

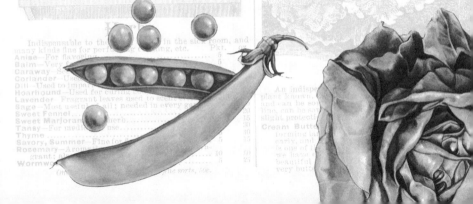

-W. Atlee Burpee & Co.

'Salad Bush' cucumber

Time- and space-

saving ways to reap

heaps from a patch

of soil or a pot.

by Robin Sweetser

2. KEEP SEEDLINGS COMING

Succession planting keeps the garden in continual production. Whenever one crop is harvested, have seedlings ready to transplant in its place. For best results, use quick-maturing varieties to fit several crops into one season and spread out the harvest.

3. PUT PLANTS CLOSE TOGETHER

"Intercropping" means growing two or more crops together to save space. Plants should be placed close enough so that their leaves will touch, shading the ground between them when they are fully mature. This will keep weeds down and conserve moisture, eliminating the need to mulch and weed. As the plants begin to crowd out their neighbors, harvest the early-maturing ones, leaving room for the others to develop. For example, pair lettuce with longer-season vegetables such as broccoli, peppers, or tomatoes.

4. PLANT COMPANIONS, NOT COMPETITORS

Some intercropping partners thrive if their roots occupy a different depth of soil. Pairing shallow-rooted vegetables, such as bush beans, with deeply rooted beets makes good use of space without creating root competition. Similarly, planting heavy feeders such as cabbage or cucumbers with light-feeding carrots or beans reduces the competition for soil nutrients. The best intercropping partners are

SUNSHINE SECRETS

Most vegetables need a minimum of 6 hours of sunlight a day. These are exceptions:

Leafy greens (lettuce and spinach) grow well in part shade.

Beets, garlic, peas, and radishes can get by on 4 hours of sun a day.

Corn, eggplant, peppers, and tomatoes require 8 hours of sun per day to bear the most fruit.

29

companion plants that make different demands while complementing each other.

5. GROW UP

▨ Lay out your garden plot with the fence, trellis, or wall at the north side. By planting the tallest plants there, you will avoid shading the smaller ones. Vining plants, if left to sprawl, take up valuable space in a small garden, so help them grow up. Cucumbers will eagerly climb a nylon net fence, with the subsequent bonus result that the dangling fruits grow straighter and are easier to pick. Tomatoes produce more fruit and ripen earlier if kept off the ground on a trellis or in a wire cage. Peas and pole beans naturally reach for the sky and will cover a wire fence or twine around a tripod of poles. Some heavier plants, such as cantaloupes, melons, and winter squashes, may need help in climbing, so tie their vines to the structure to get them going in the right direction. Support the fruit with slings to keep them from tearing off the vine too soon.

Plot It Out

Good soil, adequate sunshine, and sufficient drainage are the only requirements for a successful vegetable garden. Every garden—and every gardener—is different. Create a garden tailored to your space and needs.

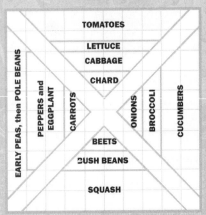

TOMATOES
LETTUCE
CABBAGE
CHARD
EARLY PEAS, then POLE BEANS
PEPPERS and EGGPLANT
CARROTS
ONIONS
BROCCOLI
CUCUMBERS
BEETS
BUSH BEANS
SQUASH

A 100-square-foot garden (10x10 feet) can easily yield a wide variety of veggies. Bisecting it with two narrow paths forms four beds that are easy to reach into and tend. (One square = one square foot.)

SITTING PRETTY (COMFORTABLY)

▨ **If you use wood, large stones, or cement or cinder blocks to enclose your raised beds, create a convenient seat to work from by placing a board across the path between the beds.**

continued

MAINTAIN YOUR COUNTRY DRIVEWAY WITH THE DR® POWER GRADER!

DR® PROFESSIONAL POWER FOR HOMEOWNERS

If you have a country driveway or private road that's difficult and/or expensive to maintain, here's what makes the DR® POWER GRADER the fastest, easiest, and simply the best do-it-yourself road-grooming solution ever —

- **PATENTED DESIGN** enables you to loosen and regrade enormous amounts of materials with minimal power. Can easily be pulled by your riding mower, ATV, or tractor!

- **POWERED ACTUATOR ▶** allows you to raise and lower the grader blade from your towing vehicle, to control how deeply you remove and regrade material.

You have precise control over the grading action with the touch of a button!

- **CARBIDE SCARIFYING TEETH ▶** loosen the hardest composite surfaces, so these materials can easily be redistributed and graded smooth.

Industrial-strength carbide teeth loosen the hardest-packed surfaces.

- **FILLS IN POTHOLES AND WASH-OUTS,** and smoothes washboard on gravel, limestone, dirt, or sand roads without hauling in new material, shoveling, or raking.

- **GRADES MORE THAN JUST YOUR DRIVEWAY.** Also excellent for leveling and smoothing new lawn areas, horse rings, beaches, and ball fields.

SO WHY SUFFER with potholes or with the continual, back-breaking repair of your country driveway?

Call for your FREE DR® POWER GRADER Catalog and DVD TODAY!

1-800-731-0493

☑ **YES!** Please send me your free information package all about the revolutionary **DR® POWER GRADER**, including factory-direct prices, and details of your 6-Month Risk-Free Trial!

Name _____
Address _____ OFA
City _____ State _____ ZIP _____
E-mail _____
DR® POWER EQUIPMENT, Dept. 58642X
127 Meigs Road, Vergennes, VT 05491
www.DRpowergrader.com

© 2007 CHP, Inc.

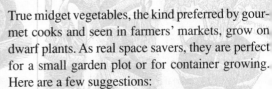

Gardening

The Mighty Midgets

'Little Finger' carrot

True midget vegetables, the kind preferred by gourmet cooks and seen in farmers' markets, grow on dwarf plants. As real space savers, they are perfect for a small garden plot or for container growing. Here are a few suggestions:

■ 'Straight 'N Narrow' **bush beans** are delicate, 5-inch-long, French gourmet beans on compact but prolific plants. For tender wax beans, try 'Goldcrop', which bears 5- to 6-inch-long pods.

■ 'Pablo' is a smooth, dark-red **beet** with a small taproot, making it perfect for harvesting as a tender baby beet. 'Little Chicago', a true baby beet, is perfect for pickling or in salads, with no slicing required. Thin plants to 1 inch apart and harvest baby beets when they reach golf-ball size. (By picking beets frequently and replanting, you can get several crops per season.)

■ 'Gonzales' **cabbage** is a tender, sweet, single-serving-size vegetable that is as big as a softball when fully grown. All-America Selections (AAS) winner 'Dynamo' is another true mini-cabbage that produces a small head on a small plant.

■ 'Little Finger' is a tiny **carrot**, only ⅝ of an inch in diameter, and 'Thumbelina', an AAS winner, is a gourmet, 1-inch, round carrot. 'MiniCor' and 'Baby Sweet' are high in soluble sugar, making them extra-sweet, true baby carrots.

DEEP THINKING

■ **Adequate soil depth is important for developing a strong, healthy root system in a container. Keep these depths in mind:**

6 INCHES lettuce, spinach, beans, and round beets

8 INCHES carrots, peas, and peppers

10 INCHES eggplant, squash, and cucumbers

12 INCHES tomatoes

MINI-MYTHS

■ **Most of the "baby" carrots available in grocery stores are full-size carrots that have been cut and shaped to look like minis.**

■ **Store-bought "baby" corn is actually immature ears that are picked before they are pollinated, just as the silk appears at the tip of the husk.**

–W. Atlee Burpee & Co.

NO PLOT? USE POTS

■ Container growing enables those without a patch of ground to enjoy harvest-fresh vegetables. Use anything that holds dirt and has drainage holes in the bottom. A 10-inch pot is perfect for lettuce or radishes. Hanging baskets work well for cherry tomatoes or strawberries. Use a 5-gallon plastic bucket for a tomato or pepper plant. A 55-gallon food-grade plastic barrel, cut in half, will make two huge planters.

THE EASIEST-EVER CONTAINER GARDEN

■ Anyone can turn an ordinary bag of potting soil into a "grow bag": Lay the bag of soil flat. Poke a few drainage holes in the top surface. Roll the bag over. Cut a few holes in the new top surface. Insert seedling plants into the holes. Water and fertilize as you would a bed. For best results, set this sack into a wheelbarrow or child's wagon and move it into and out of the sunlight as needed.

Gardening

'Dynamo' cabbage

'Sugar Ann' peas

'Eight Ball' zucchini

–photo: Veseys Seeds

34

'Golden Midget' **corn** matures at 3 feet tall and bears tiny, 4-inch-long ears.

'Midget', a pickling **cuke,** grows on 2-foot-long vines that will scramble up a trellis. To ensure that you get a space-saving plant, look for cucumbers with "bush" in the name, such as 'Salad Bush', 'Bush Crop', or 'Bush Pickle'.

Romaine 'Little Gem', red cos 'Pandero', and butterhead 'Tom Thumb' are a few of the many space-saving **lettuces** available. They're perfect for container culture or for filling bare spots between other plants.

'Minnesota Midget' is a **cantaloupe** with 3-foot-long vines that produce a multitude of melons, each only 4 inches in diameter.

For small seedless **watermelons,** try 'Extazy', which yields 4- to 5-pound fruits, or the aptly named 'Bush Sugar Baby', which produces 7-inch-wide fruits.

AAS winner 'Sugar Ann', 'Sugar Lace', and 'Sugar Bon' are dwarf **snap peas** that grow only 18 to 30 inches tall and need little or no support.

'Baby Belle' is a prolific **bell pepper** that bears 2-inch, sweet green peppers that will mature to bright red.

Although only 8 inches tall, 'Thai Hot' pepper plants will produce 2- to 3-inch-long **peppers** into the winter if brought indoors when frost threatens. They will also keep you warm: The peppers have a rating of 80,000 Scoville units (a system for measuring heat in peppers).

'Cherry Bomb' bears heart-shape 1- by 2-inch peppers that are less hot, at only 4,000 Scovilles, on compact 8-inch-tall plants.

'Eight Ball' is an AAS-winning round **zucchini** that is as big as a baseball at maturity. 'Geode' and 'Round Bush' are two other round zucchinis that grow on compact plants. All can be picked either when they are as

Gardening

'Little Chicago' beet

GET GROWING
For the names of seed companies that offer the vegetables mentioned in this article, go to **Almanac.com/garden.**

MAKE YOUR OWN MINIS

With good timing and careful planning, you can harvest tiny vegetables from full-size plants. Try these tricks:

- **Pick when petite. Many "baby" vegetables are grown on standard plants and harvested while they are still tiny. Baby beets, served greens and all, or petite summer squash picked with the flower still attached are ideal for eating long before they reach maturity.**

- **Cramp their style. Some small produce, such as mini-cabbages, come from standard plants grown closely together to keep them from reaching full size.**

small as 1 inch in diameter or after they have been allowed to grow to their full size, 3 to 4 inches across.

'Tiny Tim' and AAS winner 'Small Fry' are a couple of the **cherry tomato** varieties that are suitable for containers. 'Tumbler' was bred specifically for growing in a hanging basket. 'Micro Tom', which grows to be only 6 to 8 inches tall, is thought to be the world's smallest tomato plant. It bears a profusion of 1-inch red fruits and will thrive on a windowsill.

'Small Fry' tomato

For larger **tomatoes** on small plants, look at 'Bush Celebrity' and 'Bush Early Girl'. For something new, try 'Bush Champion', which produces 8- to 12-ounce fruits on 24-inch-tall plants.

These and other little giants promise huge success in a small garden.

☐ ☐

Robin Sweetser uses intensive gardening techniques to grow as much as she can in her postage stamp–size garden in Hillsboro, New Hampshire.

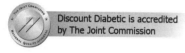

$\mathcal{S}$ecrets of the
FARMERS' MARKET

–City of Sheboygan, Wis.

The first thing to look for in a farmers' market is shade. Although fruits and veggies grow in bright sun, once removed from Mother Earth they begin to deteriorate in the same sun. If the stand is not under shade trees, it should be shaded by a cloth or roof to protect the produce and for the comfort of shoppers.

Then, consider these particulars:

IF YOU ARE SELLING . . .

GREEN BEANS: Cool them in the shade after picking, if you can't wash them immediately. Give them several rinses in cool water, remove stems and leaves, shake them dry, and pack them in baskets. When transporting, cover them with wet burlap, which allows for natural cooling through evaporation. Display them loose or in open containers.

GREENS (kale, collard, turnip, mustard, nonheading lettuce): Wash and display them slightly wet for the "dew-fresh" look. If the weather is warm, transport greens with crushed ice loosely distributed in baskets; cover with wet burlap. Discard any wilted greens before displaying. Cabbages and head lettuce should be trimmed, wet, and kept out of the sun.

POTATOES: It's all right to leave a little dirt on potatoes, especially the early crop, as they needn't be washed until ready to use. Handle fresh potatoes gently, as bruising invites rot. Keep them out of the sun. Cull any cut or rotten spuds (you can smell them). Sell by the pound or peck.

SUMMER SQUASH: Pick summer squash daily, before the weather becomes too hot. Don't allow it to become super-size; the best eating squash are the length of your hand or smaller. Scallop squash should be 4 inches or less in diameter. If blossoms adhere, all the better; they indicate freshness. Wipe any field dirt off with a damp cloth. Cool the gathered produce in a shady, ventilated place without crowding (crowding holds heat).

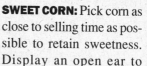

SWEET CORN: Pick corn as close to selling time as possible to retain sweetness. Display an open ear to show the kernel color and quality. Don't wash the ears, but they may need a sprinkling to keep from drying out.

TOMATOES: Pick vine-ripe ones for same-day use. Called "toppers," they are the attractors. Those that are still pale orange are "turners" that will be

fully ripe tomorrow and the next day. Display these in small baskets or one layer deep in a larger container. Cull any misshapen or bruised tomatoes. Grade by size and sell the biggest at a premium. Wipe field dirt from tomatoes with a damp cloth; wet fruit invites fungus. Keep them shaded.

APPLES: Summer apples are sold fresh from the tree; winter apples are usually stored to gain sweetness. You know your own apples; fully ripe fruit smells and sells better. Be prepared to sell by the box and in smaller quantities.

MELONS: Pick as close to full slip (ripe) and as close to your market day as possible. A cut cantaloupe to show flesh color and degree of ripeness helps customers decide; it's the same with a watermelon. Offer samples on toothpicks (don't forget paper towels). There's interest now in the smaller, seedless watermelons, but you'll always find a market for the old favorites.

PEACHES: It's hard to ignore the aroma of fresh, ripe peaches, so give them a big display. Small baskets at a set price attract customers. Don't wash them and avoid rough handling and bruising. Grade for size; price the largest at a premium. Bring your best fruit; unripe peaches don't belong at a farmers' market.

RHUBARB: Sell only your best stalks and remove the (poisonous) leaves because they wilt quickly. Keep the stalks moist and cool so that they are crisp. Sell them in bunches.

STRAWBERRIES: Smell and appearance sell strawberries. Leave the leafy caps and stems attached, and cull overripe specimens.

IF YOU ARE BUYING . . .

GREEN BEANS: There are many types of green beans, all good. Break a snap bean to determine its crispness. If not allowed to wilt in the heat, beans should stay fresh and crisp for two days. To savor the best flavor, buy only what you can use in that time.

(continued)

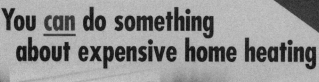

GREENS: Kale, collard, mustard, and the like are sold in bunches. The leaf is the most tender part; the stems, unless very young, are discarded (tough stems indicate age). Look for crisp, unwilted greens with a little moisture on them. Leaf lettuce should also be crisp and slightly wet, with no yellowed leaves. Cabbage and head lettuce should be firm and crisp. Avoid cabbages with mold on the stem.

POTATOES: Don't mind a little dirt on potatoes. Wash them only just before you cook them. Thin-skinned "new" potatoes have high moisture content; they are not for baking but for steaming or boiling (they're also great in potato soup). Buy mature potatoes for baking. Crops are grown during the spring and fall, and the late crop is the best for storage. Usually, every potato grower in an area has the same variety.

SUMMER SQUASH: Select small, bright, firm specimens without bruises. Tenderness is paramount; avoid oversize summer squash (zucchini, crookneck, straightneck, scallop).

SWEET CORN: The husks should be priable, and a punctured kernel will ooze milk for an indicator of freshness. The earliest corn will be the most expensive, but at the peak of the season, prices will be more reasonable.

TOMATOES: Know how you will use the tomatoes and pick the size accordingly. Select large, juicy tomatoes for hamburger slices and expect to pay more for them. Use smaller, cheaper sizes for salads or sauces. Pass by any with bruises, nicks, or dark spots, which become rotten places quickly.

APPLES: Old varieties such as 'Yellow Delicious' and 'McIntosh' are superb for eating out of hand, but it's a matter of taste; you might prefer a tart apple, like 'Granny Smith'. Local apples are often what orchardists find grow well in the region. Summer apples are softer and often used for cooking and pies, but they eat well, too.

(continued on page 45)

FIND A FARMERS' MARKET
To find a farmers' market close to you, go to **Almanac.com/garden.**

42

GET PREPARED!

WMD attacks? The US and UN say they are inevitable. Chemical train derailments? Nuclear power plant breach? What about ice storms, downed power lines? This little book is designed to help you prepare for these times. It's short, fun to read, and inexpensive. Keep it handy! **Call 1-800-247-6553** or send $14.90 check or m.o. to:

Talnik Publishing
P.O. Box 5261 • Woodridge IL 60517-0261
www.preparebook.com

Cohasset Colonials

Early American Furniture Kits

Our new catalog is filled with authentic reproductions. Make your own antiques from our kits, or let us do the finishing for you.

1-800-288-2389
FREE CATALOG

Box 548-FA, Ashburnham, MA 01430
www.cohassetcolonials.com/fa

ENJOY SOAPSTONE WARMTH
Soul-satisfying warmth from America's finest stoves

Woodstock Soapstone Stoves are beautiful, heirloom quality stoves made from nature's perfect heating material... soapstone. It holds twice as much heat as iron or steel, and radiates it gently and comfortably – more evenly than any metal stove.

Heat up to 1600 square feet (more in warmer climates). Stay comfortable during power outages – no electricity is required. Each stove is handmade and one-of-a-kind. Discover soapstone's magic warmth and never be cold again!

GAS or WOOD

FREE CATALOG

Name_____
Address_____
City/State/Zip_____
E-mail _____

Woodstock Soapstone Co., Inc.
66 Airpark Rd., Dept. 2917, West Lebanon, NH 03784

www.woodstove.com
1-888-664-8188

Food Emporium

MELONS: Use whatever method you trust to select a ripe watermelon, be it thumping or examining the stem. The bellies of some varieties turn color when ripe, but choosing one is still an act of faith. The color of the flesh and the sweetness are dictated by the variety; ask the seller what to expect.

PEACHES: This fruit is either freestone or clingstone: When a freestone peach is broken open, the stone falls free, while the stone of the clingstone clings to the flesh. "Clings" are the earliest to ripen. Lightly squeeze a peach. If it yields easily, it's ripe. Avoid any with areas of green; they'll never attain the quality of a ripe-picked peach. Freestones are usually juicier and softer, the best for fresh eating. Clingstones, being firmer, are the best for canning.

RHUBARB: Look for blemish-free, fat, crisp stalks. The all-red varieties are slightly sweeter than the mostly greenish ones and make the best pies, but greenish rhubarb makes the tartest sauce.

STRAWBERRIES: The cap and stem should be attached to the berry. Avoid overripe strawberries unless you plan to make jam the same day—and buy these at a reduced price. ☐☐

Jerry Abrams was a farm boy who planted, tended, harvested, and sold at the public market. He later became a food technologist, continuing to keep a market garden and small orchard on the side.

WHAT'S IN SEASON?
For harvest times, or what to expect when, go to **Almanac.com/garden.**

GEESE MATE FOR LIFE
Symbol of Eternal Love

Eternal love is beautifully symbolized in our Geese Mate for Life pin. Finely crafted in your choice of sterling silver or 14K yellow gold, two Canada geese are depicted majestically together in flight. As a gesture of your love, or the special bond between two people, it makes the perfect gift.

When we see the values which we hold dear as humans, adopted naturally by wild animals like geese, we are inspired by the natural wonders around us. These noble birds choose lifetime mates, and remain faithful as they travel together, flying many thousands of miles in a lifetime. Each time we see the majestic V-formation making its way across the sky, we pause to reflect on the cycles of nature - the coming winter, or the return of life in the spring. Mated geese embody many symbols and emotions that we cherish and celebrate.

The sentiments expressed by this piece are on a small card tucked inside the gift box. Shown above at actual size, available as a pin, or as a necklace with an 18-inch chain.

Silver Pin ....#X2266 ....$125.00
Silver Necklace 18" chain ...#X2267....$125.00
Gold Pin ....#X2268....$295.00
Gold Necklace 18" chain .....#X2269....$395.00

Free Priority Shipping
Satisfaction Guaranteed

Order on-line
www.GeeseMateForLife.com

Order by phone
1-800-433-2988 M-F 9:30am-5pm

Visit our store

Cross Jewelers
Jewelers to New England Since 1908
570 Congress St. Portland, ME 04101 ©07

POPPIN' FRESH

by Stacey Kusterbeck

If you love popcorn (and who doesn't?), you really ought to grow your own.

Today, some 150 years after popcorn first became a household word, most popcorn comes coated with flavor and packed to pop neatly inside expanding bags. Convenient, yes, but nothing like homegrown. Popcorn is available in a surprising number of varieties (gold, off-white, maroon, black, and calico, to name a few), each with a unique flavor. Experiment to find your favorite, using these tips from popcorn farmers and breeders.

PLANTING

Once all threat of frost has passed, plant seeds 2 to 3 inches deep. "Some people think that popcorn should be planted shallower than field corn, but there is no reason for that," says Charles P. Zangger, a North Loup, Nebraska–based popcorn breeder for 25 years. "The main thing to remember with

46

home gardening is not to plant it too thick." Plant seeds about a foot apart and make rows about 30 inches wide. Fertilize with a 17-17-17 formula; popping corn requires a bit more nitrogen, phosphorus, and sulfur than other crops.

(c o n t i n u e d)

TRADITIONAL

TIMES

According to folklore, plant corn seeds or seedlings . . .

■ when elm leaves are the size of a squirrel's ear.

■ when you can comfortably rest your bare belly on the soil.

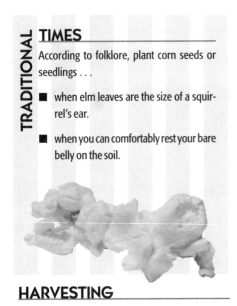

HARVESTING

Kernels mature in about 80 to 150 days, depending on the variety, but don't depend on the calendar to know when your crop is ready. There are two ways to harvest popcorn: You can pick it when it's sufficiently dried out and ready to be popped, or you can pick it earlier and then dry it out.

If you want to wait until the corn is ready for popping, and weather conditions are warm enough to allow this, the stalks and husks should be brown and the kernels should be at moisture level of about 14 percent. Popcorn ears left on the stalk will dry out in the field, and will lose about one-half a percent of their moisture each day.

Here are three ways to tell if the kernels are ready:

■ Twist and snap an ear off a stalk. The shucked ear should be firm, not pliable.

■ Grip the ear with both hands and twist it, moving your hands in opposite directions. Dry kernels will fall off very easily.

■ Press on a kernel with your fingernail. You will not be able to leave a mark on a dry kernel.

When these conditions are met, the corn is ready to be picked and probably dry enough to be popped.

Another method of harvesting is to pick the corn when it has a slightly higher moisture level and then dry it until it reaches 14 percent. If you choose this method, don't pick the popcorn before it is physiologically mature because it won't pop as well.

To test for this, pry a kernel off an ear. Hold up the pointed end (the part that was attached to the cob) and scratch away the tip. A black layer there is a sign that the corn is mature. The ears can be picked anytime after that point.

Don't leave the corn on the plant if the stalks are falling over, if freezing weather is forecast, or if it is time to plow the garden under, according to Jim Iverson, who has been breeding popcorn since 1972. He is vice president of the popcorn division at Caldwell, Idaho–based Crookham Company, a family firm that began selling popcorn seed in 1911.

Be sure to harvest your entire crop before there is any danger of freezing temperatures. "If the popcorn kernels freeze when they are at a high moisture level, they will crack internally and not pop," says Iverson. A rule of thumb: Corn can tolerate temperatures no lower than its moisture level—corn at 30 percent moisture can tolerate 30°F, for example. (Rain isn't much of a concern, as the kernels are protected by the shuck, although the

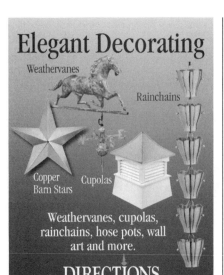

CORNY WEATHER

- If corn blades twist up, it will rain.

- If corn is hard to husk, expect a hard winter.

- Cornscateous air, which is humid and hot, is perfect for growing corn.

higher humidity level in the air after rainfall may raise the moisture level.)

CURING

If you choose to dry out your ears after they've been picked, first carefully strip away the husk from each ear. Place the ears in mesh bags to hang, or spread them out in a well-ventilated area, such as a garage or basement, at about 70°F and 70 percent humidity.

Whether you have let the corn dry out in the field or dried it out after it was picked, check the moisture level before you shell your entire crop. The goal is to reach the 14 percent level of moisture; more (too wet) or less (too dry), and the corn won't pop well. "For the home gardener, the drying part is probably the hardest thing about growing popcorn," says Steve Wetzel, vice president of purchasing for southern Indiana–based Ramsey Popcorn Company.

A simple way to test your popcorn for

Serving the Northeast

$4995.
starting at

SAFETY COMFORT & INDEPENDENCE

REMAIN IN YOUR OWN HOME

AVOID FALLING

Boston
Walk-In Bath Company

Call For a Free Brochure

(781) 229-0072

BUILT IN GRAB BAR & SHOWER

HYDROTHERAPY OPTION

AMERICAN MADE

NEUTON®...the Cleaner, Quieter, Easier Way to Mow!

FREE BAGGER for a limited time!

CLEANER than gas-powered mowers because the NEUTON® uses exhaust-free rechargeable battery power. No more gas spills, or messing with checking and changing the oil!

QUIETER! The average gas mower operates at an ear-splitting 85 decibels! The NEUTON® produces one-quarter the noise!

EASIER TO USE! Instead of the effort of pull-starting your gas mower, the NEUTON® starts with a gentle squeeze of its handlebar. And, at half the weight of most gas mowers, it's half the work to operate!

MOWS AN HOUR ON A SINGLE CHARGE!

TOLL-FREE 1-888-212-0740

☑ **YES!** Please send me your FREE Catalog and DVD all about the more pleasant and easier-to-use **NEUTON® Mower**, including details on how I can now receive a FREE grass bagger!

Name _____

Address _____ OFA

City _____ State _____ ZIP _____

E-mail _____

NEUTON® Power Equipment, Dept. 58638X
127 Meigs Road, Vergennes, VT 05491
www.neutonmowers.com

© 2007 CHP, Inc.

Try it for 6 Months Risk-Free!

Gardening

dryness is to drop about 20 kernels into hot cooking oil. Popcorn kernels that are too moist make dull, low-pitched popping sounds, and the flakes are round and chewy. "Many moist kernels will not pop, but instead, just split open," says Iverson. Kernels that are too dry sound like twigs snapping, and the flakes are small or nonexistent; many dry kernels don't pop at all.

"Once it's dry enough, it will pop out nice, white and fluffy," says Wetzel. Sample a few kernels every week, until you get the desired result. You will be well rewarded for the effort.

Let the ears air-dry until the kernels shell off easily—then you know that the moisture level is right. "There is a chance that you will damage the corn if you shell it when it is over the 14 percent moisture level, as the kernels are too firmly attached," says Iverson. If the corn is too

moist, he says, the kernel tears loose at the black layer, which exposes it and reduces how well it pops.

Dry popcorn kernels can be removed from the ear by hand without too much effort: Take an ear in each hand, and press and rub the ears together. If you have a

lot of ears to shell, gather friends and family to help (call it a pre-pop party)—or get a hand corn sheller. With this device, you take an ear in one hand, put the sheller around it, and turn it. The kernels will fall off. However, removing kernels by hand is the most gentle way to shell. "Steel against corn scratches the kernel and reduces the popping volume," says Iverson.

POPPING

After all of this work, pop some corn for fun and enjoy it—but be sure to save some for later. "Freshly picked popcorn will not pop as good as popcorn that is two months old," adds Iverson. "It takes time for the moisture to evenly distribute throughout the kernel."

Put your kernels in airtight plastic bags and store them in the freezer. When you want to pop some, just let the kernels warm up to room temperature and they will be ready to pop.

TAKE STALK

There are three kinds of edible corn:

- field corn, used for livestock feed and corn-related cooking products such as oil and sweeteners

- sweet corn, grown for human consumption

- popcorn

If, over time, your popcorn stops popping, it's probably too dry. Try this fix from Charles Zangger: Add two teaspoons of water to a quart of unpopped corn in an airtight container or plastic bag and shake it vigorously. Let it stand for three days and it will pop well again.

POP SOME INTO YOUR MOUTH

Get recipes for Honey Popcorn Balls, Popcorn Granola Munch, and more at **Almanac.com/food.**

POP SCIENCE

Popcorn pops because it contains a small amount of moisture and has a hard hull. As the kernel heats up, the moisture, which is stored inside a soft circle of starch, expands, putting pressure on the hull. When the hull bursts, the kernel is turned inside out, exploding the gelatinized starch, which immediately cools and forms the familiar popped shape.

If you want to munch on plain popcorn, look for seed packets marked "butterfly" kernels; these are large, light, and fluffy. If you want to make candy-coated popcorn, use "mushroom" kernels. These produce smaller, ball-shape kernels that won't break apart during the cooking process. ☐☐

Stacey Kusterbeck writes about pop culture (edible and not) from her home on Long Island in New York. She is a longtime contributor to *The Old Farmer's Almanac*.

Cultivating
CONFECTIONS

–photos: *this page*, David Cavagnaro; *opposite, top left*, Select Seeds; *opposite, top right*, Thompson & Morgan Seedsmen Inc.

Mignonette has a fragrance of raspberry or vanilla.

Dianthus has a delicious spicy-clove scent.

Heliotrope is often called cherry pie plant.

Chocolate, spice, and everything nice! "Recipes" for gardens that smell good enough to eat.

by Cynthia Van Hazinga

Fragrance was very important to our gardening grandparents. Today, garden fragrance effects come about more often by accident than by design—unless, of course, you take these suggestions.

A SWEET AND SPICY PATHWAY

Plants with strong sweet or spicy perfumes can make for a stimulating sequence of scents, but like heavily seasoned fare, too many in one place would become indigestible. Space these a few feet apart so that you can sample each individually.

The scent of heliotrope (*Heliotropium arborescens*), often called cherry pie plant, is a mixture of vanilla, sweet almonds, and cherries. This bushy, tender perennial has long-blooming sprays of flowers in shades of lavender, blue, or white. 'Marine' and 'Fragrant Delight' are scrumptious varieties; 'Alba' bears vanilla-scented white flowers. It's hardy in Zones 10 and 11.

An intensely sweet orange-spiced tea fragrance surrounds Orange Meadowbrite coneflower (*Echinacea* 'Art's Pride'). Although small (2½ to 3 feet), this drought-tolerant plant is stunning,

Chocolate cosmos scents the air with hot chocolate.

Smell is a potent wizard that transports us across thousands of miles and all the years we have lived.

–Helen Keller, American educator
(1880–1968)

Dame's rocket emits traces of clove and nutmeg.

Night phlox (above) releases a almond/honey/vanilla fragran

Orange Meadowbrite coneflowe evokes orange-spiced tea.

with its deep-orange ray florets, dark-maroon cone and orange blooms. It' hardy in Zones 4 to 9.

Dianthus, or pinks, have an even spicier clove scent Clove pink *(Dianthus plumarius)* is an antique borde pink with some fabulous ruffled cultivars (e.g., 'Beatrix') Another fragrant family member, pheasant-eyed pinks comes in shades of rose, lavender, and white with "eyes of deep pink and "pinked" petals—the jagged-edge ef fect that gave dianthus its common name. Fringed pin *(D. superbus)* is perhaps the most potent. Its delicate lilac-to-white flowers fill the air, and fringed 'Rainbov Loveliness', a hybrid from the 1920s, can perfume whole garden. Most pinks thrive in Zones 3 to 8.

For a hint of vanilla or the essence of raspberry (th fragrance is different for everyone) from summer to fal both day and night, edge your path with mignonett *(Reseda odorata)*. It's a hardy annual about a foot tal with branching stems and small spikes of yellowish green to white flowers. This "little darling" (the mean ing of its name in English) is inevitably attractive t foraging bees.

ASSORTED NIGHT CANDY

Scents can alter dramatically after dark, and many delicious-smelling flowers reach their fragrance peak at night. (During the day, plants absorb heat, which builds up fragrances; as night falls, those fragrances are released.) Many strongly scented flowers are white, to attract night pollinators, including moths and bats, but most of them tickle our appetites, too.

When the umbrella-like flower clusters of the half-hardy annual night phlox *(Zaluzianskya capensis)* explode into bloom at dusk, a delicious almond/honey/vanilla fragrance is released. One captivating variety is called 'Midnight Candy'.

Hints of vanilla, traces of lemon, and a strong note of cloves often will surround evening- or night-scented stock *(Matthiola longipetala* ssp. *bicornis).* By day, it's not impressive, but when the Sun goes down, its fragrance, from pink, mauve, or purple racemes, is quite indescribable (it's clove, yes, but quite different from the scent of pinks or carnations). Sow this annual in serial sprinkles, like lettuce; each plant lasts only a few weeks, and you will want more. Traditionally, it's grown under a window that is kept open at night or along the edge of a porch.

Traces of clove and nutmeg escape from dame's rocket *(Hesperis matronalis)* in the evening. This modest, early-summer bloomer with white or lilac flowers smells sweet by day, but come sunset, its spicy scent strengthens. It's hardy in Zones 4 to 9.

THE CHOCOHOLIC'S CORNER

If you're mad for chocolate, indulge yourself with these flowers. Set a couple of chairs nearby so that you can share this sensory experience with friends—and for heaven's sake, have some cookies on hand.

To fill the air with the aroma of premium dark chocolate, plant willow-leaf sunflowers *(Helianthus salicifolius),* a native perennial that's often confused with *H. angustifolius.* It has daisylike 2-inch gold flowers and, by summer's end, its 6- to 10-foot-tall stems provide vertical accent. This prairie plant thrives on sunshine and gets along with little water once it sinks its roots. It's hardy in Zones 6 to 9.

A bittersweet hot chocolate smell wafts from chocolate cosmos *(Cosmos atrosanguineus).* Plant this upright and bushy specimen in front of sunflowers. It has reddish-brown stems and velvety maroon flowers that recall single dahlias—no coincidentally: Cosmos is a tender perennial from Mexico, related to dahlias. It's hardy in Zones 7 to 10.

For a double dip (taste and aroma) treat yourself to an airy chocolate flower sometimes called chocolate daisy or green-eyes *(Berlandiera lyrata).* It has yellow, daisylike flowers with red-striped undersides, but it's the brown stamens that smell of chocolate and taste like cocoa. The scent of this night bloomer is strongest in the morning, but the stamens exude a mouthwatering scent as the temperature rises. This small, water-thrifty native perennial is perfect for edging. It's hardy in Zones 7 to 9.

The last bonbon in this box stands

RUG SALE!

braided-texture area rugs & accessories
Just 30 mins. from Route 128

www.rugfactorystore.com

CHECK OUT OUR MONTHLY SALES!

50% OFF
all in-store items
see website for dates

Open Mon-Sat 9-5 / 401-724-6840
560 Mineral Spring Ave. Pawtucket, RI

Viyella is, as always, an intimate
blend of natural fibers. It is soft, warm, light, and supremely comfortable. Its fine blend of 80% long staple cotton and 20% merino wool affords the unique combination of luxury and practicality. Viyella is produced solely by William Hollins & Company Ltd., world-famous for superb British textile craftsmanship since 1784. Reg. sizes Small- XXL. Tall sizes L-3XL. Robes also available.

MILLER BROS. NEWTON
Fine Men's Clothier for 150 Years

www.mbnmenswear.com
105 Main St., Keene, NH • 888-256-1170

NEW DR® LEAF and LAWN VACUUM
— turns your riding mower into a powerful yard clean-up machine!

- **VACUUMS** leaves, grass clippings, pine cones, pine needles, nuts, and twigs from your lawn using an incredible 85 mph suction force!

- **SHREDS** most everything it vacuums. Reduces the volume of leaves by 90%.

- **DUMPS OR BAGS** collected material.

- **CHIPS** fallen tree branches and prunings up to 2" thick with built-in chipper.

Call TOLL-FREE

1-800-731-0493

☑ **YES!** Please rush me a **FREE DVD and Catalog** with full details, including your 6-Month Risk-Free Trial offer, low, factory-direct prices, and seasonal savings now in effect.

Name _____

Address _____ OFA

City _____ State _____ Zip _____

E-mail _____

DR® POWER EQUIPMENT, Dept. 58641X
127 Meigs Road, Vergennes, VT 05491

www.DRleafvac.com
© 2007 CHP, Inc.

FREE DVD! SEE IT IN ACTION!

PLUS NEW WALK-BEHIND MODELS FOR SMALLER PROPERTIES!
Get into tight spots. Power up hills. The easiest-handling walk-behind ever!

Gardening

apart: If you have a wall or trellis—even a tripod—drape it with a chocolate vine *(Akebia quinata)*. This semi-evergreen climber blooms in early spring, with small, hanging, chocolate/vanilla-scented, mauve (almost brown) flowers in racemes up to 5 inches long among graceful, five-lobe leaflets. (It's also known as fiveleaf akebia.) Native to forest margins in East Asia, it quickly twines to 30 to 40 feet and may become invasive, so prune after it flowers. It's hardy in Zones 5 to 9.

THE NOSE KNOWS

Our sense of smell is said to be the most primitive of our senses, yet we register a scent in a half-second—nearly twice as fast as we feel pain. There is a close relationship between taste and smell. We detect food aromas through receptors at the back of our throats in a process called retronasal olfaction.

What we call the taste of food is mostly smell. "We smell before we taste," says Ken Purzycki, a fragrance consultant. He can name the chemical behind every scent: "For instance, the same chemicals are found in lemons as in lemon verbena—after all, the same chemicals are found throughout nature, but they're very complex."

Without a sense of smell, we would sharply limit ourselves to the basic taste sensations: sweet, salty, sour, and bitter. Thank goodness our very discriminating noses can differentiate between thousands of different scents and flavors. ☐☐

Cynthia Van Hazinga, a longtime contributor to *The Old Farmer's Almanac*, divides her time between Hillsborough, New Hampshire, and New York City.

Why wait ten months?

Now you can have rich, dark compost _in just 14 days!_

With the amazing ComposTumbler, you'll have bushels of crumbly, ready-to-use compost — _in just 14 days!_ (And, in the ten months it takes to make compost the old way, your ComposTumbler can produce _hundreds of pounds_ of rich food for your garden!)

Say good-bye to that messy, open compost pile (and to the flies, pests, and odors that come along with it!) Bid a happy farewell to the strain of trying to turn over heavy, wet piles with a pitchfork.

Compost the Better Way

Compost-making with the ComposTumbler is neat, quick and easy!

Gather up leaves, old weeds, kitchen scraps, lawn clippings, etc. and toss them into the roomy 18-bushel drum. Then, once each day, give the ComposTumbler's _gear-driven_ handle a few easy spins.

The ComposTumbler's Magic

Inside the ComposTumbler, carefully positioned mixing fins blend materials, pushing fresh mixture to the core where the temperatures are the hottest (up to 160°) and the composting bacteria most active.

After just 14 days, open the door, and you'll find an abundance of dark, sweet-smelling "garden gold" — ready to enrich and feed your garden!

NEW SMALLER SIZE!

Now there are 2 sizes. The 18-bushel original ComposTumbler and the NEW 9.5-bushel Compact ComposTumbler. Try either size risk-free for 30 days!

See for yourself! Try the ComposTumbler risk-free with our 30-Day Home Trial!

Call Toll-Free 1-800-880-2345

Visit us at
www.compostumbler.com

ComposTumbler®

The choice of more than 250,000 gardeners

☐ YES! Please rush FREE information on the ComposTumbler, including special savings and 30-Day Home Trial.

Name _____

Address _____

City _____

State _____ ZIP _____

MAIL TO:
ComposTumbler
30 Wright Ave., Dept. 42018C
Lititz (Lancaster Co.), PA 17543

© 2008 PBM Group

CONTAINER MANIA

one another, holding others upright, peeking and creeping through in odd places, or simply making one another look good.

■ **Look into new materials.** Check

Plants in pots are all the rage—and for good reason. They are easy to care for and movable (if they're not too large), and add a decorative accent in just about any spot. As you pick your pots and plantings, keep these ideas in mind.

■ **Combine eye-catching mixes** of annuals, perennials, flower bulbs, and even vegetables.

■ **Group several containers** for impact. Too often, people use the same container in the same place every year—for instance, one big container by the front door. Instead, put seven—even ten—containers there.

■ **Create balance,** then add a zinger. Choose plants that go together but don't quite match—this repetition of related colors ties the big picture together. Three to five colors work nicely as a base, but don't stop there. Toss in a zinger, something oddball that is just "off" enough in color or texture to punch up everything else a notch.

For example, start with a selection of one or more of the following, as illustrated in the photo at right: variegated cannas with multi-striped leaves of green, orange, gold, and pink; magenta-and-gold coleuses; hot-pink-and-green caladiums; hot-pink pentas; and even-pinker trailing petunias. For the kicker, add taxicab-yellow lantanas. As the plants mature, they take on a life of their own.

■ **Go for intertwining plants.** The best plantings are those in which the plants fall in love—growing intertwined, looping through

–photo: Netherlands Flower Bulb Information Center

out fiberglass, resin, and synthetic containers. They are lightweight, can overwinter outdoors without cracking, and are often fashioned after old estate designs, mimicking stone, terra-cotta, and cast iron.

■ **Bring life to dead zones.** Use containers to soften places where no soil or garden is available—side yards, walkways, decks, next to garage walls, or cemented areas bounded by a chain-link fence.

–Netherlands Flower Bulb Information Center

FOR POT LUCK

Container gardening offers hundreds of possibilities for small spaces. We asked the authors of *The Bountiful Container* (Workman Publishing, 2002), Rose Marie Nichols McGee and Maggie Stuckey, for some tips.

–Workman Publishing

■ *What are the "musts" of container gardening?*

MAGGIE: Fluffy soil that drains well and vigilance about watering and replacing fertilizer that washes away.

■ *What is the best soil for containers?*

ROSE MARIE: Half peat and half perlite or vermiculite is a good mix.

MAGGIE: I pick up the bag and gauge its lightness. The lighter, the better.

■ *Are diseases and insects less of a problem with container gardens?*

MAGGIE: Yes, by a huge factor. You will avoid soilborne pathogens, and slugs are less of a problem.

■ *What is the most unusual container you have planted?*

MAGGIE: A wooden salad bowl with mesclun. It made me giggle every time I looked at it.

ROSE MARIE: A collection of old zinc buckets and tubs. One bucket had a staked tomato plant with lemon cucumber vines spilling out of it.

–Doreen G. Howard

□□

Symbolic Meanings of Herbs, Flowers, and Trees

Aloe .... Healing, protection, affection
Angelica .... Inspiration
Arborvitae ..... Unchanging friendship
Bachelor's button .. Single blessedness
Basil .... Good wishes, love
Bay .... Glory
Black-eyed Susan .... Justice
Carnation ...... Alas for my poor heart
Chamomile .... Patience
Chives .... Usefulness
Clover, white .... Think of me
Coriander .... Hidden worth
Cumin .... Fidelity
Fennel .... Flattery
Fern .... Sincerity
Geranium, oak-leaved .. True friendship
Goldenrod .... Encouragement
Heliotrope .... Eternal love
Holly .... Hope
Hollyhock .... Ambition
Honeysuckle .... Bonds of love
Horehound .... Health
Hyssop .... Sacrifice, cleanliness
Ivy .... Friendship, continuity
Lady's-mantle .... Comforting
Lavender .... Devotion, virtue
Lemon balm .... Sympathy
Marjoram .... Joy, happiness
Mint .... Eternal refreshment
Morning glory .... Affectation
Nasturtium .... Patriotism
Oak .... Strength
Oregano .... Substance
Pansy .... Thoughts
Parsley .... Festivity
Pine .... Humility

Poppy, red .... Consolation
Rose .... Love
Rosemary .... Remembrance
Rue .... Grace, clear vision
Sage .... Wisdom, immortality
Salvia, blue .... I think of you
Salvia, red .... Forever mine
Savory .... Spice, interest
Sorrel .... Affection
Southernwood .... Constancy, jest
Sweet pea .... Pleasures
Sweet woodruff .... Humility
Tansy .... Hostile thoughts
Tarragon .... Lasting interest
Thyme .... Courage, strength
Valerian .... Readiness
Violet .... Loyalty, devotion
Violet, blue .... Faithfulness
Violet, yellow .... Rural happiness
Willow .... Sadness
Zinnia ..... Thoughts of absent friends

Looking for some 'local color'?

FREE CATALOG
Call today and mention code **OFA07**

Find it at WEBS – *America's Largest Yarn Store!*

Knitters, Weavers & Spinners...
Visit our beautiful 5,000 sq. ft.
store in Northampton, MA
Or on-line at: **www.yarn.com**
Ask about our famous yarn discounts!

800.367.9327

WEBS
America's Yarn Store™

75 SERVICE CENTER RD · NORTHAMPTON, MA

1-12 Stone Mother's Basket

Born from the tradition of the Nantucket Lightship Basket, we present the ***Original Mother's Basket*** with each flower representing your child's birth month. Handcrafted 14K gold pendant, synthetic stones, and 14K gold chain. *$200-$312*
(based on number of stones)

Cranberry Jewelers

554 Rte. 28, Harwich Port, Cape Cod, MA 02646
Toll free **1-866-286-5036**
www.cranberryjewelers.net

HAULS LIKE A DUMP TRUCK
YET IT HANDLES WITH EASE!

PROFESSIONAL POWER FOR HOMEOWNERS

DR

Try out the **DR® POWERWAGON** – the heavy-duty, easy-handling, self-propelled hauler for your yard, barn, woodlot or garden – for 6 months **RISK-FREE!**

FREE DVD!
SEE IT IN ACTION!

- **HAUL** up to 800 lbs...up or down hills, over rough, even soft, wet ground!

- **UNLOAD** it like a dump truck without shoveling or tedious hand labor. Optional *powered* lift available.

- **ENJOY** the easy handling of 4 speeds, Power Reverse, Electric-Starting, and Zero-Radius-Turning!

CALL TOLL-FREE TODAY!

1-800-731-0493

☑ **YES**, please send me **FREE** details of the **DR® POWERWAGON** including how I can try one out for 6 months **RISK-FREE!**

Name_____
Address _____ OFA
City _____ State _____ ZIP _____
Email_____
DR® POWER EQUIPMENT, Dept. 58637X
127 Meigs Road, Vergennes, VT 05491
www.DRpowerwagon.com

©2007 CHP, Inc.

Country Cookin'

-Elizabeth Whiting & Associates/CORBIS

Straight From the Farm

-background: Philip Nealey/Photodisc Red/Getty;
farm families: courtesy photos

FARM WAYS

Robin and Mark Way have run Rumbleway Farm, a 62-acre organic farm in Conowingo, Maryland, since 1992. With their children—Samantha (age 12), Melissa (10), and Matthew (6)—they raise grass-fed chickens, turkeys, and ducks, as well as cattle, goats, and rabbits, and sell the meat at the farm and in nearby grocery co-ops. (The Ways process the poultry and rabbit on-site; the beef and goat are handled by a USDA-certified butcher.) In the summer, they plant a large vegetable garden and, come fall, Robin cans much of the harvest. The couple enjoys hosting home-cooked community dinners at their farm during the winter, as well as holding a Farm Day each September for visitors.

Mark Way with children Matthew, Melissa, and Samantha

(c o n t i n u e d)

Robin Way

Cream of Mushroom Soup
Robin makes this for community dinners.

1 pound white button
   mushrooms, wiped
   clean
½ cup (1 stick) butter
1 teaspoon lemon juice
1 small onion, chopped
½ cup all-purpose flour
3½ cups chicken stock
1 cup heavy cream
1 teaspoon salt
¼ teaspoon pepper

Remove the mushroom stems and set aside. Slice the caps. Melt the butter in a pan over medium heat. Add the sliced mushrooms and lemon juice and cook until the mushrooms are tender. Reduce the heat and remove the mushrooms with a slotted spoon, leaving the butter in the pan. Set aside. Add the mushroom stems and onion to the pan with the butter and cook until tender. Stir in the flour and cook 1 minute. Gradually stir in the stock and cook until thick, stirring constantly. Remove from the heat and blend the mixture in a blender, half at a time, until smooth. Pour the mixture into a pot and add the cream, salt and pepper, and reserved mushroom slices. Reheat and serve. **Makes 4 to 6 servings.**

■ ■ ■

HARVESTING HISTORY

Robert and Donna Kimball own Beech Hill Farm, a ninth-generation family farm and former dairy farm in Hopkinton, New Hampshire. Today, with help from their daughter Holly and her husband, Peter, they operate an ice cream stand, a gardener's shop, a museum, and a pavilion in the newly renovated barn buildings. Robert raises vegetables, tends to the corn for the annual corn mazes, and maintains the nature

Donna and Robert Kimball

trails around the property. Donna's Farm House baked goods are made on-site (her breads, cookies, and apple pound cakes are favorites). In summer, she tends sunflowers and gladiolus to sell at the farm and the local farmers' market. In the fall, the farm offers pumpkins for sale.

(c o n t i n u e d)

The Kimballs' daughter Holly and her family

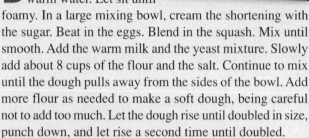

Fall Harvest Squash Rolls

These rolls have been served at Kimball family Thanksgiving dinners as far back as anyone can remember.

4 tablespoons dry yeast
1 cup very warm water
1⅓ cups vegetable shortening
1 cup sugar
4 large eggs
2 cups cooked and mashed winter squash
2 cups warm milk
8 cups flour, plus extra as needed
2 teaspoons salt

Dissolve the yeast in the warm water. Let sit until foamy. In a large mixing bowl, cream the shortening with the sugar. Beat in the eggs. Blend in the squash. Mix until smooth. Add the warm milk and the yeast mixture. Slowly add about 8 cups of the flour and the salt. Continue to mix until the dough pulls away from the sides of the bowl. Add more flour as needed to make a soft dough, being careful not to add too much. Let the dough rise until doubled in size, punch down, and let rise a second time until doubled.

Divide the dough into four equal parts, then divide each quarter into 12 pieces. Shape each piece into a ball and place them all in greased 9-inch cake pans, touching. Let rise until doubled. Preheat the oven to 375°F. Bake for 20 minutes or until lightly browned. Remove from the pans and let cool. **Makes 4 dozen rolls.**

■ ■ ■

COMMUNITY SPIRITS

Moie and Jim Crawford have owned and operated New Morning Farm, a 95-acre organic vegetable farm in Hustontown, Pennsylvania, since 1976. They grow about 40 crops, including berries, herbs, and vegetables, and raise about 250 laying hens. Over the years, they have operated a farm stand, organized two farmers' markets, and started a wholesale marketing cooperative with local organic farmers. They also run an apprenticeship program to help aspiring farmers get started.

Jim and Moie Crawford

(c o n t i n u e d)

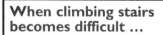

2008

Tangy Slaw

This slaw is great at a barbecue.

2 cups shredded red cabbage
2 cups shredded green cabbage
½ cup finely diced red bell pepper
juice of ½ lime
2 tablespoons chopped fresh cilantro
2 teaspoons maple syrup
1 teaspoon prepared horseradish
½ cup toasted pecans

In a large bowl, mix together the cabbages and pepper. Combine the lime juice, cilantro, maple syrup, and horseradish in a small bowl. Pour the dressing over the vegetables and mix. Shortly before serving, add the pecans. **Makes 6 servings.**

■ ■ ■

GETTING THEIR GOAT

Diane Thompson and Dan Workman settled in British Columbia's remote Nazko Valley after moving south from the Arctic to fulfill a lifelong dream: to build a farm. They started Riversong Farm in 1995. They have chickens, pigs, milk goats, horses, guardian dogs, a donkey, and a llama, but cashmere goats, which they raise for chevon (meat) and cashmere fiber, are their main focus. The goats are tough, hardy animals, comfortable even when temperatures drop to –45°F. The couple operates a bed-and-breakfast cabin for folks who want to experience farm life or explore the surrounding wilderness.

Diane Thompson

Dan's Greek-Style Chevon

Since goat meat has very little fat, it is best cooked with a slow, moist heat. Note: Lamb or beef can be substituted for goat meat. Serve over rice or with your favorite side dish.

2 pounds goat meat, cut into cubes
1 clove garlic, minced
2 tablespoons olive oil
4 tomatoes, chopped
1 green bell pepper, cubed (optional)
1/2 cup sliced black olives
1 or 2 medium onions, cut into large
    pieces
1 tablespoon oregano
1 to 2 teaspoons salt
1/2 teaspoon pepper
1 bay leaf
½ cup cubed feta cheese (optional)

Brown the cubed meat and garlic in the olive oil. Add everything else

Does Herbal Medicine Work?

A few years ago I was in a drug store and overheard a woman say to the pharmacist, *"I've tried herbs, and they just don't work."* Being an herbal doctor, I was furious. But I took a deep breath and after talking to this woman, I realized she was right. The herbal medicine she was talking about, in fact most herbal products, DON'T WORK!

My name is Dr. Richard Schulze and let me assure you that Herbs are God's gifts to us, for our healing and health, and **HERBS DO WORK!** I can't tell you how many times I've bought a product only to discover it wasn't made well, or doesn't work very well, or work at all. An old friend of mine says the world is full of high-quality advertising, but low-quality products. From tools to televisions, how well something works depends totally on how well it was made. <u>Well, in my business I make the best</u>; the highest <u>Quality</u>, most <u>Potent</u> and most <u>Effective</u> herbal products, **THAT WORK**!

3 Reasons Why My Herbal Formula WORK!

1. <u>QUALITY AMERICAN ORGANIC HERBS</u> Like vegetables and fruits, all herbs are not the same. Most manufacturers use cheap, filthy herbs from India and China. I do not! I use only the purest and most potent, American-grown, <u>organic</u> and wild-harvested herbs to make my formulae. **<u>Potent Herbs Create Powerful Health</u>**.

2. <u>MORE HERBS IN THE VAT</u> Most manufacturers use the standard formula of 10% herbs in the vat when making extracts. I FILL THE VATS TO THE VERY TOP! This is not rocket science—**<u>More Herbs Equals Stronger Products</u>**!

3. <u>PROVEN CLINICAL EXPERIENCE</u> My formulae are not some herbal *hypothesis* or textbook *theories*. They were <u>proven</u> in a <u>real clinic</u> with <u>real patients</u>. My California clinic spanned three decades where I helped thousands of people create powerful health naturally. **Today, my herbal formulae are proven effective with millions of customers** <u>just like you</u>.

except the feta cheese, if using, and simmer in a slow cooker (or in a pot on the back of a wood cookstove) for 3 to 4 hours, or until the meat is tender. Add the feta cheese and serve. **Makes 6 servings.**

■ ■ ■

A FAMILY AFFAIR

The house that Sara and Mark Seppanen own in Lake Norden, South Dakota, was built in 1898. Mark's parents took it over in the 1950s, and Sara and Mark bought it from them in 1993. Today, the couple—with their children Elsie (17), Leonard (8), Martin (6), Elaine (5), Julie (3), and Joseph (1)—have 320 acres sown with corn, wheat, soybeans, and alfalfa; a dairy cow; a small herd of beef cattle; four registered quarter horses; two border collies; and a few cats. The

The Seppanen family

older children milk the cow, Little Lady, for table milk; feed the calves and horses; and get corn from the silo for the corn-burning stove. The younger ones pitch in playfully. "Farming teaches the children so many valuable things," says Sara, who is originally from Massachusetts. "Animal care, how to grow crops, the care and repair of machinery . . . I didn't realize that a farmer needs to know so much!"

Potatoes on the Grill

Serve with grilled steak, grilled onions and/or mushrooms, and a green salad.

4 potatoes, washed
½ cup sour cream
2 tablespoons butter, softened
2 tablespoons olive oil
½ onion, peeled and sliced
3 cloves garlic, minced
½ teaspoon each: marjoram, parsley, basil, oregano
½ teaspoon salt
¼ teaspoon pepper

Light the grill. Slice the potatoes in half lengthwise, then into ¼-inch-thick pieces. In a large bowl, combine the sour cream, butter, olive oil, onion, garlic, herbs, salt, and pepper. Add the potatoes and stir to coat.

Spray a 2-foot length of aluminum foil with cooking spray and place the potato mixture in the center, spreading

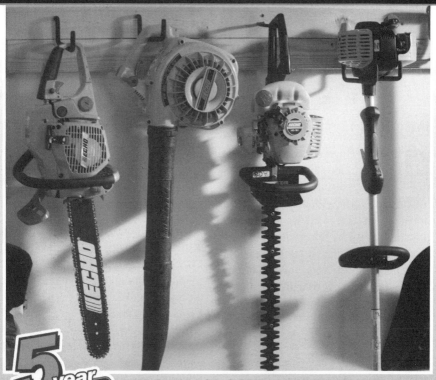

lengthwise. Bring the sides of the foil together and fold to make a seam at center top, then fold to seal at one end. Add ⅓ cup of water to the open end, then seal. Grill for 30 to 40 minutes. Check for doneness with a fork. **Makes 4 servings.**

■ ■ ■

DELICIOUS DECADES

Billie and Billy Whitfield of Clovis, New Mexico, started their married life by developing 10 acres of land into a small farm with a three-bedroom house, a cistern, well irrigation, and livestock. Five children and 50 years later, they have a small garden and grow peaches, apricots, and nectarines. Billie has been active in the Curry County Extension Homemakers Club,

Billie Whitfield

and this recipe was published in the club's cookbook.

Frontier Beef Jerky

A few pieces will tide you over 'til dinner. Place the unsliced meat in the freezer for about half an hour so that it becomes firm; this will make it easier to slice thin.

2 tablespoons liquid smoke
2 tablespoons Worcestershire sauce
1 teaspoon garlic powder
1 teaspoon salt
½ teaspoon pepper
1 pound lean beef, sliced (³⁄₁₆- to ¼-inch thick)

In a small bowl, combine all the ingredients, except the beef. Stir to mix well. Place the meat three or four layers deep in a non-aluminum container, spooning the liquid smoke mixture over each layer. Cover tightly; marinate 6 to 12 hours in the refrigerator, stirring occasionally. Preheat the oven to 200°F, line a large baking sheet with foil, and place a metal cooling rack over the sheet. Remove the meat from the container and place the strips on the rack. Dry in the oven, turning a few times, for 4 to 10 hours, or until the meat is dark and fibrous and forms sharp points when bent. **Makes about 30 pieces.** ☐☐

Mare-Anne Jarvela is senior editor at *The Old Farmer's Almanac* and a country cook herself.

STILL HUNGRY?

More recipes from these families—Ranch Breakfast, Rabbit Stew, Apple Dumplings, Chocolate Chip Doughnuts, and Hunter's Chicken—are available at **Almanac.com/food.**

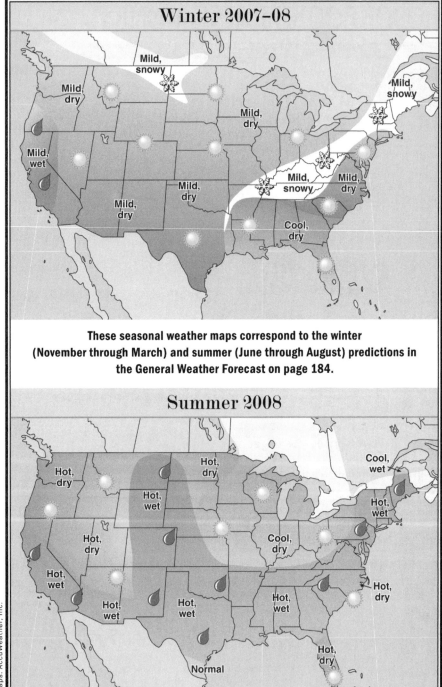

Winter 2007–08

Mild, snowy

Mild, dry

Mild, wet

Mild, snowy

Mild, dry

Mild, dry

Mild, dry

Mild, snowy

Mild, dry

Cool, dry

These seasonal weather maps correspond to the winter (November through March) and summer (June through August) predictions in the General Weather Forecast on page 184.

Summer 2008

Hot, dry

Hot, dry

Hot, wet

Cool, wet

Hot, wet

Hot, dry

Hot, wet

Cool, dry

Hot, wet

Hot, wet

Hot, wet

Hot, dry

Hot, dry

Normal

–maps: AccuWeather, Inc.

To Patrons

A Time Capsule of the Years

Someday the Almanac that you now hold in your hands will be a collector's item of inestimable value. In a few years, perhaps decades, long after this edition has outlived its primary purpose, someone will happen upon it and delight in his good fortune.

It happens all the time.

Throughout the year, we hear from people who have discovered old editions of this Almanac. With a mix of excitement, awe, and anticipation, they share the details of their finds:

■ "I was cleaning out my grandmother's attic, and there in the drawer of an old bureau was a bunch of *Old Farmer's Almanacs.*"

■ "I got some really old Almanacs at a garage sale."

■ "In an old icehouse, we found five *Old Farmer's Almanacs,* dogeared and faded, hanging on a nail."

■ "I picked up an 1862 edition at a used-book store."

A few of them want to sell us their old copies (thanks, but we have all we need). A few more want to sell their finds to anybody and ask *us* to assign a dollar value—sight unseen, no less. We leave that task to used-book dealers and the like. The vast majority of Almanac finders are keepers—and we are grateful for that. To them (and us) the old editions are priceless time capsules, offering a glimpse into another era, a different way of life.

For example, where but in our Almanac would you learn these things (all true, by the way; if you would like to know more, go to Almanac.com/extras):

■ the recipe for "easy and safe puke" (it's an antidote to poisoning), 1830

■ how to make butter by wrapping cream in a napkin or clean cloth and burying it a foot or so deep in the earth for 12 to 24 hours, 1889

■ about the Chrysler Bell Victory Siren, which made "the loudest continuous noise ever created by mechanical means—a noise equal to the shouting potential of 4,000 million ordinary men," 1964

■ advice on when to shop for what to save money (watches in February, canned goods in August), 1977

■ the pencil test to see how many children you'll have, 1989

■ when 99.3% of college students bathe (men on Saturday, women on Tuesday, neither on Sunday), 1995

■ the way to "iron" your face to prevent wrinkles, 2001

Even the advertisements mark time. These actually appeared:

■ "Tombstones direct to you, $9.95," 1948

■ "100-Year-Old Gypsy Bait Oil Makes Fish Bite: Catch 300 big fish or money back," 1958

■ "Eyeglasses by mail, limited to folks 40 years or older," 1971

continued

■ "Rooster Pills, for men who feel run down, worn out, and just plain uninterested," 1979

Speaking of great finds, some of you may have discovered the all-new *Old Farmer's Almanac for Kids,* Volume 2. It began appearing in book and specialty stores in July. (Can't find it? Go to shop.Almanac.com.) In addition to fun facts and stories about nature, gardening, sports, astronomy, weather, and more, Volume 2 has kids' calendar pages, with trivia and timeless wisdom for every day of every year. Plus, our Web site Almanac4kids.com has an all-new, fun—and free!—Activity Guide designed so that kids, parents, grandparents, and teachers can make the most of the Almanac for Kids itself. (To so many of you who helped to make Volume 1 a huge success: Thank you!)

Finally, we have an all-new Almanac experience for traditional Almanac users: a new face and new features at Almanac.com. Check it out and tell us what you think.

Read, use, and enjoy this Almanac. When the year is done, put it somewhere safe but out of sight so that, in a few years, it can be discovered and appreciated all over again.

J. S., June 2007

However, it is by our works and not our words that we would be judged. These, we hope, will sustain us in the humble though proud station we have so long held in the name of

Your obedient servant,

THE 2008 EDITION OF

The Old Farmer's Almanac

Established in 1792 and published every year thereafter

ROBERT B. THOMAS (1766–1846), *Founder*

YANKEE PUBLISHING INC.

EDITORIAL AND PUBLISHING OFFICES

P.O. Box 520, 1121 Main Street, Dublin, NH 03444
Phone: 603-563-8111 • Fax: 603-563-8252

EDITOR *(13th since 1792):* Janice Stillman
ART DIRECTOR: Margo Letourneau
SENIOR/INTERNET EDITOR: Mare-Anne Jarvela
COPY EDITOR: Jack Burnett
SENIOR ASSOCIATE EDITOR: Heidi Stonehill
RESEARCH EDITOR: Martie Majoros
ASSISTANT EDITOR: Sarah Perreault
WEATHER GRAPHICS AND CONSULTATION:
AccuWeather, Inc.

DIRECTOR, PRODUCTION AND NEW MEDIA:
Paul Belliveau
PRODUCTION DIRECTOR: Susan Gross
PRODUCTION MANAGER: David Ziarnowski
SENIOR PRODUCTION ARTISTS: Lucille Rines,
Rachel Kipka, Sarah Heineke

WEB SITE: ALMANAC.COM

WEB DESIGNER: Lou S. Eastman
PROGRAMMING: Reinvented, Inc.

CONTACT US

We welcome your questions and comments about articles in and topics for this Almanac. Mail all editorial correspondence to Editor, The Old Farmer's Almanac, P.O. Box 520, Dublin, NH 03444-0520; fax us at 603-563-8252; or send e-mail to us at almanac@yankeepub.com. *The Old Farmer's Almanac* can not accept responsibility for unsolicited manuscripts and will not acknowledge any hard-copy queries or manuscripts that do not include a stamped and addressed return envelope.

The newsprint in this edition of *The Old Farmer's Almanac* consists of 23 percent recycled content. All printing inks used are soy-based. This product is recyclable. Consult local recycling regulations for the right way to do it.

Thank you for buying this Almanac!
We hope you find it new, useful, and entertaining.
Thanks, too, to everyone who had a hand in it,
including advertisers, distributors, printers, and
sales and delivery people.

OUR CONTRIBUTORS

Bob Berman, our astronomy editor, is the director of Overlook Observatory in Woodstock and Storm King Observatory in Cornwall, both in New York. In 1976, he founded the Catskill Astronomical Society. Bob will go a long way for a good look at the sky: He has led many aurora and eclipse expeditions, venturing as far as the Arctic and Antarctic.

Castle Freeman Jr., who lives in southern Vermont, has been writing the Almanac's Farmer's Calendar essays for more than 25 years. The essays come out of his longtime interest in wildlife and the outdoors, gardening, history, and the life of rural New England. His most recent book is *My Life and Adventures* (St. Martin's Press, 2002).

George Greenstein, Ph.D., who has been the Almanac's astronomer for more than 30 years, is the Sidney Dillon Professor of Astronomy at Amherst College in Amherst, Massachusetts. His research has centered on cosmology, pulsars, and other areas of theoretical astrophysics, and on the mysteries of quantum mechanics. He has written three books and many magazine articles on science for the general public.

Celeste Longacre, our astrologer, often refers to astrology as "the world's second-oldest profession." A New Hampshire native, she has been a practicing astrologer for more than 25 years: "It is a study of timing, and timing is everything." Her book, *Love Signs* (Sweet Fern Publications, 1999), is available on her Web site, www.yourlovesigns.com.

Michael Steinberg, our meteorologist, has been forecasting weather for the Almanac since 1996. In addition to having college degrees in atmospheric science and meteorology, he brings a lifetime of experience to the task: He began making weather predictions when he attended the only high school in the world with weather Teletypes and radar.

A free catalog you should

HEAR about

Risk-FREE 45-day Home Trial

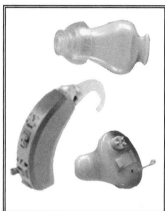

Reported by *The Wall Street Journal*
EarMate-4000 hearing aid results:

★ "Sound was crisp and clear."

★ "With different tip sizes to choose from, this fit our ears the best, resulting in minimal feedback."

★ "45-day money-back trial."

http://webreprints.djreprints.com/1005421313607.html

World's Best Hearing Value!

★ FREE catalog

★ 100% Risk-FREE offer

★ 45-day home trial

★ Ready to use

★ Compare to hearing aids costing $1,000 or more

FREE Hearing Aid Catalog!

Choose from many high-quality hearing aids at remarkably low prices. Order easily by mail from a family business with over 450,000 satisfied customers and 27 years selling hearing aids by mail.

www.HearingHelpExpress.com/15349

Call for your FREE Catalog!

1-800-782-6316

ext. 15-349

Don't pay another dime until you clip and mail this coupon for your free information!

☑ **YES!** Please rush me a free shop-at-home catalog. I understand there is no obligation and I get FREE shipping.

Dr/Mr/Mrs/Ms _____

Address _____

City/State/Zip _____

Mail to: **Hearing Help Express**
105 North First St., Dept 15-349
DeKalb, IL 60115-0586

Free Shipping!

THE 2008 EDITION OF

The Old Farmer's Almanac
Established in 1792 and published every year thereafter

Robert B. Thomas (1766–1846), *Founder*

YANKEE PUBLISHING INC.
P.O. Box 520, 1121 Main Street, Dublin, NH 03444
Phone: 603-563-8111 • Fax: 603-563-8252

GROUP PUBLISHER: John Pierce
PUBLISHER *(23rd since 1792):* Sherin Wight
EDITOR IN CHIEF: Judson D. Hale Sr.

ADVERTISING RATES AND INFORMATION
800-729-9265
Almanac.com/advertising
PRODUCTION ARTIST: Janet Calhoun

Classified Advertising
Gallagher Group • 203-263-7171

PUBLIC RELATIONS
Quinn/Brein • 206-842-8922

**TO PURCHASE ALMANAC PRODUCTS OR
FOR MAIL-ORDER INQUIRIES**
800-ALMANAC
Subscription to *The Old Farmer's Almanac:*
3 years, $24.95 (plus $4.95 s/h)

TO SELL ALMANAC PRODUCTS
Cindy Schlosser, 800-729-9265, ext. 126,
or Stacey Korpi, ext. 160.

NATIONAL DISTRIBUTOR
Curtis Circulation Company
New Milford, NJ

BOOKSTORE DISTRIBUTOR
Houghton Mifflin Company
Boston, MA

The Old Farmer's Almanac publications are
available for sales promotions or premiums.
Contact MeadWestvaco, 800-333-1125.

Jamie Trowbridge, *President;* Judson D. Hale Sr., John Pierce
Senior Vice Presidents; Jody Bugbee, Judson D. Hale Jr.,
Sherin Wight, *Vice Presidents.*

PRINTED IN U.S.A.

We're looking for people to—

Write Children's Books

By Patricia Pfitsch

If you've ever dreamed of writing for publication, this may be your best chance to turn that dream into a reality. If you qualify and show promise, we'll teach you—the same way I was taught—how to break into one of the most rewarding of all markets for new writers.

The $3 billion children's market

The continued success of publications for young people has led to a growing *need* for new writers to help create the $3 billion worth of children's books published each year, plus stories and articles for more than 600 magazines.

"But am I good enough?"

My dream of writing professionally while raising three kids on a farm was once bogged down in the same kind of uncertainty you may have experienced.

Then, an ad for the Institute seemed to offer the writing and selling skills I needed. I passed its test and entered into a richly rewarding relationship with an author-instructor, which was a major turning point in my life—as I hope it will be in yours.

The at-home training that has launched more successful children's authors than any other

The Institute of Children's Literature has successfully trained more new writers to meet the needs of this market than any other institution. Its unique program turned my dream into reality, and I became one of more than 11,000 Institute graduates who have published children's stories, articles, and books, including prestigious award winners. Now I'm using my skills at the Institute to train promising new writers.

Our test and professional evalution are fre

The promise that paid off

The Institute made exactly the same promise to me that it will make to you if you demonstrate basic writing aptitude:

You will complete at least one manuscript suitable to submit to editors by the time you finish the course.

With skill, empathy, and tough love when needed, my Institute instructor helped me complete and sell three of my course assignments, which, I later discovered, was not unusual.

Now, as a nationally published author of 7 children's books and over 500 stories and articles, I enjoy helping aspiring writers—as *I* was helped—to change their dreams into bright reality

Patricia Pfitsch, a graduate of our course, has published 552 stories and articles, plus 7 books, includin 3 award-winning novels and an Edgar nominee. She also an instructor at the Institute.

A nationally published author or editor is your one-on-one writing and selling coach

If you are accepted, you will be assigned a personal instructor who is a successful author and who becomes your energizing spark plug and deeply committed writing and selling coach.

We all work the same way. When you've finished an assignment at *your* pace, you send it to me. I edit it line-by-line and send you a detailed letter explaining my edits.

I point out your strengths, help eliminate weaknesses, and even show you how to turn bits of your everyday life into saleable writing. You push and I pull, and between us both, you learn how to write—and how to sell what you write.

We are the living proof

Among my fellow instructors, 30 are graduates of the Institute—all nationally published authors. One is a former bank teller, another came from nursing, and several were busy raising children. The wide range of backgrounds they represent is typical of Institute students.

What they shared in common was a dream and the willingness to take the first step toward realizing it. We're showered with letters like these:

"Little did I suspect I was about to be offered a new lease on life," writes Maribel de Suarez, Vega Baja, PR. "While still a student, I sold Assignment 5 and another piece for $1,750 and bought a computer. When I turned 80, I sold a collection of 15 stories and another book. . . . It was a dream come true. . . ."

"A whole new world"

"My first two published pieces were Institute assignments," says Michelle Barone, Denver, CO. "You have opened up a whole new world for me."

"I started the course when I was pregnant with my third child," writes C. Hope Flinchbaugh, York, PA. "Since then, I've been published in 13 magazines, and published a novel. . . . My instructor was the teacher of my dreams."

Don't let your dream die— send for your free test today!

If a writing life is the one you long for, here's your chance to test that dream. The Institute offers a revealing aptitude test for children's writing based on its 38 years of experience, and it's free.

If you pass, it's because you have the aptitude to make it in the world of writing for children. It takes work, it takes commitment, it takes courage—but you can do it.

Just fill out and mail the coupon below to receive your free test and 32-page introduction to our course, *Writing for Children and Teenagers,* and 80 of our instructors.

There is no obligation.

Institute of Children's Literature
93 Long Ridge Road
West Redding, CT 06896-0812

Yes, please send me your free *Aptitude Test for Children's Writing* and illustrated brochure. I understand I'm under no obligation, and no salesperson will visit me.

Please circle one and print name clearly:

Mr. Mrs. Ms. Miss   G1380

Name

Street

City

State   Zip

Recommended for college credits by the Connecticut Board for State Academic Awards and approved by the Connecticut Commissioner of Higher Education.

© COPYRIGHT © ICL 2007, A DIVISION OF WRITER'S INSTITUTE, INC.

by Bob Berman

Since Galileo's time, millions of people h.

telescope. If astronomy is a new hobby

Durable and trouble-free, a refractor telescope (shown with an optional star prism for easy viewing) never needs adjustment.

THROUGH THE LOOKING GLASS

ighted in owning a

, look-y here.

RULE 1: Ignore claims about power or magnification.

Most people equate "high power"—say, 300× or 600× (expressed as "300 power" and "600 power," respectively)—with "better telescope," but the importance of magnification is often exaggerated. Most celestial objects look best (clearer, sharper, and with no portion of the target outside the field of view) through a modest, 50× to 120× eyepiece. Higher power only makes an image blurrier, thanks to our atmosphere's fuzziness.

Any eyepiece with any power can be inserted into any telescope. (Yes, *the power lies in the eyepiece.*) Some companies include a 450× eyepiece to satisfy customers who suffer from "high-poweritis," but that degree of magnification produces an image that is dark and blurry.

(continued)

RULE 2: Focus on the tube: the fatter, the better.

Rather than ask about a telescope's power, inquire instead about its size. The answer, expressed in inches, will be more meaningful than any information about magnification. The diameter, or aperture, reveals a telescope's true value: specifically, how much light its lens or mirror can gather. For example, a telescope, or tube, that is 10 inches in diameter gathers, or lets in, more light than one that is 6 inches in diameter. *(The length of the tube is unimportant.)* To better understand this principle, look through the wrong end of several telescopes of different diameters.

RULE 3: Curb your enthusiasm—at first.

Most people who get a telescope expect to see billions of heavenly bodies right from their own backyard. In fact, *there are only about a dozen objects in the sky that appear spectacular;* everything else looks colorless, smudgy, and blurry, including all of the galaxies and nearly every nebula. (High power won't alter a smudgy view; under excessive high power, even the Moon would appear blurry.)

Some amateur astronomers love the faint smudges, and they train their eyes to recognize subtle features, such as tiny dark streaks on galaxies (also known as dust lanes, or spaces between spiral stellar arms) and dark nebulae thousands of light-years across. The majority of raw beginners will not be impressed by the thousands of galaxies and nebulae that could be viewed through a small telescope because they do not know what they are—yet.

Most novice astronomers use a telescope to view the Moon (except in its full phase, when its craters and mountains seem to vanish because the Sun is shining straight "down" on it), Jupiter, Saturn, a few nebulae, and a few double stars. Backyard amateurs rarely use their telescopes for seeing single stars. Half of the stars in the

'SCOPE STYLES

Galileo's telescopes were re‌fractors, the simplest type‌. The user peers through a‌ eyepiece and literally look‌ through the instrument (or‌ star prism, an accesso‌ that eliminates the need ‌ bend the neck or crouch‌

A reflector telescope (*top right*) uses mirrors to collect light. A refractor telescope (*right,* with a star prism) uses a lens to collect and focus light.

Most novice astronomers use a telescope to view the Moon, Jupiter, Saturn, and a few nebulae.

sky are double stars; they look single to the naked eye, but their beautiful contrasting colors are visible through a telescope. To find any of these, you must know where in the sky to look.

RULE 4: Start small.

It's probably a safe bet that, over the centuries, countless telescopes have ended up in attics, gathering dust. If astronomy is a new interest, *make your first telescope a relatively inexpensive one*—say, under $500. Something at that price will display exquisite images when pointed at the appropriate targets; just don't expect colorful swirling galaxies and nebulae that resemble the photos in magazines. And remember: You can always upgrade.

Many beginners look for portability and ease of setup, but those conveniences too often define telescopes that are too flimsy to provide a steady image.

If you want a hassle-free, durable instrument that never needs adjustment, get a refractor. This kind of telescope uses a lens to collect and focus light. You can buy a 2.4-inch (60mm) beginner's refractor for as little as $100. If you can afford more, get one that is at least 3 inches in diameter (about 75mm). A 4-inch (100mm) model would be better, while a 5-inch (125mm) one, although expensive, would be ideal.

A reflector telescope uses mirrors to collect light and "reflect" images. A 6- to 10-inch model with a motor drive to track sky objects automatically as they move during the night is a wonderful tool. But this type is large and must be carried in and out of the house for each use.

Isaac Newton invented the reflector, which uses mirrors to gather light. The user looks through the side of the tube and sees the image through a series of reflections. These are good instruments in the 6- to 12-inch size, but they are not easily portable.

Today, many amateur astronomers prefer catadioptic, or mixed-type, instruments. These have lenses and mirrors and "fold," or bounce, the light back and forth to produce a portable (albeit pricey) instrument with a short tube, which also serves well for terrestrial uses such as bird watching.

(c o n t i n u e d)

RULE 5: Open both eyes.

One of the most undervalued tools on the amateur astronomer's shelf is a pair of binoculars. *Binoculars are un-beatable for delivering a bright image* (brighter than that of most telescopes!), *a wide field, and a stereo-scopic view.* In fact, binoculars are a better choice for some objects than, say, the Keck Telescopes, which are state-of-the-art, ground-based telescopes on Hawaii's Mauna Kea extinct volcano. Binocular magnifications are too low for viewing planets well, but they are fine for sighting loose star clusters and for sweeping the Milky Way. Keep this in mind:

- Binoculars over 10× cause images to shake too much, so avoid them.

- Image-stabilized binoculars are preferable, but they are expensive.

- In order to have an image that is bright enough for astronomical use, make sure that the second number in the specs (as in 7×35, expressed as "seven power") is at least four times greater than the first. However, any binoculars whose second number is 30 or higher and whose magnification is 7 to 10 can provide satisfying views of many celestial phenomena.

RULE 6: Join a club.

Local astronomy clubs exist in nearly every part of the country and welcome enthusiasts of all experience levels. Most clubs hold monthly sky-observing sessions with impressive telescopes. *A club is one of the best ways to explore the wonders of the night sky and learn more about the equipment.* Many clubs have electronic newsletters, with articles and all sorts of astronomical advice; if a newsletter is offered, be sure to sign up.

(c o n t i n u e d)

RED LIGHT

It takes at least ten minute to acquire night vision (tha is, to see well in the dark) and a red light enables you to read a star chart withou losing that dark sensitivit Pick up a red LED flashligh in a hardware or home sup ply store, or use red cell phone and rubber bands t cover a flashlight.

GREEN LIGHT

Red lasers do not cast beam into the sky, bu green ones do, especiall at a dark site away fro artificial lights. They loo "cool" and allow a know edgeable stargazer t point out celestial object to friends. However, neve point any laser at a pe son's eyes or aim a gree laser at an airplane. Yo can harm the eyes of th pilots or passengers, an it is a federal offense.

It doesn't play games, take pictures, or give you the weather.

The Jitterbug™ developed with Samsung®. It's the cell phone that's changing all the rules.

For people like me, who want a phone that's easy to see, easy to hear, and easy to use. Over the years, cell phones have become smaller and smaller with so many complicated features. They are harder to program and harder to use. But the Jitterbug Cell Phone has simplified everything, so it's not only easy to use, it's easy to try. No crowded malls, no waiting in line, no confusing sales people, or complicated plans. Affordable and convenient cell phone service is only a toll-free phone call away.

Questions about Jitterbug? Try our pre-recorded Jitterbug Toll-Free Hotline **1-800-230-9045.**

The new Jitterbug™ Cell Phone makes calling simple!
- Available in OneTouch™ or Full Dial model
- Large, bright, easy-to-see display and buttons
- Push "Yes" to call directly from personal phone list
- Soft ear cushion and louder volume for better sound quality
- Hearing aid compatible
- Familiar dial tone confirms service
- Service as low as $10 a month*
- Access help wherever you go

Why pay for minutes you'll never use!		
	Simple 30 Plan	Simple 60 Plan
Monthly Price	$15.00	$20.00
Included Minutes/Month	30	60
Operator Assistance	24/7	24/7
911 Access	FREE	FREE
Long Distance Calls	No add'l charge	No add'l charge
Calls from Anywhere in US	No add'l charge	No add'l charge
Nationwide Coverage	Yes	Yes
Trial Period	30 days	30 days

Available in a simple 12-button Dial Phone and an even simpler 3-button OneTouch Phone for easy access to the operator, the number of your choice, and 911.

Service as low as $10 a month and a 30-day money-back guarantee.**
If you've ever wanted the security and convenience of a cell phone, but never wanted the fancy features and minutes you don't need… Jitterbug is for you. Like me, you'll soon be telling your friends about Jitterbug. Call now… this product is not available in stores!

Jitterbug™ Cell Phone Item# BU-4722
Call now for our lowest price.
Please mention promotional code 33400.

1-866-540-0297
www.jitterbugdirect.com

brought to you by

for Boomers and Beyond™

1998 Ruffin Mill Road
Colonial Heights, VA 23834

*Not including government taxes, assessment surcharges, and activation fee.
**Applies to phone only, provided talk time usage is fewer than 30 minutes. Usage charges may apply.

Only a handful of major observatories make their telescopes available to the public, although many schools and science museums have telescopes and programs and open nights throughout the year. Contact the science or astronomy departments.

HOW TO AVOID THE WIGGLES

Telescopes belong on a lawn, not on a wooden deck or pavement, although pavement is better than a deck. A deck vibrates, even if you can't feel it. Pavement heats up during the day and, as the heat from it dissipates after sundown, this warm air acts like the wiggly air you see rising from a radiator or woodstove to distort an image as seen through a telescope.

Telescopes also should not be used at an open window. The same warm air principle distorts the view: Heat from the house escapes through the open window, making for turbulent air. Avoid closed windows, too, as the quality of the glass will distort an image.

SEE FOR YOURSELF

As a calendar of the heavens, *The Old Farmer's Almanac* provides accurate sighting times for a variety of celestial events and highlights throughout the year (see pages 98, 100, 102–104, and 114–141). For planet viewing times in your area, go to Almanac.com/astronomy.

Bob Berman is the Almanac's astronomy editor. His latest book is *Shooting for the Moon* (Lyons Press 2007).

Eclipses

■ There will be four eclipses in 2008, two of the Sun and two of the Moon. Solar eclipses are visible only in certain areas and require eye protection to be viewed safely. Lunar eclipses are technically visible from the entire night side of Earth, but during a penumbral eclipse, the dimming of the Moon's illumination is slight.

FEBRUARY 7: annular eclipse of the Sun. This eclipse will not be visible from North America.

FEBRUARY 20–21: total eclipse of the Moon. The entire eclipse can be seen from eastern and central North America. The Moon enters Earth's umbral shadow on February 20 at 8:43 P.M. EST, and the eclipse becomes total at 10:01 P.M. EST. Totality ends at 10:52 P.M. EST, and the umbral phase ends at 12:09 A.M. EST on February 21. The penumbral phase (only) will occur over western North America, at the time of moonrise; it will be difficult to see changes in the Moon's appearance.

AUGUST 1: total eclipse of the Sun. In North America, totality will be visible only from arctic Canada. The partial phase will be visible from extreme northeastern areas of North America, where the Sun will rise partially eclipsed.

AUGUST 16: partial eclipse of the Moon. This eclipse will not be visible from North America.

Full-Moon Dates (Eastern Time)				
	2008	**2009**	**2010**	**2011**	**2012**
Jan.	22	10	30	19	9
Feb.	20	9	28	18	7
Mar.	21	10	29	19	8
Apr.	20	9	28	17	6
May	19	9	27	17	5
June	18	7	26	15	4
July	18	7	25	15	3
Aug.	16	5	24	13	1&31
Sept.	15	4	23	12	29
Oct.	14	4	22	11	29
Nov.	13	2	21	10	28
Dec.	12	2 & 31	21	10	28

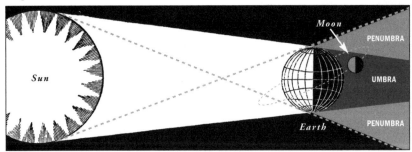

In a lunar eclipse *(above)*, Earth is between the Sun and the Moon. The umbra is the central dark part of the shadow created during an eclipse. The penumbra is the area of partial darkness surrounding the umbra. During a total lunar eclipse, the Moon passes through the umbra.

Total Solar Eclipse Dates, 2009–15	
DATE	**REGIONS WITH VISIBLE TOTALITY**
2009 July 22	India, China, central Pacific Ocean
2010 July 11	South Pacific Ocean, southern South America
2012 November 13	Northern Australia, South Pacific Ocean
2015 March 20	North Atlantic Ocean, Norwegian Sea

Black Listed Cancer Treatment Could Save Your Life

As unbelievable as it seems the key to stopping many cancers has been around for over 30 years. Yet it has been banned. Blocked. And kept out of your medicine cabinet by the very agency designed to protect your health—the FDA.

In 1966, the senior oncologist at a prominent New York hospital rocked the medical world when he developed a serum that **"shrank cancer tumors in 45 minutes!"** 90 minutes later they were gone... Headlines hit every major paper around the world. Time and again this life saving treatment worked miracles, but the FDA ignored the research and hope he brought and shut him down.

You read that right. He was not only shut down—but also forced out of the country where others benefited from his discovery. How many other treatments have they been allowed to hide?

Decades ago, European research scientist Dr. Johanna Budwig, a six-time Nobel Award nominee, discovered a totally natural formula that not only protects against the development of cancer, but has helped people all over the world diagnosed with incurable cancer—now lead normal lives.

After 30 years of study, Dr. Budwig discovered that the blood of seriously ill cancer patients was deficient in certain substances and nutrients. Yet, healthy blood always contained these ingredients. It was the lack of these nutrients that allowed cancer cells to grow wild and out of control.

It has been shown that by simply eating a combination of two natural and delicious foods (found on page 134) not only can cancer be prevented—but in some cases it was actually healed! "Symptoms of cancer, liver dysfunction, and diabetes were completely alleviated." Remarkably, what Dr. Budwig discovered was a totally natural way for eradicating cancer.

However, when she went to publish these results so that everyone could benefit—**she was blocked by manufacturers with heavy financial stakes!** For over 10 years now her methods have proved effective—yet she is denied publication—blocked by the giants who don't want you to read her words.

What's more, the world is full of expert minds like Dr. Budwig who have pursued cancer remedies and come up with remarkable natural formulas and diets that work for hundreds and thousands of patients. *How to Fight Cancer & Win* author William Fischer has studied these methods and revealed their secrets for you—so that you or someone you love may be spared the horrors of conventional cancer treatments.

As early as 1947, Virginia Livingston, M.D., isolated a cancer-causing microbe. She noted that every cancer sample analyzed contained it.

This microbe—a bacteria that is actually in each of us from birth to death—multiplies and promotes cancer when the immune system is weakened by disease, stress, or poor nutrition. Worst of all, the microbes secrete a special hormone protector that short-circuits our body's immune system—allowing the microbes to grow undetected for years. No wonder so many patients are riddled with cancer by the time it is detected. But there is hope even for them...

Throughout the pages of *How to Fight Cancer & Win* you'll meet real people who were diagnosed with cancer—suffered through harsh conventional treatments—turned their backs on so called modern medicine—only to be miraculously healed by natural means! Here is just a sampling of what others have to say about the book.

"We purchased *How to Fight Cancer & Win*, and immediately my husband started following the recommended diet for his just diagnosed colon cancer. He refused the surgery that our doctors advised. Since following the regime recommended in the book he has had no problems at all, cancerwise. If not cured, we believe the cancer has to be in remission." —*Thelma B.*

"As a cancer patient who has been battling lymphatic cancer on and off for almost three years now, I was very pleased to stumble across *How to Fight Cancer & Win*. The book was inspiring, well-written and packed with useful information for any cancer patient looking to maximize his or her chances for recovery." —*Romany S.*

"I've been incorporating Dr. Budwig's natural remedy into my diet and have told others about it. Your book is very informative and has information I've never heard about before. Thanks for the wonderful information." —*Molly G.*

Claim your book today and you will be one of the lucky few who no longer have to wait for cures that get pushed "underground" by big business and money hungry giants.

To get your copy of *How to Fight Cancer & Win* go to www.agorahealthbooks.com/P6H96 or call **1-888-821-3609 and ask for code P6H96** to order by credit card. Or write "Fight Cancer—Dept. P6H96" on a plain piece of paper with your name, address, phone number (in case we have a question about your order) and mail it with a check for $19.95 plus $5.00 shipping to: **Agora Health Books, Dept. P6H96, P.O. Box 925 Frederick, MD 21705-9838**

If you are not completely satisfied, return the book within one year for a complete and total refund—no questions asked. This will probably be the most important information you and your loved ones receive—so order today!

ID#P6H96

Bright Stars

Transit Times

■ This table shows the time (EST or EDT) and altitude of a star as it transits the meridian (i.e., reaches its highest elevation while passing over the horizon's south point) at Boston on the dates shown. The transit time on any other date differs from that of the nearest date listed by approximately four minutes per day. To find the time of a star's transit for your location, convert its time at Boston using Key Letter C.*

Star	Constellation	Magnitude	Time of Transit (EST/EDT) ☞ Bold = P.M. ☞ Light = A.M.						Altitude (degrees)
			Jan. 1	Mar. 1	May 1	July 1	Sept. 1	Nov. 1	
Altair	Aquila	0.8	**12:51**	8:55	5:55	1:56	**9:48**	**5:48**	56.3
Deneb	Cygnus	1.3	**1:42**	9:46	6:46	2:46	**10:39**	**6:39**	92.8
Fomalhaut	Psc. Aus.	1.2	**3:57**	**12:01**	9:01	5:01	12:53	**8:54**	17.8
Algol	Perseus	2.2	**8:07**	**4:11**	**1:12**	9:12	5:08	1:08	88.5
Aldebaran	Taurus	0.9	**9:35**	**5:39**	**2:39**	10:39	6:35	2:36	64.1
Rigel	Orion	0.1	**10:13**	**6:17**	**3:17**	11:17	7:14	3:14	39.4
Capella	Auriga	0.1	**10:15**	**6:19**	**3:19**	11:19	7:15	3:16	93.6
Bellatrix	Orion	1.6	**10:24**	**6:28**	**3:28**	11:28	7:24	3:25	54.0
Betelgeuse	Orion	var. 0.4	**10:54**	**6:58**	**3:58**	11:58	7:54	3:55	55.0
Sirius	Can. Maj.	−1.4	**11:43**	7:47	4:48	**12:48**	8:44	4:44	31.0
Procyon	Can. Min.	0.4	12:41	**8:41**	**5:41**	**1:42**	9:38	5:38	52.9
Pollux	Gemini	1.2	12:47	**8:47**	**5:47**	**1:48**	9:44	5:44	75.7
Regulus	Leo	1.4	3:10	**11:10**	**8:10**	**4:11**	**12:07**	8:07	59.7
Spica	Virgo	var. 1.0	6:26	2:31	**11:27**	**7:27**	**3:23**	11:23	36.6
Arcturus	Boötes	−0.1	7:17	3:21	12:18	**8:18**	**4:14**	**12:14**	66.9
Antares	Scorpius	var. 0.9	9:30	5:34	2:34	**10:31**	**6:27**	**2:27**	21.3
Vega	Lyra	0	11:38	7:42	4:42	12:38	**8:34**	**4:34**	86.4

Rise and Set Times

■ To find the time of a star's rising at Boston on any date, subtract the interval shown at right from the star's transit time on that date; add the interval to find the star's setting time. To find the rising and setting times for your city, convert the Boston transit times above using the Key Letter* shown at right before applying the interval. The directions in which the stars rise and set, shown for Boston, are generally useful throughout the United States.

Deneb, Algol, Capella, and Vega are circumpolar stars—they never set but appear to circle the celestial north pole.

Star	Interval (h. m.)	Rising Key	Rising Dir.	Setting Key	Setting Dir.
Altair	6 36	B	EbN	E	WbN
Fomalhaut	3 59	E	SE	D	SW
Aldebaran	7 06	B	ENE	D	WNW
Rigel	5 33	D	EbS	B	WbS
Bellatrix	6 27	B	EbN	D	WbN
Betelgeuse	6 31	B	EbN	D	WbN
Sirius	5 00	D	ESE	B	WSW
Procyon	6 23	B	EbN	D	WbN
Pollux	8 01	A	NE	E	NW
Regulus	6 49	B	EbN	D	WbN
Spica	5 23	D	EbS	B	WbS
Arcturus	7 19	A	ENE	E	WNW
Antares	4 17	E	SEbE	A	SWbW

*The values of Key Letters are given in the Time Corrections table (page 235).

–Beth Krommes

Find more heavenly details at Almanac.com.

The Visible Planets

■ Listed here for Boston are viewing suggestions for and the rise and set times (EST/EDT) of Venus, Mars, Jupiter, and Saturn on specific days each month, as well as when it is best to view Mercury. Approximate rise and set times for other days can be found by interpolation. Use the Key Letters at the right of each listing to convert the times for other localities **(see pages 110 and 235).** For all planet rise and set times by zip code, visit **Almanac.com/astronomy.**

Venus

The brightest planet is best seen in January and December. It starts 2008 shining conspicuously in the predawn twilight and meets Jupiter on February 1. By late February, it is next to Mercury, low and inconspicuous, where it remains that way until vanishing in April. The cloud-covered world reemerges as an evening star in September and can be glimpsed by southern observers. Others can look for it low in the west, 40 minutes after sunset, during October. December begins with a Venus-Jupiter-Moon conjunction and ends with the planet 25 degrees high as evening twilight fades.

Jan. 1	rise	4:11	D	Apr. 1	rise	5:54	C	July 1	**set**	**8:52**	E	Oct. 1	**set**	**7:35**	B
Jan. 11	rise	4:33	E	Apr. 11	rise	5:43	C	July 11	**set**	**8:56**	E	Oct. 11	**set**	**7:27**	A
Jan. 21	rise	4:51	E	Apr. 21	rise	5:31	B	July 21	**set**	**8:56**	E	Oct. 21	**set**	**7:24**	A
Feb. 1	rise	5:07	E	May 1	rise	5:20	B	Aug. 1	**set**	**8:49**	D	Nov. 1	**set**	**7:26**	A
Feb. 11	rise	5:17	E	May 11	rise	5:11	B	Aug. 11	**set**	**8:39**	D	Nov. 11	**set**	**6:35**	A
Feb. 21	rise	5:20	E	May 21	rise	5:06	A	Aug. 21	**set**	**8:27**	C	Nov. 21	**set**	**6:50**	A
Mar. 1	rise	5:19	D	June 1	rise	5:05	A	Sept. 1	**set**	**8:13**	C	Dec. 1	**set**	**7:09**	A
Mar. 11	rise	6:14	D	June 11	**set**	**8:24**	E	Sept. 11	**set**	**7:59**	B	Dec. 11	**set**	**7:30**	A
Mar. 21	rise	6:06	D	June 21	**set**	**8:40**	E	Sept. 21	**set**	**7:46**	B	Dec. 21	**set**	**7:52**	A
												Dec. 31	**set**	**8:12**	B

Mars

Mars is brightest on January 1, still ablaze from its biennial close approach to Earth two weeks earlier. Retrograding in Taurus, Mars fades in January from magnitude –1.5 to –0.6. It dims again in February and yet again in March, as it moves into Gemini. The red planet remains high at nightfall, but it is no longer very bright in April and less so in May, as it moves into Cancer and passes near the Beehive star cluster for three days, starting on the 22nd. By June, in Leo, it is a dull magnitude 1.6. Mars is difficult to see in August and is lost in the Sun's glare from September onward.

Jan. 1	**set**	**6:55**	E	Apr. 1	**set**	**2:38**	E	July 1	**set**	**11:02**	D	Oct. 1	**set**	**7:09**	B
Jan. 11	**set**	**6:02**	E	Apr. 11	**set**	**2:16**	E	July 11	**set**	**10:37**	D	Oct. 11	**set**	**6:46**	B
Jan. 21	**set**	**5:13**	E	Apr. 21	**set**	**1:53**	E	July 21	**set**	**10:11**	D	Oct. 21	**set**	**6:24**	B
Feb. 1	**set**	**4:26**	E	May 1	**set**	**1:31**	E	Aug. 1	**set**	**9:43**	C	Nov. 1	**set**	**6:02**	A
Feb. 11	**set**	**3:50**	E	May 11	**set**	**1:08**	E	Aug. 11	**set**	**9:17**	C	Nov. 11	**set**	**4:44**	A
Feb. 21	**set**	**3:18**	E	May 21	**set**	**12:43**	E	Aug. 21	**set**	**8:51**	C	Nov. 21	**set**	**4:27**	A
Mar. 1	**set**	**2:52**	E	June 1	**set**	**12:17**	E	Sept. 1	**set**	**8:23**	C	Dec. 1	**set**	**4:13**	A
Mar. 11	**set**	**3:27**	E	June 11	**set**	**11:52**	D	Sept. 11	**set**	**7:58**	B	Dec. 11	rise	7:00	E
Mar. 21	**set**	**3:03**	E	June 21	**set**	**11:28**	D	Sept. 21	**set**	**7:33**	B	Dec. 21	rise	6:55	E
												Dec. 31	rise	6:49	E

☞ **Bold = P.M.**   ☞ Light = A.M.

–Illustrated by Beth Krommes

Jupiter

♃ **For Northern Hemisphere observers, Jupiter is** never more than one-third of the way up in the sky this year. On February 1, it has a predawn meeting with Venus. Rising two hours earlier each month, it appears before midnight at the beginning of June. At opposition on July 9, it blazes at magnitude –2.7 all night. After a conjunction with Venus and the Moon on December 1, Jupiter is low in the sky.

Jan. 1......rise 6:44 E	Apr. 1......rise 2:53 E	July 1......**rise 8:47** E	Oct. 1......**set 11:30** A
Jan. 11.....rise 6:14 E	Apr. 11....rise 2:18 E	July 11......set 5:15 A	Oct. 11......set 10:54 A
Jan. 21.....rise 5:44 E	Apr. 21....rise 1:41 E	July 21......set 4:29 A	Oct. 21......set 10:21 A
Feb. 1......rise 5:11 E	May 1......rise 1:03 E	Aug. 1 ......set 3:40 A	Nov. 1......**set 9:45** A
Feb. 11.....rise 4:39 E	May 11....rise 12:21 E	Aug. 11 ...set 2:56 A	Nov. 11....set 8:13 A
Feb. 21.....rise 4:08 E	May 21 ....rise **11:40** E	Aug. 21 ...set 2:13 A	Nov. 21....set 7:43 A
Mar. 1 .....rise 3:39 E	June 1 ......rise **10:55** E	Sept. 1 ....set 1:28 A	Dec. 1......set 7:13 A
Mar. 11 ...rise 4:06 E	June 11 ....rise **10:13** E	Sept. 11 ...set 12:44 A	Dec. 11....set 6:44 A
Mar. 21 ...rise 3:32 E	June 21 ....rise **9:30** E	Sept. 21 ...set 12:06 A	Dec. 21....set 6:16 A
			Dec. 31.....set 5:48 A

Saturn

♄ **With its shiny rings now more edgewise than** they've been for ten years, Saturn is bright but not brilliant. The planet looks conspicuous to the naked eye and glorious through a telescope. In January, it is high by 11:00 P.M. The ringed world reaches opposition on February 24, when it is closest to Earth and shines at magnitude 0.2 all night. It is visible most of the night throughout spring but becomes an evening-only object in June and July. Saturn vanishes into evening twilight in August, reemerges in the predawn east in the autumn, and begins to rise before midnight in December.

Jan. 1........**rise 9:02** B	Apr. 1 ......set 5:13 D	July 1........**set 11:16** D	Oct. 1......rise 4:40 B
Jan. 11.....**rise 8:21** B	Apr. 11.....set 4:33 D	July 11......**set 10:39** D	Oct. 11....rise 4:07 B
Jan. 21.....**rise 7:39** B	Apr. 21.....set 3:53 D	July 21......**set 10:02** D	Oct. 21....rise 3:33 B
Feb. 1......**rise 6:52** B	May 1.......set 3:13 D	Aug. 1 ......**set 9:21** D	Nov. 1......rise 2:56 B
Feb. 11.....**rise 6:09** B	May 11.....set 2:34 D	Aug. 11.....**set 8:45** D	Nov. 11....rise 1:21 B
Feb. 21.....**rise 5:25** B	May 21.....set 1:55 D	Aug. 21.....**set 8:08** D	Nov. 21....rise 12:45 B
Mar. 1 ......set 6:20 D	June 1.......set 1:13 D	Sept. 1.......**set 7:28** D	Dec. 1 .....rise 12:09 B
Mar. 11.....set 6:39 D	June 11.....set 12:31 D	Sept. 11 ...rise 5:46 B	Dec. 11.....**rise 11:28** A
Mar. 21.....set 5:58 D	June 21 .....**set 11:53** D	Sept. 21 ...rise 5:13 B	Dec. 21....**rise 10:50** B
			Dec. 31 ....**rise 10:11** B

Mercury

☿ **Mercury is best seen when it's at least five degrees above the horizon, 35 minutes after sunset or before** sunrise, and when its brightness exceeds magnitude 0.5. Look in the western sky from January 12–28 and from April 25 to May 16. In the predawn eastern sky, look in mid-July and during the last half of October. Mercury joins brilliant Jupiter in the evening sky on December 30 and 31.

DO NOT CONFUSE ■ *Saturn with Leo's brightest star, Regulus, from February through June. Saturn is brighter.* ■ *Jupiter with Venus in late January and early February, and from late November through early December. Venus is always brighter.* ■ *Mercury with Venus in late February. Venus is brighter.* ■ *Mercury with Taurus's star Aldebaran in late June and early July. Both are reddish, but Mercury is brighter and lower.*

The Twilight Zone

How to determine the length of twilight and the times of dawn and dark.

■ Twilight is the time preceding sunrise and again following sunset, when the sky is partially illuminated. The three ranges of twilight are defined according to the Sun's position below the horizon. Civil twilight occurs when the Sun is between the horizon and 6 degrees below the horizon (visually, the horizon is clearly defined). Nautical twilight occurs when the Sun is between 6 and 12 degrees below the horizon (the horizon is indistinct). Astronomical twilight occurs when the Sun is between 12 and 18 degrees below the horizon (sky illumination is imperceptible). When the Sun is at 18 degrees (dawn or dark) or below, there is no illumination.

LENGTH OF TWILIGHT (hours and minutes)

LATITUDE	Jan. 1 to Apr. 10	Apr. 11 to May 2	May 3 to May 14	May 15 to May 25	May 26 to July 22	July 23 to Aug. 3	Aug. 4 to Aug. 14	Aug. 15 to Sept. 5	Sept. 6 to Dec. 31
25°N to 30°N	1 20	1 23	1 26	1 29	1 32	1 29	1 26	1 23	1 20
31°N to 36°N	1 26	1 28	1 34	1 38	1 43	1 38	1 34	1 28	1 26
37°N to 42°N	1 33	1 39	1 47	1 52	1 59	1 52	1 47	1 39	1 33
43°N to 47°N	1 42	1 51	2 02	2 13	2 27	2 13	2 02	1 51	1 42
48°N to 49°N	1 50	2 04	2 22	2 42	—	2 42	2 22	2 04	1 50

TO DETERMINE THE LENGTH OF TWILIGHT: The length of twilight changes with latitude and the time of year and is independent of time zones. Use the **Time Corrections** table, **page 235**, to find the latitude of your city or the city nearest you. Use that figure in the chart above with the appropriate date to calculate the length of twilight in your area.

TO DETERMINE WHEN DAWN OR DARK WILL OCCUR: Calculate the sunrise/sunset times for your locality, using the instructions in **How to Use This Almanac, page 110.** Subtract the length of twilight from the time of sunrise to determine when dawn breaks. Add the length of twilight to the time of sunset to determine when dark descends.

E X A M P L E :

Boston, Mass. (latitude 42°22')

Sunrise, August 1	5:37 A.M. EDT
Length of twilight	− 1 52
Dawn breaks	3:45 A.M.
Sunset, August 1	8:04 P.M. EDT
Length of twilight	+ 1 52
Dark descends	9:56 P.M.

Principal Meteor Showers

SHOWER	BEST VIEWING	POINT OF ORIGIN	DATE OF MAXIMUM*	PEAK RATE (/HR.)**	ASSOCIATED COMET
Quadrantid	Predawn	N	Jan. 4	80	—
Lyrid	Predawn	S	Apr. 22	12	Thatcher
Eta Aquarid	Predawn	SE	May 4	20	Halley
Delta Aquarid	Predawn	S	July 30	10	—
Perseid	Predawn	NE	Aug. 11–13	75	Swift-Tuttle
Draconid	Late evening	NW	Oct. 9	6	Giacobini-Zinner
Orionid	Predawn	S	Oct. 21–22	25	Halley
Taurid	Late evening	S	Nov. 9	6	Encke
Leonid	Predawn	S	Nov. 18	20	Tempel-Tuttle
Andromedid	Late evening	S	Nov. 25–27	5	Biela
Geminid	All night	NE	Dec. 13–14	65	—
Ursid	Predawn	N	Dec. 22	12	Tuttle

*May vary by one or two days in either direction.   **Approximate.*

Astronomical Glossary

Aphelion (Aph.): The point in a planet's orbit that is farthest from the Sun.

Apogee (Apo.): The point in the Moon's orbit that is farthest from Earth.

Celestial Equator (Eq.): The imaginary circle around the celestial sphere that can be thought of as the plane of Earth's equator projected out onto the sphere.

Celestial Sphere: An imaginary sphere projected into space that represents the entire sky, with an observer on Earth at its center. All celestial bodies other than Earth are imagined as being on its inside surface.

Conjunction: The time at which two or more celestial bodies appear closest in the sky. **Inferior (Inf.):** Mercury or Venus is between the Sun and Earth. **Superior (Sup.):** The Sun is between a planet and Earth. Actual dates for conjunctions are given in the **Right-Hand Calendar Pages, 115–141;** the best times for viewing the closely aligned bodies are given in the **SKY WATCH** section of the **Left-Hand Calendar Pages, 114–140.**

Declination: The celestial latitude of an object in the sky, measured in degrees north or south of the celestial equator; analogous to latitude on Earth. The Almanac gives the Sun's declination at noon.

Eclipse, Lunar: The full Moon enters the shadow of Earth, which cuts off all or part of the sunlight reflected off the Moon. **Total:** The Moon passes completely through the **umbra** (central dark part) of Earth's shadow. **Partial:** Only part of the Moon passes through the umbra. **Penumbral:** The Moon passes through only the **penumbra** (area of partial darkness surrounding the umbra). **See page 98** for more eclipse information.

Eclipse, Solar: Earth enters the shadow of the new Moon, which cuts off all or part of the Sun's light. **Total:** Earth passes through the umbra (central dark part) of

the Moon's shadow, resulting in totality for observers within a narrow band on Earth. **Annular:** The Moon appears silhouetted against the Sun, with a ring of sunlight showing around it. **Partial:** The Moon blocks only part of the Sun.

Ecliptic: The apparent annual path of the Sun around the celestial sphere. The plane of the ecliptic is tipped $23\frac{1}{2}°$ from the celestial equator.

Elongation: The difference in degrees between the celestial longitudes of a planet and the Sun. **Greatest Elongation (Gr. Elong.):** The greatest apparent distance of a planet from the Sun, as seen from Earth.

Epact: A number from 1 to 30 that indicates the Moon's age on January 1 at Greenwich, England; used for determining the date of Easter.

Equinox: When the Sun crosses the celestial equator. This event occurs two times each year: **Vernal** is around March 21 and **Autumnal** is around September 23.

Evening Star: A planet that is above the western horizon at sunset and less than 180° east of the Sun in right ascension.

Golden Number: A number in the 19-year cycle of the Moon, used for determining the date of Easter. (Approximately every 19 years, the Moon's phases occur on the same dates.) Add 1 to any given year and divide by 19; the remainder is the Golden Number. If there is no remainder, the Golden Number is 19.

Greatest Illuminated Extent (Gr. Illum. Ext.): When the maximum surface area of a planet is illuminated as seen from Earth.

Julian Period: A period of 7,980 years beginning January 1, 4713 B.C. It provides a chronological basis for the study of ancient history. To find the Julian year, add 4,713 to any year.

Midnight: Astronomical midnight is the time when the Sun is opposite its highest point in the sky (noon). Midnight is neither A.M. nor P.M., although 12-hour digital clocks typically display midnight as 12:00 A.M. On a 24-hour time cycle, 00:00, rather than 24:00, usually indicates midnight.

Moon on Equator: The Moon is on the celestial equator.

Moon Rides High/Runs Low: The Moon is highest above or farthest below the celestial equator.

Moonrise/Moonset: When the Moon rises above or sets below the horizon.

Moon's Phases: The changing appearance of the Moon, caused by the different angles at which it is illuminated by the Sun. **First Quarter:** Right half of the Moon is illuminated. **Full:** The Sun and the Moon are in opposition; the entire disk of the Moon is illuminated. **Last Quarter:** Left half of the Moon is illuminated. **New:** The Sun and the Moon are in conjunction; the entire disk of the Moon is darkened.

Moon's Place, Astronomical: The actual position of the Moon within the constellations on the celestial sphere. **Astrological:** The astrological position of the Moon within the zodiac, according to calculations made more than 2,000 years ago. Because of precession of the equinoxes and other factors, this is not the Moon's actual position in the sky.

Morning Star: A planet that is above the eastern horizon at sunrise and less than 180° west of the Sun in right ascension.

Node: Either of the two points where a celestial body's orbit intersects the ecliptic. **Ascending:** When the body is moving from south to north of the ecliptic. **Descending:** When the body is moving from north to south of the ecliptic.

Occultation (Occn.): When the Moon or a planet eclipses a star or planet.

Opposition: The Moon or a planet appears on the opposite side of the sky from the Sun (elongation 180°).

Perigee (Perig.): The point in the Moon's orbit that is closest to Earth.

Perihelion (Perih.): The point in a planet's orbit that is closest to the Sun.

Precession: The slowly changing position of the stars and equinoxes in the sky resulting from variations in the orientation of Earth's axis.

Right Ascension (R.A.): The celestial longitude of an object in the sky, measured eastward along the celestial equator in hours of time from the vernal equinox; analogous to longitude on Earth.

Roman Indiction: A number within a 15-year cycle, established January 1, A.D. 313, as a fiscal term. Add 3 to any given year in the Christian era and divide by 15; the remainder is the Roman Indiction. If there is no remainder, it is 15.

Solar Cycle: In the Julian calendar, a period of 28 years, at the end of which the days of the month return to the same days of the week.

Solstice, Summer: The Sun reaches its greatest declination (23½°) north of the celestial equator, around June 21. **Winter:** The Sun reaches its greatest declination (23½°) south of the celestial equator, around December 21.

Stationary (Stat.): The brief period of apparent halted movement of a planet against the background of the stars shortly before it appears to move backward/westward (retrograde motion) or forward/eastward (direct motion).

Sun Fast/Slow: When a sundial reading is ahead of (fast) or behind (slow) clock time.

Sunrise/Sunset: The visible rising and setting of the upper edge of the Sun's disk across the unobstructed horizon of an observer whose eyes are 15 feet above ground level.

Twilight: For definitions of civil, nautical, and astronomical twilight, **see page 104.** □□

How to Use This Almanac

The calendar pages (114–141) are the heart of *The Old Farmer's Almanac*. They present sky sightings and astronomical data for the entire year and are what make this book a true almanac, a "calendar of the heavens." In essence, these pages are unchanged since 1792, when Robert B. Thomas published his first edition. The long columns of numbers and symbols reveal all of nature's precision, rhythm, and glory—providing an astronomical look at the year 2008.

Why We Have Seasons

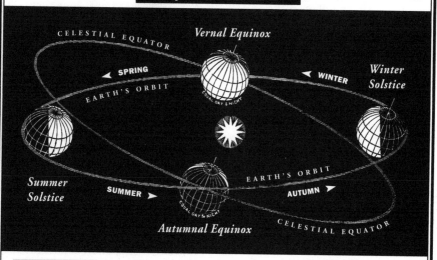

THE SEASONS OF 2008

Spring . . . . March 20, 1:48 A.M. EDT	Autumn . . . . . . September 22, 11:44 A.M. EDT
Summer . . . . June 20, 7:59 P.M. EDT	Winter . . . . December 21, 7:04 A.M. EST

■ The seasons occur because as Earth revolves around the Sun, its axis remains tilted at 23.5 degrees from the perpendicular. This tilt causes different latitudes on Earth to receive varying amounts of sunlight throughout the year.

In the Northern Hemisphere, the summer solstice (around June 21) marks the beginning of summer and occurs when the North Pole is tilted toward the Sun. The winter solstice (around December 21) marks the beginning of winter and occurs when the North Pole is tilted away from the Sun.

The equinoxes occur when the hemispheres equally face the Sun and receive equal amounts (12 hours each) of daylight and darkness. The vernal equinox (around March 21) marks the beginning of spring; the autumnal equinox (around September 23) marks the beginning of autumn. In the Southern Hemisphere, the seasons are the reverse of those in the Northern Hemisphere.

continued

The Left-Hand Calendar Pages • 114–140

A SAMPLE MONTH

SKY WATCH ☆ *The box at the top of each Left-Hand Calendar Page describes the best times to view celestial highlights, including conjunctions, meteor showers, and planets. (The dates on which select astronomical events occur appear on the Right-Hand Calendar Pages.)*

1 2 3 4 5 6 7 8

All times are given in Eastern Standard Time. ☞ **Bold = P.M.** ☞ Light = A.M.

Day of Year	Day of Month	Day of Week	Rises h. m.	Key	Sets h. m.	Key	Length of Day h. m.	Sun Fast m.	Declination of Sun ° '	High Tide Times Boston		Rises h. m.	Key	Sets h. m.	Key	Place	Age
1	1	M.	7:14	E	**4:22**	A	9 08	12	22 s.59	8¾	9½	**2:14**	A	5:40	E	TAU	12
2	2	Tu.	7:14	E	**4:23**	A	9 09	12	22 54	9¾	**10½**	**3:12**	A	6:46	E	AUR	13
3	3	W.	7:14	E	**4:24**	A	9 10	11	22 49	10½	**11¾**	**4:19**	A	7:40	E	GEM	14

The Left-Hand Calendar Pages (detail above) contain daily Sun and Moon rise and set times, the length of day, high tide times, the Moon's place and age, and more for Boston. Examples of how to calculate astronomical times are shown below.

1 To calculate the sunrise/sunset times for your locale: Each sunrise/sunset time is assigned a Key Letter whose value is given in minutes in the **Time Corrections** table on **page 235**. Find your city in the table, or the city nearest you, and add or subtract those minutes to/from Boston's sunrise or sunset time given.

E X A M P L E :

■ To find the time of sunrise in Denver, Colorado, on the first day of the month:

Sunrise, Boston, with Key Letter E (above)	7:14 A.M. EST
Value of Key Letter E for Denver (p. 235)	+ 7 minutes
Sunrise, Denver	7:21 A.M. MST

2 To determine your city's length of day, find the sunrise/sunset Key Let-

ATTENTION, READERS: *All times given in this edition of the Almanac are for Boston, Massachusetts, and are in Eastern Standard Time (EST), except from 2:00 A.M., March 9, until 2:00 A.M., November 2, when Eastern Daylight Time (EDT) is given. Key Letters (A–E) are provided so that you can calculate times for other localities.*

ter values for your city on **page 235**. Add or subtract the sunset value to/from Boston's length of day. Then simply *reverse* the sunrise sign (from minus to plus, or plus to minus) and add or subtract this value to/from the result of the first step.

E X A M P L E :

■ To find the length of day in Richmond, Virginia:

Length of day, Boston (above)	9h. 08m.
Sunset Key Letter A for Richmond (p. 239)	+ 41m.
Reverse sunrise Key Letter E for	9h. 49m.
Richmond (p. 239, +11 to −11)	− 11m.
Length of day, Richmond	9h. 38m.

3 Use the Sun Fast column to change sundial time to clock time in Boston. A sundial reads natural time, or Sun time, which is neither Standard nor Daylight time except by coincidence. To get Boston clock time, *subtract* the minutes given in the Sun Fast column (except where the number is preceded by an asterisk [*], in which case *add* the minutes) and use Key Letter C in the table on **page 235** to convert the time to your city.

E X A M P L E :

■ To change sundial time to clock time in Boston, or Salem, Oregon:

Sundial reading	
(Boston or Salem)	**12:00 noon**
Subtract Sun Fast (p. 110)	− 12 minutes
Clock time, Boston	**11:48 A.M. EST**
Use Key Letter C for Salem	
(p. 238)	+ 27 minutes
Clock time, Salem	**12:15 P.M. PST**

Longitude of city	Correction minutes
58°–76°	0
77°–89°	+1
90°–102°	+2
103°–115°	+3
116°–127°	+4
128°–141°	+5
142°–155°	+6

E X A M P L E :

■ To determine the time of moonrise in Lansing, Michigan:

Moonrise, Boston,	
with Key Letter A (p. 110)	**2:14 P.M. EST**
Value of Key Letter A	
for Lansing (p. 237)	+ 52 minutes
Correction for Lansing	
longitude, 84°33'	+ 1 minute
Moonrise, Lansing	**3:07 P.M. EST**

Use the same procedure to determine the time of moonset.

4 This column gives the degrees and minutes of the Sun from the celestial equator at noon EST or EDT.

5 This column gives the approximate times of high tides in Boston. For example, the first high tide occurs at 8:45 A.M. and the second occurs at 9:30 P.M. the same day. (A dash indicates that high tide occurs after midnight and so is recorded on the next day.) Figures for calculating high tide times and heights for localities other than Boston are given in the **Tide Corrections** table on **page 240.**

6 To calculate the moonrise/moonset times for localities other than Boston, follow the example in the next column, making a correction for longitude (see table, above right). For the longitude of your city, see **page 235.** (Note: A dash in the moonrise/moonset columns indicates that rise or set times occur on or after midnight and are recorded on the next day.)

7 The Moon's Place is its *astronomical* placement in the heavens. (This should not be confused with the Moon's *astrological* place in the zodiac, as explained on **page 228.**) All calculations in this Almanac are based on astronomy, not astrology, except for the information on **pages 228–230.**

In addition to the 12 constellations of the zodiac, this column may indicate others: Auriga **(AUR),** a northern constellation between Perseus and Gemini; Cetus **(CET),** which lies south of the zodiac, just south of Pisces and Aries; Ophiuchus **(OPH),** a constellation primarily north of the zodiac but with a small corner between Scorpius and Sagittarius; Orion **(ORI),** a constellation whose northern limit first reaches the zodiac between Taurus and Gemini; and Sextans **(SEX),** which lies south of the zodiac except for a corner that just touches it near Leo.

8 The last column gives the Moon's Age, which is the number of days since the previous new Moon. (The average length of the lunar month is 29.53 days.)

continued

CALENDAR

The Right-Hand Calendar Pages • 115–141

A SAMPLE MONTH

- Weather prediction rhyme.
- Civil holidays and astronomical events.
- Sundays and special holy days.
- The bold letter is the Dominical Letter (from A to G), a traditional ecclesiastical designation for Sunday determined by the date on which the first Sunday falls. For 2008, a leap year, the Dominical Letter is **F** through February. It then reverts to **E** for the rest of the year.
- Symbols for notable celestial events. (See opposite page for explanations.)
- High tide heights, in feet, at Boston.
- Proverbs, poems, and adages.
- Noteworthy historical events, folklore, and legends.
- Religious feasts. A ᵀ indicates a major feast that the church has this year temporarily transferred to a date other than its usual one. This is to avoid conflict with Sundays, Holy Week, Easter Week, and other observances that take precedence.

Day of Month	Day of Week	Dates, Feasts, Fasts, Aspects, Tide Heights	Weather
1	Fr.	Lammas Day • New ● • **Eclipse** ☉ • ☾ AT ☋	*Moist*
2	Sa.	Cookies baked successfully on a vehicle's dashboard during heat wave, Bedford, N.H., 2006 • { 11.5 / 10.2	*at*
3	**E**	12th S. af. P. • ☌ ♄ ☾ • Gray squirrels have second litters now.	*foist.*
4	M.	☾ ON EQ. • ☌ ♂ ☾ • Pres. Carter signed bill to create U.S. Dept. of Energy, 1977	*Thunder*
5	Tu.	Cornerstone for pedestal of Statue of Liberty laid, 1884	*rattles*
6	W.	**Transfiguration** • U.S. dropped atomic bomb on Hiroshima, Japan, 1945 • { 10.0 / 10.0	*the*
7	Th.	107°F, Waco, Tex., 1988 • *Lightning brings heat.*	*china.*
8	Fr.	**St. Dominic** • "Canada's Hundred Days" began, WWI, 1918 • { 8.8 / 9.5	*Nothing*
9	Sa.	First Smokey Bear poster produced, 1944 • { 8.3 / 9.2	*could*
10	**E**	13th S. af. P. • ☾ AT APO. • Tides { 8.0 / 9.1	*be*
11	M.	**St. Clare** • Dog days end. • First prisoners arrived at Alcatraz, 1934 • { 7.9 / 9.1	*finah!*
12	Tu.	☾ RUNS LOW • 232-day baseball strike began, causing World Series to be canceled, 1994	*Coolish,*
13	W.	☌ ♃ ☾ • ☌ ♀ ♄ • *They that walk much in the sun will be tanned at last.* • { 8.1 / 9.6	*then*
14	Th.	Major power outage in N.E. North America, 2003	*warmish,*
15	Fr.	**Assumption** • ☌ ☿ ♄ • ♆ AT ☍ • Tides { 8.8 / 10.1	*then*
16	Sa.	**Full Sturgeon** ○ • **Eclipse** ☾ • ☾ AT ☊ • ☌ ♆ ☾	*lightning-*
17	**E**	14th S. af. P. • Cat Nights commence. • Tides { 9.5 / —	*stormish.*
18	M.	☾ ON EQ. • ☌ ⛢ ☾ • Gov. J. White found his Roanoke (N.C.) settlement deserted, 1590	*Sweet!*
19	Tu.	Hurricane Bob hit New England, 1991 • Tides { 10.5 / 10.2	*Can't*
20	W.	President Benjamin Harrison born, 1833 • *The resolved mind has no cares.*	*be*
21	Th.	*Mona Lisa* was stolen, 1911 • Hawaii became 50th state, 1959 • { 10.2 / 10.6	*beat!*
22	Fr.	Nat Turner's slave rebellion began, 1831 • { 9.8 / 10.7	*Pack*
23	Sa.	☌ ☿ ♀ • *Ranger I* lunar probe launched, 1961 • Tides { 9.4 / 10.6	*a*
24	**E**	15th S. af. P. • *The bad gardener quarrels with his rake.*	*picnic,*
25	M.	**St. Bartholomew**ᵀ • ☾ RIDES HIGH • Hummingbirds migrate south. • { 8.8 / 10.5	*but*
26	Tu.	☾ AT PERIG. • 100-mph winds, Lake County, Ind., 1965	*bring*

☞ *For explanations of Almanac terms, see the glossaries on pages 106, 142, and 242.*

Predicting Earthquakes

■ Note the dates in the **Right-Hand Calendar Pages** when the Moon rides high or runs low. The date of the high begins the most likely five-day period of earthquakes in the Northern Hemisphere; the date of the low indicates a similar five-day period in the Southern Hemisphere. Also noted are the two days each month when the Moon is on the celestial equator, indicating the most likely time for earthquakes in either hemisphere.

■ Throughout the **Right-Hand Calendar Pages** are groups of symbols that represent notable celestial events. The symbols and names of the principal planets and aspects are:

☉	**Sun**	♆	**Neptune**
☽ ● ☾	**Moon**	♇	**Pluto**
☿	**Mercury**	☌	**Conjunction (on the**
♀	**Venus**		**same celestial**
⊕	**Earth**		**longitude)**
♂	**Mars**	☊	**Ascending node**
♃	**Jupiter**	☋	**Descending node**
♄	**Saturn**	☍	**Opposition (180 degrees**
♅	**Uranus**		**from Sun)**

E X A M P L E :

♂♀♄ on the thirteenth day of the month (see opposite page) means that on that date a conjunction (♂) of Venus (♀) and Saturn (♄) occurs: They are aligned along the same celestial longitude and appear to be closest together in the sky.

Earth at Perihelion and Aphelion

■ Perihelion: January 2, 2008. Earth will be 91,401,587 miles from the Sun. Aphelion: July 4, 2008. Earth will be 94,513,190 miles from the Sun.

2008 Calendar Highlights

Movable Religious Observances

Septuagesima Sunday	**January 20**
Shrove Tuesday	**February 5**
Ash Wednesday	**February 6**
Palm Sunday	**March 16**
Good Friday	**March 21**
Easter	**March 23**
First day of Passover	**April 20**
Orthodox Easter	**April 27**
Rogation Sunday	**April 27**
Ascension Day	**May 1**
Whitsunday–Pentecost	**May 11**
Trinity Sunday	**May 18**
Corpus Christi	**May 25**
First day of Ramadan	**September 2**
Rosh Hashanah	**September 30**
Yom Kippur	**October 9**
First Sunday of Advent	**November 30**
First day of Chanukah	**December 22**

Chronological Cycles

Dominical Letter	**F/E**
Epact	**22**
Golden Number (Lunar Cycle)	**14**
Roman Indiction	**1**
Solar Cycle	**1**
Year of Julian Period	**6721**

–Beth Krommes

Eras

ERA	YEAR	BEGINS
Byzantine	7517	September 14
Jewish (A.M.)*	5769	September 30
Chinese (Lunar) [Year of the Rat]	4706	February 7
Roman (A.U.C.)	2761	January 14
Nabonassar	2757	April 21
Japanese	2668	January 1
Grecian (Seleucidae)	2320	September 14 (or October 14)
Indian (Saka)	1930	March 21
Diocletian	1725	September 11
Islamic (Hegira)*	1429	January 10
	1430	December 29

Year begins at sunset the evening before.

SKY WATCH ☆ *Mercury has its year's-best morning showing during the first 24 days of the month. It's bright in the predawn east, but it can't approach the dazzle of higher-up Venus. The crescent Moon has a close encounter with Venus on the 5th, then floats below Mercury on the 8th, 40 minutes before sunrise. With its orbit temporarily more oval than usual, the Moon is at its farthest distance of the year—about 252,705 miles—on the 9th. A week later, Saturn makes a comeback and rises by 1:00 A.M. The big story is Mars, now brightening rapidly in Gemini and rising by 8:30 P.M at midmonth. The evening sky finds Jupiter sinking; it's conspicuous early in the month but very low by Thanksgiving.*

◐	**Last Quarter**	1st day	17th hour	18th minute
●	**New Moon**	9th day	18th hour	3rd minute
◑	**First Quarter**	17th day	17th hour	33rd minute
○	**Full Moon**	24th day	9th hour	30th minute

To use this page, see p. 110; for Key Letters, see p. 235; for Tide Tables, see p. 240.
After 2:00 A.M. on November 4, Eastern Standard Time is given. ☞ **Bold = P.M.** ☞ Light = A.M.

Day of Year	Day of Month	Day of Week	☼ Rises h. m.	Key	☼ Sets h. m.	Key	Length of Day h. m.	Sun Fast m.	Declination of Sun ° ′	High Tide Times Boston		☾ Rises h. m.	Key	☾ Sets h. m.	Key	☾ Place	☾ Age
305	1	Th.	7:17	D	**5:38**	B	10 21	32	14s.27	4¾	5	**11:51**	B	**2:03**	E	CAN	21
306	2	Fr.	7:19	D	**5:37**	B	10 18	32	14 46	6	6¼	—	–	**2:30**	E	CAN	22
307	3	Sa.	7:20	D	**5:36**	B	10 16	32	15 05	7	7¼	1:00	B	**2:53**	D	LEO	23
308	4	**G**	6:21	D	**4:34**	B	10 13	32	15 24	7	7¼	1:05	C	**2:13**	D	LEO	24
309	5	M.	6:22	D	**4:33**	B	10 11	32	15 43	7¾	8¼	2:08	D	**2:31**	C	LEO	25
310	6	Tu.	6:24	D	**4:32**	B	10 08	32	16 01	8½	9	3:10	D	**2:49**	C	VIR	26
311	7	W.	6:25	D	**4:31**	B	10 06	32	16 19	9¼	9¾	4:12	E	**3:08**	B	VIR	27
312	8	Th.	6:26	D	**4:30**	A	10 04	32	16 36	10	10½	5:14	E	**3:30**	B	VIR	28
313	9	Fr.	6:27	D	**4:29**	A	10 02	32	16 53	10½	11	6:18	E	**3:55**	A	LIB	0
314	10	Sa.	6:29	D	**4:28**	A	9 59	32	17 10	11	11¾	7:21	E	**4:26**	A	LIB	1
315	11	**G**	6:30	D	**4:27**	A	9 57	32	17 27	11¾	—	8:24	E	**5:03**	A	SCO	2
316	12	M.	6:31	D	**4:26**	A	9 55	32	17 43	12¼	12¼	9:23	E	**5:49**	A	OPH	3
317	13	Tu.	6:33	D	**4:25**	A	9 52	31	17 59	1	**1**	10:16	E	**6:44**	A	SAG	4
318	14	W.	6:34	D	**4:24**	A	9 50	31	18 15	1¾	1¾	11:01	E	**7:46**	A	SAG	5
319	15	Th.	6:35	D	**4:23**	A	9 48	31	18 31	2½	2½	11:39	E	**8:52**	B	SAG	6
320	16	Fr.	6:36	D	**4:22**	A	9 46	31	18 46	3¼	3¼	**12:10**	E	**10:02**	B	CAP	7
321	17	Sa.	6:37	D	**4:21**	A	9 44	31	19 01	4	4¼	**12:36**	D	**11:12**	B	CAP	8
322	18	**G**	6:39	D	**4:20**	A	9 41	31	19 15	5	5¼	**1:00**	D	—	–	AQU	9
323	19	M.	6:40	D	**4:19**	A	9 39	30	19 29	5¾	6¼	**1:22**	D	12:24	C	AQU	10
324	20	Tu.	6:41	D	**4:19**	A	9 38	30	19 43	6¾	7¼	**1:45**	C	1:37	D	PSC	11
325	21	W.	6:42	D	**4:18**	A	9 36	30	19 56	7½	8	**2:09**	B	2:53	E	PSC	12
326	22	Th.	6:44	D	**4:17**	A	9 33	30	20 09	8½	9	**2:37**	B	4:13	E	PSC	13
327	23	Fr.	6:45	D	**4:17**	A	9 32	29	20 22	9¼	10	**3:13**	A	5:36	E	ARI	14
328	24	Sa.	6:46	D	**4:16**	A	9 30	29	20 34	10¼	10¾	**3:58**	A	7:00	E	TAU	15
329	25	**G**	6:47	D	**4:16**	A	9 29	29	20 46	11	11¾	**4:55**	A	8:19	E	TAU	16
330	26	M.	6:48	D	**4:15**	A	9 27	29	20 58	**12**	—	**6:04**	A	9:27	E	AUR	17
331	27	Tu.	6:49	E	**4:14**	A	9 25	28	21 09	12¾	12¾	**7:19**	B	10:20	E	GEM	18
332	28	W.	6:50	E	**4:14**	A	9 24	28	21 19	1½	1¾	**8:35**	B	11:00	E	CAN	19
333	29	Th.	6:52	E	**4:14**	A	9 22	28	21 30	2½	2¾	**9:47**	C	11:31	E	CAN	20
334	30	Fr.	6:53	E	**4:13**	A	9 20	27	21s.39	3½	3¾	**10:55**	C	11:56	D	LEO	21

NOVEMBER HATH 30 DAYS • 2007

The woodland foliage now
Is gathered by the wild November blast. –J. Howard Bryant

Day of Month	Day of Week	Dates, Feasts, Fasts, Aspects, Tide Heights	Weather
1	Th.	All Saints' • ☿ STAT. • Architect James Renwick Jr. born, 1818 • { 9.2 10.2	*Bright*
2	Fr.	All Souls' • Storm blocked Ben Franklin's view of a lunar eclipse, 1743 • Tides { 8.9 9.7	*and*
3	Sa.	Sadie Hawkins Day • ☽ AT ☋ • ☌♄☽ • Tides { 8.9 9.4	*still:*
4	G	**23rd S. af. P.** • **U.S. Daylight Saving Time ends, 2:00 A.M.**	*Raindrops*
5	M.	☽ ON EQ. • ☌♀☽ • Pres. FDR won third term in office, 1940 • Tides { 9.3 9.2	*fill*
6	Tu.	**Election Day** • Canada's second national Thanksgiving Day after confederation, 1879	*the*
7	W.	*In the decay of the Moon, a cloudy morning bodes a fair afternoon.* • Tides { 9.7 9.2	*lakes,*
8	Th.	☌☿☽ • ☿ GR. ELONG. (19° WEST) • William Frost's electric insect destroyer patented, 1910	*then*
9	Fr.	**New** ● • ☽ AT APO. • Great fire in Boston raged for two days, 1872 • { 10.0 9.1	*turn*
10	Sa.	*Sesame Street* debuted on television, 1969 • Tides { 10.0 8.9	*to*
11	G	**24th S. af. P.** • **Veterans Day** • Tides { 10.0 —	*flakes.*
12	M.	Indian Summer • ☌♃☽ • Lobsters move to offshore waters. • { 8.8 9.9	*Streams*
13	Tu.	☽ RUNS LOW • Newfoundland co-proprietorship granted to David Kirke, 1637 • { 8.6 9.8	*are*
14	W.	Melville's *Moby Dick* first published in U.S., 1851 • Actress Veronica Lake born, 1919 • { 8.5 9.7	*hardly*
15	Th.	♂ STAT. • *When the Sun is highest, it casts the least shadow.* • Tides { 8.3 9.5	*flowing,*
16	Fr.	6" snow, Tucson, Ariz., 1958 • Crab apples are ripe now. • { 8.3 9.4	*their*
17	Sa.	St. Hugh of Lincoln • ☌♆☽ • Athlete Bob Mathias born, 1930	*pulses*
18	G	**25th S. af. P.** • ☽ AT ☊ • Tides { 8.7 9.4	*slowing;*
19	M.	☽ ON EQ. • ☌♅☽ • Lincoln's Gettysburg Address, 1863 • { 9.2 9.5	*Again,*
20	Tu.	City of Moose Jaw, Sask., incorporated, 1903 • { 9.9 9.7	*it's*
21	W.	Mayflower Compact signed by Pilgrim settlers, 1620 • Skunks hibernate now.	*snowing.*
22	Th.	**Thanksgiving** • *The company makes the feast.* • { 11.2 10.2	*But*
23	Fr.	St. Clement • ☽ AT PERIG. • Comedian Harpo Marx born, 1888 • { 11.7 10.4	*just*
24	Sa.	**Full Beaver** ○ • ♅ STAT. • Tides { 12.1 10.4	*before*
25	G	**26th S. af. P.** • 160-mph winds, Mt. Washington, N.H., 1950 • { 12.2 10.3	*all*
26	M.	☽ RIDES HIGH • Stan Berenstain, "Berenstain Bears" cocreator, died, 2005 • { 12.1 —	*freezes*
27	Tu.	☌♂☽ • Basketball's Wilt Chamberlain hit 18 field goals in a row, 1963 • Tides { 10.1 11.7	*up,*
28	W.	First recorded U.S. auto race, Ill., 1895 • Storm on Lake Superior caused 20- to 40-foot-high waves, 1960	*it*
29	Th.	*Forsaken by the wind, you must use your oars.* • { 9.5 10.6	*eases*
30	Fr.	St. Andrew • ☽ AT ☋ • Lucille Ball married Desi Arnaz, 1940 • { 9.3 10.0	*up.*

Celebration is a communal experience of joy. –Jean Vanier

Farmer's Calendar

■ It was only a few years ago that up-to-date Enhanced 911 wireless telephone service for emergency response arrived in this neighborhood. Formerly, emergency calls went to a local dispatch center that summoned responders who, you hoped, knew where you were and how to get there. The new service is more efficient. It relies not only on responders knowing their beat, but also on precise, minutely detailed maps locating every dwelling in town.

Those maps revealed the unappreciated magnitude and complexity of the local road system—unappreciated by me, anyhow. I was surprised to learn what a wealth of ways we have for such a small place. We have high roads, low roads, back roads, way-back roads, highways, byways, lanes. Until the advent of E911 service, many of our roads had been nameless and unknown to all but those who lived on them.

Giving names is a mysterious and powerful act. Almost, to name a thing is to call it into being. Certainly in this town there seem to be an awful lot more roads than there used to be. Upper Eager Road, Sears Road—who knew of them before E911? Like Adam in the Garden of Eden, we set out to assign names to our surroundings. And like Adam, we got a little more than we bargained for.

SKY WATCH ☆ *The Geminid meteors will be best after the Moon sets on the evening of December 13. Venus loses some of its height and dazzle in the predawn sky but remains prominent. The headliner is Mars, retrograding in Gemini, arriving at its closest and brightest of the year on the 18th and at opposition on the 24th. Mars is exceptionally high up at midnight, not far from the zenith. The year's 13th full Moon rises on the 23rd at sunset, right next to Mars, making a striking sight. Winter begins with the solstice on the 22nd, at 1:08 A.M., although the year's earliest sunset occurs two weeks earlier.*

◑	**Last Quarter**	1st day	7th hour	44th minute
●	**New Moon**	9th day	12th hour	40th minute
◐	**First Quarter**	17th day	5th hour	18th minute
○	**Full Moon**	23rd day	20th hour	16th minute
◑	**Last Quarter**	31st day	2nd hour	51st minute

To use this page, see p. 110; for Key Letters, see p. 235; for Tide Tables, see p. 240. All times are given in Eastern Standard Time. ☞ **Bold = P.M.** ☞ Light = A.M.

Day of Year	Day of Month	Day of Week	Rises h. m.	Key	Sets h. m.	Key	Length of Day h. m.	Sun Fast m.	Declination of Sun ° ′	High Tide Times Boston		Rises h. m.	Key	Sets h. m.	Key	Place	Age
335	1	Sa.	6:54	E	**4:13**	A	9 19	27	21s.49	4½	4¾	12:00	C	**12:17**	D	LEO	22
336	2	**G**	6:55	E	**4:13**	A	9 18	27	21 58	5¼	5¾	—	–	**12:36**	C	LEO	23
337	3	M.	6:56	E	**4:12**	A	9 16	26	22 07	6¼	6¾	1:03	D	**12:54**	C	VIR	24
338	4	Tu.	6:57	E	**4:12**	A	9 15	26	22 15	7¼	7½	2:04	E	**1:13**	B	VIR	25
339	5	W.	6:58	E	**4:12**	A	9 14	25	22 23	8	8½	3:06	E	**1:34**	B	VIR	26
340	6	Th.	6:59	E	**4:12**	A	9 13	25	22 30	8¾	9¼	4:09	E	**1:58**	B	VIR	27
341	7	Fr.	7:00	E	**4:12**	A	9 12	25	22 37	9¼	10	5:13	E	**2:27**	A	LIB	28
342	8	Sa.	7:01	E	**4:12**	A	9 11	24	22 43	10	10¾	6:16	E	**3:02**	A	SCO	29
343	9	**G**	7:02	E	**4:12**	A	9 10	24	22 49	10¾	11¼	7:17	E	**3:46**	A	SCO	0
344	10	M.	7:03	E	**4:12**	A	9 09	23	22 55	11¼	12	8:12	E	**4:39**	A	OPH	1
345	11	Tu.	7:03	E	**4:12**	A	9 09	23	23 01	**12**	—	9:00	E	**5:39**	A	SAG	2
346	12	W.	7:04	E	**4:12**	A	9 08	22	23 05	12¾	12¾	9:40	E	**6:45**	B	SAG	3
347	13	Th.	7:05	E	**4:12**	A	9 07	22	23 09	1¼	1¼	10:12	E	**7:54**	B	CAP	4
348	14	Fr.	7:06	E	**4:12**	A	9 06	21	23 13	2	**2**	10:40	D	**9:03**	C	CAP	5
349	15	Sa.	7:07	E	**4:13**	A	9 06	21	23 16	2¾	2¾	11:04	D	**10:13**	C	AQU	6
350	16	**G**	7:07	E	**4:13**	A	9 06	20	23 19	3½	3¾	11:25	D	**11:23**	C	AQU	7
351	17	M.	7:08	E	**4:13**	A	9 05	20	23 21	4½	4¾	11:47	C	—	–	PSC	8
352	18	Tu.	7:09	E	**4:13**	A	9 04	19	23 23	5¼	5¾	**12:09**	C	12:35	D	PSC	9
353	19	W.	7:10	E	**4:14**	A	9 04	19	23 25	6¼	6¾	**12:35**	B	1:50	E	PSC	10
354	20	Th.	7:10	E	**4:14**	A	9 04	18	23 26	7	7¾	**1:05**	B	3:08	E	ARI	11
355	21	Fr.	7:11	E	**4:15**	A	9 04	18	23 26	8	8¾	**1:44**	A	4:30	E	ARI	12
356	22	Sa.	7:11	E	**4:15**	A	9 04	17	23 26	9	9¾	**2:35**	A	5:50	E	TAU	13
357	23	**G**	7:11	E	**4:16**	A	9 05	17	23 26	10	10½	**3:38**	A	7:04	E	TAU	14
358	24	M.	7:11	E	**4:16**	A	9 05	16	23 25	10¾	11½	**4:51**	A	8:04	E	AUR	15
359	25	Tu.	7:12	E	**4:17**	A	9 05	16	23 24	11¾	—	**6:09**	B	8:52	E	GEM	16
360	26	W.	7:12	E	**4:18**	A	9 06	15	23 22	12½	12½	**7:25**	B	9:28	E	CAN	17
361	27	Th.	7:12	E	**4:18**	A	9 06	15	23 20	1¼	1½	**8:37**	C	9:56	D	LEO	18
362	28	Fr.	7:13	E	**4:19**	A	9 06	14	23 17	2	2¼	**9:46**	D	10:19	D	LEO	19
363	29	Sa.	7:13	E	**4:20**	A	9 07	14	23 13	3	**3**	**10:50**	D	10:39	D	LEO	20
364	30	**G**	7:14	E	**4:21**	A	9 07	13	23 09	3¾	**4**	**11:54**	D	10:58	C	VIR	21
365	31	M.	7:14	E	**4:21**	A	9 07	13	23s.05	4½	**5**	—	–	11:17	B	VIR	22

DECEMBER HATH 31 DAYS • 2007

Good-by, kind year, we walk no more together,
But here in quiet happiness we part. –Sarah Doudney

Day of Month	Day of Week	Dates, Feasts, Fasts, Aspects, Tide Heights	Weather
1	Sa.	☌♄☾ • Temperature rose 80 degrees in one day, Kipp, Mont., 1896 • Tides {9.1 / 9.4	*Mercy,*
2	G	**1st S. of Advent** • ☾ ON EQ. • Tides {9.0 / 9.0	*it's*
3	M.	First public performance of G. Gershwin's "Concerto in F," Carnegie Hall, N.Y.C., 1925 • {9.1 / 8.7	*mild,*
4	Tu.	*One eyewitness is better than two hear-so's.* • {9.2 / 8.5	*but*
5	W.	First day of Chanukah • ☌♀☾ • Tides {9.3 / 8.5	*turning*
6	Th.	St. Nicholas • ☾ AT APO. • 362 killed in coal mine explosion, Monongah, W. Va., 1907	*wild!*
7	Fr.	St. Ambrose • **National Pearl Harbor Remembrance Day** • Tides {9.7 / 8.6	*On*
8	Sa.	American Bird Banding Association formed, first such society in U.S., 1909 • Tides {9.8 / 8.6	*every*
9	G	**2nd S. of Advent** • New ● • Tides {9.9 / 8.6	*rooftop*
10	M.	St. Eulalia • ☾ RUNS LOW • Winterberry fruits especially showy now. • {10.0 / 8.6	*snow*
11	Tu.	Canada granted legislative independence from Britain, 1931	*is*
12	W.	Orange soil discovered on Moon by *Apollo 17* astronauts, 1972 • Beware the Pogonip. • {8.6 / 10.0	*piled*
13	Th.	St. Lucia • *Lucy light, Lucy light, Shortest day and longest night.* • {8.6 / 10.0	*like*
14	Fr.	Halcyon Days • ☌♆☾ • Tilt-a-Whirl trademark registered, 1926	*wedding*
15	Sa.	☾ AT ☊ • Sioux chief Sitting Bull killed, 1890 • {8.8 / 9.7	*cake!*
16	G	**3rd S. of Advent** • ☌♅☾ • Tides {9.1 / 9.5	*Sunny*
17	M.	☾ ON EQ. • ☿ IN SUP. ☌ • Airport renamed for Bob Hope, Burbank, Calif., 2003	*break*
18	Tu.	♂ CLOSEST APPROACH • 13th Amendment, prohibiting slavery, went into effect, 1865 • {9.8 / 9.3	*to*
19	W.	Ember Day • Fictional Robinson Crusoe left island after 28 years, 1686 • {10.2 / 9.3	*hit*
20	Th.	☌♇☉ • ♄ STAT. • *Tomorrow never comes.* • {10.7 / 9.4	*the*
21	Fr.	St. Thomas • Ember Day • Actress Jane Fonda born, 1937 • {11.1 / 9.5	*malls,*
22	Sa.	Ember Day • **Winter Solstice** • ☾ AT PERIG. • Tides {11.5 / 9.7	*roast*
23	G	**Full Cold** ○ • ☾ RIDES HIGH • ☌♂☾ • ☌♃☉ • {11.8 / 9.9	*the*
24	M.	♂ AT ☍ • Fire at Library of Congress destroyed 35,000 volumes, 1851	*chestnuts,*
25	Tu.	**Christmas Day** • –57°F, Fort Smith, N.W.T., 1917	*deck*
26	W.	St. Stephen • **Boxing Day (Canada)** • **First day of Kwanzaa** • Tides {9.9 / 11.5	*the*
27	Th.	St. John • ☾ AT ☋ • Carry Nation smashed Hotel Carey bar, Wichita, Kans., 1900	*halls!*
28	Fr.	Holy Innocents • ☌♄☾ • Tides {9.6 / 10.4	*Cryogenic*
29	Sa.	☾ ON EQ. • *A cake eaten in peace is worth two in trouble.* • Tides {9.4 / 9.8	*cold*
30	G	**1st S. af. Ch.** • Golfer Tiger Woods born, 1975	*abates*
31	M.	St. Sylvester • C. B. Darrow received patent for *Monopoly* game, 1935 • {9.0 / 8.6	*in '08!*

Farmer's Calendar

■ For as long as there have been weather prognosticators, apparently, there have been those who loved to mock them. Benjamin Franklin was known to poke fun at weather prediction—a business he himself was very much in. Writing in 1737 in *Poor Richard's Almanack,* Franklin gave an ironic defense of his forecasts. The promised weather would turn up, he assured readers; it was merely a matter of *when.* "We modestly desire only the favorable allowance of a day or two before and a day or two after the precise day" whose weather Poor Richard was predicting, wrote Ben. And "if it does not come to pass accordingly, let the fault be laid upon the printer."

Our attitude toward weather prediction and those who practice it is complex. On the one hand, we follow the forecasters closely and rely on them implicitly. On the other hand, we feel a perverse little satisfaction on the rare occasions when they're wrong. We almost seem to want the forecaster to fail. Why?

Perhaps we're ambivalent about the forecasts just because they're so good. We want there to be a realm of our experience that has a power, a mystery beyond our control and understanding. To the extent that scientific forecasting makes that mystery less in the case of the weather, we may accept it, but we won't entirely like it.

SKY WATCH ☆ *Mars, in the evening sky, shines at its brightest of the year at magnitude –1.5. It briefly equals the brilliance of the brightest star, Sirius; both shine gloriously after 8:00 P.M., with ruddy Mars high and blue Sirius much lower. By the end of the month, Mars has lost half its light. Saturn, bright but not dazzling in Leo, rises around 8:30 P.M. Mercury hovers next to the thin crescent Moon on the 9th and is best seen about 40 minutes after sunset from the 12th to the 28th, about 10 degrees high in the southwest. Venus rules the predawn sky at magnitude –4 and is close to Jupiter at the end of the month. Earth reaches perihelion, its annual position closest to the Sun, on the 2nd.*

●	**New Moon**	8th day	6th hour	37th minute
◐	**First Quarter**	15th day	14th hour	46th minute
○	**Full Moon**	22nd day	8th hour	35th minute
◑	**Last Quarter**	30th day	0 hour	3rd minute

To use this page, see p. 110; for Key Letters, see p. 235; for Tide Tables, see p. 240. All times are given in Eastern Standard Time. ☞ **Bold = P.M.** ☞ Light = A.M.

Day of Year	Day of Month	Day of Week	Rises h. m.	Key	Sets h. m.	Key	Length of Day h. m.	Sun Fast m.	Declination of Sun ° '	High Tide Times Boston	Rises h. m.	Key	Sets h. m.	Key	Place	Age
1	1	Tu.	7:14	E	4:22	A	9 08	13	23 s.00	5½ 6	12:56	E	11:37	B	VIR	23
2	2	W.	7:14	E	4:23	A	9 09	12	22 55	6¼ 7	1:59	E	12:00	B	VIR	24
3	3	Th.	7:14	E	4:24	A	9 10	12	22 50	7¼ 7¾	3:02	E	12:27	A	LIB	25
4	4	Fr.	7:14	E	4:25	A	9 11	11	22 44	8 8¾	4:06	E	1:00	A	LIB	26
5	5	Sa.	7:14	E	4:26	A	9 12	11	22 38	8¾ 9½	5:08	E	1:41	A	SCO	27
6	6	**F**	7:14	E	4:27	A	9 13	10	22 31	9½ 10¼	6:05	E	2:31	A	OPH	28
7	7	M.	7:14	E	4:28	A	9 14	10	22 23	10¼ 11	6:56	E	3:30	A	SAG	29
8	8	Tu.	7:14	E	4:29	A	9 15	9	22 15	11 11½	7:39	E	4:35	A	SAG	0
9	9	W.	7:13	E	4:30	A	9 17	9	22 07	11½ —	8:14	E	5:44	B	SAG	1
10	10	Th.	7:13	E	4:31	A	9 18	8	21 59	12¼ 12¼	8:44	E	6:55	B	CAP	2
11	11	Fr.	7:13	E	4:32	A	9 19	8	21 50	12¾ 1	9:08	D	8:05	C	CAP	3
12	12	Sa.	7:13	E	4:33	A	9 20	8	21 40	1½ 1¾	9:31	D	9:15	D	AQU	4
13	13	**F**	7:12	E	4:34	A	9 22	7	21 30	2¼ 2½	9:52	C	10:26	D	PSC	5
14	14	M.	7:12	E	4:35	A	9 23	7	21 19	3 3¼	10:13	C	11:38	D	PSC	6
15	15	Tu.	7:11	E	4:37	A	9 26	7	21 09	3¾ 4¼	10:37	B	—	–	PSC	7
16	16	W.	7:11	E	4:38	A	9 27	6	20 58	4¾ 5¼	11:05	B	12:53	E	ARI	8
17	17	Th.	7:10	E	4:39	A	9 29	6	20 46	5¾ 6¼	11:39	A	2:11	E	ARI	9
18	18	Fr.	7:10	E	4:40	A	9 30	5	20 34	6¾ 7½	12:22	A	3:30	E	TAU	10
19	19	Sa.	7:09	E	4:41	A	9 32	5	20 22	7¾ 8½	1:18	A	4:44	E	TAU	11
20	20	**F**	7:09	E	4:43	A	9 34	5	20 09	8¾ 9½	2:26	A	5:49	E	AUR	12
21	21	M.	7:08	E	4:44	A	9 36	5	19 56	9¾ 10½	3:41	B	6:41	E	GEM	13
22	22	Tu.	7:07	E	4:45	A	9 38	4	19 42	10½ 11¼	4:58	B	7:22	E	CAN	14
23	23	W.	7:07	D	4:46	A	9 39	4	19 28	11½ —	6:14	B	7:54	E	CAN	15
24	24	Th.	7:06	D	4:48	A	9 42	4	19 14	12 12¼	7:25	C	8:19	D	LEO	16
25	25	Fr.	7:05	D	4:49	A	9 44	4	18 59	12¾ 1	8:33	D	8:41	D	LEO	17
26	26	Sa.	7:04	D	4:50	A	9 46	3	18 44	1½ 1¾	9:38	D	9:01	C	LEO	18
27	27	**F**	7:03	D	4:51	A	9 48	3	18 29	2¼ 2½	10:42	E	9:20	C	VIR	19
28	28	M.	7:03	D	4:53	A	9 50	3	18 14	3 3½	11:46	E	9:40	B	VIR	20
29	29	Tu.	7:02	D	4:54	A	9 52	3	17 58	3¾ 4¼	—	–	10:02	B	VIR	21
30	30	W.	7:01	D	4:55	A	9 54	2	17 42	4½ 5¼	12:49	E	10:27	A	LIB	22
31	31	Th.	7:00	D	4:57	A	9 57	2	17 s.25	5½ 6	1:53	E	10:57	A	LIB	23

JANUARY HATH 31 DAYS • 2008

In pearls and rubies rich, the hawthorns show,
While through the ice the crimson berries glow. –Ambrose Philips

Day of Month	Day of Week	Dates, Feasts, Fasts, Aspects, Tide Heights	Weather
1	Tu.	**New Year's Day • Holy Name •** Patriot Betsy Ross born, 1752	*Bright*
2	W.	⊕ AT PERIHELION • 14°F on Haleakala summit, Hawaii, 1876 • Tides {9.0 8.0	*and*
3	Th.	☾ AT APO. • First free kindergarten opened, Florence, Mass., 1876 • {9.1 7.9	*melting,*
4	Fr.	**St. Elizabeth Ann Seton •** Jacob Grimm, of Brothers Grimm fame, born, 1785 • {9.2 8.0	*then*
5	Sa.	Twelfth Night • ☌♀☾ • *A closed mouth gathers no foot.*	*a*
6	**F**	**Epiphany** • ☾ RUNS LOW • Morse's telegraph demonstrated, 1838	*belting!*
7	M.	Distaff Day • Plough Monday • Philadelphia, Pa., got 18" snow, 1821 • {10.0 8.6	*Cold*
8	Tu.	New ● • Astronomer Galileo Galilei died, 1642 • Tides {10.2 8.8	*enough*
9	W.	*Jack Frost in Janiveer / Nips the nose of the nascent year.*	*to*
10	Th.	**Islamic New Year** • ☌♆☾ • Thomas Paine's *Common Sense* published, 1776	*make*
11	Fr.	☾ AT ☊ • American League adopted "designated hitter" rule, 1973 • Tides {9.2 10.4	*us*
12	Sa.	☌♅☾ • *Set not your loaf in till the oven's hot.*	*blanch;*
13	**F**	**1st S. af. Ep.** • ☾ ON EQ. • Tides {9.7 10.0	*watch*
14	M.	*Huygens* space probe landed on largest of Saturn's moons, Titan, 2005 • Tides {9.9 9.7	*out*
15	Tu.	Molasses flooded the streets of Boston, 1919 • {10.0 9.3	*for*
16	W.	Red Lake Band of Chippewas first tribe in U.S. to issue tribal license plates, Minn., 1974 • {10.1 9.0	*an*
17	Th.	Ben Franklin born, 1706 • Canada's last ex-slave, John Baker, died, 1871	*avalanche!*
18	Fr.	Bacteria announced as cause of Legionnaire's disease (Legionellosis), 1977 • {10.4 8.7	*Freezin'*
19	Sa.	☾ AT PERIG. • OCCN. ♂☾ • Confederate general Robert E. Lee born, 1807	*beyond*
20	**F**	**Septuagesima** • ☾ RIDES HIGH • Tides {10.9 9.2	*reason.*
21	M.	**Martin Luther King Jr.'s Birthday (observed)** • *The mind is the man.*	*Another*
22	Tu.	**St. Vincent • Full Wolf** ○ • ☿ GR. ELONG. (19° EAST) • {11.3 9.8	*blast*
23	W.	Rock and Roll Hall of Fame inducted first members, 1986	*is*
24	Th.	☾ AT ☋ • 38" of snow on Cape Cod after a 2-day blizzard, 2005 • {9.9 11.1	*barely*
25	Fr.	**Conversion of Paul** • ☌♄☾ • Tides {10.0 10.7	*past:*
26	Sa.	**Sts. Timothy & Titus** • ☾ ON EQ. • Rocky Mountain Nat'l Park, Colo., est., 1915	*Avast!*
27	**F**	**Sexagesima** • More than 60 nations signed the Outer Space Treaty, 1967 • {9.7 9.6	*How*
28	M.	**St. Thomas Aquinas** • ☿ STAT. • *The wind in one's face makes one wise.*	*long*
29	Tu.	Emily H. Warner became the first female pilot of a U.S. commercial airline, 1973 • Tides {9.2 8.4	*can*
30	W.	☾ AT APO. • ♂ STAT. • Raccoons mate now. • Tides {9.0 7.9	*it*
31	Th.	Germany informed U.S. that on February 1 unrestricted submarine warfare would begin, 1917 • {8.8 7.6	*last?*

Farmer's Calendar

■ When a real, old-fashioned winter gets going properly, there is no day without its snow. The northeasters and other big storms that give the New England winter its fame are the stars of the show, the opera divas whom the multitudes turn out to see. Less celebrated but also essential to the whole effect is the supporting cast, the mezzo-sopranos and baritones who fill in the dramatic spaces around the grandees. In the production that is winter in the hill country, this secondary role belongs to the elusive nocturnal visitations of what you might call baker's snow.

In the deepest winter, and especially on the hilltops, each morning reveals a light fall of snow, even when the night has been clear. This snow won't amount to an inch, and so dry and soft is it that its removal calls less for a shovel than for a feather duster. The Lord of Winter is not a king, but a baker who each night sifts down over the fields, woods, and homesteads the finest, whitest flour in his shop.

To be sure, winter in these parts isn't quite what it was. You don't get this casual, throwaway snow every winter morning anymore, just as you don't get as many storms that mean business. That's not all bad. For my part, I don't mind not having to shovel out from under a two-footer every week, but I confess I miss the little baker's snows.

SKY WATCH ☆ *Venus and Jupiter are close together in the southeast, in Sagittarius, on the 1st. This spectacle is best seen around 6:30 A.M. On the 4th, the crescent Moon hovers below them. Venus gets lower each morning; when it meets Mercury from the 24th to month's end, the duo is only 5 degrees above the horizon at 6:00 A.M. Throughout the month, Mars is easy to view at nightfall. The planet resumes direct (eastward) motion in Taurus, but loses half its light, as Earth races away at 66,000 mph. Saturn, at its closest point of the year, reaches opposition on the 24th, in Leo, at magnitude 0.2. A total lunar eclipse on the 20th will be visible from North America. (See page 98 for eclipse times.)*

● **New Moon**	6th day	22nd hour	44th minute
◐ **First Quarter**	13th day	22nd hour	33rd minute
○ **Full Moon**	20th day	22nd hour	30th minute
◑ **Last Quarter**	28th day	21st hour	18th minute

To use this page, see p. 110; for Key Letters, see p. 235; for Tide Tables, see p. 240. All times are given in Eastern Standard Time. ☞ **Bold = P.M.** ☞ Light = A.M.

Day of Year	Day of Month	Day of Week	☼ Rises h. m.	Key	☼ Sets h. m.	Key	Length of Day h. m.	Sun Fast m.	Declination of Sun ° ′	High Tide Times Boston		☾ Rises h. m.	Key	☾ Sets h. m.	Key	☾ Place	☾ Age
32	1	Fr.	6:59	D	**4:58**	A	9 59	2	17 s.08	6½	7	2:56	E	11:35	A	SCO	24
33	2	Sa.	6:58	D	**4:59**	A	10 01	2	16 51	7¼	8	3:55	E	**12:21**	A	OPH	25
34	3	**F**	6:57	D	**5:01**	A	10 04	2	16 33	8¼	9	4:49	E	**1:16**	A	SAG	26
35	4	M.	6:56	D	**5:02**	A	10 06	2	16 16	9	9¾	5:35	E	**2:19**	A	SAG	27
36	5	Tu.	6:54	D	**5:03**	A	10 09	2	15 58	9¾	10½	6:13	E	**3:28**	B	SAG	28
37	6	W.	6:53	D	**5:04**	A	10 11	2	15 39	10½	11	6:45	E	**4:39**	B	CAP	0
38	7	Th.	6:52	D	**5:06**	A	10 14	2	15 21	11¼	11¾	7:12	D	**5:51**	C	CAP	1
39	8	Fr.	6:51	D	**5:07**	B	10 16	1	15 02	**12**	—	7:35	D	**7:03**	D	AQU	2
40	9	Sa.	6:50	D	**5:08**	B	10 18	1	14 43	12¼	12½	7:57	D	**8:15**	D	AQU	3
41	10	**F**	6:48	D	**5:10**	B	10 22	1	14 24	1	1¼	8:19	C	**9:29**	E	PSC	4
42	11	M.	6:47	D	**5:11**	B	10 24	1	14 04	1¾	2	8:42	B	**10:44**	E	PSC	5
43	12	Tu.	6:46	D	**5:12**	B	10 26	1	13 44	2½	3	9:08	B	—	–	PSC	6
44	13	W.	6:45	D	**5:14**	B	10 29	1	13 24	3¼	4	9:40	A	**12:01**	E	ARI	7
45	14	Th.	6:43	D	**5:15**	B	10 32	1	13 04	4¼	5	10:19	A	**1:18**	E	TAU	8
46	15	Fr.	6:42	D	**5:16**	B	10 34	1	12 43	5¼	6	11:10	A	**2:33**	E	TAU	9
47	16	Sa.	6:40	D	**5:17**	B	10 37	1	12 22	6½	7¼	**12:11**	A	**3:40**	E	TAU	10
48	17	**F**	6:39	D	**5:19**	B	10 40	2	12 02	7½	8¼	**1:22**	A	**4:35**	E	AUR	11
49	18	M.	6:38	D	**5:20**	B	10 42	2	11 40	8½	9¼	**2:37**	B	**5:18**	E	GEM	12
50	19	Tu.	6:36	D	**5:21**	B	10 45	2	11 19	9½	10¼	**3:52**	B	**5:53**	E	CAN	13
51	20	W.	6:35	D	**5:23**	B	10 48	2	10 58	10½	11	**5:04**	C	**6:20**	D	LEO	14
52	21	Th.	6:33	D	**5:24**	B	10 51	2	10 36	11¼	11¾	**6:14**	D	**6:43**	D	LEO	15
53	22	Fr.	6:32	D	**5:25**	B	10 53	2	10 14	**12**	—	**7:20**	D	**7:04**	C	LEO	16
54	23	Sa.	6:30	D	**5:26**	B	10 56	2	9 52	12½	12¾	**8:25**	E	**7:23**	C	VIR	17
55	24	**F**	6:29	D	**5:28**	B	10 59	2	9 30	1	1¼	**9:30**	E	**7:43**	B	VIR	18
56	25	M.	6:27	D	**5:29**	B	11 02	2	9 08	1¾	2	**10:34**	E	**8:04**	B	VIR	19
57	26	Tu.	6:26	D	**5:30**	B	11 04	3	8 46	2¼	2¾	**11:39**	E	**8:28**	B	VIR	20
58	27	W.	6:24	D	**5:31**	B	11 07	3	8 23	3	3½	—	–	**8:56**	A	LIB	21
59	28	Th.	6:22	D	**5:32**	B	11 10	3	8 01	3¾	4½	**12:42**	E	**9:30**	A	SCO	22
60	29	Fr.	6:21	D	**5:34**	B	11 13	3	7 s.38	4¾	5½	**1:43**	E	**10:12**	A	SCO	23

FEBRUARY HATH 29 DAYS • 2008

Snow falling and night falling fast, oh, fast
In a field I looked into going past. –Robert Frost

Day of Month	Day of Week	Dates, Feasts, Fasts, Aspects, Tide Heights	Weather
1	Fr.	St. Brigid • ☌♀♃ • First auto insurance policy issued, 1898	*Groundhogs*
2	Sa.	Candlemas • Groundhog Day • Actor Boris Karloff died, 1969 • {8.9 / 7.7	*shiver,*
3	**F**	**Quinquagesima** • ☾ RUNS LOW • Tides {9.2 / 7.9	*stay*
4	M.	☌♃☾ • ☌♀☾ • 96-hour surgical operation began, 1951 • {9.5 / 8.3	*indoors.*
5	Tu.	St. Agatha • Shrove Tuesday • *Newer is truer.* • {9.9 / 8.7	*Snow*
6	W.	Ash Wednesday • **New** ● • **Eclipse** ⊙ • ☿ IN INF. ☌	*is*
7	Th.	**Chinese New Year** • ☾ AT ☊ • Ballet introduced to United States, 1827	*reaching*
8	Fr.	Schenectady, N.Y., attacked by French and Indians, 1690 • Tides {10.7 / —	*second*
9	Sa.	☾ ON EQ. • ☌♅☾ • Canada expelled 13 Soviet diplomats for spying, 1978 • {10.0 / 10.7	*floors!*
10	**F**	**1st S. in Lent** • ☌♆⊙ • Tides {10.3 / 10.6	*Not*
11	M.	Barbara Harris became first female Episcopal bishop, 1989 • *Every time a sheep bleats, it loses a mouthful.*	*a*
12	Tu.	Abe Lincoln born, 1809 • –47°F, Camp Clarke, Nebr., 1899 • {10.6 / 9.7	*good*
13	W.	Ember Day • ☾ AT PERIG. • N.Y.C. mayor R. Giuliani made honorary knight, 2002	*time*
14	Th.	Sts. Cyril & Methodius • **Valentine's Day** • Tides {10.3 / 8.8	*to*
15	Fr.	Ember Day • Susan B. Anthony born, 1820 • Winter's back breaks.	*be*
16	Sa.	Ember Day • ☾ RIDES HIGH • ☌♂☾ • Tides {10.1 / 8.5	*a*
17	**F**	**2nd S. in Lent** • *Nude Descending a Staircase* outraged viewers, 1913	*snow*
18	M.	**George Washington's Birthday (observed)** • ☿ STAT. • Tides {10.4 / 9.1	*maker:*
19	Tu.	First practical U.S. coal-burning locomotive *(York)* tested, York, Pa., 1831 • {10.7 / 9.5	*There's*
20	W.	**Full Snow** ○ • **Eclipse** ☾ • ☾ AT ☋ • {10.8 / 9.8	*two*
21	Th.	☌♄☾ • Activist Malcolm X assassinated in N.Y.C., 1965 • Tides {10.8 / 10.1	*more*
22	Fr.	☾ ON EQ. • George Washington born, 1732 • Tides {10.6 / —	*feet*
23	Sa.	U.S. soldiers raised flag on Mt. Suribachi, Iwo Jima, Japan, 1945 • Tides {10.1 / 10.3	*on*
24	**F**	**3rd S. in Lent** • ♄ AT ☍ • Tides {10.1 / 9.9	*every*
25	M.	St. Matthias[T] • ☌☿♀ • 18" snow, Society Hill, S.C., 1914 • Tides {9.9 / 9.4	*acre!*
26	Tu.	Robert Penn Warren first to be designated U.S. "Poet Laureate Consultant in Poetry," 1986 • {9.6 / 8.8	*Call*
27	W.	☾ AT APO. • Children's television icon Mister (Fred) Rogers died, 2003 • {9.3 / 8.3	*it*
28	Th.	Colorado Territory created, 1861 • Tides {9.0 / 7.9	*Heap*
29	Fr.	**Leap Day** • *He who leaps high must take a long run.*	*Year!*

A caress is better than a career. –Elisabeth Marbury

Farmer's Calendar

■ All in the space of 15 seconds, a coyote trots out of the woods and into the road, sees me, stops, looks me up and down, and trots on across the road, over the stone wall, and into the pines. It's a moment that is rare and brief, and like all encounters with wild predators, it has about it an element of the uncanny.

What is it about these creatures that makes our fleeting glimpses of them so charged? Not their looks. This coyote might have been the neighbor's German shepherd, an animal to which it is genetically quite close. In size, color, and form the two canines are very similar, but in their presence, they are utterly unlike. The wild cousin has a vibration, a hyper-vitality that separates it from the domestic. The coyote was nobody's pet, nobody's companion. I wasn't part of its life; it wasn't part of mine.

Except in that quick meeting. There, across 50 feet of woodland road, we were for an instant connected. And in that instant, in the look that passed from the coyote to me, I saw the factor that set it apart from other like creatures: intensity. That look was not casual. It belonged to a being that was alert and focused on a level far beyond the tame. It came from a mind altogether simple and rigorous. The coyote in our quick exchange asked two questions. Can I eat you? Can you eat me?

SKY WATCH ☆ *Mars, in Gemini, is now high overhead by 7:00 P.M. It hovers near the Moon on the 14th but dims from brilliant to merely bright. Saturn, out all night in Leo, fades slightly as its rings tilt increasingly edgewise. On the 18th, Leo's brightest star, Regulus, can be seen between the Moon and Saturn. Jupiter, in Sagittarius all year, brightens slightly and starts rising before 4:00 A.M. Venus becomes lower and will be very difficult to see from now until the fall. On the 5th, it bunches up with the Moon, Mercury, and Neptune, but the trio is only 4 degrees high at 6:00 A.M. and difficult to observe. Spring begins with the vernal equinox on the 20th, at 1:48 A.M.*

●	**New Moon**	7th day	12th hour	14th minute
◐	**First Quarter**	14th day	6th hour	46th minute
○	**Full Moon**	21st day	14th hour	40th minute
◑	**Last Quarter**	29th day	17th hour	47th minute

To use this page, see p. 110; for Key Letters, see p. 235; for Tide Tables, see p. 240.
After 2:00 A.M. on March 9, Eastern Daylight Time is given. ☞ **Bold = P.M.** ☞ Light = A.M.

Day of Year	Day of Month	Day of Week	Rises h. m.	Key	Sets h. m.	Key	Length of Day h. m.	Sun Fast m.	Declination of Sun ° '	High Tide Times Boston		Rises h. m.	Key	Sets h. m.	Key	Place	Age
61	1	Sa.	6:19	D	5:35	B	11 16	3	7 s. 15	5¾	6½	2:39	E	11:03	A	OPH	24
62	2	**E**	6:18	D	5:36	B	11 18	3	6 53	6½	7½	3:27	E	**12:02**	A	SAG	25
63	3	M.	6:16	D	5:37	B	11 21	4	6 30	7½	8¼	4:09	E	**1:08**	B	SAG	26
64	4	Tu.	6:14	D	5:39	B	11 25	4	6 06	8½	9	4:43	E	**2:18**	B	CAP	27
65	5	W.	6:13	D	5:40	B	11 27	4	5 43	9¼	9¾	5:12	E	**3:30**	C	CAP	28
66	6	Th.	6:11	D	5:41	B	11 30	4	5 20	10	10½	5:37	D	**4:43**	C	AQU	29
67	7	Fr.	6:09	D	5:42	B	11 33	5	4 56	10¾	11¼	6:00	D	**5:57**	D	AQU	0
68	8	Sa.	6:08	D	5:43	B	11 35	5	4 33	11½	11¾	6:22	C	**7:11**	E	PSC	1
69	9	**E**	7:06	D	6:45	B	11 39	5	4 09	1¼	—	7:45	C	**9:28**	E	PSC	2
70	10	M.	7:04	D	6:46	B	11 42	5	3 46	1½	2	8:11	B	**10:47**	E	PSC	3
71	11	Tu.	7:03	C	6:47	B	11 44	6	3 22	2¼	2¾	8:41	B	—	–	ARI	4
72	12	W.	7:01	C	6:48	B	11 47	6	2 59	3	3¾	9:19	A	12:06	E	ARI	5
73	13	Th.	6:59	C	6:49	B	11 50	6	2 35	4	4¾	10:06	A	**1:23**	E	TAU	6
74	14	Fr.	6:58	C	6:50	B	11 52	6	2 11	5	5¾	11:05	A	**2:33**	E	TAU	7
75	15	Sa.	6:56	C	6:52	B	11 56	7	1 48	6	7	**12:12**	A	**3:32**	E	AUR	8
76	16	**E**	6:54	C	6:53	B	11 59	7	1 24	7¼	8	**1:25**	B	**4:18**	E	GEM	9
77	17	M.	6:52	C	6:54	B	12 02	7	1 00	8½	9¼	**2:39**	B	**4:54**	E	CAN	10
78	18	Tu.	6:51	C	6:55	B	12 04	7	0 36	9½	10	**3:50**	C	**5:23**	E	CAN	11
79	19	W.	6:49	C	6:56	C	12 07	8	0 s. 13	10½	11	**4:59**	D	**5:47**	D	LEO	12
80	20	Th.	6:47	C	6:57	C	12 10	8	0 N. 11	11¼	11¾	**6:06**	D	**6:08**	D	LEO	13
81	21	Fr.	6:45	C	6:58	C	12 13	8	0 35	12	—	**7:11**	D	**6:28**	C	VIR	14
82	22	Sa.	6:44	C	7:00	C	12 16	9	0 58	12¼	12¾	**8:16**	E	**6:47**	C	VIR	15
83	23	**E**	6:42	C	7:01	C	12 19	9	1 22	1	1¼	**9:20**	E	**7:08**	B	VIR	16
84	24	M.	6:40	C	7:02	C	12 22	9	1 46	1½	2	**10:25**	E	**7:31**	B	VIR	17
85	25	Tu.	6:38	C	7:03	C	12 25	10	2 09	2	2½	**11:29**	E	**7:57**	A	LIB	18
86	26	W.	6:37	C	7:04	C	12 27	10	2 33	2¾	3¼	—	–	**8:29**	A	LIB	19
87	27	Th.	6:35	C	7:05	C	12 30	10	2 56	3½	4	12:31	E	**9:07**	A	SCO	20
88	28	Fr.	6:33	C	7:06	C	12 33	10	3 19	4¼	4¾	**1:28**	E	**9:54**	A	OPH	21
89	29	Sa.	6:31	C	7:08	C	12 37	11	3 43	5	5¾	**2:19**	E	**10:49**	A	SAG	22
90	30	**E**	6:30	C	7:09	C	12 39	11	4 06	6	6¾	**3:03**	E	**11:51**	A	SAG	23
91	31	M.	6:28	B	7:10	C	12 42	11	4 N. 29	7	7¾	**3:40**	E	**12:58**	B	SAG	24

March hath 31 days • 2008

In March is good grafting, the skillful do know,
So long as the wind in the east do not blow. –Thomas Tusser

Day of Month	Day of Week	Dates, Feasts, Fasts, Aspects, Tide Heights	Weather
1	Sa.	St. David • ☾ RUNS LOW • Yellowstone National Park created, 1872 • {8.7 / 7.5	*Winds*
2	E	4th S. in Lent • ☌♃☾ • Tides {8.8 / 7.7	*ululate*
3	M.	☿ GR. ELONG. (27° WEST) • *March comes in with adder heads and goes out with peacock tails.* • {9.0 / 8.0	*while*
4	Tu.	Lincoln inaugurated as U.S. president for second term, 1865 • Tides {9.4 / 8.6	*snowflakes*
5	W.	St. Piran • ☌☿☾ • OCCN. ♀☾ • ☌♆☾	*accumulate!*
6	Th.	☾ AT ☊ • ☌♆♀ • City of Toronto, Ont., incorporated, 1834 • {10.4 / 9.8	*So*
7	Fr.	St. Perpetua • New ● • *No remedy but patience.* • {10.7 / 10.3	*cold*
8	Sa.	☾ ON EQ. • ☌♅☉ • ☌☿♆ • K. Grahame, *The Wind in the Willows* author, born, 1859	*it's*
9	E	5th S. in Lent • Daylight Saving Time begins, 2:00 A.M. • {10.9 / —	*hard*
10	M.	Pure Monday • ☾ AT PERIG. • Ulysses S. Grant became Lt. Gen. of Union Army, 1864	*to*
11	Tu.	Bank of Canada issued its first series of bank notes, 1935 • Tides {11.2 / 10.3	*believe*
12	W.	Boston Celtics' Larry Bird scored 60 points in basketball game vs. Atlanta Hawks, 1985 • {11.1 / 9.8	*we'll*
13	Th.	Planet Uranus discovered by Sir William Herschel, 1781	*be*
14	Fr.	☾ RIDES HIGH • ☌♂☾ • Jack Ruby guilty of murdering Lee Harvey Oswald, 1964	*relieved,*
15	Sa.	Beware the ides of March. • *After dinner sit awhile, After supper walk a mile.*	*but*
16	E	Palm Sunday • Sunday of Orthodoxy • {9.9 / 8.6	*Spring*
17	M.	St. Patrick's Day • –50°F, Snake River, Wyo., 1906 • {9.9 / 8.9	*has*
18	Tu.	☾ AT ☋ • Composer Nikolay Rimsky-Korsakov born, 1844 • {10.1 / 9.3	*sunshine*
19	W.	☌♄☾ • Chipmunks emerge from hibernation now. • Tides {10.2 / 9.7	*up*
20	Th.	Maundy Thursday • Vernal Equinox • Tides {10.3 / 10.0	*her*
21	Fr.	Good Friday • Full Worm ○ • ☾ ON EQ. • {10.3 / —	*sleeve.*
22	Sa.	Stamp Act passed by English Parliament, 1765 • {10.2 / 10.1	*And*
23	E	Easter • ☌☿♀ • *Better keep peace than make peace.* • Tides {10.2 / 9.9	*though*
24	M.	Easter Monday • Boston archbishop Sean O'Malley elevated to cardinal, 2006	*we're*
25	Tu.	Italian explorer Giovanni da Verrazano arrived off Outer Banks of N.C., 1524 • Tides {10.0 / 9.2	*wary,*
26	W.	☾ AT APO. • Popeye statue unveiled during spinach festival, Crystal City, Tex., 1937 • {9.8 / 8.8	*we*
27	Th.	Yuri Gagarin, first man in space, died, 1968 • {9.5 / 8.4	*know*
28	Fr.	☾ RUNS LOW • Wilt Chamberlain played his last pro basketball game, 1973 • {9.2 / 8.0	*this*
29	Sa.	First wedding at the White House, 1812 • Tides {8.9 / 7.8	*snow*
30	E	2nd S. of Easter • ☌♃☾ • *Even reckoning makes long friends.*	*is*
31	M.	St. Joseph[T] • United Farm Workers founder Cesar Chavez born, 1927	*temporary!*

Farmer's Calendar

■ Sugaring season. The sap gatherers are busy among the maples. Steam billows round the clock from the sugarhouses. For a couple of weeks, people all over northern New England turn out to take their share of the woods' annual bounty of maple syrup and sugar. Some operate on a huge scale, drawing truckloads of sap from the sugarbushes. Others are amateurs who sugar for fun. Both are subject to what might be called maple sugaring's ruling ratio: You have to boil an awful lot of sap to get an awful little of syrup.

The backyard sugarer ignores this rule at his peril. I learned that some years ago when our family decided to make our own syrup. We had a big sugar maple in the yard, we had a bucket, and if we didn't have a proper evaporator, we had a kitchen range. We tapped the tree, collected the sap, and set to boiling.

We boiled and boiled. And boiled. The kitchen filled with steam. We boiled on. For hours we stumbled blindly through the fog, eventually to wind up with about a cup of syrup. What we had not counted on was the gummy film that covered the kitchen, deposited by the evaporation of gallons and gallons of sugar-rich sap. So sticky was our kitchen ceiling that the cats and dogs, and even the smaller children, could walk around up there easily, like houseflies.

Listen to the Farmer's Calendar at Almanac.com.

THE FOURTH MONTH • 2008

SKY WATCH ☆ *Mars, still in Gemini, remains high up at nightfall. It fades this month, but not as dramatically as before, reaching magnitude 1.1 by month's end. Jupiter brightens to –2.4 as it starts to rise before 2:00* A.M. *The Moon dangles just below Jupiter on the 27th. Saturn's shiny rings turn even more sideways, causing its brightness to dim further to a still-respectable magnitude 0.6 by the end of the month. It's visible most of the night, but at least a 30× telescope is needed to see the famous rings. Meanwhile, Mercury begins its best evening apparition of the year during the month's final week, shining low in the west at magnitude –1.4 about 35 minutes after sunset.*

●	**New Moon**	5th day	23rd hour	55th minute
◐	**First Quarter**	12th day	14th hour	32nd minute
○	**Full Moon**	20th day	6th hour	25th minute
◑	**Last Quarter**	28th day	10th hour	12th minute

To use this page, see p. 110; for Key Letters, see p. 235; for Tide Tables, see p. 240.
All times are given in Eastern Daylight Time. ☞ **Bold = P.M.** ☞ Light = A.M.

Day of Year	Day of Month	Day of Week	☼ Rises h. m.	Key	☼ Sets h. m.	Key	Length of Day h. m.	Sun Fast m.	Declination of Sun ° '	High Tide Times Boston		☾ Rises h. m.	Key	☾ Sets h. m.	Key	☾ Place	☾ Age
92	1	Tu.	6:26	B	**7:11**	C	12 45	12	4N.52	8	**8½**	4:10	E	**2:08**	B	CAP	25
93	2	W.	6:25	B	**7:12**	C	12 47	12	5 15	8¾	**9½**	4:36	E	**3:19**	C	CAP	26
94	3	Th.	6:23	B	**7:13**	C	12 50	12	5 38	9¾	**10¼**	5:00	D	**4:32**	D	AQU	27
95	4	Fr.	6:21	B	**7:14**	D	12 53	13	6 01	10½	**11**	5:23	C	**5:46**	D	PSC	28
96	5	Sa.	6:19	B	**7:15**	D	12 56	13	6 24	11¼	**11½**	5:46	C	**7:03**	E	PSC	0
97	6	**E**	6:18	B	**7:17**	D	12 59	13	6 47	**12**	—	6:11	B	**8:22**	E	PSC	1
98	7	M.	6:16	B	**7:18**	D	13 02	13	7 09	12¼	**1**	6:40	B	**9:44**	E	ARI	2
99	8	Tu.	6:14	B	**7:19**	D	13 05	14	7 32	1	**1¾**	7:16	A	**11:06**	E	ARI	3
100	9	W.	6:13	B	**7:20**	D	13 07	14	7 54	2	**2½**	8:01	A	—	–	TAU	4
101	10	Th.	6:11	B	**7:21**	D	13 10	14	8 17	2¾	**3½**	8:57	A	12:21	E	TAU	5
102	11	Fr.	6:09	B	**7:22**	D	13 13	15	8 39	3¾	**4½**	10:03	A	1:25	E	AUR	6
103	12	Sa.	6:08	B	**7:23**	D	13 15	15	9 00	4¾	**5½**	11:16	B	2:16	E	GEM	7
104	13	**E**	6:06	B	**7:24**	D	13 18	15	9 22	5¾	**6¾**	**12:30**	B	2:56	E	CAN	8
105	14	M.	6:05	B	**7:26**	D	13 21	15	9 44	7	**7¾**	**1:42**	C	3:27	E	CAN	9
106	15	Tu.	6:03	B	**7:27**	D	13 24	16	10 05	8¼	**8¾**	**2:51**	C	3:52	D	LEO	10
107	16	W.	6:01	B	**7:28**	D	13 27	16	10 26	9¼	**9¾**	**3:57**	D	4:14	D	LEO	11
108	17	Th.	6:00	B	**7:29**	D	13 29	16	10 47	10	**10½**	**5:02**	D	4:34	C	LEO	12
109	18	Fr.	5:58	B	**7:30**	D	13 32	16	11 08	11	**11¼**	**6:05**	D	4:53	C	VIR	13
110	19	Sa.	5:57	B	**7:31**	D	13 34	16	11 28	11½	**11¾**	**7:09**	E	5:13	B	VIR	14
111	20	**E**	5:55	B	**7:32**	D	13 37	17	11 49	**12¼**	—	**8:13**	E	5:35	B	VIR	15
112	21	M.	5:54	B	**7:33**	D	13 39	17	12 09	12¼	**1**	**9:18**	E	6:00	A	LIB	16
113	22	Tu.	5:52	B	**7:35**	D	13 43	17	12 29	1	**1½**	**10:20**	E	6:30	A	LIB	17
114	23	W.	5:51	B	**7:36**	D	13 45	17	12 49	1½	**2¼**	**11:20**	E	7:06	A	SCO	18
115	24	Th.	5:49	B	**7:37**	D	13 48	17	13 09	2¼	**2¾**	—	–	7:50	A	OPH	19
116	25	Fr.	5:48	B	**7:38**	D	13 50	18	13 28	3	**3½**	12:13	E	8:42	A	SAG	20
117	26	Sa.	5:46	B	**7:39**	D	13 53	18	13 47	3¾	**4¼**	12:59	E	9:40	A	SAG	21
118	27	**E**	5:45	B	**7:40**	D	13 55	18	14 06	4½	**5¼**	1:37	E	10:44	B	SAG	22
119	28	M.	5:43	B	**7:41**	D	13 58	18	14 25	5¼	**6**	2:09	E	11:51	B	CAP	23
120	29	Tu.	5:42	B	**7:42**	D	14 00	18	14 44	6¼	**7**	2:36	E	**1:00**	C	CAP	24
121	30	W.	5:41	B	**7:44**	D	14 03	18	15N.02	7¼	**7¾**	3:00	D	**2:10**	C	AQU	25

APRIL HATH 30 DAYS • 2008

Blossom of the almond trees,
April's gift to April's bees. –Edwin Arnold

Day of Month	Day of Week	Dates, Feasts, Fasts, Aspects, Tide Heights	Weather
1	Tu.	**Annunciation**[T] • **All Fools'** • Musician Scott Joplin died, 1917 • {9.1 8.5	*Solar,*
2	W.	☾ at ☊ • ☌♆☾ • ♇ stat. • U.S. Mint established, 1792 • {9.5 9.1	*then*
3	Th.	**St. Richard of Chichester** • 148 tornadoes in 13 states, 1974 • {9.9 9.8	*doler;*
4	Fr.	☾ on Eq. • ☌☉☾ • ☌♀☾ • *Ben Hur* won 11 Academy Awards, 1960	*must*
5	Sa.	**New ●** • Women granted the right to vote in British Columbia, 1917 • {10.7 11.1	*this*
6	**E**	**3rd S. of Easter** • *A mill can not grind with the water that is past.*	*month*
7	M.	☾ at perig. • Booker T. Washington first African-American on a postage stamp, 1940 • {11.6 10.8	*be*
8	Tu.	85°F in N.Y.C. due to record heat wave, 1929 • {11.8 10.6	*so*
9	W.	Sir Winston Churchill declared honorary U.S. citizen, 1963 • Tides {11.8 10.3	*bipolar?*
10	Th.	The American Society for the Prevention of Cruelty to Animals incorporated, 1866	*Wondrously*
11	Fr.	☾ rides high • U.S. Navy bought its first commissioned submarine, USS *Holland,* 1900	*warm,*
12	Sa.	occn. ♂☾ • *Follow love and it will flee thee; Flee love and it will follow thee.*	*followed*
13	**E**	**4th S. of Easter** • Thomas Jefferson born, 1743	*by*
14	M.	James Cash Penney opened his first store, Kemmerer, Wyo., 1902 • {9.8 9.0	*thunderousy*
15	Tu.	☾ at ☋ • ☌♄☾ • *When dogwood blooms are plentiful, expect a cold winter.*	*storms:*
16	W.	☿ in sup. ☌ • Two ships exploded in harbor, Texas City, Tex., 1947 • Tides {9.7 9.6	*Boom!*
17	Th.	☾ on Eq. • Lewis M. Norton patented a vat for forming pineapple-shape cheese, 1810 • {9.7 9.9	*Rain's*
18	Fr.	Catherine Ndereba, of Kenya, won her fourth Boston Marathon, 2005 • Tides {9.7 10.1	*a-fallin',*
19	Sa.	Surgeon's Loch Ness monster hoax photo taken, 1934	*streams*
20	**E**	**First day of Passover** • **Full Pink** ○ • {9.6 —	*a-risin',*
21	M.	50-lb. 8-oz. African pompano caught, Daytona Beach, Fla., 1990 • Tides {10.2 9.4	*but*
22	Tu.	First substantial human eye replacement, Houston, Tex., 1969 • Tides {10.2 9.2	*there's*
23	W.	**St. George** • ☾ at apo. • *Kindnesses, like grain, increase by sowing.* • {10.1 9.0	*hope*
24	Th.	Almanac maker Robert B. Thomas born, 1766 • Tides {9.9 8.7	*on*
25	Fr.	**St. Mark** • ☾ runs low • United Negro College Fund incorporated, 1944 • {9.6 8.5	*the*
26	Sa.	John Wilkes Booth, assassin of Pres. Lincoln, killed, 1865 • Tides {9.4 8.3	*horizon.*
27	**E**	**Rogation S.** • **Orthodox Easter** • ☌♃☾	*Daffodils*
28	M.	*Vows made in storms are forgotten in calms.* • {9.1 8.3	*garland*
29	Tu.	☾ at ☊ • occn. ♆☾ • Poplars leaf out about now. • {9.1 8.6	*the*
30	W.	Franklin D. Roosevelt became the first president to appear on television, 1939 • Tides {9.2 9.1	*hills.*

You can not shake hands with a clenched fist. –Indira Gandhi

Farmer's Calendar

■ An April day with the grass coming in green and a soft wind blowing among the daffodils is a perfect time to seize the leaf rake and set to cleaning up outdoors. Another, similar, April day—also perfect. A third? Slightly less perfect. A fourth such day begins to feel like work.

It feels like work because it is work. Leaf raking is a task of a magnitude and a futility rivaling the labor of Sisyphus, the unfortunate inmate of hell in Greek myth who eternally rolled his boulder up the hill, to have it eternally roll back down again. Last year's leaves, pasted to the ground by the snows, cling tenaciously and require vigorous raking. Raked, freed from the earth, they toss themselves gaily in the breeze; they caper and shy about like wild colts. Chasing them with your rake, gathering them into piles, watching as they escape and frisk away, and raking them back to the pile is a job less like bringing order to a disordered setting than it is like herding boisterous and unruly young stock.

You're a kind of drover or wrangler of leaves, with the difference that at the end of your drive there is no railhead where you ship the critters off to Chicago. There is only a task abandoned rather than completed, as you contemplate the many leaves that escaped your rake—and their successors, this year's leaves, multiplying overhead.

CALENDAR

CALENDAR

SKY WATCH ☆ *The best time to see Mercury is on the 6th, at about 35 minutes after sunset, when the charbroiled planet floats next to the crescent Moon, 12 degrees high in the west. Although Mercury remains visible until the 26th, it is only one-tenth as bright by then, at magnitude 2.0, and hidden by the twilight. Mars, halfway up the western sky at nightfall, crosses into Cancer and floats in front of the famous Beehive star cluster from the 22nd to the 24th. This fine sight is best viewed through binoculars. Saturn is highest at nightfall and appears above the Moon on the 12th. Jupiter, at magnitude –2.5, rises by midnight at month's end. Venus is too close to the Sun to be seen.*

● **New Moon**	5th day	8th hour	18th minute
◐ **First Quarter**	11th day	23rd hour	47th minute
○ **Full Moon**	19th day	22nd hour	11th minute
◑ **Last Quarter**	27th day	22nd hour	57th minute

To use this page, see p. 110; for Key Letters, see p. 235; for Tide Tables, see p. 240.
All times are given in Eastern Daylight Time. ☞ **Bold = P.M.** ☞ Light = A.M.

Day of Year	Day of Month	Day of Week	☼ Rises h. m.	Key	☼ Sets h. m.	Key	Length of Day h. m.	Sun Fast m.	Declination of Sun ° '	High Tide Times Boston		☾ Rises h. m.	Key	☾ Sets h. m.	Key	☾ Place	☾ Age
122	1	Th.	5:39	B	**7:45**	D	14 06	18	15N.21	8¼	**8¾**	3:23	D	**3:21**	D	AQU	26
123	2	Fr.	5:38	B	**7:46**	D	14 08	19	15 38	9	**9½**	3:45	C	**4:35**	D	PSC	27
124	3	Sa.	5:37	A	**7:47**	D	14 10	19	15 56	10	**10¼**	4:09	B	**5:52**	E	PSC	28
125	4	**E**	5:35	A	**7:48**	D	14 13	19	16 13	10¾	**11**	4:36	B	**7:14**	E	PSC	29
126	5	M.	5:34	A	**7:49**	D	14 15	19	16 30	11¾	—	5:09	A	**8:37**	E	ARI	0
127	6	Tu.	5:33	A	**7:50**	D	14 17	19	16 47	12	**12½**	5:50	A	**9:58**	E	TAU	1
128	7	W.	5:31	A	**7:51**	D	14 20	19	17 03	12¾	**1½**	6:43	A	**11:10**	E	TAU	2
129	8	Th.	5:30	A	**7:52**	D	14 22	19	17 19	1½	**2¼**	7:48	A	—	–	TAU	3
130	9	Fr.	5:29	A	**7:53**	D	14 24	19	17 35	2½	**3¼**	9:01	A	12:09	E	GEM	4
131	10	Sa.	5:28	A	**7:55**	D	14 27	19	17 51	3½	**4¼**	10:18	B	12:54	E	GEM	5
132	11	**E**	5:27	A	**7:56**	D	14 29	19	18 06	4½	**5¼**	11:32	B	1:28	E	CAN	6
133	12	M.	5:26	A	**7:57**	D	14 31	19	18 22	5½	**6½**	**12:43**	C	1:56	D	LEO	7
134	13	Tu.	5:25	A	**7:58**	D	14 33	19	18 36	6¾	**7½**	**1:50**	D	2:19	D	LEO	8
135	14	W.	5:24	A	**7:59**	E	14 35	19	18 50	7¾	**8¼**	**2:55**	D	2:39	D	LEO	9
136	15	Th.	5:23	A	**8:00**	E	14 37	19	19 04	8¾	**9¼**	**3:58**	E	2:59	C	VIR	10
137	16	Fr.	5:22	A	**8:01**	E	14 39	19	19 18	9¾	**10**	**5:02**	E	3:18	B	VIR	11
138	17	Sa.	5:21	A	**8:02**	E	14 41	19	19 31	10½	**10½**	**6:05**	E	3:40	B	VIR	12
139	18	**E**	5:20	A	**8:03**	E	14 43	19	19 44	11¼	**11¼**	**7:09**	E	4:04	B	VIR	13
140	19	M.	5:19	A	**8:04**	E	14 45	19	19 57	11¾	—	**8:12**	E	4:32	A	LIB	14
141	20	Tu.	5:18	A	**8:05**	E	14 47	19	20 09	12	**12½**	**9:12**	E	5:06	A	SCO	15
142	21	W.	5:17	A	**8:06**	E	14 49	19	20 22	12½	**1¼**	**10:08**	E	5:47	A	SCO	16
143	22	Th.	5:16	A	**8:07**	E	14 51	19	20 33	1¼	**1¾**	**10:56**	E	6:37	A	SAG	17
144	23	Fr.	5:16	A	**8:08**	E	14 52	19	20 45	1¾	**2½**	**11:36**	E	7:34	A	SAG	18
145	24	Sa.	5:15	A	**8:08**	E	14 53	19	20 56	2½	**3¼**	—	–	8:36	B	SAG	19
146	25	**E**	5:14	A	**8:09**	E	14 55	19	21 06	3¼	**4**	12:10	D	9:41	B	CAP	20
147	26	M.	5:13	A	**8:10**	E	14 57	19	21 16	4	**4¾**	12:38	D	10:48	B	CAP	21
148	27	Tu.	5:13	A	**8:11**	E	14 58	18	21 26	4¾	**5½**	1:03	D	11:55	C	CAP	22
149	28	W.	5:12	A	**8:12**	E	15 00	18	21 36	5¾	**6¼**	1:25	D	**1:04**	D	AQU	23
150	29	Th.	5:12	A	**8:13**	E	15 01	18	21 45	6½	**7¼**	1:46	D	**2:14**	D	PSC	24
151	30	Fr.	5:11	A	**8:14**	E	15 03	18	21 54	7½	**8**	2:08	C	**3:27**	E	PSC	25
152	31	Sa.	5:10	A	**8:14**	E	15 04	18	22N.02	8½	**9**	2:33	B	**4:44**	E	PSC	26

May hath 31 days • 2008

The song of Nature is forever,
Her joyous voices falter never. –Joyce Vance Cheney

Day of Month	Day of Week	Dates, Feasts, Fasts, Aspects, Tide Heights	Weather
1	Th.	**Ascension** • May Day • ☾ ON EQ. • ☌♅☾	*Lightning*
2	Fr.	**Sts. Philip & James**[T] • Golfer Kelly Gibson born, 1964 • { 9.8 10.5	*flashing,*
3	Sa.	**Invention of the Holy Cross** • ♄ STAT. • { 10.2 11.1	*raindrops*
4	E	**1st S. af. Asc.** • *A cold May is kindly, And fills the barn finely.*	*splashing,*
5	M.	Cinco de Mayo • New ● • ☾ AT PERIG. • { 10.6 12.0	*spring*
6	Tu.	☌☿☾ • John Gorrie patented an ice machine, 1851 • Tides { 10.6 —	*unfurls*
7	W.	American Medical Association founded, 1847 • { 12.1 10.5	*its*
8	Th.	**St. Julian of Norwich** • ☾ RIDES HIGH • Grapefruit-size hail, Dallas, Tex., 1981	*flowery*
9	Fr.	**St. Gregory of Nazianzus** • ♃ STAT. • { 11.7 9.9	*fashions.*
10	Sa.	☌♂☾ • Victoria Woodhull first woman to be nominated for U.S. president, 1872 • { 11.2 9.6	*Kissed*
11	E	**Whit S.** • **Pentecost** • Three • Tides { 10.6 9.4	*by*
12	M.	☾ AT ☋ • ☌♄☾ • *Many a truth is spoken in jest.* • Chilly • { 10.1 9.4	*mist*
13	Tu.	A New Brunswick earthquake measured 3.9 on the Richter scale, 1983 • Saints • Tides { 9.7 9.4	*or*
14	W.	Ember Day • ☾ ON EQ. • ☿ GR. ELONG. (22° EAST) • Tides { 9.4 9.6	*sunlight-*
15	Th.	Johannes Kepler verified his Third Law of Planetary Motion, 1618 • Tides { 9.2 9.8	*dappled,*
16	Fr.	Ember Day • Fire broke out at tire dump, Saint-Amable, Que., 1990 • { 9.2 9.9	*blossoms*
17	Sa.	Ember Day • First Kentucky Derby held, Louisville, Ky., 1875 • { 9.1 10.0	*burst*
18	E	**Trinity** • 116°F, Death Valley, Calif., 2006 • { 9.1 10.1	*on*
19	M.	**St. Dunstan** • **Vesak** • Victoria Day (Canada) • Full Flower ○	*peach*
20	Tu.	☾ AT APO. • NFL president Joseph Carr died, 1939 • { 9.0 —	*and*
21	W.	U.S. merchant ship *Robin Moor* sunk by U-boat, 1941	*apple.*
22	Th.	☾ RUNS LOW • Barry Bishop's team reached summit of Mt. Everest, 1963 • Tides { 10.1 8.8	*Every*
23	Fr.	*Turnips like a dry bed but a wet head.* • Pirate Captain Kidd hanged, 1701 • { 10.0 8.7	*orchard's*
24	Sa.	☌♃☾ • Second U.S. manned orbital space flight, *Aurora 7,* 1962 • Tides { 9.8 8.6	*a*
25	E	**Corpus Christi** • *Star Wars* released, 1977 • { 9.7 8.6	*Monet,*
26	M.	Memorial Day (observed) • ☾ AT ☊ • ☌♆☾ • ☿ STAT. • ♆ STAT.	*a*
27	Tu.	Golden Gate B[illegible] San Francisco opened to pedes[illegible] only, 1937 • Tides { 9.4 9.0	*dazzling*
28	W.	Vietnam War sol[illegible] buried in Tomb of the Unknowns (later ID'd and exhumed), Arlington, Va., 1984	*display*
29	Th.	☾ ON EQ. • ☌♅☾ • *Generous minds are all of kin.* • { 9.4 9.8	*for*
30	Fr.	Massive flooding of Columbia River caused dike break that destroyed Vanport, Oreg., 1948	*Memorial*
31	Sa.	**Visit. of Mary** • *Beware of the door that has too many keys.* • Tides { 9.6 10.9	*Day.*

Farmer's Calendar

■ "Each animal is thought to have a proper pleasure," writes Aristotle, "as it has a proper function." It's an arresting thought, coming from one of the first systematic observers in history—and still the most versatile of them all. Aristotle (384–322 B.C.) wrote about practically everything, from physics, astronomy, botany, and anatomy to logic, poetry, and psychology.

In general, Aristotle's method of thought seems to have been to find, in the diverse and particular objects of his inquiry, characteristic traits; and then reason by analogy from them to higher and more universal conclusions. Thus his remarks on animals' pleasures are part of his larger argument about the happy life, proper to mankind, which turns out to be not a search for pleasure but virtuous, rational action.

Even today, we can learn from Aristotle's practice of reasoning from concrete observation. For example, as I look out the window, I observe a small red dog exploring the new lawn. He sniffs and roots about, at last flipping over on his back and rolling to and fro ecstatically in the warm spring grass. Is he pursuing his proper pleasure? It sure looks that way. I don't always feel I know what virtue and happiness really are, and I'm not completely sure Aristotle did either; but if that dog isn't happy, then nothing ever was.

THE SIXTH MONTH • 2008

SKY WATCH ☆ *Mars and Saturn are now evening-only objects. The red planet crosses into Leo in midmonth, fades to below magnitude 1.5, and becomes a medium-bright "star." Saturn does better at magnitude 0.8, slightly brighter than the star Regulus, next to it. The Moon is close to Mars on the 7th and near Saturn the next night. Mercury and Venus are hidden behind the Sun's glare, but Jupiter emerges as the summer's dominant planet. The giant world, shining at a blazing –2.7, rises before 11:00 P.M. and meets the Moon on the 19th. The two will grab the world's attention that night as they parade together in the midnight sky. Summer begins with the solstice on the 20th, at 7:59 P.M.*

● **New Moon**	3rd day	15th hour	23rd minute
◐ **First Quarter**	10th day	11th hour	4th minute
○ **Full Moon**	18th day	13th hour	30th minute
◑ **Last Quarter**	26th day	8th hour	10th minute

To use this page, see p. 110; for Key Letters, see p. 235; for Tide Tables, see p. 240.
All times are given in Eastern Daylight Time. ☞ **Bold = P.M.** ☞ Light = A.M.

Day of Year	Day of Month	Day of Week	☼ Rises h. m.	Key	☼ Sets h. m.	Key	Length of Day h. m.	Sun Fast m.	Declination of Sun ° '	High Tide Times Boston		☾ Rises h. m.	Key	☾ Sets h. m.	Key	☾ Place	☾ Age
153	1	**E**	5:10	A	**8:15**	E	15 05	18	22N.11	9½	**9¾**	3:02	B	**6:06**	E	ARI	27
154	2	M.	5:10	A	**8:16**	E	15 06	18	22 18	10½	**10¾**	3:39	A	**7:28**	E	ARI	28
155	3	Tu.	5:09	A	**8:17**	E	15 08	17	22 25	11¼	**11½**	4:26	A	**8:46**	E	TAU	0
156	4	W.	5:09	A	**8:17**	E	15 08	17	22 32	**12¼**	—	5:26	A	**9:53**	E	TAU	1
157	5	Th.	5:08	A	**8:18**	E	15 10	17	22 38	12½	**1¼**	6:38	A	**10:45**	E	GEM	2
158	6	Fr.	5:08	A	**8:19**	E	15 11	17	22 44	1¼	**2¼**	7:56	B	**11:25**	E	GEM	3
159	7	Sa.	5:08	A	**8:19**	E	15 11	17	22 50	2¼	**3**	9:14	B	**11:56**	E	CAN	4
160	8	**E**	5:08	A	**8:20**	E	15 12	17	22 56	3¼	**4**	10:29	C	—	–	LEO	5
161	9	M.	5:08	A	**8:21**	E	15 13	16	23 00	4¼	**5**	11:39	D	12:22	D	LEO	6
162	10	Tu.	5:07	A	**8:21**	E	15 14	16	23 05	5¼	**5¾**	**12:46**	D	12:43	D	LEO	7
163	11	W.	5:07	A	**8:22**	E	15 15	16	23 09	6¼	**6¾**	**1:51**	D	1:04	C	VIR	8
164	12	Th.	5:07	A	**8:22**	E	15 15	16	23 12	7¼	**7¾**	**2:54**	E	1:23	C	VIR	9
165	13	Fr.	5:07	A	**8:23**	E	15 16	16	23 15	8¼	**8½**	**3:58**	E	1:44	B	VIR	10
166	14	Sa.	5:07	A	**8:23**	E	15 16	15	23 18	9	**9¼**	**5:01**	E	2:07	B	VIR	11
167	15	**E**	5:07	A	**8:23**	E	15 16	15	23 20	10	**10**	**6:05**	E	2:34	A	LIB	12
168	16	M.	5:07	A	**8:24**	E	15 17	15	23 22	10¾	**10¾**	**7:06**	E	3:06	A	LIB	13
169	17	Tu.	5:07	A	**8:24**	E	15 17	15	23 24	11½	**11½**	**8:03**	E	3:46	A	SCO	14
170	18	W.	5:07	A	**8:24**	E	15 17	15	23 26	**12¼**	—	**8:53**	E	4:33	A	OPH	15
171	19	Th.	5:08	A	**8:25**	E	15 17	14	23 26	12	**12¾**	**9:36**	E	5:28	A	SAG	16
172	20	Fr.	5:08	A	**8:25**	E	15 17	14	23 26	12¾	**1½**	**10:12**	E	6:29	B	SAG	17
173	21	Sa.	5:08	A	**8:25**	E	15 17	14	23 26	1½	**2**	**10:41**	E	7:34	B	SAG	18
174	22	**E**	5:08	A	**8:25**	E	15 17	14	23 26	2	**2¾**	**11:07**	D	8:40	B	CAP	19
175	23	M.	5:08	A	**8:25**	E	15 17	13	23 25	2¾	**3½**	**11:29**	D	9:47	C	CAP	20
176	24	Tu.	5:09	A	**8:25**	E	15 16	13	23 24	3½	**4¼**	**11:50**	D	10:54	D	AQU	21
177	25	W.	5:09	A	**8:25**	E	15 16	13	23 22	4¼	**5**	—	–	**12:02**	D	PSC	22
178	26	Th.	5:10	A	**8:26**	E	15 16	13	23 20	5¼	**5¾**	12:11	C	**1:11**	D	PSC	23
179	27	Fr.	5:10	A	**8:26**	E	15 16	13	23 17	6	**6½**	12:34	C	**2:25**	E	PSC	24
180	28	Sa.	5:10	A	**8:25**	E	15 15	12	23 14	7	**7½**	1:00	B	**3:42**	E	PSC	25
181	29	**E**	5:11	A	**8:25**	E	15 14	12	23 11	8	**8½**	1:32	B	**5:01**	E	ARI	26
182	30	M.	5:11	A	**8:25**	E	15 14	12	23N.07	9	**9¼**	2:12	A	**6:20**	E	TAU	27

 Customize this table to your location at Almanac.com/MyAlmanac.

Beneath a willow long forsook,
The fisher seeks his custom'd nook. –Thomas Warton

Farmer's Calendar

■ Nature mostly goes by the book, but not always. Cutting the grass in a shady corner, I found a flower that was new to me. That discovery itself wasn't unusual; each year a couple of unknown wildflowers come my way. It's worth taking the time to get out the guidebook and identify them. (It's also an excuse to quit mowing the lawn.) Sometimes a new species takes a bit of tracking down, but eventually it finds its place and its name in the pages of the book.

Not this time. The specimen at hand was a slender, six-inch stem, leafless, branched once, with a single flower at the end of each branch. The inch-wide flowers had six slim white petals, green striped outside. What was it? I went through my wildflower guide, then I went through it backward, then I turned it upside down and went through it again. The mystery flower looked most like goldthread, a small buttercup of the north woods; but it was bigger than the book said goldthread ought to be.

I never did put a name to it. Now, maybe it was a great rarity, or even a species new to science. But my curiosity has its limits. I decided it was merely a plant that had too many petals or too few—a plant that didn't know how to behave. I wrote it off. In the end, its refusal to take its place in the taxonomic scheme made it not more interesting, but less.

Day of Month	Day of Week	Dates, Feasts, Fasts, Aspects, Tide Heights	Weather
1	E	3rᵭ ☉. af. ℟. • K. Close won Scripps Howard National Spelling Bee, 2006	*Nature*
2	M.	Congress granted citizenship to Native Americans born in the U.S., 1924 • Tides { 10.0 / 11.9 }	*plays*
3	Tu.	New ● • ☾ AT PERIG. • *New York Times* won its first Pulitzer Prize, 1918 • { 10.2 / 12.1 }	*the*
4	W.	☾ RIDES HIGH • Psychologist Dr. Ruth Westheimer born, 1928	*Anvil*
5	Th.	St. Boniface • Orthodox Ascension • Tides { 12.2 / 10.3 }	*Chorus,*
6	Fr.	D-Day, 1944 • *He who bathes in June, Will sing a merry tune.* • { 12.0 / 10.2 }	*booming*
7	Sa.	♂○☾ • ☿ IN INF. ♂ Graceland opened to public, 1982 • { 11.6 / 10.1 }	*over*
8	E	4tᴴ ☉. af. ℟. • ☾ AT ☌ Bald Eagle Protection Act passed, 1940	*field*
9	M.	Shavuot • ♂♄☾ • ♀ IN SUP. ♂ • Tides { 10.6 / 9.8 }	*and*
10	Tu.	☾ ON EQ. • U.S. Marines landed at Guantánamo Bay, Cuba, 1898 • { 10.0 / 9.7 }	*forest,*
11	W.	St. Barnabas • Actor DeForest Kelley died, 1999 • { 9.4 / 9.6 }	*while*
12	Th.	Harry Houdini escaped straightjacket, head downward, 40' above ground, N.Y.C., 1923	*commencement*
13	Fr.	*The bread never falls but on its buttered side.* • { 8.7 / 9.7 }	*speakers*
14	Sa.	St. Basil • Tractor-trailer accident unleashed 9 million honeybees, Bear Trap Canyon, Mont., 2004	*bore*
15	E	5tᴴ ☉. af. ℟. • Orthodox Pentecost • Tides { 8.6 / 9.8 }	*us.*
16	M.	☾ AT APO. • First issue of *Klondike Nugget* published, Dawson, Yukon, 1898	*Intensifying*
17	Tu.	Plow and gun combo patented, 1862 • Tides { 8.6 / 10.0 }	*solstice*
18	W.	Full Strawberry ○ • ☾ RUNS LOW • 3.47" rain in an hour, Atlanta, Ga., 1991	*sun;*
19	Th.	☿ STAT. • *The fly that playeth too long in the candle, singeth his wings at last.* • { 10.1 / 8.7 }	*summer's*
20	Fr.	Summer Solstice • ♂♃☾ • ♇ AT ☌ • Tides { 10.1 / 8.8 }	*begun.*
21	Sa.	President-to-be Richard Nixon married Thelma Catherine ("Pat") Ryan, 1940 • Tides { 10.1 / 8.9 }	*Road*
22	E	6tᴴ ☉. af. ℟. • Orthodox All Saints' • ☾ AT ☋	*trip!*
23	M.	OCCN. ♆ ☾ • Hail accumulated a foot deep in El Dorado, Kans., 1951	*Weather's*
24	Tu.	Nativ. John the Baptist • Midsummer Day • { 9.8 / 9.3 }	*sweller,*
25	W.	☾ ON EQ. • ♂☽☾ • Harness racing driver Joe O'Brien born, 1917 • { 9.7 / 9.6 }	*feller!*
26	Th.	United Nations charter signed, San Francisco, 1945	*Bring*
27	Fr.	♁ STAT. • First flight of XB-19 bomber, 1941 • { 9.4 / 10.3 }	*a*
28	Sa.	St. Irenaeus • Labor Day became an official U.S. holiday, 1894 • { 9.3 / 10.7 }	*sweater*
29	E	7tᴴ ☉. af. ℟. • *Two things do prolong thy life: a quiet heart and a loving wife.*	*and*
30	M.	Sts. Peter & Paulᵀ • Tunguska fireball in sky, Russia, 1908 • { 9.4 / 11.4 }	*umbreller.*

A hen is only an egg's way of making other eggs. –Samuel Butler

C A L E N D A R

SKY WATCH ☆ In the evening sky, dim orange Mars passes near Leo's blue star Regulus from the 1st to the 3rd. At nightfall on the 4th, Regulus, Mars, and Saturn form a short straight line, with Saturn highest and Mars in the middle. The crescent Moon is below them. Mars is closest to Saturn on the 10th and 11th, somewhat low in the west at nightfall. In the opposite side of the sky, Jupiter is at its brightest of the year at magnitude −2.7. It reaches opposition on the 9th and hovers at its closest to Earth one night later. Mercury, low in the predawn east during the first half of the month, will be brightest at midmonth. Earth reaches aphelion, its position farthest from the Sun in 2008, on the 4th.

●	New Moon	2nd day	22nd hour	19th minute
◑	First Quarter	10th day	0 hour	35th minute
○	Full Moon	18th day	3rd hour	59th minute
◐	Last Quarter	25th day	14th hour	42nd minute

*To use this page, see p. 110; for Key Letters, see p. 235; for Tide Tables, see p. 240.
All times are given in Eastern Daylight Time.* ☞ **Bold = P.M.** ☞ Light = A.M.

Day of Year	Day of Month	Day of Week	☼ Rises h. m.	Key	☼ Sets h. m.	Key	Length of Day h. m.	Sun Fast m.	Declination of Sun ° '	High Tide Times Boston		☽ Rises h. m.	Key	☽ Sets h. m.	Key	☽ Place	☽ Age
183	1	Tu.	5:12	A	**8:25**	E	15 13	12	23 N.03	10	10¼	3:05	A	**7:32**	E	TAU	28
184	2	W.	5:12	A	**8:25**	E	15 13	12	22 58	11	11¼	4:11	A	**8:31**	E	GEM	0
185	3	Th.	5:13	A	**8:25**	E	15 12	11	22 53	**12**	—	5:27	B	**9:17**	E	GEM	1
186	4	Fr.	5:13	A	**8:24**	E	15 11	11	22 48	12¼	**1**	6:47	B	**9:53**	E	CAN	2
187	5	Sa.	5:14	A	**8:24**	E	15 10	11	22 42	1¼	**1¾**	8:06	C	**10:22**	D	CAN	3
188	6	**E**	5:15	A	**8:24**	E	15 09	11	22 36	2	**2¾**	9:20	C	**10:45**	D	LEO	4
189	7	M.	5:15	A	**8:23**	E	15 08	11	22 29	3	**3½**	10:31	D	**11:07**	C	LEO	5
190	8	Tu.	5:16	A	**8:23**	E	15 07	11	22 22	3¾	**4½**	11:38	D	**11:27**	B	LEO	6
191	9	W.	5:17	A	**8:23**	E	15 06	10	22 15	4¾	**5¼**	**12:43**	E	**11:48**	B	VIR	7
192	10	Th.	5:17	A	**8:22**	E	15 05	10	22 07	5¾	**6**	**1:48**	E	—	–	VIR	8
193	11	Fr.	5:18	A	**8:22**	E	15 04	10	21 59	6½	**7**	**2:52**	E	12:10	B	VIR	9
194	12	Sa.	5:19	A	**8:21**	E	15 02	10	21 51	7½	**7¾**	**3:56**	E	12:36	A	LIB	10
195	13	**E**	5:20	A	**8:21**	E	15 01	10	21 42	8½	**8¾**	**4:58**	E	1:06	A	LIB	11
196	14	M.	5:21	A	**8:20**	E	14 59	10	21 33	9½	**9½**	**5:57**	E	1:43	A	SCO	12
197	15	Tu.	5:21	A	**8:19**	E	14 58	10	21 23	10¼	**10¼**	**6:50**	E	2:28	A	OPH	13
198	16	W.	5:22	A	**8:19**	E	14 57	10	21 13	11	**11**	**7:35**	E	3:20	A	SAG	14
199	17	Th.	5:23	A	**8:18**	E	14 55	9	21 03	11¾	**11¾**	**8:13**	E	4:20	A	SAG	15
200	18	Fr.	5:24	A	**8:17**	E	14 53	9	20 52	12¼	—	**8:45**	E	5:25	B	SAG	16
201	19	Sa.	5:25	A	**8:16**	E	14 51	9	20 41	12½	**1**	**9:11**	E	6:32	B	CAP	17
202	20	**E**	5:26	A	**8:16**	E	14 50	9	20 30	1	**1¾**	**9:35**	D	7:39	C	CAP	18
203	21	M.	5:27	A	**8:15**	E	14 48	9	20 18	1¾	**2¼**	**9:56**	D	8:46	D	AQU	19
204	22	Tu.	5:28	A	**8:14**	E	14 46	9	20 06	2½	**3**	**10:17**	C	9:54	D	PSC	20
205	23	W.	5:29	A	**8:13**	E	14 44	9	19 53	3¼	**3½**	**10:39**	B	11:03	D	PSC	21
206	24	Th.	5:29	A	**8:12**	E	14 43	9	19 41	4	**4¼**	**11:03**	B	**12:13**	E	PSC	22
207	25	Fr.	5:30	A	**8:11**	D	14 41	9	19 28	4¾	**5¼**	**11:31**	B	**1:27**	E	PSC	23
208	26	Sa.	5:31	A	**8:10**	D	14 39	9	19 15	5¾	**6**	—	–	**2:44**	E	ARI	24
209	27	**E**	5:32	A	**8:09**	D	14 37	9	19 01	6¾	**7**	12:07	A	**4:01**	E	ARI	25
210	28	M.	5:33	A	**8:08**	D	14 35	9	18 47	7¾	**8**	12:53	A	**5:14**	E	TAU	26
211	29	Tu.	5:34	A	**8:07**	D	14 33	9	18 32	8¾	**9**	1:51	A	**6:17**	E	TAU	27
212	30	W.	5:35	A	**8:06**	D	14 31	9	18 18	10	**10**	3:02	A	**7:08**	E	GEM	28
213	31	Th.	5:36	A	**8:05**	D	14 29	9	18 N.03	10¾	**11**	4:20	B	**7:48**	E	GEM	29

JULY HATH 31 DAYS • 2008

The "green things growing" whisper me
Of many an earth-old mystery. –Eben Eugene Rexford

Day of Month	Day of Week	Dates, Feasts, Fasts, Aspects, Tide Heights	Weather
1	Tu.	**Canada Day** • ☾ at perig. • ☌ ☿ ☾ • ☿ gr. elong. (22° west)	*Fireworks*
2	W.	**New** ● • ☾ rides high • *Time enough lost the ducks.* • Tides { 9.8 11.9	*fizzle*
3	Th.	Dog Days begin. • Samuel de Champlain founded what was later called Quebec City, Que., 1608	*under*
4	F.	**Independence Day** • ⊕ at aphelion • Tides { 11.9 10.2	*drizzle.*
5	Sa.	☾ at ☋ • 113°F at Midale and Yellow Grass, Sask., 1937 • Tides { 11.8 10.3	*String*
6	**E**	**8th S. af. P.** • ☌ ♂ ☾ • ☌ ♄ ☾ • Tides { 11.4 10.2	*a*
7	M.	☾ on eq. • First six enlisted women transferred from Naval Reserve to regular U.S. Navy, 1948	*hammock,*
8	Tu.	Sieur de Monts National Monument (now, Acadia National Park), Maine, est. 1916 • { 10.4 10.0	*loll*
9	W.	♃ at ☍ • Inventor Elias Howe born, 1819 • { 9.7 9.8	*and*
10	Th.	Cornscateous air is everywhere. • Tides { 9.1 9.6	*laze;*
11	Fr.	☌ ♂ ♄ • Fred Baldasare first to swim English Channel underwater (with scuba gear), 1962	*these*
12	Sa.	*The brave flea dares to eat his breakfast on the lip of a lion.* • Tides { 8.3 9.4	*are*
13	**E**	**9th S. af. P.** • Montreal hosted first baseball All-Star game outside U.S., 1982	*days*
14	M.	**Bastille Day** • ☾ at apo. • Armadillos mate now. • Tides { 8.1 9.5	*for*
15	Tu.	**St. Swithin** • ☾ runs low • *Elbow grease gives the best polish.* • { 8.2 9.7	*slothful*
16	W.	Black-eyed Susans in bloom now. • Tides { 8.4 9.9	*ways.*
17	Th.	☌ ♃ ☾ • Last 400 Woolworth's dept. stores closed, 1997 • Tides { 8.6 10.1	*Stay*
18	Fr.	**Full Buck** ○ • *Do not speak of secrets in a field that is full of little hills.* • { 8.8 —	*away*
19	Sa.	☾ at ☊ • Teacher Christa McAuliffe selected to ride in space shuttle, 1985 • { 10.2 9.0	*from*
20	**E**	**10th S. af. P.** • occn. ♆ ☾ • Tides { 10.3 9.3	*midday's*
21	M.	World-record cold temperature, –128.6°F, Vostok Station, Antarctica, 1983 • { 10.3 9.5	*blaze.*
22	Tu.	**St. Mary Magdalene** • ☾ on eq. • ☌ ♅ ☾ • { 10.2 9.8	*Thunder's*
23	W.	First U.S. swimming school opened, Boston, Mass., 1827 • Tides { 10.0 10.0	*tympani*
24	Th.	Adult gypsy moths emerge now. • Tides { 9.8 10.2	*outboom*
25	Fr.	**Sts. James & Christopher** • SS *Andrea Doria* collided with SS *Stockholm*, 1956	*the*
26	Sa.	**St. Anne** • General Samuel Houston died, 1863	*symphony.*
27	**E**	**11th S. af. P.** • *The cow knows not what her tail is worth till she has lost it.*	*Pitter,*
28	M.	Nine coal miners rescued after being trapped for 77 hours in flooded Quecreek Mine, Somerset, Pa., 2002	*patter,*
29	Tu.	**St. Martha** • ☾ rides high • ☾ at perig. • ☿ in sup. ☌	*gutters*
30	W.	*The wind in the west suits everyone best.* • Tides { 9.3 11.3	*clatter*
31	Th.	**St. Ignatius of Loyola** • Inventor John Ericsson born, 1803	*incessantly.*

Farmer's Calendar

■ Midsummer belongs to the insects. Bugs, flies, bees, and moths abound in buzzing, fluttering, creeping legions everywhere. Most we ignore; some we greet with affection. Some we don't.

Very much in the last category is the eastern tent caterpillar larva, a pestiferous species that destroys trees by devouring their young leaves as it swathes their boughs in yards and yards of shabby gray silk, the larva's shelter, or nest. The eastern tent caterpillar's adult form is a small, brown moth with cream-colored stripes that looks like something you'd buy in a high-class chocolate shop.

The guilty caterpillar is itself a pretty thing: a couple of inches long, and mostly black, with a white stripe down its back and vivid blue flanks. The creatures look like fancy antique enamelwork: animated Fabergé snuffboxes. If you were to come upon one or two in the course of a summer, you'd find them charming. As it is, however, they arrive in a tidal wave. Their nests make the woods look like the set of a bad horror movie. They crawl about everywhere. Most disconcerting, they fall from the trees in a steady patter all day long. They land on your head, your shoulder. They plunge down your collar. As rarities, tent caterpillars would be a welcome part of summer. Swimming in your glass of lemonade, they are otherwise.

C
A
L
E
N
D
A
R

SKY WATCH ☆ *The 1st brings a total solar eclipse to Russia, Mongolia, and China. (See page 98.) Sky-spectacle seekers in the Western Hemisphere must wait until the 11th, when the Perseid meteor shower delivers the year's best shooting stars. The fireworks will be excellent between 1:30 A.M. and dawn on the 12th, when a meteor a minute should cross the sky. Mars and Saturn vanish into the Sun's glare. Jupiter alone rules the southern sky: The giant world sets after midnight. Neptune is at opposition on the 15th, in Capricornus, but it shines only at magnitude 7.8, requiring a telescope to be seen.*

●	**New Moon**	1st day	6th hour	13th minute
◐	**First Quarter**	8th day	16th hour	20th minute
○	**Full Moon**	16th day	17th hour	16th minute
◑	**Last Quarter**	23rd day	19th hour	50th minute
●	**New Moon**	30th day	15th hour	58th minute

To use this page, see p. 110; for Key Letters, see p. 235; for Tide Tables, see p. 240. All times are given in Eastern Daylight Time. ☞ **Bold = P.M.** ☞ Light = A.M.

Day of Year	Day of Month	Day of Week	☀ Rises h. m.	Key	☀ Sets h. m.	Key	Length of Day h. m.	Sun Fast m.	Declination of Sun ° '	High Tide Times Boston		☾ Rises h. m.	Key	☾ Sets h. m.	Key	☾ Place	☾ Age
214	1	Fr.	5:37	A	**8:04**	D	14 27	9	17 N.48	11¾	—	5:39	B	**8:20**	D	CAN	0
215	2	Sa.	5:38	A	**8:02**	D	14 24	9	17 32	12	12¾	6:56	C	**8:46**	D	LEO	1
216	3	**E**	5:40	A	**8:01**	D	14 21	9	17 17	12¾	1½	8:10	D	**9:09**	D	LEO	2
217	4	M.	5:41	A	**8:00**	D	14 19	10	17 01	1¾	2¼	9:20	D	**9:30**	C	LEO	3
218	5	Tu.	5:42	A	**7:59**	D	14 17	10	16 44	2½	3	10:27	E	**9:51**	B	VIR	4
219	6	W.	5:43	A	**7:57**	D	14 14	10	16 27	3¼	3¾	11:33	E	**10:13**	B	VIR	5
220	7	Th.	5:44	A	**7:56**	D	14 12	10	16 11	4¼	4½	**12:39**	E	**10:37**	B	VIR	6
221	8	Fr.	5:45	A	**7:55**	D	14 10	10	15 53	5	5¼	**1:44**	E	**11:06**	A	VIR	7
222	9	Sa.	5:46	A	**7:53**	D	14 07	10	15 36	6	6¼	**2:47**	E	**11:40**	A	LIB	8
223	10	**E**	5:47	A	**7:52**	D	14 05	10	15 18	6¾	7	**3:48**	E	—	—	SCO	9
224	11	M.	5:48	A	**7:51**	D	14 03	10	15 00	7¾	8	**4:43**	E	12:22	A	OPH	10
225	12	Tu.	5:49	A	**7:49**	D	14 00	11	14 42	8¾	9	**5:31**	E	1:11	A	SAG	11
226	13	W.	5:50	A	**7:48**	D	13 58	11	14 24	9¾	9¾	**6:12**	E	2:09	A	SAG	12
227	14	Th.	5:51	B	**7:46**	D	13 55	11	14 06	10½	10½	**6:46**	E	3:12	B	SAG	13
228	15	Fr.	5:52	B	**7:45**	D	13 53	11	13 47	11¼	11¼	**7:14**	E	4:19	B	CAP	14
229	16	Sa.	5:53	B	**7:43**	D	13 50	11	13 28	11¾	—	**7:39**	D	5:27	B	CAP	15
230	17	**E**	5:54	B	**7:42**	D	13 48	12	13 09	12	12½	**8:01**	D	6:35	C	AQU	16
231	18	M.	5:55	B	**7:40**	D	13 45	12	12 49	12½	1	**8:23**	C	7:44	D	AQU	17
232	19	Tu.	5:56	B	**7:39**	D	13 43	12	12 30	1¼	1¾	**8:44**	C	8:53	D	PSC	18
233	20	W.	5:57	B	**7:37**	D	13 40	12	12 10	2	2½	**9:08**	B	10:04	E	PSC	19
234	21	Th.	5:58	B	**7:36**	D	13 38	12	11 50	2¾	3	**9:35**	B	11:18	E	PSC	20
235	22	Fr.	6:00	B	**7:34**	D	13 34	13	11 29	3½	4	**10:08**	A	**12:33**	E	ARI	21
236	23	Sa.	6:01	B	**7:33**	D	13 32	13	11 09	4½	4¾	**10:49**	A	**1:50**	E	ARI	22
237	24	**E**	6:02	B	**7:31**	D	13 29	13	10 48	5½	5¾	**11:42**	A	**3:03**	E	TAU	23
238	25	M.	6:03	B	**7:29**	D	13 26	14	10 27	6½	6¾	—	—	**4:08**	E	TAU	24
239	26	Tu.	6:04	B	**7:28**	D	13 24	14	10 06	7½	8	12:46	B	**5:02**	E	AUR	25
240	27	W.	6:05	B	**7:26**	D	13 21	14	9 45	8¾	9	2:00	B	**5:45**	E	GEM	26
241	28	Th.	6:06	B	**7:24**	D	13 18	14	9 24	9¾	10	3:17	B	**6:19**	E	CAN	27
242	29	Fr.	6:07	B	**7:23**	D	13 16	15	9 03	10¾	11	4:34	C	**6:47**	D	CAN	28
243	30	Sa.	6:08	B	**7:21**	D	13 13	15	8 41	11½	11¾	5:48	C	**7:10**	D	LEO	0
244	31	**E**	6:09	B	**7:19**	D	13 10	15	8 N.19	12¼	—	6:59	D	**7:32**	C	LEO	1

AUGUST HATH 31 DAYS • 2008

Small summer insects chirp amid the blades
That rattle with a sharp metallic sound. –James Berry Bensel

Day of Month	Day of Week	Dates, Feasts, Fasts, Aspects, Tide Heights	Weather
1	Fr.	Lammas Day • New ● • Eclipse ⊙ • ☾ AT ☋	*Moist*
2	Sa.	Cookies baked successfully on a vehicle's dashboard during heat wave, Bedford, N.H., 2006 • {11.5 / 10.2	*at*
3	E	12th S. af. P. • ☌♄☾ • Gray squirrels have second litters now.	*foist.*
4	M.	☾ ON EQ. • ☌♂☾ • Pres. Carter signed bill to create U.S. Dept. of Energy, 1977	*Thunder*
5	Tu.	Cornerstone for pedestal of Statue of Liberty laid, 1884	*rattles*
6	W.	Transfiguration • U.S. dropped atomic bomb on Hiroshima, Japan, 1945 • {10.0 / 10.0	*the*
7	Th.	107°F, Waco, Tex., 1988 • *Lightning brings heat.*	*china.*
8	Fr.	St. Dominic • "Canada's Hundred Days" began, WWI, 1918 • {8.8 / 9.5	*Nothing*
9	Sa.	First Smokey Bear poster produced, 1944 • {8.3 / 9.2	*could*
10	E	13th S. af. P. • ☾ AT APO. • Tides {8.0 / 9.1	*be*
11	M.	St. Clare • Dog days end. • First prisoners arrived at Alcatraz, 1934 • {7.9 / 9.1	*finah!*
12	Tu.	☾ RUNS LOW • 232-day baseball strike began, causing World Series to be canceled, 1994	*Coolish,*
13	W.	☌♃☾ • ☌♀♄ • *They that walk much in the sun will be tanned at last.* • {8.1 / 9.6	*then*
14	Th.	Major power outage in N.E. North America, 2003	*warmish,*
15	Fr.	Assumption • ☌☿♄ • ♆ AT ☍ • Tides {8.8 / 10.1	*then*
16	Sa.	Full Sturgeon ○ • Eclipse ☾ • ☾ AT ☊ • ☌♆☾	*lightning-*
17	E	14th S. af. P. • Cat Nights commence. • Tides {9.5 / —	*stormish.*
18	M.	☾ ON EQ. • ☌♅☾ • Gov. J. White found his Roanoke (N.C.) settlement deserted, 1590	*Sweet!*
19	Tu.	Hurricane Bob hit New England, 1991 • Tides {10.5 / 10.2	*Can't*
20	W.	President Benjamin Harrison born, 1833 • *The resolved mind has no cares.*	*be*
21	Th.	*Mona Lisa* was stolen, 1911 • Hawaii became 50th state, 1959 • {10.2 / 10.6	*beat!*
22	Fr.	Nat Turner's slave rebellion began, 1831 • {9.8 / 10.7	*Pack*
23	Sa.	☌☿♀ • *Ranger I* lunar probe launched, 1961 • Tides {9.4 / 10.6	*a*
24	E	15th S. af. P. • *The bad gardener quarrels with his rake.*	*picnic,*
25	M.	St. Bartholomew[T] • ☾ RIDES HIGH • Hummingbirds migrate south. • {8.8 / 10.5	*but*
26	Tu.	☾ AT PERIG. • 100-mph winds, Lake County, Ind., 1965	*bring*
27	W.	Largest trade at time in NBA history, 11 players changed teams, 1999 • Tides {9.0 / 10.7	*a*
28	Th.	St. Augustine of Hippo • *Tom Thumb* train raced horse, 1830 • {9.3 / 10.9	*brolly;*
29	Fr.	St. John the Baptist • ☾ AT ☋ • Tides {9.8 / 11.1	*chilly,*
30	Sa.	New ● • Hotline between White House and Kremlin installed, 1963 • {10.2 / 11.1	*by*
31	E	16th S. af. P. • ☾ ON EQ. • *Be first at the feast and last at the fight.*	*golly!*

Farmer's Calendar

■ Sometime around the middle of this month, the hummingbirds will have departed, and, once again, I won't know it. At this place last year we had a pair. They turned up in mid-May, poised on blurred, invisible wings before the first garden flowers, dipping and sipping fastidiously at the red plastic hummingbird feeder by the window, zooming away. They loved the bee balm best, and the phlox, but they also loved the brightly colored feeder, which I kept filled with a sugar-water solution. It holds about a cup. Early in the summer the little birds were at the feeder constantly, emptying the reservoir in a single day. By early August, their visits had dropped off, and I filled the feeder only every three to four days. Perhaps the pair was in training as the time of their southern migration approached. The frail and tiny hummingbird is among the hardiest of birds. It's a marathoner, an epic migrator, making its way from New England to Central America.

That's a long haul, and it takes a long time. Thus, the hummingbirds get an early start. By mid-August, I realized that our pair was gone, the feeder unvisited. I wondered exactly when they had taken off and where they were when I missed them. That happens every year: I wait for the hummingbirds to decamp, but the event remains unrecorded. It's hard to watch for an absence.

THE NINTH MONTH • 2008

SKY WATCH ☆ *Brilliant Venus, bright Mercury, dim Mars, and the Moon all meet, on the 1st, in the west about 40 minutes after sunset, but the conjunction is too low to view for those who live north of the Carolinas. Observers in South Texas and Florida can see it readily, as well as the close conjunction of Venus and Mars, with Mercury to their left, on the 10th and 11th. The entire world will notice Jupiter blazing in the south all month, from nightfall until 11:00* P.M. *Uranus reaches opposition on the night of the 12th–13th, in Aquarius, at a barely visible magnitude 5.7. The Moon floats near Uranus the next night. Autumn begins with the equinox on the 22nd, at 11:44* A.M.

◐	**First Quarter**	7th day	10th hour	4th minute
○	**Full Moon**	15th day	5th hour	13th minute
◑	**Last Quarter**	22nd day	1st hour	4th minute
●	**New Moon**	29th day	4th hour	12th minute

To use this page, see p. 110; for Key Letters, see p. 235; for Tide Tables, see p. 240.
All times are given in Eastern Daylight Time. ☞ **Bold = P.M.** ☞ Light = A.M.

Day of Year	Day of Month	Day of Week	☼ Rises h. m.	Key	☼ Sets h. m.	Key	Length of Day h. m.	Sun Fast m.	Declination of Sun ° '	High Tide Times Boston		☾ Rises h. m.	Key	☾ Sets h. m.	Key	☾ Place	☾ Age
245	1	M.	6:10	B	**7:18**	D	13 08	16	7 N.57	12½	**1**	8:08	D	**7:53**	B	VIR	2
246	2	Tu.	6:11	B	**7:16**	D	13 05	16	7 35	1¼	**1¾**	9:16	E	**8:15**	B	VIR	3
247	3	W.	6:12	B	**7:14**	D	13 02	16	7 13	2	**2½**	10:22	E	**8:39**	B	VIR	4
248	4	Th.	6:13	B	**7:13**	D	13 00	17	6 51	2¾	**3**	11:28	E	**9:06**	A	VIR	5
249	5	Fr.	6:14	B	**7:11**	D	12 57	17	6 29	3½	**3¾**	**12:33**	E	**9:38**	A	LIB	6
250	6	Sa.	6:15	B	**7:09**	D	12 54	17	6 07	4½	**4½**	**1:36**	E	**10:16**	A	SCO	7
251	7	**E**	6:16	B	**7:07**	D	12 51	18	5 44	5¼	**5½**	**2:33**	E	**11:03**	A	SCO	8
252	8	M.	6:17	B	**7:06**	C	12 49	18	5 22	6¼	**6½**	**3:24**	E	**11:57**	A	OPH	9
253	9	Tu.	6:19	B	**7:04**	C	12 45	18	4 59	7¼	**7½**	**4:08**	E	—	–	SAG	10
254	10	W.	6:20	B	**7:02**	C	12 42	19	4 37	8¼	**8¼**	**4:44**	E	12:57	B	SAG	11
255	11	Th.	6:21	B	**7:00**	C	12 39	19	4 14	9	**9¼**	**5:15**	E	2:03	B	CAP	12
256	12	Fr.	6:22	B	**6:59**	C	12 37	19	3 51	9¾	**10**	**5:41**	E	3:10	B	CAP	13
257	13	Sa.	6:23	B	**6:57**	C	12 34	20	3 28	10½	**10¾**	**6:04**	D	4:18	C	CAP	14
258	14	**E**	6:24	B	**6:55**	C	12 31	20	3 05	11¼	**11½**	**6:26**	D	5:28	D	AQU	15
259	15	M.	6:25	B	**6:53**	C	12 28	20	2 42	11¾	—	**6:48**	C	6:38	D	PSC	16
260	16	Tu.	6:26	B	**6:52**	C	12 26	21	2 19	12¼	**12½**	**7:12**	B	7:50	E	PSC	17
261	17	W.	6:27	B	**6:50**	C	12 23	21	1 56	12¾	**1¼**	**7:38**	B	9:04	E	PSC	18
262	18	Th.	6:28	B	**6:48**	C	12 20	21	1 32	1½	**2**	**8:10**	B	10:21	E	ARI	19
263	19	Fr.	6:29	C	**6:46**	C	12 17	22	1 09	2½	**2¾**	**8:49**	A	11:38	E	ARI	20
264	20	Sa.	6:30	C	**6:45**	C	12 15	22	0 46	3¼	**3½**	**9:38**	A	12:54	E	TAU	21
265	21	**E**	6:31	C	**6:43**	C	12 12	23	0 N.22	4¼	**4½**	**10:39**	A	**2:02**	E	TAU	22
266	22	M.	6:32	C	**6:41**	C	12 09	23	0 S.01	5¼	**5½**	**11:49**	A	**2:59**	E	AUR	23
267	23	Tu.	6:33	C	**6:39**	C	12 06	23	0 24	6¼	**6½**	—	–	**3:44**	E	GEM	24
268	24	W.	6:34	C	**6:37**	C	12 03	24	0 48	7½	**7¾**	1:04	B	**4:20**	E	CAN	25
269	25	Th.	6:36	C	**6:36**	C	12 00	24	1 11	8½	**8¾**	2:19	B	**4:49**	D	CAN	26
270	26	Fr.	6:37	C	**6:34**	C	11 57	24	1 35	9½	**9¾**	3:32	C	**5:13**	D	LEO	27
271	27	Sa.	6:38	C	**6:32**	B	11 54	25	1 58	10¼	**10¾**	4:43	D	**5:36**	C	SEX	28
272	28	**E**	6:39	C	**6:30**	B	11 51	25	2 21	11¼	**11½**	5:52	D	**5:57**	C	LEO	29
273	29	M.	6:40	C	**6:29**	B	11 49	25	2 45	11¾	—	6:59	D	**6:18**	B	VIR	0
274	30	Tu.	6:41	C	**6:27**	B	11 46	26	3 S.08	12¼	**12½**	8:06	E	**6:41**	B	VIR	1

SEPTEMBER HATH 30 DAYS • 2008

It is the summer's great last heat,
It is the fall's first chill: They meet. –Sarah Morgan Bryan Piatt

Day of Month	Day of Week	Dates, Feasts, Fasts, Aspects, Tide Heights	Weather
1	M.	**Labor Day** • ☌♀☾ • ☌☿☾ • Tides {10.9 / 10.5	*Moppets*
2	Tu.	**First day of Ramadan** • ☌♂☾ • Tides {10.6 / 10.5	*are*
3	W.	☌♄☉ • *Viking 2* landed on Mars, 1976 • {10.1 / 10.3	*mopin'*
4	Th.	Thieves stole $2 million in art from Montreal Museum of Fine Arts, 1972 • Tides {9.6 / 10.0	*as*
5	Fr.	First Continental Congress opened, 1774 • {9.1 / 9.7	*schools*
6	Sa.	Martha Jefferson, wife of Thomas, died, 1782 • {8.6 / 9.3	*reopen.*
7	**E**	**17th S. af. P.** • ☾ AT APO. • ♃ STAT. • {8.2 / 9.1	*Nights*
8	M.	☾ RUNS LOW • Percy Saltzman first meteorologist to appear on Canadian television, 1952 • {7.9 / 8.9	*are*
9	Tu.	**St. Omer** • ☌♃☾ • ♇ STAT. • Tides {7.8 / 8.9	*crisp,*
10	W.	*September rain good for crops and vines.* • Tides {7.9 / 9.1	*and*
11	Th.	☿ GR. ELONG. (27° EAST) • ☌☿♀ • ☌♀♂ • Tides {8.2 / 9.5	*apples*
12	Fr.	☾ AT ☊ • ☌☿♂ • OCCN. ♆☾ • ♅ AT ☍ • {8.7 / 9.8	*crisper;*
13	Sa.	Halford Mackinder's team first Europeans to summit Mt. Kenya, 1899 • Tides {9.2 / 10.1	*in*
14	**E**	**18th S. af. P.** • George Handel finished composing *Messiah*, 1741 • {9.7 / 10.4	*the*
15	M.	**Holy Cross**[T] • **Full Harvest** ○ • ☾ ON EQ. • ☌♅☾ • {10.2 / —	*wind,*
16	Tu.	*Only a fool tests the depth of the water with both feet.*	*there's*
17	W.	Ember Day • Alabama's Heather Whitestone became first deaf Miss America, 1994 • {10.6 / 11.0	*just*
18	Th.	After 7 years, G. Meegan finished walk from S. America's tip to Prudhoe Bay, Alaska, 1983 • {10.5 / 11.2	*a*
19	Fr.	Ember Day • ☾ AT PERIG. • ☌☿♂ • Tides {10.2 / 11.2	*whisper*
20	Sa.	**St. Eustace** • Ember Day • Peoria, Ill., had its first recorded summer freeze, 1991	*of*
21	**E**	**19th S. af. P.** • Farmer bought Stonehenge for £6,600, 1915	*what's*
22	M.	**St. Matthew**[T] • Harvest Home • **Autumnal Equinox** • ☾ RIDES HIGH	*coming.*
23	Tu.	N.Y. Knickerbocker Base Ball Club organized, 1845	*Rain*
24	W.	☿ STAT. • Alberta fires turned Sun and Moon blue in Northeast, 1950 • {8.9 / 10.2	*drumming,*
25	Th.	☾ AT ☋ • *No pear falls into a shut mouth.* • {9.2 / 10.3	*warm*
26	Fr.	Australia won America's Cup, first time in 132 years that the U.S. did not win, 1983 • {9.6 / 10.4	*but*
27	Sa.	**St. Vincent de Paul** • ☌♄☾ • 109-mph winds, Chatham, Mass., 1985	*steady,*
28	**E**	**20th S. af. P.** • ☾ ON EQ. • Woodchucks hibernate now.	*mutters,*
29	M.	**St. Michael** • **New** ● • *A fog can not be dispelled with a fan.* • {10.5 / —	*"Get*
30	Tu.	**St. Sophia** • **Rosh Hashanah** • Tides {10.3 / 10.6	*ready."*

Outer space is no place for a person of breeding. –Violet B. Carter

Farmer's Calendar

■ No tree in the woods is a better friend to man than the common ash. It hasn't the maple's beauty or the oak's prestige, and it isn't a cabinetmaker's tree. But its strong wood has a straight, open grain and is easily worked for tool handles, sports equipment, baskets, and many other utilitarian applications. The spears of Homer's warrior princes in the *Iliad*—the first superheroes—had their shafts made of ash.

In the lore of wood burning, the ash has a unique place. It's supposed to make the best cordwood because it will burn as well green as it will seasoned. "Ash wood new or ash wood old / Is fit for a king with a crown of gold," went the old-timers' woodpile rhyme. Is it true? I can't say, but I can testify to one way in which the excellence of ash as fuel is plain: in the splitting. This was borne in on me a couple of years back when a fine, tall, forest-grown ash came down near our place, leaving me with a straight, nearly clear log more than a foot thick and 25 feet long. I cut it into rounds for splitting and went to work. Never, in several decades of beating away on hardwood chunks, have I had an easier time. The ash billets flew apart on a single stroke, often into three or four pieces. I split my ash chunks with an axe, but I believe I might have split them with a stern look.

OCTOBER

The Tenth Month • 2008

SKY WATCH ☆ *Jupiter remains conspicuous this month in the south the first few hours after nightfall, fading slightly to magnitude –2.1. Venus returns, and each night, about 40 minutes after sunset, the cloud-covered world is a bit higher in the west. It's up 6 degrees on the 1st and 10 degrees on the 31st. Mercury has its best morning apparition of 2008 during the last half of the month. About 40 minutes before sunrise, the innermost world stands 6 degrees high at magnitude 1, on the 13th. It continues to brighten and hovers higher each morning: By the 27th, Mercury's brilliance has doubled to magnitude –0.8. It stands 10 degrees up and is readily seen to the left of the thin crescent Moon.*

◐	**First Quarter**	7th day	5th hour	4th minute
○	**Full Moon**	14th day	16th hour	2nd minute
◑	**Last Quarter**	21st day	7th hour	55th minute
●	**New Moon**	28th day	19th hour	14th minute

To use this page, see p. 110; for Key Letters, see p. 235; for Tide Tables, see p. 240.
All times are given in Eastern Daylight Time. ☞ **Bold = P.M.** ☞ Light = A.M.

Day of Year	Day of Month	Day of Week	☼ Rises h. m.	Key	☼ Sets h. m.	Key	Length of Day h. m.	Sun Fast m.	Declination of Sun ° ′	High Tide Times Boston		☾ Rises h. m.	Key	☾ Sets h. m.	Key	☾ Place	☾ Age
275	1	W.	6:42	C	**6:25**	B	11 43	26	3 s.31	1	**1¼**	9:12	E	**7:07**	B	VIR	2
276	2	Th.	6:43	C	**6:23**	B	11 40	26	3 54	1¾	**1¾**	10:18	E	**7:37**	A	LIB	3
277	3	Fr.	6:44	C	**6:22**	B	11 38	27	4 17	2¼	**2½**	11:22	E	**8:13**	A	LIB	4
278	4	Sa.	6:45	C	**6:20**	B	11 35	27	4 41	3	**3¼**	**12:22**	E	**8:56**	A	SCO	5
279	5	**E**	6:47	C	**6:18**	B	11 31	27	5 04	3¾	**4**	**1:15**	E	**9:47**	A	OPH	6
280	6	M.	6:48	C	**6:17**	B	11 29	27	5 27	4¾	**4¾**	**2:02**	E	**10:45**	A	SAG	7
281	7	Tu.	6:49	C	**6:15**	B	11 26	28	5 50	5½	**5¾**	**2:41**	E	**11:47**	B	SAG	8
282	8	W.	6:50	C	**6:13**	B	11 23	28	6 13	6½	**6¾**	**3:13**	E	—	–	SAG	9
283	9	Th.	6:51	C	**6:12**	B	11 21	28	6 35	7½	**7¾**	**3:41**	E	12:52	B	CAP	10
284	10	Fr.	6:52	C	**6:10**	B	11 18	29	6 58	8¼	**8½**	**4:05**	D	1:59	B	CAP	11
285	11	Sa.	6:53	C	**6:08**	B	11 15	29	7 21	9	**9¼**	**4:28**	D	3:07	C	AQU	12
286	12	**E**	6:54	C	**6:07**	B	11 13	29	7 43	9¾	**10¼**	**4:50**	C	4:16	D	PSC	13
287	13	M.	6:56	D	**6:05**	B	11 09	29	8 06	10½	**11**	**5:13**	B	5:28	D	PSC	14
288	14	Tu.	6:57	D	**6:03**	B	11 06	30	8 28	11¼	**11¾**	**5:38**	B	6:42	E	PSC	15
289	15	W.	6:58	D	**6:02**	B	11 04	30	8 50	**12**	—	**6:08**	B	7:59	E	PSC	16
290	16	Th.	6:59	D	**6:00**	B	11 01	30	9 12	12½	**12¾**	**6:46**	A	9:19	E	ARI	17
291	17	Fr.	7:00	D	**5:59**	B	10 59	30	9 34	1¼	**1½**	**7:33**	A	10:38	E	TAU	18
292	18	Sa.	7:01	D	**5:57**	B	10 56	30	9 56	2	**2¼**	**8:32**	A	11:51	E	TAU	19
293	19	**E**	7:03	D	**5:56**	B	10 53	31	10 18	3	**3¼**	**9:40**	A	**12:53**	E	TAU	20
294	20	M.	7:04	D	**5:54**	B	10 50	31	10 39	4	**4¼**	**10:55**	B	**1:43**	E	GEM	21
295	21	Tu.	7:05	D	**5:53**	B	10 48	31	11 00	5	**5¼**	—	–	**2:22**	E	GEM	22
296	22	W.	7:06	D	**5:51**	B	10 45	31	11 21	6¼	**6½**	12:10	C	**2:52**	E	CAN	23
297	23	Th.	7:07	D	**5:50**	B	10 43	31	11 42	7¼	**7½**	1:23	C	**3:18**	D	LEO	24
298	24	Fr.	7:09	D	**5:48**	B	10 39	31	12 03	8¼	**8¾**	2:33	D	**3:40**	D	LEO	25
299	25	Sa.	7:10	D	**5:47**	B	10 37	32	12 24	9¼	**9½**	3:41	D	**4:01**	C	LEO	26
300	26	**E**	7:11	D	**5:45**	B	10 34	32	12 44	10	**10½**	4:48	D	**4:22**	B	VIR	27
301	27	M.	7:12	D	**5:44**	B	10 32	32	13 04	10¾	**11¼**	5:54	E	**4:44**	B	VIR	28
302	28	Tu.	7:13	D	**5:43**	B	10 30	32	13 24	11½	—	6:59	E	**5:09**	B	VIR	0
303	29	W.	7:15	D	**5:41**	B	10 26	32	13 44	12	**12**	8:05	E	**5:38**	A	VIR	1
304	30	Th.	7:16	D	**5:40**	B	10 24	32	14 03	12½	**12¾**	9:10	E	**6:11**	A	LIB	2
305	31	Fr.	7:17	D	**5:39**	B	10 22	32	14 s.23	1¼	**1¼**	10:11	E	**6:52**	A	SCO	3

OCTOBER HATH 31 DAYS • 2008

This day is done, and the darkness
Falls from the wings of Night. –Henry Wadsworth Longfellow

Day of Month	Day of Week	Dates, Feasts, Fasts, Aspects, Tide Heights	Weather
1	W.	St. Gregory • ☌♂☾ • ☌♀☾ • Tides {10.0 / 10.5}	*Up*
2	Th.	President Woodrow Wilson suffered a paralytic stroke, 1919 • Tides {9.7 / 10.3}	*north,*
3	Fr.	*The stillest tongue can be the truest friend.* • {9.3 / 10.0}	*leaves*
4	Sa.	St. Francis of Assisi • Dr. Benjamin Church investigated for espionage, 1775 • {8.8 / 9.6}	*are*
5	**E**	**21st S. af. P.** • ☾ runs low • ☾ at apo. • {8.4 / 9.3}	*peaking;*
6	M.	☿ in inf. ☌ • Mag. 2.0 earthquake near Keene, N.H., 2004	*the*
7	Tu.	☌♃☾ • Musical *Cats* opened on Broadway, 1982	*color's*
8	W.	N.Y. Yankees' Don Larsen pitched first perfect baseball game in World Series history, 1956 • {7.9 / 8.9}	*leaking*
9	Th.	Yom Kippur • ☾ at ☊ • Hailstorms caused $7.5 million in crop damage, Mont., 1944	*south,*
10	Fr.	occn. ♆☾ • *Deeds are fruits, words are leaves.*	*bringing*
11	Sa.	T. Edison completed his first invention to be patented, an electrical vote recorder, 1868 • {9.1 / 9.7}	*summer*
12	**E**	**22nd S. af. P.** • ☾ on Eq. • ☌♅☾ • Tides {9.7 / 10.0}	*heat.*
13	M.	**Columbus Day** • **Thanksgiving Day (Canada)** • Tides {10.3 / 10.3}	*Trees*
14	Tu.	Sukkoth • **Full Hunter's** ○ • Queen Eliz. II began Canadian tour, 1977 • {10.9 / 10.5}	*are*
15	W.	☿ stat. • Andy Green first to break sound barrier in a land-based vehicle, at 763.035 mph, 1997	*like*
16	Th.	*In October dung your field, And your land its wealth shall yield.* • {10.5 / 11.6}	*torches.*
17	Fr.	St. Ignatius of Antioch • ☾ at perig. • Tides {10.4 / 11.7}	*We*
18	Sa.	St. Luke • St. Luke's little summer. • Tides {10.2 / 11.6}	*sleep*
19	**E**	**23rd S. af. P.** • ☾ rides high • Tides {9.8 / 11.2}	*on*
20	M.	Jacqueline Kennedy married Greek shipping magnate Aristotle Onassis, 1968 • {9.4 / 10.8}	*porches,*
21	Tu.	M. Owen set typing speed record, 170 wpm, 1918	*sweating,*
22	W.	☾ at ☋ • ☿ gr. elong. (18° west) • 100°F, Los Angeles, Calif., 1965 • {9.1 / 10.1}	*almost*
23	Th.	*There's no catching trout with dry breeches.*	*forgetting…*
24	Fr.	Statesman Daniel Webster died, 1852 • Tides {9.5 / 9.9}	*then*
25	Sa.	☾ on Eq. • ☌♄☾ • Little brown bats hibernate now. • Tides {9.9 / 9.9}	*awake*
26	**E**	**24th S. af. P.** • Gunfight at the O.K. Corral, Tombstone, Ariz., 1881	*to*
27	M.	☌☿☾ • *Saturn 1* first launched, 1961 • Tides {10.4 / 9.7}	*flakes.*
28	Tu.	Sts. Simon & Jude • New ● • First Lady Abigail Adams died, 1818	*It's*
29	W.	First ballpoint pens sold, for $12.50 at Gimbel's, N.Y.C., 1945 • Tides {10.4 / —}	*trick*
30	Th.	*Fear nothing but your own conscience.* • Tides {9.4 / 10.3}	*and*
31	Fr.	All Hallows' Eve • St. Wolfgang • Tides {9.2 / 10.2}	*treat.*

Farmer's Calendar

■ *October 25.* A day of slate and lead, compounded of blues and grays and mixed by a cold, damp wind from the north that rides along the very edge of snow. High time to get things put away, covered up, battened down, and ready for the real winter that this day presages.

The winter's firewood is in the shed. It stands in long, head-high racks—ten-foot walls that look a little like enormous honeycombs. They take up about half the shed. Today I must see to the other half. I will put away the chain saw, the axe, the sledgehammer, and the steel wedges. I'll hang up the garden tools on their nails or prop them in the corner out of the way. I'll put the paint cans, gas cans, and coffee cans full of nails and other hardware on shelves.

After the shed is properly straightened, I'll sweep the whole place, clearing out the blown-in leaves, the sawdust, cobwebs, and other dirt. That done, I'll linger for a moment in the pleasurable contemplation of the neatness I have produced. And I will reflect on the effort that happily spends hours tidying a humble outbuilding, the home of mice and spiders, while the nearby house, where the people dwell, remains an unredeemed wilderness, a disaster area. The paradox of household order is that often you make it most effectively where it's least needed.

SKY WATCH ☆ As evening twilight fades on the 1st, the crescent Moon and brilliant Venus hover side by side, 10 degrees high in the southwest. Two nights later, on the 3rd, the Moon dangles beneath Jupiter. During the month's final 10 days, Venus approaches Jupiter and floats below it on the 29th and 30th. The Moon closes the month hanging below the planet pair; all three brightest nighttime objects gather in the deepening twilight. Mercury concludes its fine autumn apparition during the first four days of the month, now just 6 degrees high at magnitude –0.9, low in the east just before dawn. At midmonth, Saturn rises before 1:30 A.M.; it is halfway to the zenith at dawn, in the southeast.

◑ **First Quarter**	5th day	23rd hour	3rd minute
○ **Full Moon**	13th day	1st hour	17th minute
◐ **Last Quarter**	19th day	16th hour	31st minute
● **New Moon**	27th day	11th hour	55th minute

To use this page, see p. 110; for Key Letters, see p. 235; for Tide Tables, see p. 240.
After 2:00 A.M. on November 2, Eastern Standard Time is given. ☞ **Bold = P.M.**　☞ Light = A.M.

Day of Year	Day of Month	Day of Week	Rises h. m.	Key	Sets h. m.	Key	Length of Day h. m.	Sun Fast m.	Declination of Sun ° ′	High Tide Times Boston		Rises h. m.	Key	Sets h. m.	Key	Place	Age
306	1	Sa.	7:18	D	**5:37**	B	10 19	32	14 s.42	2	**2**	11:07	E	**7:40**	A	OPH	4
307	2	**E**	6:20	D	**4:36**	B	10 16	32	15 01	1½	**1¾**	10:56	E	**7:35**	A	SAG	5
308	3	M.	6:21	D	**4:35**	B	10 14	32	15 20	2¼	**2½**	11:37	E	**8:35**	A	SAG	6
309	4	Tu.	6:22	D	**4:34**	B	10 12	32	15 38	3¼	**3¼**	**12:12**	E	**9:39**	B	SAG	7
310	5	W.	6:23	D	**4:32**	B	10 09	32	15 56	4	**4**	**12:40**	E	**10:43**	B	CAP	8
311	6	Th.	6:25	D	**4:31**	B	10 06	32	16 14	4¾	**5**	**1:05**	E	**11:49**	B	CAP	9
312	7	Fr.	6:26	D	**4:30**	A	10 04	32	16 32	5¾	**6**	**1:28**	D	—		AQU	10
313	8	Sa.	6:27	D	**4:29**	A	10 02	32	16 49	6½	**6¾**	**1:50**	D	12:56	C	AQU	11
314	9	**E**	6:28	D	**4:28**	A	10 00	32	17 06	7¼	**7¾**	**2:12**	C	2:04	D	PSC	12
315	10	M.	6:30	D	**4:27**	A	9 57	32	17 23	8¼	**8½**	**2:36**	B	3:16	D	PSC	13
316	11	Tu.	6:31	D	**4:26**	A	9 55	32	17 39	9	**9½**	**3:04**	B	4:31	E	PSC	14
317	12	W.	6:32	D	**4:25**	A	9 53	31	17 55	9¾	**10¼**	**3:38**	B	5:50	E	ARI	15
318	13	Th.	6:33	D	**4:24**	A	9 51	31	18 11	10½	**11**	**4:22**	A	7:11	E	ARI	16
319	14	Fr.	6:35	D	**4:23**	A	9 48	31	18 27	11¼	—	**5:17**	A	8:30	E	TAU	17
320	15	Sa.	6:36	D	**4:22**	A	9 46	31	18 42	12	**12¼**	**6:25**	A	9:39	E	TAU	18
321	16	**E**	6:37	D	**4:21**	A	9 44	31	18 57	12¾	**1**	**7:40**	B	10:36	E	GEM	19
322	17	M.	6:38	D	**4:20**	A	9 42	31	19 12	1¾	**2**	**8:58**	B	11:20	E	GEM	20
323	18	Tu.	6:40	D	**4:20**	A	9 40	30	19 26	2¾	**3**	**10:13**	C	11:54	E	CAN	21
324	19	W.	6:41	D	**4:19**	A	9 38	30	19 39	3¾	**4**	**11:25**	C	**12:22**	D	LEO	22
325	20	Th.	6:42	D	**4:18**	A	9 36	30	19 53	4¾	**5¼**	—		**12:45**	D	LEO	23
326	21	Fr.	6:43	D	**4:17**	A	9 34	30	20 06	5¾	**6¼**	12:34	D	**1:07**	C	LEO	24
327	22	Sa.	6:44	D	**4:17**	A	9 33	30	20 18	6¾	**7¼**	1:41	D	**1:27**	C	VIR	25
328	23	**E**	6:46	D	**4:16**	A	9 30	29	20 31	7¾	**8¼**	2:46	E	**1:49**	B	VIR	26
329	24	M.	6:47	D	**4:16**	A	9 29	29	20 44	8½	**9**	3:51	E	**2:13**	B	VIR	27
330	25	Tu.	6:48	D	**4:15**	A	9 27	29	20 55	9¼	**10**	4:56	E	**2:40**	A	VIR	28
331	26	W.	6:49	E	**4:15**	A	9 26	28	21 06	10	**10½**	6:00	E	**3:12**	A	LIB	29
332	27	Th.	6:50	E	**4:14**	A	9 24	28	21 17	10½	**11¼**	7:02	E	**3:50**	A	SCO	0
333	28	Fr.	6:51	E	**4:14**	A	9 23	28	21 27	11¼	—	8:00	E	**4:36**	A	SCO	1
334	29	Sa.	6:52	E	**4:13**	A	9 21	27	21 37	12	**12**	8:51	E	**5:29**	A	OPH	2
335	30	**E**	6:54	E	**4:13**	A	9 19	27	21 s.46	12½	**12½**	9:35	E	**6:27**	A	SAG	3

NOVEMBER HATH 30 DAYS • 2008

The soft wind and the yellow leaves
Are having their last dance together. –Harriet Eleanor Hamilton-King

Day of Month	Day of Week	Dates, Feasts, Fasts, Aspects, Tide Heights	Weather
1	Sa.	All Saints' • Sadie Hawkins Day • ☌♀☾ • Tides { 8.9 9.9	*Rain*
2	E	Daylight Saving Time ends, 2:00 A.M. • ☾ RUNS LOW • ☾ AT APO. • ♆ STAT.	*descends*
3	M.	All Souls'[T] • ☌♃☾ • Poet and outlaw Black Bart's last robbery, Calif., 1883	*like*
4	Tu.	Election Day • T. S. Eliot won Nobel Prize for literature, 1948 • { 8.2 9.1	*curtains*
5	W.	☾ AT ☊ • 78-mph winds, Block Island, R.I., 1894 • Tides { 8.1 9.0	*closing*
6	Th.	OCCN. ♆☾ • *The novelty of noon is out of date by night.*	*a*
7	Fr.	Alexander Mackenzie became the second prime minister of Canada, 1873 • Tides { 8.5 9.0	*show:*
8	Sa.	☾ ON EQ. • ☌♅☾ • Black bears head to winter dens now.	*there's*
9	E	26th S. af. P. • T. Roosevelt first to travel outside U.S. while president, 1906	*snow*
10	M.	*Choice food and costly fare do make the back go bare.*	*up*
11	Tu.	St. Martin of Tours • Veterans Day • Tides { 10.8 10.0	*north,*
12	W.	Indian Summer • Lobsters move to offshore waters. • { 11.4 10.2	*but*
13	Th.	Full Beaver ○ • Sammy Davis Jr. married May Britt, 1960	*the*
14	Fr.	☾ AT PERIG. • Louis Timothée became first salaried librarian in "U.S.," 1732 • { 12.0 10.3	*south*
15	Sa.	☾ RIDES HIGH • Sadie Hawkins Day debuted in Al Capp's *Li'l Abner* comic strip, 1937 • { 12.0 —	*gets*
16	E	27th S. af. P. • Crab apples are ripe now. • { 10.1 11.8	*a*
17	M.	St. Hugh of Lincoln • Queen Mary I died, 1558	*hosing!*
18	Tu.	☾ AT ☋ • *Ice in November Brings mud in December.* • { 9.7 10.8	*Sunbeams*
19	W.	Leonard Bernstein named music director of N.Y. Philharmonic, 1957 • Tides { 9.5 10.3	*on*
20	Th.	Fire destroyed most of business district in Oceana, W.Va., 1907 • Tides { 9.4 9.8	*football*
21	Fr.	☾ ON EQ. • ☌♄☾ • Skunks hibernate now. • { 9.5 9.5	*teams;*
22	Sa.	Storm began that left 56" of snow in Randolph, N.H., 1943 • Tides { 9.7 9.3	*losers,*
23	E	28th S. af. P. • *LIFE* debuted, 1936 • { 9.9 9.1	*winners*
24	M.	First transcontinental flight by a woman began, Mineola, N.Y., 1930 • Tides { 10.0 9.1	*shovel*
25	Tu.	☿ IN SUP. ☌ • *A man must lose a feather to win a goose.*	*out,*
26	W.	First major football game played indoors, Chicago Coliseum, Ill., 1896 • Tides { 10.2 9.0	*then*
27	Th.	Thanksgiving • New ● • ♅ STAT. • Tides { 10.2 8.9	*shovel*
28	Fr.	Banff Hot Springs Reserve (later, Banff National Park), Alta., est., 1885 • Tides { 10.1 8.8	*in*
29	Sa.	☾ RUNS LOW • ☾ AT APO. • Writer C. S. Lewis born, 1898	*turkey*
30	E	1st S. of Advent • ☌♀♃ • Tides { 8.7 9.9	*dinners!*

You can't have everything. Where would you put it? –Steven Wright

Farmer's Calendar

■ Weather signs needn't be folklore: They can appear in modern dress. Years ago, on first moving to the Vermont foothills from farther south, and knowing little of serious winter weather, I took note of the effort made in the fall by the road crew in my town to mark the local culverts and smaller bridges. They planted slender sapling poles where a stream or drainage cut passed under a roadway. Evidently the poles were for the benefit of the snowplows. They warned the drivers to avoid the culverts when clearing the roads of snow. Very well. But why, I asked myself, did the marker poles have to be nine feet tall?

When the first winter storm arrived that year—and then the second, and the third—when ramparts of plowed snow reared beside the roads and only the top foot of the marker poles showed above them, I found I had discovered a very plausible weather predictor of a particular kind. We are told to observe how deeply chipmunks bury the nuts they gather in the fall as a clue to the severity of the winter to come. Deeply buried nuts mean a cold winter. In the same spirit, I have learned to notice the length of the poles that the town cuts each year to mark the culverts. If those poles are five feet long, I await the winter without anxiety. Poles over seven feet long, however, are cause for alarm.

DECEMBER

THE TWELFTH MONTH • 2008

SKY WATCH ☆ *The year's most striking conjunction blazes on the 1st, an hour after sunset as Venus, Jupiter, and the Moon form a brilliant triangle, 15 degrees high up, in the southwest. The two planets stay reasonably close together for a few more nights. The Geminid meteors on the 13th are washed out by an exceptionally high, bright, and large Moon: The year's closest lunar approach happens five hours before the full Moon, on the 12th. Expect unusually strong tides. Meanwhile, Saturn starts to rise before midnight beginning at midmonth. The ringed planet hovers next to the Moon from midnight to dawn on the night of the 18th–19th. Winter begins with the solstice on the 21st at 7:04* A.M.

◐	**First Quarter**	5th day	16th hour	26th minute
○	**Full Moon**	12th day	11th hour	37th minute
◑	**Last Quarter**	19th day	5th hour	29th minute
●	**New Moon**	27th day	7th hour	22nd minute

To use this page, see p. 110; for Key Letters, see p. 235; for Tide Tables, see p. 240.
All times are given in Eastern Standard Time. ☞ **Bold = P.M.** ☞ Light = A.M.

Day of Year	Day of Month	Day of Week	☼ Rises h. m.	Key	☼ Sets h. m.	Key	Length of Day h.	m.	Sun Fast m.	Declination of Sun °	'	High Tide Times Boston		☾ Rises h. m.	Key	☾ Sets h. m.	Key	☾ Place	☾ Age
336	1	M.	6:55	E	**4:13**	A	9	18	27	21 s.	56	1¼	**1¼**	10:11	E	**7:29**	B	SAG	4
337	2	Tu.	6:56	E	**4:12**	A	9	16	26	22	05	2	**2**	10:42	E	**8:33**	B	CAP	5
338	3	W.	6:57	E	**4:12**	A	9	15	26	22	13	2½	**2¾**	11:07	D	**9:37**	B	CAP	6
339	4	Th.	6:58	E	**4:12**	A	9	14	25	22	21	3¼	**3½**	11:30	D	**10:41**	D	CAP	7
340	5	Fr.	6:59	E	**4:12**	A	9	13	25	22	29	4¼	**4¼**	11:52	D	**11:47**	D	AQU	8
341	6	Sa.	7:00	E	**4:12**	A	9	12	25	22	35	5	**5¼**	**12:13**	C	—	–	PSC	9
342	7	**E**	7:01	E	**4:12**	A	9	11	24	22	42	5¾	**6¼**	**12:35**	C	12:54	D	PSC	10
343	8	M.	7:01	E	**4:12**	A	9	11	24	22	48	6¾	**7¼**	**1:00**	B	2:05	E	PSC	11
344	9	Tu.	7:02	E	**4:12**	A	9	10	23	22	54	7½	**8**	**1:30**	B	3:20	E	PSC	12
345	10	W.	7:03	E	**4:12**	A	9	09	23	22	59	8¼	**9**	**2:08**	A	4:39	E	ARI	13
346	11	Th.	7:04	E	**4:12**	A	9	08	22	23	04	9¼	**10**	**2:57**	A	5:59	E	TAU	14
347	12	Fr.	7:05	E	**4:12**	A	9	07	22	23	08	10	**10¾**	**3:59**	A	7:15	E	TAU	15
348	13	Sa.	7:06	E	**4:12**	A	9	06	21	23	12	11	**11¾**	**5:14**	A	8:20	E	GEM	16
349	14	**E**	7:06	E	**4:12**	A	9	06	21	23	15	**12**	—	**6:34**	B	9:11	E	GEM	17
350	15	M.	7:07	E	**4:13**	A	9	06	21	23	18	12½	**12¾**	**7:54**	C	9:51	E	CAN	18
351	16	Tu.	7:08	E	**4:13**	A	9	05	20	23	21	1½	**1¾**	**9:11**	C	10:22	D	CAN	19
352	17	W.	7:08	E	**4:13**	A	9	05	20	23	23	2½	**2¾**	**10:23**	D	10:48	D	LEO	20
353	18	Th.	7:09	E	**4:14**	A	9	05	19	23	25	3½	**3¾**	**11:32**	D	11:11	C	LEO	21
354	19	Fr.	7:09	E	**4:14**	A	9	05	19	23	26	4¼	**4¾**	—	–	11:32	C	VIR	22
355	20	Sa.	7:10	E	**4:15**	A	9	05	18	23	26	5¼	**5¾**	12:38	E	11:54	B	VIR	23
356	21	**E**	7:11	E	**4:15**	A	9	04	18	23	26	6¼	**6¾**	1:44	E	**12:17**	B	VIR	24
357	22	M.	7:12	E	**4:16**	A	9	04	17	23	26	7¼	**7¾**	2:49	E	**12:42**	B	VIR	25
358	23	Tu.	7:12	E	**4:16**	A	9	04	17	23	25	8	**8¾**	3:53	E	**1:13**	A	LIB	26
359	24	W.	7:12	E	**4:17**	A	9	05	16	23	24	8¾	**9½**	4:56	E	**1:49**	A	LIB	27
360	25	Th.	7:12	E	**4:17**	A	9	05	16	23	23	9½	**10¼**	5:55	E	**2:32**	A	SCO	28
361	26	Fr.	7:13	E	**4:18**	A	9	05	15	23	20	10¼	**11**	6:48	E	**3:23**	A	OPH	29
362	27	Sa.	7:13	E	**4:19**	A	9	06	15	23	17	11	**11½**	7:34	E	**4:20**	A	SAG	0
363	28	**E**	7:13	E	**4:20**	A	9	07	14	23	14	11½	—	8:12	E	**5:22**	B	SAG	1
364	29	M.	7:13	E	**4:20**	A	9	07	14	23	10	12¼	**12¼**	8:44	E	**6:25**	B	SAG	2
365	30	Tu.	7:14	E	**4:21**	A	9	07	13	23	06	12¾	**12¾**	9:11	E	**7:29**	B	CAP	3
366	31	W.	7:14	E	**4:22**	A	9	08	13	23 s.	03	1½	**1½**	9:35	E	**8:33**	B	CAP	4

DECEMBER HATH 31 DAYS • 2008

Then, heigh-ho, the holly!
This life is most jolly! –William Shakespeare

Day of Month	Day of Week	Dates, Feasts, Fasts, Aspects, Tide Heights	Weather
1	M.	St. Andrew[T] • ☌♃☾ • OCCN. ♀☾ • Tides { 8.6 9.8	*Shopping*
2	Tu.	St. Viviana • ☾ AT ☊ • Environmental Protection Agency established, 1970	*leaves*
3	W.	☌♆☾ • Final run of luxury train *20th Century Limited* finished, 1967 • Tides { 8.5 9.4	*us*
4	Th.	Temperature dropped 34 degrees in 20 minutes, Livingston, Mont., 1972 • Tides { 8.5 9.2	*sopping.*
5	Fr.	☌♂☉ • American League for Physical Culture formed, 1929 • { 8.7 9.0	*White*
6	Sa.	St. Nicholas • ☾ ON EQ. • ☌♅☾ • Tides { 8.9 8.9	*wool*
7	E	**2nd S. of Advent** • **Nat'l Pearl Harbor Remembrance Day**	*dropping;*
8	M.	U.S. declared war on Japan, 1941 • Tides { 9.8 9.1	*bundle*
9	Tu.	Football's Bob Waterfield made five field goals in one game, 1951 • Tides { 10.4 9.3	*up*
10	W.	St. Eulalia • *No snowflake ever falls in the wrong place.* • Tides { 11.0 9.6	*tight!*
11	Th.	Winterberry fruits especially showy now. • { 11.5 9.8	*You'll*
12	Fr.	Our Lady of Guadalupe • **Full Cold** ○ • ☾ AT PERIG. • { 11.9 10.0	*need*
13	Sa.	St. Lucia • ☾ RIDES HIGH • Dartmouth College chartered, Hanover, N.H., 1769	*a*
14	E	**3rd S. of Advent** • Halcyon Days • Tides { 12.1 —	*fur*
15	M.	☾ AT ☋ • Groundbreaking ceremonies for Jefferson Memorial, Washington, D.C., 1938	*piece*
16	Tu.	Mag. ~8.1 earthquake in northeast Ark., 1811 • { 10.1 11.4	*or*
17	W.	Ember Day • First rendezvous of two manned spacecraft, *Gemini 6* and *Gemini 7*, 1965	*lots*
18	Th.	☾ ON EQ. • ☌♄☾ • Giant panda Basi's 25th birthday celebration, China, 2005 • { 9.9 10.1	*of*
19	Fr.	Ember Day • Beware the Pogonip. • Tides { 9.7 9.5	*fleece*
20	Sa.	Ember Day • *May you have warmth in your igloo, oil in your lamp, and peace in your heart.*	*when*
21	E	**4th S. of Advent** • **Winter Solstice** • Tides { 9.6 8.6	*looking*
22	M.	St. Thomas[T] • First day of Chanukah • ☌♇☉ • { 9.5 8.4	*at*
23	Tu.	8-yr.-old Richard Knecht set world record for consecutive sit-ups at 25,222, 1972 • Tides { 9.6 8.4	*the*
24	W.	Frontiersman Kit Carson born, 1809 • Tides { 9.7 8.4	*holiday*
25	Th.	**Christmas Day** • *At Christmas meadows green, at Easter covered with frost.*	*lights!*
26	Fr.	St. Stephen • ☾ RUNS LOW • ☾ AT APO. • ☌♆♀ • { 9.9 8.5	*Pour*
27	Sa.	St. John • New ● • Architect Gustave Eiffel died, 1923 • Tides { 10.0 8.6	*the*
28	E	**1st S. af. Ch.** • ☌☿☾ • Tides { 10.0 —	*wine:*
29	M.	Holy Innocents[T] • Islamic New Year • ☌♃☾ • { 8.7 10.0	*Here's*
30	Tu.	☾ AT ☊ • U.S. and Mexico signed the Gadsden Purchase Treaty, 1853 • { 8.8 9.9	*cheers*
31	W.	St. Sylvester • ☌☿♃ • ☌♆☾ • ☌♀☾ • { 8.8 9.8	*to '09!*

Farmer's Calendar

■ Old garden plans afford a unique view of their subject, which is not only a patch of earth but also the history of an individual's effort to make it fruitful.

I have garden plans going back to 1978. Originally, drawing them let me avoid planting the same crop in the same place on our small vegetable plot in successive years. So much for the plans' utility; but by now they also have an archaeological interest. I get them out from time to time and study them for what they show of a garden—and a gardener—that is past.

I find our gardens to have had a rhythmic base of reliable vegetables that recur regularly, and a treble line of more exotic fare that comes and goes. Peas, beans, tomatoes, carrots, pumpkins, and marigolds are constants over 30 years; while potatoes, melons, lettuces, and others come in, linger, depart, and reappear in a more complex figure.

The plans show the composition of the garden, but they also show its success and failure. It all comes back: the year slugs ate the beans (1988); the unexpected bumper crop of fennel (1990: How much fennel do you *need,* really?). Especially in the deep winter, when the garden seems so remote, these fading documents give pleasure. And they're so easy to make. Let us omit the tiresome work with spade and hoe and become planners only.

Glossary of Almanac Oddities

■ Many readers have expressed puzzlement over the rather obscure notations that appear on our **Right-Hand Calendar Pages, 115–141.** These "oddities" have long been fixtures in the Almanac, and we are pleased to provide some definitions. (Once explained, they may not seem so odd after all!)

–Beth Krommes

Ember Days: The four periods formerly observed by the Roman Catholic and Anglican churches for prayer, fasting, and the ordination of clergy are called Ember Days. Specifically, these are the Wednesdays, Fridays, and Saturdays that follow in succession following (1) the First Sunday in Lent; (2) Whitsunday–Pentecost; (3) the Feast of the Holy Cross, normally September 14; and (4) the Feast of St. Lucia, December 13. The word *ember* is perhaps a corruption of the Latin *quatuor tempora,* "four times."

Folklore has it that the weather on each of the three days foretells the weather for the next three months; that is, for September's Ember Days, Wednesday forecasts the weather for October, Friday for November, and Saturday for December.

Distaff Day (January 7): This was the first day after Epiphany (January 6), when women were expected to return to their spinning following the Christmas holiday. A distaff is the staff that women used for holding the flax or wool in spinning. (Hence the term "distaff" refers to women's work or the maternal side of the family.)

Plough Monday (January): Traditionally, the first Monday after Epiphany was called Plough Monday because it was the day that men returned to their plough, or daily work, following the Christmas holiday. (Every few years, Plough Monday and Distaff Day fall on the same day.) It was customary at this time for farm laborers to draw a plough through the village, soliciting money for a "plough light," which was kept burning in the parish church all year. One proverb notes that

> *"Yule is come and Yule is gone,*
> *and we have feasted well;*
> *so Jack must to his flail again*
> *and Jenny to her wheel."*

Three Chilly Saints (May): Mamertus, Pancras, and Gervais were three early Christian saints. Because their feast days, on May 11, 12, and 13, respectively, are traditionally cold, they have come to be known as the Three Chilly Saints. An old French saying translates to: "St. Mamertus, St. Pancras, and St. Gervais do not pass without a frost."

Midsummer Day (June 24): To the farmer, this day is the midpoint of the growing season, halfway between planting and harvest. (Midsummer Eve is an occasion for festivity and celebrates fertility.) The Anglican church considered it a "Quarter Day," one of the four major divisions of the liturgical year. It also marks the feast day of St. John the Baptist.

Cornscateous Air (July): First used by early almanac makers, this term signifies warm, damp air. Though it signals ideal climatic conditions for growing corn, it poses a danger to those affected by asthma and other respiratory problems.

Dog Days (July 3–August 11): These are the hottest and most unhealthy days of the year. Also known as Canicular Days, their name derives from the Dog Star, Sirius. The traditional 40-day period of Dog Days coincides with the heliacal (at sunrise) rising of Sirius.

Lammas Day (August 1): Derived from the Old English *hlaf maesse,* meaning "loaf mass," Lammas Day marked the beginning of the harvest. Traditionally, loaves of bread were baked from the first-ripened grain and brought to the churches to be consecrated. Eventually, "loaf mass" became "Lammas." In Scotland, Lammastide fairs became famous as the time when trial marriages could be made. These marriages could end after a year with no strings attached.

Cat Nights Begin (August 17): This term harks back to the days when people believed in witches. An Irish legend says that a witch could turn into a cat and regain herself eight times, but on the ninth time, August 17, she couldn't change back, hence the saying: "A cat has nine lives." Because August is a "yowly" time for cats, this may have initially prompted the speculation about witches on the prowl.

Harvest Home (September): In Europe and Britain, the conclusion of the harvest each autumn was once marked by festivals of fun, feasting, and thanksgiving known as "Harvest Home." It was also a time to hold elections, pay workers, and collect rents. These festivals usually took place around the autumnal equinox. Certain groups in this country, particularly the Pennsylvania Dutch, have kept the tradition alive.

St. Luke's Little Summer (October): A spell of warm weather that occurs about the time of the saint's feast day, October 18, this period is sometimes referred to as Indian summer.

Indian Summer (November): A period of warm weather following a cold spell or a hard frost, Indian summer can occur between St. Martin's Day (November 11) and November 20. Although there are differing dates for its occurrence, for more than 200 years the Almanac has adhered to the saying "If All Saints' brings out winter, St. Martin's brings out Indian summer." Some say that the term comes from the early Native Americans, who believed that the condition was caused by a warm wind sent from the court of their southwestern god, Cautantowwit.

Halcyon Days (December): About two weeks of calm weather often follow the blustery winds of autumn's end. Ancient Greeks and Romans believed these occured around the time of the winter solstice, when the halcyon, or kingfisher, was brooding. In a nest floating on the sea, the bird was said to have charmed the wind and waves so that the waters were especially calm during this period.

Beware the Pogonip (December): The word *pogonip* is a meteorological term used to describe an uncommon occurrence—frozen fog. The word was coined by Native Americans to describe the frozen fogs of fine ice needles that occur in the mountain valleys of the western United States and Canada. According to their tradition, breathing the fog is injurious to the lungs. □ □

Holidays and Observances

For Movable Religious Observances, see page 113.

Jan. 17	Benjamin Franklin's Birthday
Jan. 19	Robert E. Lee Day *(Ark., Fla., Ky., La., S.C.)*
Feb. 2	Groundhog Day
Feb. 5	Mardi Gras *(Baldwin & Mobile counties, Ala.; La.)*
Feb. 12	Abraham Lincoln's Birthday
Feb. 14	Valentine's Day
Feb. 15	Susan B. Anthony's Birthday *(Fla., Wis.)* National Flag of Canada Day
Mar. 2	Texas Independence Day
Mar. 4	Town Meeting Day *(Vt.)*
Mar. 15	Andrew Jackson Day *(Tenn.)*
Mar. 17	St. Patrick's Day Evacuation Day *(Suffolk Co., Mass.)*
Mar. 31	Seward's Day *(Alaska)*
Apr. 2	Pascua Florida Day
Apr. 21	Patriots Day *(Maine, Mass.)* San Jacinto Day *(Tex.)*
Apr. 22	Earth Day
Apr. 25	National Arbor Day
May 5	Cinco de Mayo
May 8	Truman Day *(Mo.)*
May 11	Mother's Day
May 17	Armed Forces Day
May 19	Victoria Day *(Canada)*
May 22	National Maritime Day
June 5	World Environment Day
June 11	King Kamehameha I Day *(Hawaii)*
June 14	Flag Day
June 15	Father's Day
June 17	Bunker Hill Day *(Suffolk Co., Mass.)*
June 19	Emancipation Day *(Tex.)*
June 20	West Virginia Day
July 1	Canada Day
July 24	Pioneer Day *(Utah)*
Aug. 4	Colorado Day Civic Holiday *(Canada)*
Aug. 16	Bennington Battle Day *(Vt.)*
Aug. 19	National Aviation Day
Aug. 26	Women's Equality Day
Sept. 7	Grandparents Day
Sept. 9	Admission Day *(Calif.)*
Sept. 11	Patriot Day
Sept. 17	Constitution Day
Oct. 6	Child Health Day
Oct. 9	Leif Eriksson Day
Oct. 13	Native Americans' Day *(S.Dak.)* Thanksgiving Day *(Canada)*
Oct. 18	Alaska Day
Oct. 24	United Nations Day
Oct. 31	Halloween Nevada Day
Nov. 4	Election Day Will Rogers Day *(Okla.)*
Nov. 11	Remembrance Day *(Canada)*
Nov. 19	Discovery Day *(Puerto Rico)*
Nov. 28	Acadian Day *(La.)*
Dec. 7	National Pearl Harbor Remembrance Day
Dec. 15	Bill of Rights Day
Dec. 17	Wright Brothers Day
Dec. 26	Boxing Day *(Canada)* First day of Kwanzaa

Federal Holidays

Jan. 1	New Year's Day
Jan. 21	Martin Luther King Jr.'s Birthday *(observed)*
Feb. 18	George Washington's Birthday *(observed)*
May 26	Memorial Day *(observed)*
July 4	Independence Day
Sept. 1	Labor Day
Oct. 13	Columbus Day *(observed)*
Nov. 11	Veterans Day
Nov. 27	Thanksgiving Day
Dec. 25	Christmas Day

2007

January
S	M	T	W	T	F	S
	1	2	3	4	5	6
7	8	9	10	11	12	13
14	15	16	17	18	19	20
21	22	23	24	25	26	27
28	29	30	31			

February
S	M	T	W	T	F	S
				1	2	3
4	5	6	7	8	9	10
11	12	13	14	15	16	17
18	19	20	21	22	23	24
25	26	27	28			

March
S	M	T	W	T	F	S
				1	2	3
4	5	6	7	8	9	10
11	12	13	14	15	16	17
18	19	20	21	22	23	24
25	26	27	28	29	30	31

April
S	M	T	W	T	F	S
1	2	3	4	5	6	7
8	9	10	11	12	13	14
15	16	17	18	19	20	21
22	23	24	25	26	27	28
29	30					

May
S	M	T	W	T	F	S
		1	2	3	4	5
6	7	8	9	10	11	12
13	14	15	16	17	18	19
20	21	22	23	24	25	26
27	28	29	30	31		

June
S	M	T	W	T	F	S
					1	2
3	4	5	6	7	8	9
10	11	12	13	14	15	16
17	18	19	20	21	22	23
24	25	26	27	28	29	30

July
S	M	T	W	T	F	S
1	2	3	4	5	6	7
8	9	10	11	12	13	14
15	16	17	18	19	20	21
22	23	24	25	26	27	28
29	30	31				

August
S	M	T	W	T	F	S
			1	2	3	4
5	6	7	8	9	10	11
12	13	14	15	16	17	18
19	20	21	22	23	24	25
26	27	28	29	30	31	

September
S	M	T	W	T	F	S
						1
2	3	4	5	6	7	8
9	10	11	12	13	14	15
16	17	18	19	20	21	22
23	24	25	26	27	28	29
30						

October
S	M	T	W	T	F	S
	1	2	3	4	5	6
7	8	9	10	11	12	13
14	15	16	17	18	19	20
21	22	23	24	25	26	27
28	29	30	31			

November
S	M	T	W	T	F	S
				1	2	3
4	5	6	7	8	9	10
11	12	13	14	15	16	17
18	19	20	21	22	23	24
25	26	27	28	29	30	

December
S	M	T	W	T	F	S
						1
2	3	4	5	6	7	8
9	10	11	12	13	14	15
16	17	18	19	20	21	22
23	24	25	26	27	28	29
30	31					

2008

January
S	M	T	W	T	F	S
		1	2	3	4	5
6	7	8	9	10	11	12
13	14	15	16	17	18	19
20	21	22	23	24	25	26
27	28	29	30	31		

February
S	M	T	W	T	F	S
					1	2
3	4	5	6	7	8	9
10	11	12	13	14	15	16
17	18	19	20	21	22	23
24	25	26	27	28	29	

March
S	M	T	W	T	F	S
						1
2	3	4	5	6	7	8
9	10	11	12	13	14	15
16	17	18	19	20	21	22
23	24	25	26	27	28	29
30	31					

April
S	M	T	W	T	F	S
		1	2	3	4	5
6	7	8	9	10	11	12
13	14	15	16	17	18	19
20	21	22	23	24	25	26
27	28	29	30			

May
S	M	T	W	T	F	S
				1	2	3
4	5	6	7	8	9	10
11	12	13	14	15	16	17
18	19	20	21	22	23	24
25	26	27	28	29	30	31

June
S	M	T	W	T	F	S
1	2	3	4	5	6	7
8	9	10	11	12	13	14
15	16	17	18	19	20	21
22	23	24	25	26	27	28
29	30					

July
S	M	T	W	T	F	S
		1	2	3	4	5
6	7	8	9	10	11	12
13	14	15	16	17	18	19
20	21	22	23	24	25	26
27	28	29	30	31		

August
S	M	T	W	T	F	S
					1	2
3	4	5	6	7	8	9
10	11	12	13	14	15	16
17	18	19	20	21	22	23
24	25	26	27	28	29	30
31						

September
S	M	T	W	T	F	S
	1	2	3	4	5	6
7	8	9	10	11	12	13
14	15	16	17	18	19	20
21	22	23	24	25	26	27
28	29	30				

October
S	M	T	W	T	F	S
			1	2	3	4
5	6	7	8	9	10	11
12	13	14	15	16	17	18
19	20	21	22	23	24	25
26	27	28	29	30	31	

November
S	M	T	W	T	F	S
						1
2	3	4	5	6	7	8
9	10	11	12	13	14	15
16	17	18	19	20	21	22
23	24	25	26	27	28	29
30						

December
S	M	T	W	T	F	S
	1	2	3	4	5	6
7	8	9	10	11	12	13
14	15	16	17	18	19	20
21	22	23	24	25	26	27
28	29	30	31			

2009

January
S	M	T	W	T	F	S
				1	2	3
4	5	6	7	8	9	10
11	12	13	14	15	16	17
18	19	20	21	22	23	24
25	26	27	28	29	30	31

February
S	M	T	W	T	F	S
1	2	3	4	5	6	7
8	9	10	11	12	13	14
15	16	17	18	19	20	21
22	23	24	25	26	27	28

March
S	M	T	W	T	F	S
1	2	3	4	5	6	7
8	9	10	11	12	13	14
15	16	17	18	19	20	21
22	23	24	25	26	27	28
29	30	31				

April
S	M	T	W	T	F	S
			1	2	3	4
5	6	7	8	9	10	11
12	13	14	15	16	17	18
19	20	21	22	23	24	25
26	27	28	29	30		

May
S	M	T	W	T	F	S
					1	2
3	4	5	6	7	8	9
10	11	12	13	14	15	16
17	18	19	20	21	22	23
24	25	26	27	28	29	30
31						

June
S	M	T	W	T	F	S
	1	2	3	4	5	6
7	8	9	10	11	12	13
14	15	16	17	18	19	20
21	22	23	24	25	26	27
28	29	30				

July
S	M	T	W	T	F	S
			1	2	3	4
5	6	7	8	9	10	11
12	13	14	15	16	17	18
19	20	21	22	23	24	25
26	27	28	29	30	31	

August
S	M	T	W	T	F	S
						1
2	3	4	5	6	7	8
9	10	11	12	13	14	15
16	17	18	19	20	21	22
23	24	25	26	27	28	29
30	31					

September
S	M	T	W	T	F	S
		1	2	3	4	5
6	7	8	9	10	11	12
13	14	15	16	17	18	19
20	21	22	23	24	25	26
27	28	29	30			

October
S	M	T	W	T	F	S
				1	2	3
4	5	6	7	8	9	10
11	12	13	14	15	16	17
18	19	20	21	22	23	24
25	26	27	28	29	30	31

November
S	M	T	W	T	F	S
1	2	3	4	5	6	7
8	9	10	11	12	13	14
15	16	17	18	19	20	21
22	23	24	25	26	27	28
29	30					

December
S	M	T	W	T	F	S
		1	2	3	4	5
6	7	8	9	10	11	12
13	14	15	16	17	18	19
20	21	22	23	24	25	26
27	28	29	30	31		

CALENDAR

The Diabetes Healer Drug Companies Want to Keep Secret

Doctors have been trained to prescribe drugs to treat diabetes. It's no wonder that sales of diabetes drugs totaled $8.1 billion dollars last year. The trouble with drugs is they treat the *symptoms* of diabetes...not the underlying *cause*. Diabetes drugs can also have serious side effects and increase risk factors for other diseases.

Now, a medically sound program is available that treats the underlying cause of diabetes by enabling your body to metabolize sugar. It allows your body to heal itself naturally... helping you **normalize blood sugar levels, reduce insulin resistance, reverse neuropathy, improve vision and improve balance**. In addition, people report more energy and faster healing.

It's called *"The Diabetes Prescription"* and is based on documented scientific principles that lower blood sugar and help reverse symptoms... allowing diabetics to gain control of their lives and feel better than they ever thought possible.

"The Diabetes Prescription" activates your body's built-in healers once you start eating the right combination of foods. It works for both Type 1 and Type 2 diabetes... and can make a huge difference in how you feel both physically and mentally. As you begin to feel better, you'll find yourself with a new outlook on life.

"The Diabetes Prescription" can also help your overall health by reducing risk factors for other diseases. It can **lower blood pressure, lower cholesterol and reduce triglyceride levels**. It can also **improve your circulation** and **help cleanse clogged arteries**. What's more, it can **help numb feet regain a level of feeling**.

The health-saving principles revealed in "The Diabetes Prescription" have been repeatedly proven effective in numerous scientific studies by top health authorities around the world... from such respected institutions as Harvard University, UCLA, and the U.S. Government Human Nutrition Research Center.

"The Diabetes Prescription" is based on documented scientific principles that can help:
- **Reverse neuropathy**
- **Strengthen your eyesight**
- **Make blood sugar levels go from high risk to normal**
- **Heal cuts and scrapes faster**
- **Boost your energy**
- **Control sugar cravings**

In addition, you learn valuable tips on vitamins and supplements every diabetic should be aware of, such as:
- **The #1 vitamin for blood sugar problems**
- **Which vitamins and supplements you don't need to take**
- **The most important mineral for diabetics**
- **What natural supplement is good for both blood pressure and blood sugar**
- **The liquid supplement that reduces triglycerides**
- **What supposedly 'healthy' drink is repeatedly connected to diabetes**
- **What easy to do non-exercise lowers fasting glucose levels, lowers blood pressure, cholesterol and triglycerides and can reduce your waistline**
- **How to lose weight without feeling hungry**
- **and much more**

If you or someone you know have diabetes, *"The Diabetes Prescription"* can be life changing. Right now, as part of a special introductory offer, you can receive *"The Diabetes Prescription"* direct from the publisher for only $12.95 plus $2.00 postage and handling. It is not available in stores. It comes with a 90 day money back guarantee. If you are not 100% satisfied, simply return it for a full refund – no questions asked.

Order an extra copy for family or friend and SAVE. You can order 2 for only $20 total.

HERE'S HOW TO ORDER: Simply PRINT your name and address and the words "Diabetes Prescription" on a piece of paper and mail it along with a check or money order to: Leader Health Publishers, Dept. DH331, P.O. Box 8347, Canton, OH 44711. VISA, MasterCard, Discover or American Express send card number and expiration date. Act now. Orders are fulfilled on a first come first served basis.

©2008 Leader Health Publishers

Best Fishing Days and Times

■ **The best times to fish are when the fish are naturally most active. The Sun,** Moon, tides, and weather all influence fish activity. For example, fish tend to feed more at sunrise and sunset. During a full Moon, tides are higher than average and fish tend to feed more. However, most of us go fishing when we can get the time off, not because it is the best time. But there *are* best times, according to fishing lore:

The Best Fishing Days for 2008, when the Moon is between new and full:

January 8–22
February 6–20
March 7–21
April 5–20
May 5–19
June 3–18
July 2–18
August 1–16
August 30–September 15
September 29–October 14
October 28–November 13
November 27–December 12
December 27–31

■ One hour before and one hour after high tides, and one hour before and one hour after low tides. (The times of high tides for Boston are given on pages 114–140; also see pages 240–241. Inland, the times for high tides correspond with the times when the Moon is due south. Low tides are halfway between high tides.)

■ During the "morning rise" (after sunup for a spell) and the "evening rise" (just before sundown and the hour or so after).

■ When the barometer is steady or on the rise. (But even during stormy periods, the fish aren't going to give up feeding. The smart fisherman will find just the right bait.)

■ When there is a hatch of flies—caddis flies or mayflies, commonly. (The fisherman will have to match *his* fly with the hatching flies or go fishless.)

■ When the breeze is from a westerly quarter rather than from the north or east.

■ When the water is still or rippled, rather than during a wind.

Tackle-Box Checklist

- ❏ Fishing line
- ❏ Bobbers
- ❏ Swivels, to keep fishing line from twisting
- ❏ Leaders
- ❏ Sinkers
- ❏ Different sizes of hooks
- ❏ Pliers, to help remove hooks
- ❏ Stringer, to hold all the fish you catch
- ❏ Sharp knife
- ❏ Ruler/scale
- ❏ Flashlight
- ❏ First-aid kit
- ❏ Insect repellent
- ❏ Sunscreen

trout

catfish

salmon

New lure's catch rate may be too high for some tournaments.

Out-fishes other bait 19 to 4 in one contest.

Uses aerospace technology to mimic a real fish.

ORLANDO, FL— A small company in Connecticut has developed a new lure that mimics the motion of a real fish so realistically eight professionals couldn't tell the difference between it and a live shad when it "swam" toward them on retrieval. The design eliminates wobbling, angled swimming and other unnatural motions that problem other hard bait lures. It swims upright and appears to propel itself with its tail.

Curiously, the company may have designed it too well. Tournament fishermen who have used it said it's possible officials will not allow it in contests where live bait is prohibited. They claim it swims more realistically than anything they have ever seen. If so, that would hurt the company's promotional efforts. Winning tournaments is an important part of marketing a new lure.

Fish would probably prefer to see it restricted. I watched eight veteran fishermen test the new lure (called The KickTail®) on a lake outside Orlando FL for about four hours. Four used the KickTail and four used a combination of their favorite lures and shiners (live bait). The four using the KickTail caught 41 fish versus 14 for the other four. In one boat the KickTail won 19 to 4. The KickTail also caught bigger fish, which suggests it triggers larger, less aggressive fish to strike.

The KickTail's magic comes from a patented technology that breaks the tail into five segments. As water rushes by on retrieval, a little-known principle called aeronautical flutter causes the tail to wag left and right, as if the lure were propelling itself with its tail. Unlike other hard baits,

Swims with its tail.

New lure swims like a real fish--nearly triples catch in Florida contest.

the head remains stationary—only the tail wags. A company spokesman told me this.

"Marine biologists will tell you that the more a lure swims like a real fish, the more fish it will catch. Well, the only live thing the KickTail doesn't do is breathe. It's always swimming wild and free. Fish can't stand it. We've seen fish that have just eaten go for the KickTail. It's like having another potato chip."

Whether you fish for fun or profit, if you want a nearly 3 to 1 advantage, I would order now before the KickTail becomes known. The company even guarantees a refund, if you don't catch more fish and return the lures within 30 days. There are three versions: a floater, a diver and a "dying shad" with a weed guard. Each lure costs $9.95 and you must order at least two. There is also a "Super 10-Pack" with additional colors for only $79.95, a savings of almost $20.00. S/h is only $7.00 no matter how many you order.

To order call **1-800-873-4415** (Ask for item # kt), or click **www.ngc sports.com** anytime or day or send a check or M.O. (or cc number and exp. date) to NGC Sports **(Dept. KT-1133)** 60 Church Street, Yalesville, CT 06492. CT add sales tax. The KickTail is four inches long and works in salt and fresh water.

KTS-8A   © NGC Worldwide, Inc. 2007 **Dept. KT-1133**

by Ann Thurlow

How to Wash You

I f you're like most people, you've probably heard this more than once: "Wash
your hands—and use lots of soap and hot
water!"

As it turns out, the temperature of the
water has little or no effect on a good scrub's
germ-fighting abilities. "If the water you use is
hot enough to actually kill germs, it will burn
you," says Dr. Lamont Sweet, Chief Health
Officer for the Canadian province of Prince
Edward Island. "The purpose of hand washing
is to rinse germs away. For that, you need lots
of soap and lots of water. The temperature of
the water is more a matter of comfort." Warm
water tends to make soap lather better and feels
better, he says, but cold water will do the job.

Washing your hands properly is one very
simple way to keep yourself healthy. In fact,
according to Sweet, it is one of the most
effective ways to avoid colds, influenza,
and gastrointestinal disorders. "But," he
says, "you have to do it right." He recommends this method:

Allow two minutes. Put effort into scrubbing
not only palms and fingers, but also the backs
of hands and the skin between fingers, which
are places where germs can continue to reside.

Sweet specifically advises a good
cleansing . . .

- before and after your hands are nea
  your face

- before eating and cooking, and, if you
  smoke, before lighting up

- after using the bathroom, changing di
  apers, blowing your nose or sneezing
  into a hand, handling any kind of mea
  or garbage, and touching animals o
  cleaning up after them

So, be good to yourself and everyone around you—wash your hands

The U.S. Standard
The U.S. Centers for Disease Control and
Prevention recommends a vigorous 20
second scrub, once hands are lathered

Hands

When Soap Won't Suffice

For those sticky—and stinky—situations when ordinary soap just won't work, try these cleaning agents (followed by soap and water):

To remove pine tar or pitch, rub with a dab of mayonnaise, toothpaste, bacon grease, or peanut butter.

To remove car or bicycle grease, wash with dish detergent or baking soda.

To eliminate the smell of fish, wipe your fingers with a piece of lemon.

To eliminate the aroma of garlic from your hands, rub them on a stainless-steel pot or with cool, used coffee grounds, or full-strength vinegar.

To eliminate onion odor on your fingers, rub them with vinegar before and after slicing onions.

To remove beet stains, scrub your skin with a piece of raw potato.

To keep beneath your nails clean when gardening, scratch them on a bar of soap before heading out into the garden. (Washing up will be easier, too.)

PANTRY Potions

The first known hand cream, a substance that consisted of tallow (sheep or cattle fat), pig fat, and potato starch, was unearthed by archaeologists in England and is believed to date from A.D. 2. Here are some reliable, old-fashioned (but not that old) alternatives:

■ To relieve cracked skin on your hands, rub with calendula oil or wrap in a vinegar-soaked towel for 20 to 30 minutes.

■ To soothe dry skin on your hands and feet, massage with vegetable shortening and cover with cotton gloves or socks overnight.

■ To tone your hands, wash with cucumber juice.

■ To moisturize your hands, rub with honey.

■ To soften your hands, wash with mashed boiled potatoes (plain, or mashed with milk).

■ To condition your hands, massage them with egg whites.

nn Thurlow is a writer and scrupulous hand washer. She lives with a very understanding man and a very **e**manding cat in Charlottetown, Prince Edward Island.

Hexafoo on You!

ric Claypoole sees ghosts and brings them back to life. His specters are not from the grave; they are pale outlines of once-bright barn stars that adorned the sturdy barns of German immigrants known collectively as the Pennsylvania Dutch. He revives the symbols before they fade into obscurity and, in so doing, keeps a tradition alive with his paintbrush.

Claypoole learned his sign-painting skills from his father, beginning some 30 years ago. His dad, the late Johnny Claypoole, was a world-renowned hex sign painter whose work can still be seen on barns in Berks County, Pennsylvania, as well as on the elephant house at the Philadelphia Zoo. Today, 48-year-old Eric is the country's only professional barn star painter, restoring old stars and creating new ones—mostly on weekends. (During the week, he works as a carpenter, restoring and renovating old buildings.) His canvases are the sides and gables of old barns; his "ghosts" are raised patterns in wood that once bore a painted star, created perhaps more than 150 years ago. The paint, long since faded, protected the wood from weathering. This preserved wood, which sometimes stands as little as $\frac{3}{16}$ of an inch in profile, defines the original star pattern.

Working on a ladder or perched on a plank stretched between two ladders, Claypoole paints in freehand, true to the folk art's origins. Each star begins with four coats of white base paint. Then, using a level and square, he marks out the pattern. He applies the colors one at a time, eliminating the need to balance multiple brushes and paint containers. He lets each color dry before adding the next one; a single 5- to 6-foot-diameter star may take him 8 to 10 hours to finish, depending on the complexity of the pattern. The oil-based enamel lettering paints

The star on this stone barn in Lenhartsville, Pennsylvania, is the oldest yet restored by Eric Claypoole.

–photos: courtesy Eric Claypoole
–hex sign illustrations: Margo Letourneau

*Barn stars and hex signs a
big mystery? No more.*

by Đeb Martin

A traditional hex sign design, the single distelfink is a symbol of good luck and happiness. The heart implies love; the tulips, faith.

What's the Hex?

The original designs that Pennsylvania's German immigrants painted on their barns came from traditional designs and motifs that decorated their homes in Europe. Interpretations may vary from one artist to the next, but most symbols represent common themes such as health, bounty, faith, and love.

The terms "hex sign" and "barn star" are often used interchangeably, but they represent different images. Traditional barn stars tend to feature geometric patterns. Hex signs typically feature more complex shapes, making them harder to paint from the rungs of a ladder. These signs are painted on signboard to be mounted on a barn or elsewhere.

153

The tulip, a characteristic feature of Pennsylvania Dutch folk art, appears on pottery, quilts, and furniture.

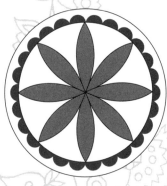

In general, a rosette design symbolizes good fortune. Red petals indicate strength.

MAGIC OR MYSTERY?

Some of the owners of barns with stars restored by Eric Claypoole have curious tales to tell. Read about three of them, as well as tours and events in the area, at **Almanac.com/extras**.

154

that Claypoole uses keep his stars shining bright for many years. His first barn star, painted in 1974, "still looks good," he says, adding that the paint is fading, but not peeling.

These days, although barn stars are "really a one-of-a-kind piece of artwork," according to Kutztown realtor Jeff Sicher, the decoration has more cultural than monetary value. More important, the stars add to the region's unique flavor. To that end, to help maintain the art tradition and area's character, some of Claypoole's restorations are supported by an endowment fund administered by the Kutztown University Foundation. To Dave Fooks, director of the Dutch Hex Tour Association and executive director of the annual Kutztown Pennsylvania German Festival, who helps identify fading barn stars in need of restoration, Claypoole's work is priceless. "We can't afford to lose him," he says.

Signs of the Times

Controversy reigns as to whether hex signs have specific meanings, but these are generally accepted:

HEX SIGN	MEANING
12-pointed stars	12 months, Christ's 12 Apostles, justice
4-pointed stars	4 seasons of the year
Oak leaves or acorns	Strength
Tulips	The Holy Trinity; or faith, hope, and charity
Hearts	Love, marriage, affection
Distelfinks (goldfinches)	Good luck, happiness
Shamrocks	Good luck, Irish ancestry
Eagles	Courage, patriotism
Rosettes	Prosperity, good fortune
Sun and rain	Fertility, abundance
Rabbits	Fertility
Unicorns	Virtue and plenty
Circular chains	Long life, eternity
Scalloped borders	Smooth sailing through life

A Brief Hex-tory of the Signs

I n the late 17th century, a wave of German and Swiss immigrants seeking religious freedom arved in William Penn's settlement in the New World. The mish and Mennonites carved farms out of what is now ancaster County, while the "church" Germans (members of Lutheran, Church of Christ, and Reformed conregations) settled mainly in modern-day Berks County.

The German settlers became known as "Pennsylvania Dutch," "Dutch" probably being a corruption of *Deutsch,* ae German word for "German." They brought with them ae tradition of decorating homes, furnishings (dowry hests), books (bibles), and documents (birth certificates) with colorful symbols and elaborate lettering called *aktur.* The symbols—stars, lilies and tulips, heraldic reatures such as lions and unicorns, hearts, and stylized irds like distelfinks (goldfinches) and peacocks—gradally became part of the folk art that came to be known s hex signs.

Barn stars became popular in the mid- to late 1800s. pparently, farmers had the time and wherewithal to aint their barns. German farmers preferred red barns and ixed iron oxide with linseed oil, usually pressed from eir own flax crop, to produce the color. (The Amish and Iennonites, the "plain folk," painted their barns white d left them otherwise undecorated.)

Historians remain widely divided over how and why arn stars came into favor. They might have originated statements of cultural identity, symbols of property wnership, or good luck charms. Some believe that an uslander, or outsider, not fluent in German first suggested that the symbols were based in superstition.

Many of the earliest barn stars were six-pointed figes, or "sechserei," from the German word for six, chs. The term may have been misinterpreted as "hexei," *hex* being the German word for witch. In his 1924 ook, *Pennsylvania Beautiful,* American antiquarian 'allace Nutting (1861–1941) dubbed the decorations exafoos," a Pennsylvania Dutch word that translates "witch foot." □□

A star with six points *(top)* is said to symbolize good luck, while 12-pointed ones *(above)* can refer to the 12 months, 12 Apostles, or justice. Eight-pointed stars *(below)* indicate perseverance.

–photos: Kutztown Pennsylvania German Festival

Deb Martin enjoys spotting brightly colored barn stars and lucky hex signs as she travels the back roads near her home in southeastern Pennsylvania.

When these pets passed on, their owners could r

SECOND CO

Animals have long been believed to exist in a spirit world. Egyptian
mummified cats to accompany their human masters into their exis
tence in the afterlife. In 15th- through 17th-century Europe, feline
were believed to be witches. In the United Kingdom, the appearanc
of a shadowy, caninelike creature with glowing eyes—called a "blac
dog"—historically has been believed to foreshadow doom. Its counterpar
in South Africa, the wolhaarhond, is a shaggy beast whose entire body i
surrounded by crimson light.

Since 1811, witnesses to the spectral battle between two armies tha
occasionally occurs in the sky at sunset at Chimney Rock, North Carolina
have claimed to hear the snorts and cries of hundreds of horses ridden i:
the charge. In 1819, Washington Irving popularized the idea of the head
less horseman with his legendary short story; for some Native Americans
such apparitions have not been uncommon sights.

According to Joshua P. Warren, author of *Pet Ghosts: Anime
Encounters From Beyond the Grave* (New Page Books, 2006), these an
other animal ghosts point to the possibility of "phantimals" (phantom an
imals), paranormal creatures that appear more animal-like than humar
like, and chance encounters with them. With thanks to Mr. Warren, w
present some testimony from pet owners who have had this experience–
and offer tips for having your own encounter.

st in peace—until the animals came back.

NGS

ON LITTLE CAT FEET

Cynthia, a widow who had a deep belief in the spiritual and the afterlife, lived in Tennessee with Maximilian and Carlota, her Manx cats. The felines had been emotional pillars for Cynthia after her husband's death. When the cats died, Cynthia was devastated. To relieve her depression, she meditated on the essence of her pets and invited their spirits to return. They did! Initially, Cynthia would hear her deceased pets meowing or padding about the house. Max was the first to appear in

> ### That night was stormy, "perfect for a visitation. . . .
> ### Carly glowed slightly, a greenish-blue."

apparition. He was a shadowy form visible in the living room for a few seconds on a summer evening. Two months later, Carlota manifested. That night was stormy, "perfect for a visitation," Cynthia recalled. "Carly glowed slightly, a greenish-blue." Cynthia was most struck by how similar the animals looked to their living state (despite the aura about Carlota). "They looked," she said, "shockingly normal."

BACK FROM THE GRAVE

Nick and Dana Redfern lived with their shar-pei Charity in Texas. Shortly before the couple planned to move, Charity became ill and died, and the distraught couple buried the dog. As they departed the grave site, under a hard rain, Dana, a firm believer in life after death, called out, "Come with us, Charity! Don't stay here where it's cold and wet. Follow us home!" Nick echoed the sentiment. Later, at home, Nick detected an overpowering odor of wet dog in the garage.

In the ensuing days, the aroma recurred at different places in the house. The couple also noticed that as often as they vacuumed the living room carpet smooth, the impression of a shar-pei formed on it where Charity used to lie.

Other events followed. At least three times, Dana heard claws clicking on the floor tiles, echoing Charity's patter. Nick dreamed that Charity appeared with Susie, a deceased cairn terrier that he had owned years before. Right before that encounter, Nick had the impression of a doorbell or knock on the door sig-

nifying their entrance.

On moving day, Dana paused to reflect—and Charity came to mind. She mentally invited the beloved canine to come along. Suddenly, she realized that one of the dog's hairs was stuck to her shoe. Beside it, as a slogan on the shoe, were the words "Get a Move On." She took this to be a message from Charity.

Nick, too, had a farewell encounter. While doing a last check of a shelf, he spied a negative of a photo of Charity. "It was her way of getting the message across: 'I'm not being left behind—I'm coming with you,'" he said.

THE FEATHERED FRIEND

Gerald lived in New Mexico and longed for companionship. He found it in the form of a very vocal African Grey parrot named Snappy. Within a few months, said Gerald, "he was my best friend."

Then Gerald met Pamela. A sweeping romance grew, and Gerald started to neglect Snappy. Once, when he left Snappy with a friend while he vacationed with Pamela, Snappy, apparently inconsolable, began pulling out his feathers.

When the couple returned, they were engaged. Gerald was ecstatic—until he saw Snappy. No words or amount of physical contact could bring back the bird's spunky personality. Pamela, too, was distraught—or so it seemed.

One weekend when Gerald was away, Pamela indulged the bird with chocolate. "Snappy happy," he'd say after devouring a chunk. To maintain that mood, she fed

him more—perhaps too much. The next day, Snappy was dead.

The bird's death deeply moved Gerald. He purchased a mahogany casket and buried Snappy in the backyard.

A week later, Gerald heard the bird's familiar high-pitched voice: "Gerald and Pam." Soon after, Pamela heard the words, too. The couple took the message as good wishes and, together, spoke out loud to Snappy's spirit. Pamela asked for forgiveness and Gerald, through tears, apologized.

The couple continued hearing their names. "[It] seemed like he was conscious, maybe watching us," said Gerald.

A few days later, Gerald heard Snappy say ". . . ick and Pam." That night, he heard

the words fully formed: "Rick and Pam." Gerald woke Pamela to tell her. Hours later, the truth was revealed. Pamela had been seeing an old boyfriend named Rick. Snappy had changed Gerald's life and saved him from personal anguish—a classic theme of ghostly activity.

GHOST-HUNTING GEAR

These items may come in handy if you seek an otherworldly encounter:

■ Camera, with a variable shutter speed.

■ Compass. An electromagnetically charged apparition will cause the needle to spin or swing from true north.

■ Thermometer. Cold spots are often reported when a phantimal is about to appear.

■ Audio recorder. An electronic voice phenomenon (EVP) can usually be heard only in playback, not "live" during recording.

■ Dehumidifier. Apparitions manifest better in dry, or electrostatic, air.

■ Mirrors set so as to reflect into each other create an "infinite tunnel of images" effect.

GHOST BUSTERS, BEWARE: The existence of ghosts can not be proven (at least as far as we know). It is possible to prove only that physical phenomena occur in conjunction with the appearance or sensing of phantoms.

CHARACTERISTICS OF CLOSE ENCOUNTERS

■ Pet ghosts usually manifest only if they have a strong emotional connection to the human owner and/or to other pets.

■ If you desire a spirit to stay, vocalize that wish and reinforce it on a daily basis. If the spirit is ignored, it fades away.

■ Spectral visitors frequently mark their entrances with a traditional knock.

■ The majority of experiences happen within days or weeks of the death.

Reprinted, with permission of the publisher, from *Pet Ghosts*, © 2006 by Joshua P. Warren. Published by New Page Books, a division of Career Press, Franklin Lakes, New Jersey. 800-227-3371. All rights reserved.

TRUSTED FRIENDS FROM THE FARM.

BAG BALM® *Ointment*

A trusted friend for more than 100 years, Bag Balm is proven to help heal cuts, scrapes, chapping, galls, and hobble burns. A great sweat. At tack shops, farm, drug, and hardware stores.

If unavailable, order direct: 10 oz. can $7.99; 1 oz. can $5.50.

GREEN MOUNTAIN® *Hoof Softener*

For softening hardened, dry, pinched, or contracted hoofs and quarter cracks. At tack shops, farm, and hardware stores.

If unavailable, order direct: 10 oz. can $6.30;
28 oz. can $8.70; $6.45 non-freeze liquid pint.

TACKMASTER®

Leather cleaner, conditioner, preservative. Penetrates leather thoroughly, helps restore original life with natural oils.

If unavailable, order direct: Gallon $17.50; quart $7.80;
pint $5.00; 4 oz. $3.00.

Add $3.50 handling for your order. Prices subject to change without notice. To order, send check or money order to (no credit cards please):

DAIRY ASSOCIATION CO., INC.

P.O. BOX 145, DEPT. OFA08, LYNDONVILLE, VT 05851/TEL. 802-626-3610/WWW.BAGBALM.COM
WEST OF ROCKIES: SMITH SALES SERVICE, 16372 S. W. 72ND ST., PORTLAND, OR 97223

TOUGH ON UNRULY PROPERTY.
EASY ON YOU!

It's easy to pick up the pace with the all-new Self-Propelled DR® TRIMMER/MOWER.

All Models Feature...

- **POWERFUL ENGINES**, for TRIMMING and MOWING tough vegetation that would quickly clog and stall any hand-held trimmer.
- **DURABLE CUTTING CORDS** that hold up against fences, rocks, foundations, etc.
- **INSTANT-ADJUSTMENT** cutting height. No tools required.
- **LIFETIME-WARRANTY** on the lightweight aluminum mainframe. Plus, you can try any model for 6 months — RISK-FREE!
- **PLUS** the new Self-Propelled model has POWERED WHEELS — so it's even tougher on unruly property and easier on you!

FREE DVD! SEE IT IN ACTION!

Call TOLL-FREE:
1-800-731-0493
www.DRtrimmers.com

☑ **YES!** Please rush me a FREE DVD & Catalog...

...with full details of the New Self-Propelled DR® TRIMMER/MOWER and other models, low, factory-direct prices, and seasonal savings now in effect.

Name _____

Address _____ OFA

City _____ State _____ Zip _____

E-mail _____

DR® POWER EQUIPMENT, Dept. 58635X
127 Meigs Road, Vergennes, VT 05491

© 2007 CHP, Inc.

And the Winner Is . . .

Contests where talent is QUIRKY, fame is FLEETING, and awards are (mostly) INCIDENTAL.

We all dream about testing our mettle in a competition requiring skill, physical prowess, or quick wit and fantasize about winning something—but where and how? In honor of the 80th anniversary of the Bunion Derby (right), we searched for some of the more obscure contests held in North America. Here is a sampling of what we found, with tips and advice to give you a leg up on the competition—or at least save you from complete embarrassment.

International Rotten Sneaker Contest

WHEN: March 19, 2008

WHERE: Montpelier, Vermont

WHAT HAPPENS: Sneakers' soles, tongues, heels, toes, laces or Velcro, eyelets/grommets, and—most important—odors are evaluated for overall

by Rachel Dickinson

condition. Open to kids ages 5 to 15. Winners of regional contests compete for the national title in Vermont.

INSIDER TIP: There's no such thing as "too" rotten in this contest.

(c o n t i n u e d)

George Aldrich has judged the Rotten Sneaker Contest for years. He says that winning entries make his eyes water and his nose burn.

Bunions Across America

Wacky endurance tests were all the rage 80 years ago. People walked, talked, ran, danced, drank, ate, and even kissed in marathon competitions. One of the most famous events of the time was the Bunion Derby, the first (and last) transcontinental running race between Los Angeles and New York City, which was so called for obvious reasons.

Charles C. Pyle, the country's first sports agent, organized the grueling 3,422-mile footrace. The event's three-week training period drew 275 runners from around the world. At the sound of the starter's pistol at 3:46 P.M. on March 4, 1928, only 199 of those who had entered set off from Ascot Speedway in Los Angeles. The race was run in "laps," which meant that the runners covered a set distance every day. Forty miles per day was the average, although the shortest one-day distance was 17 miles and the longest was 74.6—and that on the next-to-last day. The runners slept in tents at night, and a cook who accompanied them provided breakfast, lunch, and dinner.

By the end of the first day, 77 runners had dropped out. Only 80 runners departed Oklahoma. By Chicago, only 65 remained. Finally, on May 26, 1928, 55 runners made the final lap into New York City. The winner, by over 15 hours, was Andy Payne, a 20-year-old Cherokee farm boy from Oklahoma. His official time was 573 hours, 4 minutes, and 34 seconds over 83 consecutive days. Payne took his $25,000 in first prize money and paid off the mortgage on the family farm.

–Oklahoma Historical Society

Left: *The eventual winner of the Bunion Derby, Andy Payne from Oklahoma*

Rotten Sneaker Contest entrants Katharine Tuck (right), 2007 winner, and McKenna Dinkel (below), the winner in 2006.

−photos: Odor-Eaters

−Walter Protzman/O. Henry Museum, Austin, Tex.

Emcee Gary Hallock (above) awards the Punniest of Show trophy to Erik Ott at the 2006 Pun-Off World Championships.

SECRET OF SUCCESS: When 7-year-old McKenna Dinkel won in 2006, she explained her strategy: "I live on a farm in Alaska, and I wore my sneakers with no socks all around the farm to make them torn up and smelly."

JUDGE'S ADVICE: George Aldrich, an odor sniffer from NASA who smells everything that goes into space, has judged the Rotten Sneaker Contest for years. Winning entries make his eyes water, his nose burn, and his head "kind of kick back." His advice to kids: "Wear sneakers with no socks or wear sneakers with the same unwashed stinky pair of socks for many months." His advice to the parents of the kids going for the top prize: "Double- or triple-bag the shoes."

PRIZES: a $2,500 U.S. Savings Bond, $100 for a new pair of sneakers, a trophy, and, last but not least, a year's supply of Odor-Eaters.

O. Henry Pun-Off World Championships

WHEN: May 17, 2008

WHERE: Austin, Texas

WHAT HAPPENS: Wordsmiths match wits in two categories of competition. In a 90-second freestyle event using prepared material, punsters battle for the title of Punniest of Show. In the High-Lies & Low-Puns portion, they twist words on a given topic in strictly timed sessions. This annual event is sponsored by the O. Henry Museum, the City of Austin, and P.U.N.Y. (Punsters Unite Nearly Yearly).

INSIDER TIP: Overcome stage fright, says Gary Hallock, master punster and founder of P.U.N.Y. "Sometimes, even the most chronic punsters are not used to entertaining big groups, and not only does this event draw a large crowd, but it's a savvy crowd, too."

SECRET OF SUCCESS: In the High-Lies & Low-Puns competition, it's all about speed, quantity, and a limber lexicon. "The best strategy for prevailing is to personalize your barb to throw your oppo-

–Kelly Quinn

–Hal Miller

Singer Steve Brooks warms up the crowd at the 2006 Pun-Off World Championships.

Casey Hodge (above left) *and Lauri Waller* (above right) *compete in the 2006 Rotary Tiller Race in Emerson, Arkansas.*

nent off his or her game," says Hallock, a former winner who has been the emcee for the Pun-Off for the past 17 years. "Twisting your wordplay into a rhetorical question or insult is a common ploy."

JUDGE'S ADVICE: Although it's said that there's no such thing as a new pun, you *can* give an old pun a new shape. Hallock says that even a "tired old shaggy dog punch line can be artfully reworked and rate well with the judges." As in most contests, the judges are inevitably influenced by costumes, props, or musical elements.

PRIZES: Varies. Sometimes medals are awarded. A trophy of a horse's behind has been given, but usually the glory of winning is enough.

World Championship Rotary Tiller Race

WHEN: June 28, 2008

WHERE: Emerson, Arkansas

WHAT HAPPENS: Contestants run behind their tiller (they don't ride it) to see who can till 200 feet of plowed ground the fastest. The tiller must have tines or blades, and an engine no bigger than 100 hp. Contestants must wear shoes. (Yes, this really is a rule.) There are men's, women's, and kids' divisions.

INSIDER TIP: "Just hope that you don't come up against the Waller family, who are like the Andretti family of tiller racing," says Bill Davey, one of the organizers.

SECRET OF SUCCESS: The fastest tillers are made from scratch, using a motorcycle engine and special tines for dry ground or mud (depending on the weather), according to Davey.

JUDGE'S ADVICE: Don't be a rule breaker. Only complete compliance gets you on the course. After the first race in 1990, when someone showed up with a souped-up engine, the organizers developed a set of guidelines that included a special division for modified tillers.

PRIZE: The first-prize winner in the men's division receives $500. Monetary prizes are awarded in other divisions as well.

(continued)

A contestant at the Watermelon Seed Spit (above) *gives it his all. Claudia Cooley* (right) *struts her stuff at the Chicken Clucking Contest.*

World Championship Watermelon Seed Spit

WHEN: June 28, 2008

WHERE: Watermelon Thump Festival, Luling, Texas

WHAT HAPPENS: The names of 20 would-be spitters are drawn from a hat, and then they line up one-by-one on the "spit way" to try to break the 1989 Luling record, which is the former *Guinness Book* world-record seed-spit of 68 feet, 9⅛ inches. "We cut up a fresh 'Black Diamond' watermelon and offer contestants the seeds," says Susan Ward, from the Luling Chamber of Commerce. Spitters get two chances to spit their seed the farthest. There are adults' and kids' divisions.

INSIDER TIP: "Each winner has their own method: Some take water or a bit of watermelon in their mouth with the seed, while others just spit," says Ward.

SECRET OF SUCCESS: Practice at home before coming to the competition.

JUDGE'S ADVICE: Don't worry about looking like a fool. Relax and enjoy yourself, but keep these tips in mind: Try to spit upward, not at the ground. Lean into the spit, wet your lips, and blow hard.

PRIZES: In the adult division, first prize is a trophy of a diver ("looks like the stance of a seed spitter," says Ward) and $500; $150 is awarded for second prize, and $100 for third. If the first-place spitter breaks the Luling record, he or she receives an additional $500.

Chicken Clucking and Rooster Calling Contest

WHEN: August 23, 2008

WHERE: Dutchess County Fair, Rhinebeck, New York

WHAT HAPPENS: Anyone who is brave enough gets on stage and clucks like a chicken and crows like a rooster.

INSIDER TIP: The 2005 chicken clucking winner, Brian Connell, says that he spent a lot of time in the barn studying and trying to imitate his chickens. "The rooster crow is a lot harder," he says, "and is a lot easier to make yourself look like a fool with."

(c o n t i n u e d)

SECRET OF SUCCESS: Don't be afraid to make a fool of yourself.

JUDGE'S ADVICE: The winner is chosen by the audience, so scratching like a chicken and flapping your arms goes a long way with the crowd.

PRIZE: $25 for first place.

International World Rock Paper Scissors (RPS) Championships

WHEN: mid-October

WHERE: Toronto, Ontario

WHAT HAPPENS: Think of the childhood pastime one, two, three, shoot! Rock beats scissors, scissors beats paper, and paper beats rock. The World RPS Society has taken the game to a new height, one that involves skill, some thought, and a whole lot of luck. The world championships also involve personas and costumes.

INSIDER TIP: When in doubt, throw paper because, according to the World RPS Society, statistically it's thrown the least number of times in competition.

SECRET OF SUCCESS: While you may think that the challenge of the game is trying to figure out what your opponent will throw, Bob "The Rock" Cooper, the 2006 world RPS champion, claims that "it's not about predicting what your opponent will throw; it's about predicting what your opponent predicts that you will throw."

JUDGE'S ADVICE: "There are subtle ways through which you can manipulate an

Top: *Referees monitor a round at the championship RPS games.* **Above:** *Champion Bob Cooper displays his winning "check."*

opponent. The art is to not let him or her know that you're eliminating one of their options or to force them into making a predictable move," says Graham Walker of the World RPS Society.

PRIZE: A total of $10,000 is awarded to the first-, second-, and third-prize winners.

Try One Yourself

If you think you have what it takes to compete in one of these contests, just Google the organization and go to its Web site for rules and entry guidelines. □□

Rachel Dickinson writes about nature, science, travel, and all things quirky from her home in upstate New York. She is the author of three nonfiction books for children, as well as *Falconer on the Edge* (Houghton Mifflin, 2008) for adults.

WHO'S FOOLING WHOM?
Can you tell a good story that's not true? Learn all about the Big Whopper Liar's Contest—when, where, and how to win—at **Almanac.com/extras.**

Soothe your stomach ... with peppermint!

Regulate your digestion ... with honey!

"Foods that 'EXPLODE' in Your Bowel!"

Plain Answers about IBS, Constipation, Diarrhea, Heartburn, Ulcers, and More!

(By Frank K. Wood)

If you suffer from bloating, cramping, chronic constipation/diarrhea, or symptoms of irritable bowel syndrome (IBS), you need *The Complete Guide to Digestive Health*. Learn about important new research that identifies which foods are your allies and which foods are your enemies, and find out which tasty beverage you should sip to soothe an irritable bowel, PLUS ...

▶ Make these simple changes and be rid of gas!

▶ Belching and bloating — they could be warning signs of up to 7 hidden health problems.

▶ Constipation? Discover a natural cure that's better than fiber!

▶ Lower blood pressure ... fewer ulcers ... less colitis ... just some of the benefits of letting yourself do this.

▶ 12 ways to ease stress and calm digestion.

▶ Does your digestive system benefit more from savory breads and cereals or from scrumptious fruits and vegetables? The answer may surprise you!

▶ Vitamins and minerals may keep you from getting colon cancer, even if this awful killer runs in your family.

▶ Drop pounds and ditch heartburn with these good fats.

▶ Heal your body, improve digestion, moisturize skin, help control weight, and it's free!

▶ Like red meat? You can still lower cancer risks by adding this to your plate.

▶ Chew this at every meal for a happy, healthy colon.

▶ How to prevent the embarrassment of a leaky bladder.

▶ Serve safe spuds ... foil wrapped potato can spell danger!

▶ These herbs may actually be better at relieving gas than some commercial products. Find out what they are.

▶ Learn about the secret "sponge" in your digestive tract that absorbs water and prevents constipation.

▶ Lower cancer risk and reduce polyps ... bone up on this mineral for healthy intestines.

Learn all these amazing secrets and more. To order a copy, just return this notice with your name and address and a check for $9.99 plus $3.00 shipping and handling to: **FC&A, Dept. IOF08B**, 103 Clover Green, Peachtree City, GA 30269. We will send you a copy of *The Complete Guide to Digestive Health.*

You get a no-time-limit guarantee of satisfaction or your money back.

You must cut out and return this notice with your order. Copies will not be accepted!

IMPORTANT — FREE GIFT OFFER EXPIRES IN 30 DAYS

All orders mailed within 30 days will receive a free gift, *Get Well and Stay Well*, **guaranteed**. Order right away!

©FC&A 2007

Winners in the 2007 Peanut Butter Recipe Contest

FIRST PRIZE

THAI CHICKEN WITH LINGUINI

1 pound chicken breasts, cut into 1-inch pieces
1 tablespoon olive oil
1 cup chicken broth
2 tablespoons honey
1 tablespoon soy sauce
1/4 cup crunchy peanut butter
1 teaspoon cornstarch
1 teaspoon ground ginger
4 green onions, sliced
2 cloves garlic, minced
1 red pepper, cut into strips

In a saucepan, sauté the chicken in the olive oil. Remove the chicken from the pan and keep warm. Add the broth, honey, and soy sauce to the pan. Whisk in the peanut butter, cornstarch, and ginger. Add the green onions and garlic, stirring constantly over low heat until blended. Add the red pepper and cooked chicken. Cook until the sauce has thickened. Serve over warm linguini. **Makes 4 to 6 servings.**

–Phyllis Klassen, Keremeos, British Columbia

SECOND PRIZE

PEANUT BUTTER SHEET CAKE

CAKE:
2 cups flour
1 teaspoon baking soda
2 cups sugar
1/2 teaspoon salt
1/2 cup vegetable oil
3/4 cup margarine
1/2 cup crunchy peanut butter
2 eggs, beaten
1 teaspoon vanilla extract
1/2 cup buttermilk

ICING:
1/2 cup evaporated milk
1 cup sugar
1 tablespoon margarine
1/2 cup crunchy peanut butter
1/2 cup miniature marshmallows
1 teaspoon vanilla extract

For the cake: Preheat the oven to 350°F. In a large bowl, mix the flour, baking soda, sugar, and salt; set aside. In a saucepan, bring the oil, margarine, peanut butter, and 1 cup of water almost to a boil (do not boil). Pour over the dry ingredients and mix well. Add the eggs, vanilla, and buttermilk. Mix well. Pour the batter into a greased and floured 15x11x1-inch pan. Bake for 15 to 18 minutes, or until a toothpick inserted into the center comes out clean.

For the icing: Combine the evaporated milk, sugar, and margarine in a saucepan. Bring to a boil and cook for 2 minutes. Remove from the heat and add the peanut butter and marshmallows, stirring until melted. Stir in the vanilla. Pour the icing over the warm cake and spread to cover. **Makes about 30 servings.**

–Martha Sparkman, Poplar Bluff, Missouri

(continued)

Have Your Best Garden Ever with the Mantis Tiller!

One-Year No-Risk Trial!

AS SEEN ON
TV

"I have to tell you, this baby works great! I have clay soil and it works just like in the video!"

G. M. - Kentucky

It cut through the grassy sod areas around the garden like a hot knife through butter. Keep up the good work! Thank you."
K. K. - Missouri

These are just some of the many yard and garden jobs the Mantis Tiller will do for you:

✓ Break ground for new garden plots

✓ Cultivate and weed around plants and between rows in existing gardens

✓ Dig holes to plant new trees or shrubs

✓ Till soil in raised beds and other small-space gardens

✓ Turn and mix debris in compost piles

Call TODAY for MORE INFORMATION and FREE DVD
1-800-366-6268 or visit: www.mantis.com
See our special offers NOW in effect!

©2007 Mantis Div. of Schiller-Pfeiffer, Inc.   DEPT MT9021

Thai-Spiced Peanut Chicken Salad Tea Sandwiches

3 cups minced, cooked chicken breast
1 cup creamy peanut butter
2 tablespoons coconut milk
2 teaspoons sugar
2 tablespoons fresh lime juice
2 teaspoons soy sauce
1/4 teaspoon chili powder
1 teaspoon minced jalapeño pepper
1/4 cup minced onion
1/4 cup finely minced cilantro
1/4 cup finely minced fresh mint leaves
1/4 cup finely minced shallot
1/4 cup thinly sliced green onion
1/2 cup finely chopped peanuts
24 thin slices firm white sandwich bread,
    crusts removed

In a large mixing bowl, combine all of the ingredients, except the bread. Divide the filling equally to make 12 sandwiches. Cut each in half diagonally and serve. **Makes 24 sandwiches.**

–Shannon Abdollmohammadi, Woodinville, Washington

Curry Chicken Peanut Soup
To save time, use canned broth and cooked chicken, cooking only until the vegetables are tender.

2 chicken breasts or 4 thighs, cut into small
    chunks

1 large can (28 oz.) diced tomatoes
2 stalks celery, chopped fine
1 large onion, chopped fine
1/2 cup diced carrots
1/2 cup cut green beans (optional)
1/2 cup loose, fresh basil leaves (or 2 to 3
    tablespoons dried)
1 cup smooth peanut butter
1 to 2 tablespoons curry powder

Put the chicken, tomatoes, celery, onion, carrots, green beans (if using), and basil into a stockpot and add 8 cups of water. Bring to a boil, cover, and simmer until the chicken is cooked through and the vegetables are tender—about 30 to 45 minutes. Put 1 cup of the broth into a bowl, and add the peanut butter a little at a time, stirring to blend. Spoon the mixture into the stockpot, stirring to prevent clumping. If the soup is too thick, add more water; if too thin, make more peanut butter mixture (using the thickened broth) and continue to add until the soup is thick enough. Add curry powder, to taste. **Makes 8 servings.**

–S. J. Wolfe, Worcester, Massachusetts

For more peanut butter recipes—both sweet and savory—go to **Almanac.com/food**.

RECIPE AND ESSAY CONTEST RULES

Cash prizes (first, $100; second, $75; third, $50) will be awarded for the best ethnic food recipe and for the best original essay on the subject "My Worst Cooking Disaster." All entries become the property of Yankee Publishing, which reserves all rights to the material. The deadline for entries is Friday, January 25, 2008. Label "Recipe Contest" or "Essay Contest" and send to The Old Farmer's Almanac, P.O. Box 520, Dublin, NH 03444; recipecontest@yankeepub.com; or essaycontest@yankeepub.com. Include your name, mailing address, and e-mail address. Winners will be announced in *The 2009 Old Farmer's Almanac* and on **Almanac.com**.

Hydrogen Peroxide Can Heal What?

Medical science has discovered that hydrogen peroxide is more than just a disinfectant, it's an amazing healer. Many doctors are using hydrogen peroxide to treat a wide variety of serious ailments such as: **heart problems, clogged arteries, chest pain, allergies, asthma, migraine headaches, vascular headaches, cluster headaches, yeast infections, type II diabetes, emphysema, chronic pain syndromes, and more.**

Average consumers are also discovering that hydrogen peroxide has tons of health, beauty and household uses. A new handbook called *"The Amazing Health and Household Uses of Hydrogen Peroxide"* is now available to the general public. It shows you home remedies using diluted hydrogen peroxide and how to mix it with ordinary household items like baking soda, lemon, vinegar and salt to help:

- Soothe ARTHRITIS PAIN
- Make SORE THROATS feel better
- Ease the pain of BEE STINGS and INSECT BITES
- Treat ATHLETE'S FOOT
- Ease the PAIN OF RHEUMATISM
- Clear up FUNGUS and MINOR INFECTIONS
- Help treat minor BURNS
- Treat BRUISES and RASHES
- Soothe ACHING MUSCLES, JOINTS & SORE FEET

Hydrogen peroxide is truly amazing. Scientists have found it is involved in virtually all of life's vital processes. It stimulates the immune system, helps your body fight off viruses, parasites and bacteria. It also regulates hormones and is involved in the production of energy in the body's cells. That's just a few of the amazing things it does.

It's also a great alternative to harsh toxic chemicals and cleaners around the house. *"The Amazing Health and Household Uses of Hydrogen Peroxide"* also shows you how to make easy peroxide recipes for:

- **A powerful bleaching formula for formica**
- **A fantastic homemade scouring powder**
- **The perfect drain cleaner for clogged drains**
- **A dishwasher detergent that makes dishes gleam**
- **An oven cleaner that eliminates elbow grease**
- **A great rust remover formula**
- **A tile cleaner that works like magic**
- **A little known formula that really cleans old porous tubs**
- **A solution to help house and garden plants flourish**
- **Use this formula to clean your pets**
- **This spray keeps a leftover salad fresher**
- **Ever wonder what happens to meats and fish before you bring them home? Here's a safety-wash for meat and fish**
- **A spray that's great for sprouting seeds**
- **Here's a sanitizing vegetable soak**
- **A denture soak that works great**
- **A tooth whitener that makes teeth sparkle**
- **A super polish for copper and brass**
- **A spot lifter for coffee, tea and wine stains**

You'll learn all this and more in this remarkable book. In addition, you also get an extensive list of qualified doctors across the United States and even some in Canada who regularly use hydrogen peroxide in their practices to treat serious ailments.

Right now you can receive a special press run of *"The Amazing Health and Household Uses of Hydrogen Peroxide"* for only $8.95 plus $2.00 postage and handling. You must be completely satisfied, or simply return it in 90 days for a <u>full refund</u>.

HERE'S HOW TO ORDER: Simply PRINT your name and address and the words "Hydrogen Peroxide" on a piece of paper and mail it along with a check or money order for only $10.95 to: THE LEADER CO., INC., Publishing Division, Dept. HPT519, P.O. Box 8347, Canton, OH 44711. VISA, MasterCard, send card number and expiration date. Act now. Orders are fulfilled on a first come, first served basis. © 2007 The Leader Co., Inc.

Winners in the 2007 Essay Contest

The Best Thing I Ever Bought at a Yard Sale

FIRST PRIZE

At a yard sale one fall afternoon, I purchased a sealed box of books for $5. Nestled among the hardbound fiction was an old diary. I read a few pages of captivating entries before looking for the owner's name on the inside cover. It was written by my grandmother! I was certain it was her, not only because she and my grandfather had unique names but also because she had written of the birth of my mother in 1925. The entries ended soon after that event, presumably because caring for an infant left little time for writing.

My grandmother is no longer living. That day, years after her death, serendipity brought me closer to her. I now know her as I hadn't before—as a young woman. How my grandmother's diary came to be in a box of old books, 2,200 miles away from where she had lived her entire life, is an enigma I marvel at daily.

–Boo Heisey, Janesville, California

SECOND PRIZE

One day I was walking home from work and noticed a tag sale at a two-story house. Upon entering, I was informed that I should feel free to sashay about the home. Each room brought a new discovery, but it was in the upstairs bedroom closet that I spotted a classic men's black wool tuxedo, complete with ties and vests, for the outrageous price of $1. I could not believe my eyes! Everything about this tux was perfect. It was even my size, 40 short. I purchased the tux and was told by the seller that it had been her father's and would be a great costume in a play. Little did she know that I would wear it on board the *Queen Elizabeth II* during a transatlantic crossing.

Later, while I was dining aboard the ocean liner, the lady sitting next to me said, "You have a beautiful tuxedo. That must have been very expensive." I responded with a twinkle in my eye: "When you are on board the QE2, what is money?"

–Charles L. Repnow, Rugby, North Dakota

THIRD PRIZE

When my five daughters were growing up, we lived on a tight budget. I usually paid up to $1.50 for secondhand clothing, but that was the limit. One day, something at a small yard sale caught my eye. On the makeshift clothesline hung the most beautiful hand-crocheted dress. It was light beige, ankle length, in excellent condition, and screamed my daughter Jessica's name. The tag said $5, but I didn't think twice as I fished into my purse to pay the lady.

Just as I thought, Jessica fell in love

It will stay in your family for centuries; it will be accurate for quite a bit longer.

The Atomic Watch from E. Howard & Co. By the time your great grandson gets it, it'll still be almost 6 million years away from losing one second.

Never set your watch again. The reason this watch is so accurate is because it gets its signal from the official U.S. Atomic Clock in Fort Collins, Colorado. The standard for time keeping throughout the U.S., the Atomic Clock uses sophisticated technology to measure the vibration of atoms, which is constant. For this reason, it is accurate to within a billionth of a second, and will take approximately 6 million years to lose a second! Until now, watches designed to receive the radio signal had to have plastic cases. Now, "America's Timekeeper" has created a high-quality analog watch in stainless steel style. The watch is designed so that it can still receive the signal– so you get traditional elegant styling with modern time keeping accuracy. Once you've selected the proper time zone, you never have to touch it again. It automatically adjusts for Daylight Savings Time, 30-day months, and leap years. It comes with the E. Howard name and a certificate of authenticity.

Designed for a lifetime of accuracy. This finely crafted watch blends past and future with an elegant, easy-to-read analog display and a handy digital readout, showing Day and Month, Seconds, or U.S. Time Zone at the touch of a button. This good-looking watch is also tough, with a scratch-resistant crystal and polished stainless steel case that's water resistant.

Try it now with our exclusive home trial. No one has sold more Atomic Watches than we have, and this is the one that meets our high standards for looks and   performance. We are so sure that you will like it too that we are offering it with our exclusive 90-day home trial. If you are not completely satisfied with the watch for any reason, simply return it within 90 days for a refund of the purchase price, and keep the atomic alarm clock as our gift.

E. Howard Continental Atomic Watch
Item # ZR-23041STS **$99.95**
FREE Radio Controlled Atomic Alarm Clock a $14.95 value.

FREE shipping a $9.95 value.
Free shipping within the contiguous 48 states only.

Please mention promotional code 33399.

For fastest service, call toll-free 24 hours a day
800-844-4216
To order by mail, please call for details
www.AtomicTimeDirect.com

1998 Ruffin Mill Road Colonial Heights, VA 23834

41432

All rights reserved. © 2007 TechnoBrands®, Inc.

---

*Call now and order the E. Howard Watch - get this Radio Controlled Atomic Alarm Clock valued at $14.95 absolutely FREE as our gift to you.   **FREE GIFT**
• Atomic radio-controlled time
• Automatically sets time and date
  • Time alarm with snooze
• Backlight for easy viewing

with the dress. As she slipped into its "laciness," she smiled from ear to ear—and that was worth so much more than five dollars.

Two weeks later, Jessica wore the dress one last time, never to remove it again. It had become her burial dress, hers forever, just as I thought it would be.

–Patricia Jones, Nevada, Missouri

HONORABLE MENTION

Over the course of some 60 years, I have visited more than a few garage sales. The one thing I have learned is that often it's not so much what folks want to sell as what they have to tell.

It was a crisp fall morning in 1976. Inside an old barn, a table of tools, a box of camping gear, and then a Boy Scout compass caught my eye. Watching me with my young son, the owner began to reminisce about his son Jack and how he grew into a man. He let it all out, reaching for an answer as to why madness half a world away had taken such a precious life. I listened with my heart and held my young son's hand a little tighter. Relieved, the man nodded and smiled, and then handed me the compass. As I removed it from its case, a small note slipped out. It read, "Jack, when you know your direction, you'll never be lost. Dad."

The compass was returned and no words were spoken. A forgotten note returned, or direction from Jack?

–Don Dostal, Carrollton, Ohio

Thanks to all who participated in the essay contest. We received many stories about great yard sale finds. Here are a few more, in brief:

■ On my boyfriend's birthday, I bought an old cigarette lighter for his collection, priced at $2. Later, I realized that it was a Zippo (his favorite), made of sterling silver, and engraved "MEH"—my initials!

■ My sister and I loved yard sales, but after her death I lost interest. One day, my daughter persuaded me to go to a few. At the first sale, she bought a straw doll. Later, she asked me about the word that was stitched into the doll's skirt. It was "Cynthia"—my sister's name.

■ I noticed a baseball, yellow with age, in a plastic container. Looking closely, I saw signatures on the ball, so I paid the seller his asking price—$5. Later, I took it to a baseball card shop, where it was determined that the ball had been autographed by the 1981 World Series Dodgers and was worth about $250.

■ An unusual cast-iron tool—elaborately decorated, stamped with its origin, and marked $25—caught my eye. It was a cigar cutter and it sang to me, so I bought it. Later, while researching my family's history, I learned that my great-grandfather had been a Cuban cigar maker. The cutter had put me in touch with my past.

■ In 1949, my parents bought an empty lot and had our old house moved onto it. Then my dad went to a garage sale—and bought the garage. Both house and garage are still in use.

ANNOUNCING THE 2008 ESSAY CONTEST TOPIC

My Worst Cooking Disaster

In 200 words or less, please tell us an amusing tale about a meal gone wrong or a kitchen calamity that you still stew about. See page 172 for contest rules.

How to Get LUCKY

Advice for anyone traversing that treacherous road to romance

There are about 90 million singles in the United States and some 14 million in Canada, but the search for a soul mate, a significant other, or a special someone isn't easy. If you find Internet dating, speed dating, and blind dating frustrating, we suggest these timeless folklorish practices. We make no guarantees that romance will come your way, but you might have more fun trying.

GALS:

- Place a peeled onion under your pillow on St. Thomas's Eve (Dec. 20, 2007; Dec. 21, 2008) and say, "Good St. Thomas do me right; bring my love to me this night."

- Throw a herring membrane (the small piece of fat from the underside of the fish's backbone) against a wall. If it adheres to it in an upright manner, the husband you get will also be so; if crooked, he will be crooked.

- Do not sit at the corner of a table, or you will never get a husband.

- On Midsummer Eve (June 23 in 2008), set out bread, cheese, and ale on a clean white tablecloth and leave the front door open. A lover (or just a hungry male) will appear.

e Old-Fashioned Way

GUYS:

For nine nights, make three notches in a gate that has five bars on it. You will see your sweetheart on the last night.

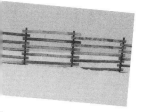

Avoid saying good night three times at the end of a date. It is unlucky.

GUYS AND GALS:

■ Do not write a love letter with red ink. It is unlucky.

■ Never court on a Friday, or you'll never meet again.

■ Throw an apple peel over your left shoulder. It will fall in the shape of the initial of your lover's name.

■ Do not wear mourning clothes when courting; you'll be doomed never to marry.

■ Meet in advance of a new Moon to be "noosed" together in matrimony.

■ Do not meet a loved one on a Sunday: Sunday's wooing draws to ruin.

■ Grasp seven cloves in your hand and think about a loved one. Then burn the cloves.

─────

Traditions relating to sitting at the corner of a table, Midsummer Eve, and cloves are adapted from *The Complete Book of Sex Magic* by Leonard R.N. Ashley (Barricade Books, 2003). All others are adapted from *A Dictionary of Superstitions,* edited by Iona Opie and Moira Tatem (Oxford University Press, 1990).

STILL LOOKING?

For hints on how to find true love on the Internet and not get caught in the Web, how to save time speed dating, and blind dating with your eyes open, plus 19 essential dos and don'ts, go to **Almanac.com/advice.**

THE WONDERS OF BLUNDERS

Proof that some errors are not mistakes—just happy accidents.

by Nick D'Alto

To avoid all mistakes in the conduct of great enterprises is beyond man's powers.

–Fabius Maximus, Roman politician
(c. 275 b.c.–203 b.c.)

Most people try to avoid making mistakes, yet psychologists say that learning from our mistakes can help us to lead happier lives. In fact, the history of innovation is filled with tales of goofs that turned into happy accidents, from penicillin (discovered when an experiment acquired bread mold) to Silly Putty (a failed attempt to invent artificial rubber) to the microwave oven (inspired when radar equipment melted a worker's chocolate bar), to name but a few.

Make no mistake about this: You can learn how to benefit from your blunders. So take note of these ten tips and timeless words of wisdom that can help us all to make successful errors.

1

When you don't get what you WANT, want what you GET.

■ In the 1930s, DuPont chemist Roy Plunkett was trying to develop a better

refrigerator. The chemical he created to be a coolant failed to perform as expected; it was too slippery. Rather than throw it out, Plunkett considered other uses. Today, we know this chemical as a nonstick coating: Teflon.

You must make your own blunders, must cheerfully accept your own mistakes as part of the scheme of things.

–Minnie Fiske, American actress
(1865–1932)

Turn a PROBLEM into a SOLUTION.

In the late 1960s, scientists at 3M Company developed a glue to paste pieces of paper together. The sheets stuck, but they came apart easily, making the glue worthless—or so it was thought until later, when an employee named Art Fry used the fickle adhesive to make bookmarks. With that, the Post-it was born.

To make mistakes as we are on the way to knowledge is far more honorable than to escape making them through never having set out to seek knowledge.

–R. C. Trench, Irish prelate (1807–86)

Remember that sometimes one WRONG can make two RIGHTS.

In 1856, while conducting experiments to find a cure for malaria, teenage lab assistant William Perkins found that one of his solutions dyed cloth. Fascinated by the failed antidote, he was inspired to sell it as a colorfast dye. This decision made him a rich man. (And years later, while using Perkins's dye to stain microscope slides, doctors did discover a malaria cure.)

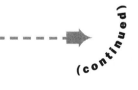

Mistakes are often the best teachers.

–James A. Froude, English historian (1818–94)

Follow your ERRORS where they LEAD you.

In 1492, Christopher Columbus set out in search of a sea route to the Far East, but instead came upon America. In 1935, while flying over the jungles of Venezuela in search of treasure below, bush pilot Jimmy Angel found the world's highest waterfall—a cataract known today as Angel Falls.

Mistakes are the portals to discovery.

–James Joyce, Irish writer (1882–1941)

(continued)

Keep an OPEN MIND.

5

■ Some of the world's leading firms pay their employees to conceive of products and services that don't—and won't—work. It's called brainstorming: setting no bounds on ideas and expectations as a way to stimulate thinking. Without the freedom of such a forum, the concepts of the bookseller without a bookstore (Amazon.com) and the warehouse as a store (Costco) might never have been developed.

Anyone who has never made a mistake has never tried anything new.

–Albert Einstein, American physicist (1879–1955)

Find the "FUN" in FUNCTIONALITY.

6

■ In 1934, while their boss was out, two DuPont chemists were horsing around, stretching strands of rubbery gum up and down the hallway. The more they pulled at the stuff, the stronger it became. Unbeknownst to them at the time, the stretching changed the material's molecular structure. Their play led to the invention of nylon.

Welcome the UNFORESEEN.

7

■ In 1953, a lab assistant at 3M Company spilled synthetic latex onto her canvas shoes. During attempts to clean off the shoes, Patsy Sherman, the chemist who had invented the synthetic latex, noticed that it repelled other liquids. This accident resulted in the fabric stain repellent known today as Scotchgard.

There is glory in a great mistake.

–Nathalia Crane, American poet (b. 1913)

If people didn't sometimes do silly things, nothing intelligent would ever get done.

–Ludwig Wittgenstein, Austrian philosopher (1889–1951)

Be FLEXIBLE.

8

■ In the 1850s, dry goods merchant Levi Strauss relocated from New York to California to sell tents to Gold Rush prospectors. When he arrived, he realized that the miners did not need tents but they could use durable trousers. Strauss's ability to adapt and turn the tent fabric into pants

USE what you KNOW.

9

In 1878, French chemist Hilaire Bernigaud de Chardonnet stumbled upon the secret for making artificial silk (rayon) when he spilled a beaker of chemicals on his lab table. Chardonnet noticed that the liquid dried into tiny fibers, like those in cloth. Only a highly trained eye would have spotted that detail—anyone else would have just overlooked an opportunity.

In the fields of observation, chance favors only the prepared mind.

–Louis Pasteur, French chemist (1822–95)

Keep TRYING.

10

"Everything's gone wrong," Thomas Edison's young lab assistant once remarked when momentarily despondent. "Not at all," replied the great inventor. "We've simply discovered 10,000* ways not to invent the light bulb."

Mistakes are a fact of life. It is the response to error that counts.

–Nikki Giovanni, American poet (b. 1943)

Experts say that mistakes enable us to practice taking risks. In the face of misfortune, remember that the idea failed—you didn't. Don't fear your foibles. Instead of disappointment, greet your occasional goofs as surprise gifts. Find the fascination in your flubs. Look for benefits in your blunders. Who knows? Your next mistake might be a happy accident just waiting to happen.

Some sources quote a different number, but it's always big!

made him a household name. Later, with modifications suggested by tailor Jacob Davis, what we know today as Levi's were born.

Every great mistake has a halfway moment, a split second when it can be recalled and perhaps remedied.

–Pearl S. Buck, American writer (1892–1973)

Rick D'Alto writes about history, science, and popular culture for *American History, Weatherwise,* and other magazines from his home on Long Island, New York.

General Weather Forecast and Report

To see maps of the forecast, turn to page 80.

Our study of solar activity suggests that a La Niña will prevail this winter, resulting in above-normal temperatures in much of the country. The coming winter will be remarkable for its lack of any prolonged cold spells, especially if the La Niña strengthens. (Only if an El Niño or neutral conditions were to develop would there be any lengthy or extreme cold spells.) Snowfall will be below normal in most areas, the exception being a rather narrow swath extending from northeast Texas into northern New England. In short, the winter of 2007–08 will be the mildest for the country as a whole.

Spring will come relatively early in most regions. Summer will be hot in most areas, but continuing drought will lead to wildfire and water management challenges in Florida and in western states.

Overall, we expect that the coming year will be the warmest of the past century.

November through March will be milder than normal, on average, in all areas, except Florida, southern portions of the Southeast and Deep South, and easternmost Texas. Snowfall will be above normal from northern New England southwestward through central Pennsylvania, the Ohio Valley, northern portions of the Deep South, and into northeast Texas, while rainfall will be above normal from Los Angeles northward to central Oregon and eastward into western Nevada. Elsewhere, precipitation and snowfall will be below normal.

April and May will be warmer than normal, on average, in all areas except Florida. Rainfall will be below normal in Florida, the Southeast, Deep South, Ohio Valley, Lower Lakes, and Texas–Oklahoma, and near or above normal in other regions.

June through August will be cooler than normal in northern Maine and in an area extending from the Great Lakes southward through the Ohio Valley and westward through most of the Heartland and Upper Midwest, near normal in the Appalachians and the southern tip of Texas, and hotter than normal elsewhere. Rainfall will be below normal from the Pacific Northwest across the Intermountain region, from the Upper Midwest south and eastward through the Ohio Valley, and in most of Florida. Rainfall elsewhere will generally be above normal.

September and October will be warmer and drier than normal in most areas. The exceptions will be Florida and the Southeast, which will be cooler than normal, while the Pacific North- and Southwest, Intermountain region, and portions of the Desert Southwest will have above normal rainfall.

How accurate was our forecast last winter?

Our forecast for the winter of 2006–07 resulted in our lowest verification scores ever, with a 61% accuracy rate on the monthly regional precipitation and a 49% accuracy rate on monthly regional temperatures. A coin toss would have beaten our monthly regional temperature forecasts by 1%. The reason our scores were so low was the exceptionally mild temperatures that persisted through much of December and the first two-thirds of January, before the turn to exceptional cold from late January through much of February. Had the cold period started a month earlier, our overall accuracy rate would have been over 75%. To our credit, we did predict that "most regions will have at least one mild month" and cautioned that "[i]f the El Niño fails to develop as expected, the very cold periods will be brief and most of the country will experience a mild winter overall, perhaps even a *very* mild winter."

We expect to do much better in our forecast for the winter of 2007–08, as we are confident that above-normal temperatures will predominate whether the La Niña that develops is weak or strong.

How We Predict the Weather

■ **We derive our weather forecasts** from a secret formula that was devised by the founder of this Almanac, Robert B. Thomas, in 1792. Thomas believed that weather on Earth was influenced by sunspots, which are magnetic storms on the surface of the Sun.

Over the years, we have refined and enhanced that formula with state-of-the-art technology and modern scientific calculations. We employ three scientific disciplines to make our long-range predictions: solar science, the study of sunspots and other solar activity; climatology, the study of prevailing weather patterns; and meteorology, the study of the atmosphere. We predict weather trends and events by comparing solar patterns and historical weather conditions with current solar activity.

Our forecasts emphasize temperature and precipitation deviations from averages, or normals. These are based on 30-year statistical averages prepared by government meteorological agencies and updated every ten years. The most-recent tabulations span the period 1971 through 2000.

We believe that nothing in the universe happens haphazardly, that there is a cause-and-effect pattern to all phenomena. However, although neither we nor any other forecasters have as yet gained sufficient insight into the mysteries of the universe to predict the weather with *total* accuracy, our results are almost always *very* close to our traditional claim of 80 percent.

U.S. Weather Regions

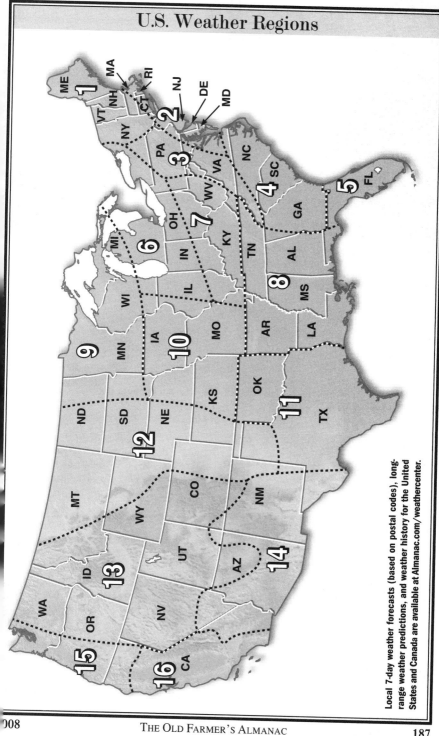

Local 7-day weather forecasts (based on postal codes), long-range weather predictions, and weather history for the United States and Canada are available at Almanac.com/weathercenter.

THE OLD FARMER'S ALMANAC

Northeast

SUMMARY: Winter will be about a degree milder than normal, on average, with slightly above-normal precipitation. Snowfall will be above normal, especially in the interior of Maine. The coldest temperatures will occur in early and late December, mid-January, and early and mid- to late February. The snowiest periods will be in mid-December, mid- and late January, and early to mid-March.

After early April snow, April and May will be slightly warmer and wetter than normal, with the season's first heat wave in late May.

Summer will be rainier and slightly hotter than normal. The hottest periods will occur in mid- to late June and mid-July.

September will be relatively dry, with near-normal temperatures. October will be unusually mild, with record warmth in midmonth.

W E A T H E R

NOV. 2007: Temp. 40° (2° above avg.); precip. 4" (0.5" above avg.). 1–3 Sunny, chilly. 4–7 Rainstorm, then sunny, cold. 8–11 Snow showers, cold. 12–17 Rain and snow, chilly. 18–27 Sunny, cool, then mild. 28–30 Heavy rain, mild.

DEC. 2007: Temp. 26° (2° above avg. north, 2° below south); precip. 3" (avg.). 1–4 Rain and snow showers, mild. 5–12 Snow showers, cold. 13–17 Very cold, then snowstorm. 18–22 Sunny, seasonable. 23–27 Snow, then very cold. 28–31 Flurries, mild.

JAN. 2008: Temp. 21° (1° above avg.); precip. 4" (1" above avg.). 1–4 Sunny, quite mild. 5–11 Snow, then sunny, cold. 12–16 Snow showers, seasonable. 17–20 Heavy snow, then sunny, very cold. 21–26 Snowstorm, then sunny, cold. 27–31 Snowstorm, then sunny, cold.

FEB. 2008: Temp. 21° (avg.); precip. 2" (0.5" below avg.). 1–5 Flurries, very cold, then seasonable. 6–11 Snow, then sunny, cold. 12–17 Periods of snow, seasonable. 18–24 Snow, then sunny, very cold. 25–29 Snow, cold.

MAR. 2008: Temp. 35° (2° above avg.); precip. 2.5" (0.5" below avg.). 1–3 Flurries, seasonable. 4–7 Snowstorm, cold. 8–10 Sunny, cold. 11–15 Rain and snow, seasonable. 16–19 Sunny, turning warm. 20–27 Rain, then sunny, warm. 28–31 Rain and snow showers.

APR. 2008: Temp. 45° (avg.); precip. 3" (0.5" below avg. north, 1" above south). 1–5 Sunny, then rain and snow, cool. 6–11 Sunny, seasonable. 12–15 Warm, t-storms. 16–22 Showers, then sunny, cool. 23–30 Rain, then sunny, cool.

MAY 2008: Temp. 57° (1° above avg.); precip. 4.5" (1" above avg.). 1–3 T-storms, warm. 4–7 Rain, then sunny, cool. 8–11 Showers, then sunny. 12–17 Showers, cool. 18–22 Sunny, turning warm. 23–29 Showers, then sunny, hot. 30–31 T-storms.

JUNE 2008: Temp. 65° (avg.); precip. 4.5" (1" above avg.). 1–6 T-storms, cool. 7–9 Sunny, seasonable. 10–14 T-storms, seasonable. 15–21 Sunny, cool, then hot. 22–26 T-storms, hot. 27–30 Showers, cool.

JULY 2008: Temp. 72° (2° above avg.); precip. 5" (1" above avg.). 1–4 Showers, cool. 5–10 Sunny, warm. 11–16 T-storms, warm. 17–21 Sunny, hot. 22–27 T-storms, then sunny, cooler. 28–31 Showers, seasonable.

AUG. 2008: Temp. 66° (1° below avg.); precip. 5" (2" above avg. north, avg. south). 1–3 Showers. 4–14 T-storms, cool. 15–17 Sunny, warm. 18–22 T-storms, then sunny, cool. 23–28 Showers. 29–31 Sunny, chilly.

SEPT. 2008: Temp. 59° (avg.); precip. 2.5" (1" below avg.). 1–5 Sunny, seasonable. 6–10 Rain, then sunny, cool. 11–14 Showers, cool. 15–19 Sunny, cold nights. 20–24 Rain, chilly. 25–30 Sunny, then showers, cool.

OCT. 2008: Temp. 53° (5° above avg.); precip. 3" (1" above avg. north, 2" below south). 1–4 Sunny, warm, then cool. 5–8 Showers, then sunny, seasonable. 9–14 Sunny, very warm. 15–22 Showers, then sunny, record warmth. 23–26 Showers, cool; snow north. 27–31 Rain, then sunny, milder.

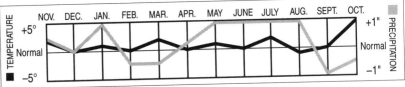

Get your local forecast at Almanac.com.

200

Atlantic Corridor

SUMMARY: Winter will be about a degree milder than normal, on average. Precipitation will be a bit above normal across southern New England and eastern Long Island and below normal elsewhere. Snowfall will be near to slightly below normal, with the snowiest periods in mid-December, mid- to late January, and mid-February. The coldest temperatures will occur in early and late December, mid-January, and early and mid-February.

April and May will be slightly warmer than normal, with above-normal rainfall north of the District of Columbia and below-normal rainfall to its south.

Summer will be rainier and slightly warmer than normal, on average. The hottest temperatures will occur in mid- to late June and mid-July.

Expect a hurricane in the last week of September. Otherwise, September and October will be slightly drier than normal, with near-normal temperatures.

NOV. 2007: Temp. 52° (4° above avg.); precip. 4.5" (1" above avg.). 1–4 Sunny, then heavy rain. 5–10 Sunny, cool. 11–16 Rain, cool; wet snow north. 17–27 Sunny, cool, then warm. 28–30 Heavy rain.

DEC. 2007: Temp. 35° (3° below avg.); precip. 3" (1" above avg. north, 1" below south). 1–9 Rain and snow, then sunny, very cold. 10–14 Flurries, then sunny, cold. 15–19 Periods of snow, cold. 20–22 Showers, seasonable. 23–26 Rain and snow, then sunny, very cold. 27–31 Flurries, seasonable.

JAN. 2008: Temp. 35° (2° above avg.); precip. 4" (0.5" above avg.). 1–4 Sunny, mild. 5–7 Rain, seasonable. 8–11 Sunny, cold. 12–15 Rain, mild. 16–19 Snow showers, cold. 20–26 Periods of snow, cold. 27–31 Rain, then sunny, seasonable.

FEB. 2008: Temp. 33° (avg.); precip. 2" (1" below avg.). 1–3 Sunny, cold. 4–8 Rain. 9–12 Sunny, cold. 13–17 Rain and snow, then sunny, cold. 18–23 Rain and snow, then sunny, cold. 24–29 Snow, then heavy rain.

MAR. 2008: Temp. 46.5° (2° above avg. north, 5° above south); precip. 2.5" (1" below avg. north, 2" below south). 1–3 Sunny, mild. 4–7 Rain, cool. 8–12 Showers. 13–17 Rain and snow, then sunny, cool. 18–22 Scattered t-storms, warm. 23–26 Sunny, mild. 27–31 Very warm, then t-storms.

APR. 2008: Temp. 53° (1° above avg.); precip. 4.5" (1" above avg.). 1–10 Sunny, seasonable. 11–15 Showers, warm. 16–22 T-storms, then sunny, cool. 23–26 Rain, cool. 27–30 Sunny, warm.

MAY 2008: Temp. 62° (avg.); precip. 4" (2" above avg. north, 2" below south). 1–3 Sunny, very warm. 4–7 T-storms, then sunny, cool. 8–14 Showers, seasonable. 15–21 Sunny, cool. 22–26 Showers, then sunny, seasonable. 27–31 T-storms, warm.

JUNE 2008: Temp. 71° (avg.); precip. 4.5" (1" above avg.). 1–4 Sunny, warm. 5–10 Scattered t-storms, cool. 11–17 Sunny. 18–26 Sunny, hot. 27–30 T-storms, then sunny, cool.

JULY 2008: Temp. 77° (1° above avg.); precip. 5" (1" above avg.). 1–6 Showers, then sunny, cool. 7–13 Showers, then sunny, hot. 14–17 T-storms, then sunny, comfortable. 18–25 Scattered t-storms, hot. 26–31 T-storms, warm.

AUG. 2008: Temp. 74° (avg.); precip. 4" (avg.). 1–7 Scattered t-storms, seasonable. 8–11 Sunny, cool. 12–18 T-storms, warm. 19–22 Sunny, cool. 23–27 Scattered showers, warm. 28–31 Rain, cool.

SEPT. 2008: Temp. 64° (3° below avg.); precip. 3" (0.5" below avg.). 1–5 Sunny, seasonable. 6–11 Rain, cool. 12–21 Showers, then sunny; chilly nights. 22–25 Heavy rain, then sunny, cool. 26–30 Showers, cool.

OCT. 2008: Temp. 59° (3° above avg.); precip. 3" (1.5" below avg. north, 0.5" above south). 1–8 Showers, then sunny, cool. 9–21 Sunny, warm. 22–31 Periods of rain, cool.

Boston
Hartford
New York
Philadelphia
Baltimore
Atlantic City
Washington
Richmond

W
E
A
T
H
E
R

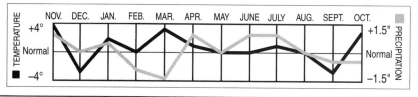

THE OLD FARMER'S ALMANAC

Appalachians

SUMMARY: Winter will be one to two degrees above normal, on average, with especially mild temperatures in November and March. Precipitation will be near normal, but the cold periods in midwinter will allow for above-normal snowfall in much of the region. The coldest periods will occur in mid- and late December, mid- to late January, and early and mid-February. Heavy snowfalls will occur in mid-December, mid- to late January, and mid- and late February.

April and May will be slightly warmer and wetter than normal, with the season's first hot temperatures in early May.

Summer will be rainier than normal, with near-normal temperatures. The hottest temperatures will occur in early and late June and in mid- and late July.

September and October will have below-normal rainfall. September will be slightly cooler than normal. October will be mild, especially in Pennsylvania and New York.

NOV. 2007: Temp. 47° (4° above avg.); precip. 4.5" (1" above avg.). 1–4 Sunny, then heavy rain. 5–9 Sunny, cool. 10–19 Periods of rain and snow, cool. 20–27 Sunny, mild. 28–30 Rain, then snow.

DEC. 2007: Temp. 31° (3° below avg.); precip. 3" (avg.). 1–3 Snow north, flurries south. 4–10 Snow showers, cold. 11–13 Sunny, mild. 14–19 Snow, cold. 20–22 Sunny, seasonable. 23–31 Snow, then sunny, cold.

JAN. 2008: Temp. 30° (2° above avg.); precip. 4" (1" above avg.). 1–6 Sunny, then rain, mild. 7–11 Snow, then sunny, cold. 12–14 Showers, mild. 15–23 Snow showers, very cold. 24–27 Rain and snow, seasonable. 28–31 Sunny, mild.

FEB. 2008: Temp. 28° (avg.); precip. 1.5" (1" below avg.). 1–4 Sunny, cold. 5–11 Rain and snow, then sunny, cold. 12–14 Snow, seasonable. 15–21 Periods of snow, cold. 22–29 Snow, then rain, turning mild.

MAR. 2008: Temp. 44° (5° above avg.); precip. 2" (1" below avg.). 1–6 Rain and snow showers, seasonable. 7–12 Sunny, then rain, warm. 13–17 Snow showers, cool. 18–28 Scattered t-storms, very warm. 29–31 Sunny, seasonable.

APR. 2008: Temp. 51° (1° above avg.); precip. 4.5" (1" above avg.). 1–10 Sunny, seasonable. 11–16 T-storms, warm. 17–22 Sunny, seasonable. 23–25 Showers, cool. 26–30 Sunny, warm.

MAY 2008: Temp. 60° (avg.); precip. 5" (1" above avg.). 1–4 Sunny, hot. 5–9 Showers, cool. 10–15 T-storms, seasonable. 16–23 Sunny, then showers, cool. 24–26 Sunny, warm. 27–31 T-storms, warm.

JUNE 2008: Temp. 67° (1° below avg.); precip. 5" (1" above avg.). 1–5 T-storms north, sunny south; hot. 6–12 T-storms, then sunny, cool. 13–22 T-storms, then sunny, warm. 23–26 T-storms, then sunny, hot. 27–30 Sunny, cool.

JULY 2008: Temp. 74° (1° above avg.); precip. 4.5" (1" above avg.). 1–6 T-storms, then sunny, cool. 7–16 Scattered t-storms, warm. 17–22 Sunny, then t-storms, hot. 23–25 Sunny, warm. 26–31 Sunny; seasonable north, hot south.

AUG. 2008: Temp. 71° (avg.); precip. 4.5" (1" above avg.). 1–6 Sunny, seasonable. 7–10 T-storms, cool. 11–17 Sunny, very warm. 18–22 T-storms, then sunny, cool. 23–28 Scattered t-storms, warm. 29–31 Rain, cool.

SEPT. 2008: Temp. 62.5° (1.5° below avg.); precip. 2.5" (1" below avg.). 1–5 Sunny, warm. 6–8 Showers, cool. 9–13 Sunny, turning warm. 14–19 Showers, then sunny, cool. 20–30 Heavy rain, then sunny, seasonable.

OCT. 2008: Temp. 57° (6° above avg. north, 2° above south); precip. 2" (1" below avg.). 1–8 Sunny, seasonable. 9–15 Sunny, warm. 16–21 Showers, then sunny, warm. 22–25 Showers, then sunny, cool. 26–31 Periods of rain, cool.

Elmira · Scranton · Harrisburg · Frederick · Roanoke · Asheville

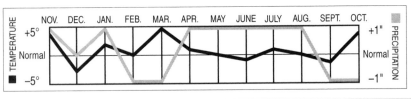

Get your local forecast at Almanac.com.

Southeast

SUMMARY: Winter will be slightly milder than normal, thanks to a mild November and March and despite colder-than-normal temperatures in December and February. Precipitation will be slightly above normal in North Carolina and below normal elsewhere, with average amounts of snow and ice. The coldest periods will be in early and late December, mid- and late January, and mid-February. Snow and ice will occur in interior locations in mid- to late January and mid-February.

April and May will be a bit warmer and drier than normal.

Summer will be slightly hotter than normal, with below-normal rainfall in eastern North Carolina and above-normal rainfall elsewhere. The hottest temperatures will occur in early June, early to mid- and late July, and early August.

September and October will be cooler and drier than normal.

NOV. 2007: Temp. 58° (3° above avg.); precip. 4" (2" above avg. north, avg. south). 1–3 Sunny, then rain, cool. 4–10 Sunny, cool. 11–16 Rain, seasonable. 17–21 Sunny, cool. 22–27 Rain, then sunny, mild. 28–30 Rain, then chilly.

DEC. 2007: Temp. 44° (3° below avg.); precip. 2" (1.5" below avg.). 1–9 Showers, then sunny, very cold. 10–14 Sunny, mild. 15–23 Periods of rain, seasonable. 24–31 Sunny, cold.

JAN. 2008: Temp. 45° (avg.); precip. 5.5" (1" above avg.). 1–3 Sunny, cool. 4–6 Rain, mild. 7–10 Sunny, cold. 11–14 Heavy rain, mild. 15–23 Snow and freezing rain, very cold north; periods of rain south. 24–31 Rain, then sunny, cold.

FEB. 2008: Temp. 43° (3° below avg.); precip. 4" (avg.). 1–4 Sunny, chilly. 5–12 Rain, then sunny, cold. 13–17 Rain, then sunny, cold. 18–23 Rain and snow, then sunny, cold. 24–29 Periods of rain, warmer.

MAR. 2008: Temp. 59° (4° above avg.); precip. 3.5" (1" below avg.). 1–4 Sunny, seasonable. 5–8 T-storms, then sunny, warm. 9–13 T-storms, then sunny, warm. 14–19 Showers, then sunny, cool. 20–29 T-storms, then sunny, warm. 30–31 Rain, then sunny.

APR. 2008: Temp. 63° (avg.); precip. 2" (1" below avg.). 1–5 Sunny, seasonable. 6–9 T-storms, then sunny, cool. 10–17 Sunny, warm. 18–21 Showers, cool. 22–24 Rain. 25–30 Sunny, cool, then warm.

MAY 2008: Temp. 71.5° (0.5° above avg.); 2.5" (1" below avg.). 1–5 Sunny, warm. 6–11 Scattered t-storms, seasonable. 12–16 T-storms, warm. 17–23 Sunny, then heavy rain, cool. 24–28 Sunny, warm. 29–31 Scattered t-storms, warm.

JUNE 2008: Temp. 77° (avg.); precip. 8" (2" above avg. north, 5" above south). 1–5 Scattered t-storms, hot. 6–9 Sunny, warm. 10–16 T-storms, cool. 17–21 Sunny north, heavy rain south; cool. 22–30 Scattered t-storms, seasonable.

JULY 2008: Temp. 81° (avg.); precip. 4" (1" below avg.). 1–8 A couple of t-storms, cool. 9–14 T-storms, hot. 15–25 T-storms, seasonable. 26–31 Sunny, hot.

AUG. 2008: Temp. 80° (1° above avg.); precip. 3" (2" below avg.). 1–3 Sunny, hot. 4–9 Scattered t-storms, seasonable. 10–16 Sunny, warm. 17–23 T-storms, then sunny, cool. 24–28 Showers, then sunny, seasonable. 29–31 Rain, cool.

SEPT. 2008: Temp. 71° (3° below avg.); precip. 3.5" (1" below avg.). 1–6 Sunny, seasonable. 7–13 Rain, then sunny, cool. 14–16 Showers, seasonable. 17–21 Sunny, cool. 22–30 Heavy rain, then sunny, seasonable.

OCT. 2008: Temp. 64.5° (2° above avg. north, 1° below south); precip. 3" (avg.). 1–10 Sunny, cool, then seasonable. 11–16 Sunny, warm. 17–22 Showers, then sunny, very warm. 23–31 Rain, cool.

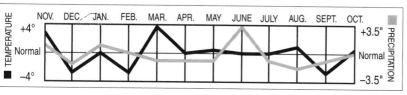

Florida

SUMMARY: Winter will be cooler than normal, especially across the south, where temperatures will be more than a degree below normal, on average. Watch for freezes in Central Florida in early to mid-December and in mid- to late February. Rainfall will be a bit above normal in the north and near normal in the south.

April and May will be drier than normal, with near-normal temperatures.

Summer will be hotter and drier than normal, with temperatures two degrees above normal, on average. The hottest periods will be in early June; early, mid-, and late July; and early and late August. South Florida will be especially dry, with an enhanced threat of wildfires.

Despite widespread t-storms in mid-September, September and October will be drier than normal overall, with below-normal temperatures.

NOV. 2007: Temp. 70° (3° above avg. north, 1° below south); precip. 3" (avg. north, 1" above south). 1–7 Rain, cool. 8–14 Sunny, turning warm. 15–21 T-storms, then sunny, cool. 22–30 Showers, cool.

DEC. 2007: Temp. 60° (3° below avg.); precip. 2" (0.5" below avg.). 1–4 Showers, then sunny, cool. 5–9 Showers, then sunny; freeze north and central. 10–17 Sunny, turning warmer. 18–23 Rain, warm. 24–30 Sunny, cool. 31 Rain.

JAN. 2008: Temp. 59° (2° below avg.); precip. 2.5" (avg.). 1–4 Showers, then sunny, cool. 5–7 T-storms, warm. 8–14 T-storms, then sunny, warm. 15–21 Showers, cool. 22–27 Sunny, warm. 28–31 Rain, cool.

FEB. 2008: Temp. 57° (4° below avg.); precip. 3.5" (1" above avg.). 1–4 Sunny, cool. 5–9 Rain, then sunny, cool. 10–12 Showers, then sunny, cool. 13–18 Showers, then sunny, cool. 19–23 Rain, then sunny, cold. 24–29 Scattered t-storms, warm.

MAR. 2008: Temp. 71° (4° above avg.); precip. 1.5" (1.5" below avg.). 1–3 Showers, cool. 4–13 Sunny, very warm. 14–18 Showers, then sunny, cool. 19–22 Sunny, warm. 23–31 T-storms, then sunny, warm.

APR. 2008: Temp. 70° (1° below avg.); precip. 1.5" (2" below avg. north, 0.5" below south). 1–7 T-storms, then sunny, warm. 8–18 Sunny, cool, then warm. 19–24 Scattered showers, seasonable. 25–30 T-storms, cool.

MAY 2008: Temp. 78° (1° above avg.); precip. 2.5" (1.5" below avg.). 1–5 Sunny, warm. 6–14 Showers north, sunny south; warm. 15–25 Scattered t-storms, seasonable. 26–31 Sunny, then t-storms, seasonable.

JUNE 2008: Temp. 83° (2° above avg.); precip. 8" (5" above avg. north, 2" below south). 1–8 Scattered t-storms, hot. 9–15 Scattered t-storms, warm. 16–22 T-storms, cool. 23–30 T-storms, then sunny, warm.

JULY 2008: Temp. 83° (avg. north, 2° above south); precip. 3.5" (3" below avg.). 1–2 Sunny, hot. 3–8 Scattered t-storms, seasonable. 9–15 Scattered t-storms, hot. 16–25 Scattered t-storms, seasonable. 26–31 Scattered t-storms, hot.

AUG. 2008: Temp. 84° (3° above avg.); precip. 4.5" (3" below avg.). 1–7 T-storms, hot. 8–16 T-storms, seasonable. 17–31 Scattered t-storms, hot.

SEPT. 2008: Temp. 79° (1° below avg.); precip. 7" (2" below avg. north, 1.5" above south). 1–8 Showers, then sunny, seasonable. 9–13 Scattered t-storms, seasonable. 14–20 Heavy t-storms, cool. 21–30 Scattered t-storms, warm.

OCT. 2008: Temp. 73° (2° below avg.); precip. 1.5" (2.5" below avg.). 1–8 Sunny north, showers south; cool. 9–13 T-storms, seasonable. 14–22 Sunny, warm. 23–28 Sunny, cool. 29–31 Rain, seasonable.

Jacksonville

Tampa

Orlando

Miami

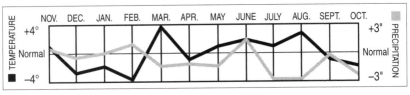

Get your local forecast at Almanac.com.

Lower Lakes

SUMMARY: Winter will be one to two degrees above normal, on average, with below-normal precipitation and near-normal snowfall. The coldest periods will be in early and mid-January and in mid-February. The heaviest widespread snowfalls will occur in mid-December, mid-January, and mid-February, with heavy lake snows in early and late December, mid-January, and early and late February.

April and May will be slightly warmer and drier than normal, despite some wet snow in late April.

Summer temperatures will be one to two degrees below normal, on average, with slightly below-normal rainfall. The hottest temperatures will occur in mid- to late June and mid-July.

September and October will be warmer and drier than normal, with late September through October being unusually warm.

NOV. 2007: Temp. 43° (3° above avg.); precip. 3" (avg.). 1–5 Rain, seasonable. 6–9 Sunny; chilly east, mild west. 10–13 Rain and snow showers, cool. 14–18 Rain and snow showers east, sunny west; cool. 19–28 Sunny, warmer. 29–30 Rain east, snow west.

DEC. 2007: Temp. 27° (2° below avg.); precip. 1.5" (1.5" below avg.). 1–10 Snow squalls, cold. 11–13 Sunny, mild. 14–19 Periods of snow, cold. 20–26 Lake snows, cold. 27–31 Flurries, milder.

JAN. 2008: Temp. 28° (2° above avg. east, 6° above west); precip. 3.5" (1" above avg.). 1–4 Sunny, mild. 5–11 Rain to snow, then lake snows, very cold. 12–13 Sunny, milder. 14–26 Snow, then lake snows, very cold. 27–31 Rain to snow, then sunny, mild.

FEB. 2008: Temp. 22.5° (avg. east, 3° below west); precip. 1.5" (0.5" below avg.). 1–10 Lake snows, cold. 11–13 Sunny, mild. 14–17 Rain and snow, then snow squalls, very cold. 18–22 Snow, then lake snows, cold. 23–29 Snow, then periods of rain, milder.

MAR. 2008: Temp. 41° (5° above avg.); precip. 2" (1" below avg.). 1–4 Rain and snow, then sunny. 5–9 Rain and snow, then sunny, cool. 10–16 Rain to snow, then sunny, cool. 17–24 Showers, warm. 25–28 T-storms, very warm. 29–31 Sunny, seasonable.

APR. 2008: Temp. 49° (2° above avg.); precip. 3" (0.5" below avg.). 1–9 Rain and snow showers, then sunny, cool. 10–18 T-storms,

warm, then cool. 19–22 Sunny, seasonable. 23–26 Rain to snow, then sunny, cool. 27–30 T-storms, warm.

MAY 2008: Temp. 58° (avg.); precip. 3.5" (avg.). 1–6 Sunny, warm, then t-storms, cool. 7–10 Sunny, seasonable. 11–14 Showers, seasonable. 15–20 Showers, then sunny, cool. 21–25 Showers, seasonable. 26–31 Scattered t-storms, very warm.

JUNE 2008: Temp. 65° (2° below avg.); precip. 2.5" (1" below avg.). 1–4 T-storms, very warm. 5–8 Showers, cool. 9–17 Sunny, cool. 18–25 Sunny, hot. 26–30 T-storms, then sunny, cool.

JULY 2008: Temp. 71° (1° below avg.); precip. 4.5" (1" above avg.). 1–6 Showers, then sunny, cool. 7–16 Scattered t-storms, warm. 17–21 Sunny, hot. 22–26 T-storms, then sunny, cool. 27–31 T-storms, seasonable.

AUG. 2008: Temp. 69° (2° below avg.); precip. 3" (1" below avg.). 1–7 Scattered t-storms, seasonable. 8–14 Showers, cool. 15–21 Sunny, cool. 22–27 Scattered t-storms, seasonable. 28–31 Sunny, cool.

SEPT. 2008: Temp. 64° (1° above avg.); precip. 1.5" (2" below avg.). 1–4 Sunny, seasonable. 5–11 T-storms, then sunny, cool. 12–19 Rain, then sunny, cool. 20–30 Showers, then sunny, very warm.

OCT. 2008: Temp. 57° (5° above avg.); precip. 0.5" (2" below avg.). 1–11 Showers, then sunny, warm. 12–20 Showers, then sunny, very warm. 21–24 Showers, then sunny, cool. 25–31 Showers, turning warmer.

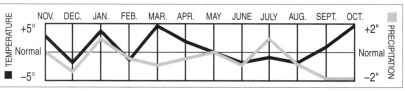

Ohio Valley

SUMMARY: Winter will be about one degree above normal, on average, with above-normal precipitation and snowfall. The coldest temperatures will occur in early and mid- to late December, mid-January, and mid-February. The snowiest periods will be in late November, mid-January, and mid-February.

April will be slightly warmer and drier than normal, on average, despite some wet snow late in the north. Temperatures and rainfall will be near normal in May, with the season's first hot spell in the beginning of the month.

Summer temperatures will be about two degrees cooler than normal, on average, with below-normal rainfall. The hottest temperatures will occur in late June, mid- to late July, and early August.

September will be relatively cool, while in October temperatures will be well above normal. Both months will be drier than normal.

NOV. 2007: Temp. 48° (3° above avg.); precip. 4" (0.5" above avg.). 1–8 Rain, then sunny, cool. 9–16 Rain and snow showers, chilly. 17–28 Sunny, turning mild. 29–30 Snow, cold.

DEC. 2007: Temp. 33° (2° below avg.); precip. 2" (1" below avg.). 1–8 Snow showers, very cold. 9–13 Sunny, seasonable. 14–16 Rain and snow. 17–26 Snow showers, very cold. 27–31 Flurries, cold.

JAN. 2008: Temp. 33° (2° above avg.); precip. 4" (1" above avg.). 1–5 Rain, mild. 6–10 Snow, then sunny, cold. 11–14 Showers, mild. 15–21 Snow, very cold. 22–26 Snow showers, cold. 27–31 Rain, then sunny, seasonable.

FEB. 2008: Temp. 29° (3° below avg.); precip 3" (avg.). 1–11 Snow showers, cold. 12–17 Snow, then sunny, very cold. 18–23 Periods of snow, cold. 24–29 T-storms, mild.

MAR. 2008: Temp. 50° (6° above avg.); precip. 4.5" (0.5" above avg.). 1–5 Rain and snow, seasonable. 6–9 Sunny, then showers, warm. 10–15 Rain, then snow, turning colder. 16–19 Sunny, warm. 20–28 T-storms, warm. 29–31 Sunny, cool.

APR. 2008: Temp. 55° (1° above avg.); precip. 2.5" (1" below avg.). 1–9 Showers, then sunny, cool. 10–17 T-storms, warm. 18–22 Sunny, cool. 23–30 Rain to snow, then sunny, seasonable.

MAY 2008: Temp. 63° (avg.); precip. 4.5" (avg.). 1–3 Sunny, hot. 4–15 Scattered t-storms, cool. 16–18 Sunny, cool. 19–23 T-storms, seasonable. 24–31 Sunny, then t-storms, seasonable.

JUNE 2008: Temp. 70° (2° below avg.); precip. 3" (1" below avg.). 1–7 T-storms, turning cooler. 8–13 Sunny, cool. 14–21 T-storms, then sunny, seasonable. 22–26 T-storms, hot. 27–30 Sunny, cool.

JULY 2008: Temp. 74° (2° below avg.); precip. 4.5" (0.5" above avg.). 1–8 Sunny, then t-storms, cool. 9–17 T-storms, seasonable. 18–21 Sunny, very warm. 22–31 Scattered t-storms, seasonable.

AUG. 2008: Temp. 72° (2° below avg.); precip. 2.5" (1" below avg.). 1–7 Scattered t-storms, warm. 8–12 Sunny, cool. 13–17 T-storms, then sunny, warm. 18–22 T-storms, then sunny, cool. 23–31 Showers, then sunny, cool.

SEPT. 2008: Temp. 65° (2° below avg.); precip. 1" (2" below avg.). 1–4 Sunny, warm. 5–10 T-storms, then sunny, cool. 11–14 Sunny, seasonable. 15–20 Showers, then sunny, cool. 21–24 Showers, then sunny, cool. 25–30 Sunny, seasonable.

OCT. 2008: Temp. 60° (4° above avg.); precip. 1" (1.5" below avg.). 1–9 Sunny, seasonable. 10–20 Sunny, warm. 21–31 Showers, cool.

Map labels: Pittsburgh, Cincinnati, Louisville, Charleston

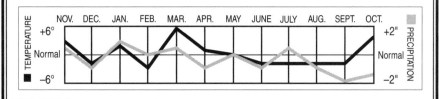

Sidebar: WEATHER

Deep South

SUMMARY: Winter will be colder than normal and precipitation will be near normal in the north and well below normal in the south. Expect the coldest temperatures in early December, early to mid- and late January, and mid-February. Snowfall will be above normal across the north, with the snowiest periods in early and mid-December, mid-January, and mid-February. Spring will arrive early, with generally warm temperatures in March.

April will be unusually warm, and May will have near-normal temperatures. Rainfall will be below normal.

Summer will be slightly hotter and wetter than normal. The hottest periods will occur in early and late June, early to mid- and late July, and mid-August.

September temperatures and rainfall will be slightly below normal, followed by an unusually warm and dry October.

NOV. 2007: Temp. 57° (2° above avg.); precip. 5" (avg.). 1–6 Scattered t-storms, seasonable. 7–10 Sunny, warm. 11–15 T-storms, seasonable. 16–21 Showers north, sunny south; cool. 22–26 Sunny, warm. 27–30 Showers, cooler.

DEC. 2007: Temp. 42° (5° below avg.); precip. 3" (2" below avg.). 1–8 Snow north, rain south, then sunny, very cold. 9–13 Showers, then sunny, warm. 14–17 Rain, then sunny. 18–21 Snow north, rain south; cold. 22–28 Rain, then sunny, cold. 29–31 Rain, seasonable.

JAN. 2008: Temp. 45° (1° above avg.); precip. 4.5" (1" above avg. north, 2" below south). 1–4 Sunny, then t-storms, warm. 5–10 Rain to snow, then sunny, cold. 11–14 Heavy t-storms. 15–19 Snow north, rain south, then sunny, cold. 20–23 Snow north, rain south, then sunny, cold. 24–31 Rain, then sunny, cold.

FEB. 2008: Temp. 40° (6° below avg.); precip. 5" (1" below avg. north, 1" above south). 1–3 Sunny, cool. 4–11 Rain to snow, then sunny, cold. 12–16 Snow north, rain south, then sunny, cold. 17–21 Rain, then sunny, chilly. 22–29 T-storms, seasonable.

MAR. 2008: Temp. 61° (5° above avg.); precip. 5" (2" above avg. north, 4" below south). 1–4 Sunny, seasonable. 5–14 T-storms, warm. 15–18 Sunny, cool. 19–27 T-storms, then sunny, very warm. 28–31 T-storms, cool.

APR. 2008: Temp. 66° (3° above avg.); precip. 2" (2.5" below avg.). 1–9 Sunny, seasonable. 10–16 Scattered t-storms, warm. 17–24 Showers, seasonable. 25–30 Sunny, cool, then warm.

MAY 2008: Temp. 71° (avg.); precip. 4.5" (0.5" below avg.). 1–10 Sunny, warm. 11–14 T-storms, then sunny, seasonable. 15–18 Showers, cool. 19–23 T-storms, seasonable. 24–31 Sunny, warm.

JUNE 2008: Temp. 79° (1° above avg.); precip. 6" (1" above avg.). 1–9 Sunny, then t-storms, hot. 10–19 T-storms, cool. 20–25 Scattered t-storms. 26–30 Sunny, hot.

JULY 2008: Temp. 81° (1° above avg.); precip. 6" (1" above avg.). 1–5 T-storms, then sunny, cool. 6–13 T-storms, then sunny, very warm. 14–25 Scattered t-storms, seasonable. 26–31 Sunny, hot.

AUG. 2008: Temp. 82° (1° above avg.); precip. 4.5" (avg.). 1–7 Scattered t-storms, seasonable. 8–11 T-storms, then sunny, cool. 12–17 Scattered t-storms, seasonable. 18–22 Scattered t-storms, hot. 23–31 Heavy t-storms, then sunny, warm.

SEPT. 2008: Temp. 75° (1° below avg.); precip. 4" (0.5" below avg.). 1–5 T-storms, then sunny, hot. 6–14 T-storms, then sunny, seasonable. 15–20 T-storms, then sunny, cool. 21–25 Heavy t-storms, then sunny, cool. 26–30 Sunny, warm.

OCT. 2008: Temp. 68° (6° above avg. north, avg. south); precip. 1" (2" below avg.). 1–5 Sunny, warm. 6–21 Showers, then sunny, very warm. 22–26 Sunny. 27–31 T-storms, cool.

Little Rock ⊙ · ⊙ Nashville · ⊙ Tupelo · Montgomery ⊙ · Shreveport ⊙ · ⊙ Jackson · Mobile ⊙ · New Orleans ⊙

WEATHER

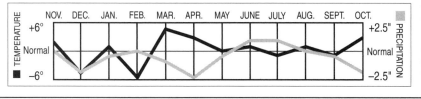

Upper Midwest

SUMMARY: Winter temperatures will be about four degrees above normal in the east and one degree above normal in the west, on average. Precipitation will be near normal, with much-below-normal snowfall. The coldest temperatures will occur in early and mid-January and mid-February. The heaviest snowfalls will occur in mid-November, mid-December, and late January.

April will be warmer and drier than normal. May will be rainier than normal, with near-normal temperatures, on average, despite a very warm beginning and end to the month.

Summer temperatures will be near normal, on average, with much-below-normal rainfall. The hottest temperatures will occur in mid- to late June and mid- and late July.

September and October will have below-normal precipitation, with above-normal temperatures. October will be one of the warmest Octobers on record.

NOV. 2007: Temp. 31.5° (7° above avg. east, avg. west); precip. 2" (avg.). 1–7 Snow showers, then sunny, mild. 8–16 Scattered showers and flurries, mild. 17–27 Snow, then sunny, warm. 28–30 Snow showers, seasonable.

DEC. 2007: Temp. 16° (2° above avg.); precip. 0.5" (0.5" below avg.). 1–7 Snow showers, then sunny, cold. 8–13 Sunny, mild. 14–21 Snow showers, cold. 22–25 Flurries, seasonable. 26–31 Sunny, mild.

JAN. 2008: Temp. 12° (3° above avg.); precip. 1.5" (0.5" above avg.). 1–3 Sunny, mild. 4–9 Snow showers, very cold. 10–12 Sunny, cold. 13–24 Flurries, very cold. 25–28 Snow showers; cold east, mild west. 29–31 Sunny, warm.

FEB. 2008: Temp. 9.5° (2° above avg. east, 5° below west); precip. 0.5" (0.5" below avg.). 1–7 Snow showers, mild. 8–9 Flurries, cold. 10–13 Snow showers, mild. 14–20 Sunny, very cold. 21–29 Snow showers, milder.

MAR. 2008: Temp. 33° (6° above avg.); precip. 2" (0.5" above avg.). 1–5 Snow showers, cold. 6–9 Sunny, mild. 10–13 Rain to snow. 14–18 Sunny, warm. 19–27 Scattered showers, very warm. 28–31 Rain and snow, then sunny, mild.

APR. 2008: Temp. 45° (4° above avg.); precip. 1.5" (0.5" below avg.). 1–4 Sunny, seasonable. 5–10 Showers, then sunny, warm. 11–15 Showers, cool. 16–22 Rain and snow, then showers, warmer. 23–25 Sunny, cool. 26–30 T-storms, seasonable.

MAY 2008: Temp. 55° (avg.); precip. 4" (1" above avg.). 1–3 T-storms, very warm. 4–8 Showers, cool. 9–12 Sunny, warm. 13–16 Rain, chilly. 17–20 Sunny, warm. 21–25 Heavy rain, then sunny, warm. 26–31 Scattered t-storms, very warm.

JUNE 2008: Temp. 64° (avg.); precip. 2" (2" below avg.). 1–6 T-storms, turning cool. 7–17 Sunny, seasonable. 18–24 Scattered t-storms, hot. 25–30 Sunny, seasonable.

JULY 2008: Temp. 71° (2° above avg.); precip. 2" (1.5" below avg.). 1–4 Sunny, warm. 5–13 Scattered t-storms, seasonable. 14–20 Sunny, hot. 21–26 Scattered t-storms, seasonable. 27–31 Sunny, hot.

AUG. 2008: Temp. 65° (2° below avg.); precip. 4" (0.5" above avg.). 1–6 Scattered t-storms, warm. 7–12 Sunny, cool. 13–25 Scattered t-storms, warm. 26–31 Rain, then sunny, warm.

SEPT. 2008: Temp. 62° (4° above avg.); precip. 2.5" (0.5" below avg.). 1–5 Sunny, warm. 6–12 Showers, cool, then warm. 13–18 Scattered t-storms, seasonable. 19–21 Sunny, warm. 22–30 T-storms, then sunny, very warm.

OCT. 2008: Temp. 55° (9° above avg.); precip. 1.5" (1" below avg.). 1–6 Scattered t-storms, warm. 7–13 Sunny, very warm. 14–20 Scattered showers, warm. 21–31 Sunny, cool, then warm.

Map labels: International Falls, Marquette, Duluth, Minneapolis, Green Bay

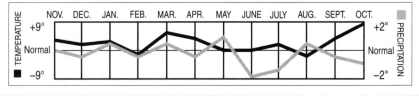

Heartland

SUMMARY: Winter will be about two degrees above normal, on average, with slightly below-normal precipitation. The coldest temperatures will occur in early December, early and mid- to late January, and mid-February. Snowfall will be near normal in Iowa and below normal elsewhere, with the heaviest snowfalls in mid-December, early to mid-January, and late February.

April and May will have above-normal temperatures, with near-normal rainfall. Early and late May will be especially warm.

Summer will be slightly cooler and drier than normal. The hottest temperatures will occur in early and mid- to late June and mid- to late July.

September will be warmer and drier than normal, with unusually hot temperatures to end the month. Unusual warmth will continue in much of October, along with below-normal rainfall.

NOV. 2007: Temp. 45° (3° above avg.); precip. 2" (0.5" below avg.). 1–9 Sunny, cool, then warm. 10–13 Rain and snow, chilly. 14–19 Sunny, mild. 20–27 Showers, then sunny, warm. 28–30 Rain, then snow showers, cold.

DEC. 2007: Temp. 29° (1° below avg.); precip. 1" (0.5" below avg.). 1–7 Snow showers, then sunny, very cold. 8–13 Sunny, mild. 14–17 Rain then sunny, cold. 18–21 Snow, then sunny, cold. 22–28 Rain, then sunny, seasonable. 29–31 Freezing rain.

JAN. 2008: Temp. 31° (5° above avg.); precip. 0.5" (0.5" below avg.). 1–4 Sunny, mild. 5–9 Rain to snow, then sunny, very cold. 10–12 Snow north, sunny south. 13–25 Snow showers, very cold. 26–31 Sunny, mild.

FEB. 2008: Temp. 26° (3° below avg.); precip. 1.5" (avg.). 1–5 Snow showers, cold. 6–9 Sunny, cold. 10–13 Sunny, mild. 14–20 Snow showers, very cold. 21–26 Snow, then sunny, mild. 27–29 Rain to snow.

MAR. 2008: Temp. 50° (7° above avg.); precip. 3" (0.5" above avg.). 1–8 Snow north, periods of rain elsewhere; seasonable. 9–13 T-storms, mild. 14–19 Sunny, turning warm. 20–25 Showers, then sunny, warm. 26–31 Showers, turning cooler.

APR. 2008: Temp. 60° (6° above avg.); precip. 3" (0.5" below avg.). 1–3 Sunny, warm. 4–8 Showers, then sunny, seasonable. 9–16 Scattered t-storms, warm. 17–19 Sunny, cool. 20–23 Rain, seasonable. 24–26 Sunny, cool. 27–30 T-storms, seasonable.

MAY 2008: Temp. 65° (1° above avg.); precip. 5" (0.5" above avg.). 1–5 Sunny, very warm. 6–10 T-storms; cool north, warm south. 11–14 Showers, cool. 15–18 Sunny, cool. 19–31 T-storms, then sunny, very warm.

JUNE 2008: Temp. 73° (avg.); precip. 3.5" (1" below avg.). 1–4 Sunny, hot. 5–10 Heavy t-storms, turning cooler. 11–12 Sunny, cool. 13–17 T-storms, cool. 18–25 Sunny, hot. 26–30 Scattered t-storms, seasonable.

JULY 2008: Temp. 76° (2° below avg.); precip. 4" (avg.). 1–5 Sunny, cool. 6–10 T-storms, then sunny, seasonable. 11–20 T-storms, then sunny, warm. 21–29 T-storms, then sunny, hot. 30–31 T-storms.

AUG. 2008: Temp. 74° (2° below avg.); precip. 3.5" (avg.). 1–7 Scattered t-storms, turning cooler. 8–11 Sunny, cool. 12–17 T-storms, then sunny, seasonable. 18–21 T-storms, then sunny, very warm. 22–31 Scattered t-storms, seasonable.

SEPT. 2008: Temp. 69° (2° above avg.); precip. 1.5" (2" below avg.). 1–6 Scattered t-storms, warm. 7–14 Sunny, warm. 15–19 Showers. 20–30 Sunny, cool, then hot.

OCT. 2008: Temp. 64° (8° above avg.); precip. 2" (1" below avg.). 1–5 Sunny, very warm. 6–12 Scattered t-storms, warm. 13–19 Sunny, very warm. 20–27 T-storms, then sunny, cool. 28–31 Showers, seasonable.

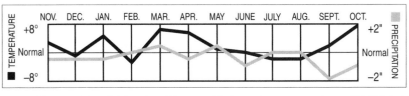

W
E
A
T
H
E
R

Texas–Oklahoma

SUMMARY: Winter will be one to two degrees warmer than normal, on average, despite a cold February. The coldest temperatures will occur in mid-January and mid-February. Precipitation will be slightly below normal, with below-normal snowfall. The most widespread snow and ice will occur across the north in mid-December and late February. March will be unusually warm, on average, despite a cool end to the month.

Unusually warm temperatures will continue in April, while May will be only a bit above normal. Rainfall will be below normal.

Summer will be near or slightly hotter than normal, with the hottest temperatures in early and late June, early and mid-July, and early, mid-, and late August. Rainfall will be above normal in most of the region.

September and October will have below-normal rainfall and above-normal temperatures.

NOV. 2007: Temp. 58° (2° above avg.); precip. 3" (avg.). 1–8 Sunny, warm. 9–14 T-storms, cool. 15–17 Sunny, warm. 18–21 T-storms, warm. 22–27 Sunny, then t-storms, warm. 28–30 Sunny, cool.

DEC. 2007: Temp. 47.5° (1° above avg. north, 2° below south); precip. 1.5" (1" above avg.). 1–4 Sunny, seasonable. 5–7 Sunny, cold. 8–14 Misty, mild. 15–22 Snow north, rain south; cool. 23–31 Sunny, mild.

JAN. 2008: Temp. 48° (2° above avg.); precip. 0.5" (1.5" below avg.). 1–4 Sunny, warm. 5–10 Rain, then sunny, cold. 11–20 Showers, then sunny, very cold. 21–31 Rain, then sunny, warm.

FEB. 2008: Temp. 44° (4° below avg.); precip. 2" (avg.). 1–3 Sunny, warm. 4–9 T-storms, then sunny, cold. 10–16 Rain, then sunny, cold. 17–21 Sunny, seasonable. 22–29 Snow north, rain south, then sunny, cool.

MAR. 2008: Temp. 65° (7° above avg.); precip. 3.5" (1" above avg.). 1–3 Sunny, turning mild. 4–12 Scattered t-storms, turning very warm. 13–21 Sunny, warm. 22–28 Scattered t-storms, very warm. 29–31 Rain, cool.

APR. 2008: Temp. 71° (5° above avg.); precip. 3.5" (0.5" above avg.). 1–11 Sunny, warm. 12–16 T-storms, then sunny, very warm. 17–21 T-storms north, sunny south; seasonable. 22–24 Sunny, warm. 25–30 T-storms, warm.

MAY 2008: Temp. 74° (1° above avg.); precip. 2" (3" below avg.). 1–7 Sunny, very warm. 8–14 Scattered t-storms, very warm. 15–21 Showers, cool north; sunny, hot south. 22–31 T-storms, then sunny, seasonable.

JUNE 2008: Temp. 81° (2° above avg. north, avg. south); precip. 4.5" (0.5" above avg.). 1–9 Sunny, hot. 10–21 Scattered t-storms, seasonable. 22–30 T-storms, then sunny, hot north; t-storms, seasonable south.

JULY 2008: Temp. 83° (avg.); precip. 4" (1" above avg.). 1–8 Scattered t-storms, hot. 9–18 Sunny, hot. 19–23 Scattered t-storms, seasonable. 24–31 Sunny, seasonable.

AUG. 2008: Temp. 82° (avg.); precip. 2" (1" above avg. north, 2" below south). 1–7 Scattered t-storms, hot. 8–13 T-storms, then less humid north; sunny, hot south. 14–19 Scattered t-storms, hot. 20–23 Sunny, hot. 24–31 T-storms, then sunny, hot.

SEPT. 2008: Temp. 76° (avg.); precip. 1.5" (2" below avg.). 1–5 Scattered t-storms, hot. 6–12 T-storms, seasonable. 13–18 Sunny north, t-storms south; seasonable. 19–26 Sunny, cool. 27–30 Sunny, hot north; t-storms south.

OCT. 2008: Temp. 72° (8° above avg. north, 2° above south); precip. 2.5" (1.5" below avg.). 1–7 Sunny, warm. 8–15 Scattered t-storms, warm. 16–21 T-storms, warm. 22–25 Sunny, warm. 26–31 T-storms, warm.

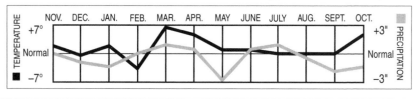

High Plains

SUMMARY: Despite a cold February, winter will be about two degrees above normal, on average. Snowfall will be near or below normal in most of the region, while precipitation will be a bit above normal in the north and a bit below normal in the south. The coldest temperatures will occur in mid-November, mid-December, and early and mid-January, with the snowiest periods in mid-November, early and mid-January, late February, and late March.

Although April temperatures will be well above normal, on average, some of the year's heaviest snow will fall in mid-month. Overall, April and May will be warmer than normal, with near-normal precipitation.

Summer temperatures and rainfall will be slightly above normal, with the hottest temperatures in mid- to late June and early and mid-July.

September and October will be warmer and drier than normal.

NOV. 2007: Temp. 37.5° (1° below avg. north, 4° above south); precip. 1" (0.5" above avg. north, 0.5" below south). 1–7 Sunny, mild. 8–12 Snow, then sunny, cold. 13–16 Sunny east, snow west. 17–22 Sunny, warm. 23–30 Snow showers, seasonable.

DEC. 2007: Temp. 31° (4° above avg.); precip. 0.2" (0.3" below avg.). 1–12 Snow showers, then sunny, warm. 13–20 Snow showers, then sunny, cold. 21–27 Sunny, turning mild. 28–31 Rain and snow showers, mild.

JAN. 2008: Temp. 27.5° (4° above avg. north, 1° above south); precip. 1" (0.5" above avg.). 1–2 Snow, very mild. 3–8 Snow showers, very cold. 9–11 Snow showers, cold. 12–15 Snow, bitter cold, then seasonable. 16–21 Snow showers, very cold. 22–31 Sunny, turning warm.

FEB. 2008: Temp. 22° (5° below avg.); precip. 0.5" (avg.). 1–2 Sunny, mild. 3–7 Snow, then sunny, cold. 8–14 Snow showers, then sunny, mild. 15–21 Snow, then sunny, mild. 22–24 Flurries, seasonable. 25–29 Snow, then sunny; cold east, mild west.

MAR. 2008: Temp. 45° (7° above avg.); precip. 1" (avg.). 1–7 Periods of snow, seasonable. 8–14 Snow north, sunny south; seasonable. 15–23 Sunny, warm. 24–26 T-storms, warm. 27–31 Snow, then sunny, cool.

APR. 2008: Temp. 53° (5° above avg.); precip. 2" (1" below avg. north, 2" above south). 1–5 Sunny, warm east; rain central; snow, cold west. 6–9 Sunny, warm. 10–17 Snow north, sunny south. 18–20 Sunny, seasonable. 21–24 Showers, then sunny, cool. 25–30 Showers, turning warmer.

MAY 2008: Temp. 59° (1° above avg.); precip. 2" (1" above avg. north, 2" below south). 1–2 Sunny, warm. 3–10 T-storms; seasonable north, hot south. 11–17 T-storms, then sunny, cool. 18–31 T-storms, warm.

JUNE 2008: Temp. 68° (1° above avg.); precip. 2.5" (0.5" below avg. north, 0.5" above south). 1–7 T-storms, then sunny, very warm. 8–15 T-storms, turning cooler. 16–22 Sunny east, t-storms west; hot. 23–30 Sunny, warm.

JULY 2008: Temp. 73° (1° above avg.); precip. 2" (avg.). 1–7 T-storms, hot, then cool. 8–19 Scattered t-storms, hot. 20–25 T-storms, then sunny, seasonable. 26–31 Scattered t-storms, warm.

AUG. 2008: Temp. 70° (1° below avg.); precip. 3" (1" above avg.). 1–7 Scattered t-storms, cool. 8–20 Scattered t-storms, warm. 21–27 T-storms, cool. 28–31 Sunny, warm.

SEPT. 2008: Temp. 62° (1° above avg.); precip. 1" (0.5" below avg.). 1–4 Scattered t-storms, hot. 5–10 T-storms, cool. 11–17 Scattered t-storms, warm. 18–22 Sunny, very warm. 23–30 Sunny, cool, then very warm.

OCT. 2008: Temp. 54° (5° above avg.); precip. 0.5" (0.5" below avg.). 1–12 Sunny, very warm. 13–19 T-storms, warm. 20–23 Sunny, seasonable. 24–31 Rain and snow, then sunny, mild.

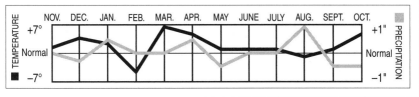

Intermountain

SUMMARY: Winter will be about one degree above normal, on average, with slightly below-normal precipitation. The coldest temperatures will occur in mid-December and early and mid-January. The most widespread snowstorms will occur in mid-November, mid-December, mid-January, and mid- and late March.

April and May will be warmer than normal, with near-normal precipitation.

Summer will be one to two degrees above normal, on average, with near- to slightly below-normal rainfall. The hottest temperatures will occur in late June, mid- and late July, and early and late August.

September and October will have above-normal temperatures, with near-normal precipitation.

NOV. 2007: Temp. 39° (avg.); precip. 1.5" (avg.). 1–6 Showers north, sunny south; mild. 7–12 Rain, then snow, turning colder. 13–18 Rain and snow showers, chilly north; sunny, mild south. 19–26 Showers, mild. 27–30 Sunny, mild.

DEC. 2007: Temp. 33° (4° above avg. north, avg. south); precip. 1" (0.5" below avg.). 1–5 Sunny, mild. 6–12 Cloudy, rain north; sunny, mild south. 13–15 Showers, mild. 16–22 Snow, then sunny, cold. 23–27 Rain, mild north; sunny, cold south. 28–31 Rain and snow, seasonable.

JAN. 2008: Temp. 29° (1° below avg.); precip. 2" (0.5" above avg.). 1–7 Snow showers, turning very cold. 8–11 Sunny, seasonable. 12–17 Snow, then sunny, cold. 18–22 Snow showers, then sunny, cold. 23–25 Heavy snow north, showers south. 26–31 Rain, then sunny, very mild.

FEB. 2008: Temp. 33° (avg.); precip. 1" (0.5" below avg.). 1–5 Sunny, mild. 6–13 Wintry mix north; sunny, mild south. 14–22 Showers, mild. 23–29 Snow showers, cold.

MAR. 2008: Temp. 45° (3° above avg.); precip. 1.5" (avg.). 1–4 Sunny, seasonable. 5–8 Flurries, seasonable. 9–13 Snow, then sunny, seasonable. 14–21 Sunny, mild. 22–25 Rain, then sunny, mild. 26–31 Snow, then sunny, seasonable.

APR. 2008: Temp. 50° (1° above avg.); precip. 1.5" (0.5" above avg.). 1–5 Rain and snow showers, then sunny, chilly. 6–8

Sunny, mild. 9–15 Snow showers, cold. 16–21 Sunny, cool. 22–30 Rain, then sunny, mild.

MAY 2008: Temp. 58° (1° above avg.); precip. 1" (1" below avg. east, 1" above west). 1–8 Showers, cool north; sunny, warm south. 9–16 Sunny, warm. 17–25 T-storms, then sunny, warm. 26–31 Rain, cool.

JUNE 2008: Temp. 68° (2° above avg.); precip. 0.2" (0.3" below avg.). 1–4 Showers, cool. 5–14 Scattered t-storms, warm. 15–20 T-storms, then sunny, cool. 21–25 Scattered t-storms, seasonable. 26–30 Sunny, hot.

JULY 2008: Temp. 74° (1° above avg.); precip. 0.5" (avg.). 1–6 Scattered t-storms, cool. 7–14 Sunny, hot. 15–25 T-storms, then sunny, warm. 26–31 Scattered t-storms, hot.

AUG. 2008: Temp. 73° (1° above avg.); precip. 1" (avg.). 1–7 Scattered t-storms, hot. 8–13 Sunny, seasonable. 14–24 Scattered t-storms, warm. 25–31 T-storms, then sunny, hot.

SEPT. 2008: Temp. 65° (3° above avg.); precip. 1" (avg.). 1–6 Sunny, very warm. 7–15 T-storms, seasonable. 16–25 Sunny, warm. 26–30 T-storms, turning cooler.

OCT. 2008: Temp. 55° (4° above avg.); precip. 1.5" (0.5" above avg.). 1–5 Sunny, warm. 6–12 T-storms, then sunny, warm. 13–18 Showers, seasonable. 19–23 Showers, cool north; sunny, mild south. 24–31 Rain, cool.

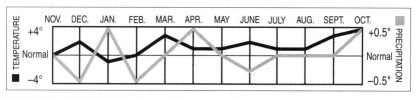

Desert Southwest

SUMMARY: Winter will be about one degree above normal in the east and two degrees above normal in the west, on average. Rainfall will be below normal, with near-normal snowfall. The coldest temperatures will occur in early and mid-January and early to mid- and late February. The snowiest periods in the north and east will be in mid- and late December, early and mid-January, and early and late February.

April and May will be warmer than normal, with near- to above-normal rainfall.

Summer will be slightly above normal, on average, with above-normal rainfall. The hottest periods will occur in mid-June, mid-July, and mid- and late August.

September will be drier than normal, with near-normal temperatures. October will be warmer and rainier than normal.

NOV. 2007: Temp. 57° (2° above avg.); precip. 0.5" (avg.). 1–8 Sunny, warm. 9–13 T-storms, cool. 14–23 Sunny, mild. 24–30 T-storms, then sunny, seasonable.

DEC. 2007: Temp. 50° (3° above avg.); precip. 0.4" (0.1" below avg.). 1–10 Sunny, seasonable. 11–17 Showers, then sunny, seasonable. 18–22 Snow northeast, showers elsewhere, then sunny, cold. 23–26 Sunny, seasonable. 27–31 Snow east, rain west, then sunny, seasonable.

JAN. 2008: Temp. 45° (2° below avg.); precip. 0.1" (0.4" below avg.). 1–2 Sunny, seasonable. 3–11 Snow east, showers west, then sunny, very cold. 12–16 Snow east, cloudy west, then sunny, cold. 17–23 Mostly cloudy, then sunny, seasonable. 24–31 Sunny, warm.

FEB. 2008: Temp. 50.5° (3° below avg. east, 4° above west); precip. 0.6" (0.1" above avg.). 1–3 Sunny, warm. 4–11 Snow east, rain west, then sunny, cold. 12–15 Sunny, seasonable. 16–25 Rain and snow showers, then sunny, seasonable. 26–29 Snow, then sunny, cold north; sunny, cold south.

MAR. 2008: Temp. 60° (3° above avg.); precip. 0.3" (0.2" below avg.). 1–9 Sunny, seasonable. 10–19 Rain and snow showers, then sunny, seasonable. 20–26 Sunny, warm. 27–31 Scattered t-storms, seasonable.

APR. 2008: Temp. 66° (2° above avg.); precip. 0.7" (0.2" above avg.). 1–8 Sunny, warm. 9–18 Sunny, cool. 19–24 Showers, then sunny, cool. 25–30 Sunny, very warm.

MAY 2008: Temp. 75° (2° above avg.); precip. 0.5" (avg.). 1–7 Sunny, turning cool. 8–18 Scattered t-storms, very warm. 19–25 Sunny, very warm. 26–31 Showers, then sunny, cool.

JUNE 2008: Temp. 84° (1° above avg.); precip. 0.3" (0.2" below avg.). 1–7 Scattered t-storms east, sunny west; comfortable. 8–10 Sunny, seasonable. 11–15 Sunny, warm. 16–24 Sunny, warm. 25–30 T-storms east; sunny, hot west.

JULY 2008: Temp. 89° (2° above avg.); precip. 1.5" (avg.). 1–6 Sunny, seasonable. 7–21 Mostly sunny, scattered t-storms, hot. 22–31 T-storms, seasonable.

AUG. 2008: Temp. 83° (2° below avg.); precip. 2.5" (1" above avg.). 1–4 T-storms, seasonable. 5–15 Mostly sunny, scattered t-storms, hot. 16–23 Scattered t-storms, seasonable. 24–31 Scattered t-storms, humid, seasonable.

SEPT. 2008: Temp. 78° (avg.); precip. 0.5" (0.5" below avg.). 1–6 Scattered t-storms, hot. 7–15 Scattered t-storms, seasonable. 16–27 Sunny, very warm. 28–30 T-storms, seasonable.

OCT. 2008: Temp. 70° (3° above avg.); precip. 1.5" (0.5" above avg.). 1–9 Sunny, warm. 10–15 T-storms, seasonable. 16–24 Sunny, warm. 25–31 T-storms, then sunny, seasonable.

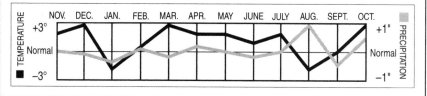

Pacific Northwest

SUMMARY: Winter will be one to two degrees above normal, on average, led by an especially mild February. The coldest periods will be in mid-December and early and mid-January. Rainfall will be below normal in Washington and above normal in Oregon and California. Snowfall will be below normal, with most of it occurring in January.

April and May rainfall will be above normal, especially in the south. Temperatures will be near or slightly above normal, on average.

Summer will be one to two degrees above normal, on average, with below-normal rainfall. The hottest temperatures will occur in early June, late July, and mid- to late August.

September and October will bring above-normal temperatures and above-normal rainfall, especially in the south.

NOV. 2007: Temp. 46° (1° below avg.); precip. 7.5" (2" above avg. north, avg. south). 1–6 Heavy rain, mild. 7–12 Light rain, seasonable. 13–20 Stormy, heavy rain. 21–25 Rain, cool. 26–30 Rainy periods, mild.

DEC. 2007: Temp. 44° (2° above avg.); precip. 6.5" (1" below avg. north, 1" above south). 1–5 Clouds, then sunny, cool. 6–14 Rainy periods, mild. 15–20 Sunny, cold. 21–27 Rain, mild. 28–31 Partly sunny, cool.

JAN. 2008: Temp. 43° (1° above avg.); precip. 7" (1" above avg.). 1–6 Rain to snow, then sunny, very cold. 7–11 Snow to rain, turning milder. 12–21 Sunny, cold. 22–31 Snow, then heavy rain, turning warm.

FEB. 2008: Temp. 48° (4° above avg.); precip. 2.5" (2.5" below avg.). 1–5 Sunny, warm. 6–14 Rain, mild. 15–18 Partly sunny, seasonable. 19–25 Rain, seasonable. 26–29 Partly sunny, cool.

MAR. 2008: Temp. 48° (1° above avg.); precip. 5" (2" below avg. north, 3.5" above south). 1–3 Sunny, seasonable. 4–12 Occasional rain, cool. 13–20 Rain, cool. 21–25 Stormy, heavy rain. 26–31 Sunny, then rain, mild.

APR. 2008: Temp. 50° (avg.); precip. 4.5" (1" below avg. north, 4" above south). 1–8 Rainy periods, seasonable. 9–14 Rain, chilly. 15–21 Partly sunny, showers, cool. 22–30 Rainy periods, cool.

MAY 2008: Temp. 56° (1° above avg.); precip. 3" (1" above avg.). 1–5 Showers, cool. 6–14 Sunny, turning hot. 15–21 T-storms, then sunny, seasonable. 22–26 Sunny, warm. 27–31 Showers, cool.

JUNE 2008: Temp. 61° (1° above avg.); precip. 1" (0.5" below avg.). 1–10 Showers, then sunny, turning hot. 11–13 Sunny, warm. 14–24 Rainy periods, cool. 25–30 Scattered t-storms, seasonable.

JULY 2008: Temp. 66° (2° above avg.); precip. 0.3" (0.2" below avg.). 1–14 Showers, then sunny, seasonable. 15–24 T-storms, then sunny, seasonable. 25–31 Showers, then sunny, warm.

AUG. 2008: Temp. 67° (2° above avg.); precip. 1" (avg.). 1–5 Sunny, warm. 6–11 T-storms, then sunny, warm. 12–19 Scattered t-storms, cool. 20–23 Sunny, very warm. 24–27 Showers, cool. 28–31 Sunny, very warm.

SEPT. 2008: Temp. 62° (1° above avg.); precip. 1.5" (1" below avg. north, 1" above south). 1–3 Sunny, hot. 4–10 T-storms, turning cool. 11–15 Sunny, seasonable. 16–21 Showers, then sunny, very warm. 22–30 Sunny, then showers, seasonable.

OCT. 2008: Temp. 55° (1° above avg.); precip. 5" (2" above avg.). 1–10 Showers, mild. 11–13 Sunny, cool. 14–18 Heavy rain, warm. 19–31 Rainy periods, seasonable.

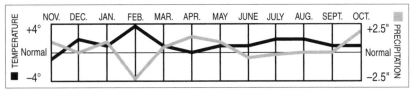

Pacific Southwest

SUMMARY: Winter be will about two degrees above normal, on average, with the coldest periods in mid-December, mid-January, and late February. Rainfall and mountain snowfall will be above normal in the north and near normal in the south. The stormiest periods will be in late January, early February, and early and mid-March.

April will be rainier than normal in the north, with near-normal rainfall in the south. Temperatures will be near normal, on average. May will be a bit warmer than normal, with near-normal rainfall.

Summer will be about one degree above normal, on average, with the hottest periods in mid-July and early to mid- and late August. Scattered t-storms in August will bring above-normal rainfall to the south.

September and October will be warmer than normal, and hot in early and mid- to late September. Rainfall will be above normal in the north and near normal in the south.

NOV. 2007: Temp. 59° (1° above avg.); precip. 0.5" (1" below avg.). 1–2 Sunny, seasonable. 3–7 Scattered showers, seasonable. 8–14 Sunny, cool. 15–19 Coastal clouds, sunny inland; seasonable. 20–30 Showers, then sunny, seasonable.

DEC. 2007: Temp. 55° (2° above avg.); precip. 3" (1" above avg.). 1–4 Sunny, seasonable. 5–12 Showers, mild. 13–15 Sunny. 16–19 Showers, cool. 20–26 Sunny, cool. 27–31 Showers, then sunny, mild.

JAN. 2008: Temp. 55° (2° above avg.); precip. 2.5" (0.5" above avg. north, 2" below south). 1–5 Showers, mild. 6–19 Sunny, cool. 20–22 Cloudy, cool. 23–27 Windy, heavy rain north; showers south; turning warmer. 28–31 Sunny, warm.

FEB. 2008: Temp. 58° (3° above avg.); precip. 4" (1" above avg.). 1–2 Sunny, warm. 3–9 Heavy rain, then showers. 10–23 Sunny, mild. 24–29 Sunny, cool.

MAR. 2008: Temp. 58° (1° above avg.); precip. 3.5" (1" above avg.). 1–7 T-storms, then sunny, seasonable. 8–15 Gusty t-storms, then sunny, mild. 16–20 Showers, then sunny, seasonable. 21–27 Heavy rain, then sunny, cool. 28–31 Showers north, sunny south; seasonable.

APR. 2008: Temp. 60° (avg.); precip. 2" (1.5" above avg. north, avg. south). 1–8 Showers, seasonable. 9–15 Rain, chilly. 16–18 Sunny, cool. 19–30 Showers, then sunny, seasonable.

San Francisco

Fresno

Los Angeles

San Diego

MAY 2008: Temp. 65° (1° above avg.); precip. 0.5" (avg.). 1–10 T-storms, then sunny, seasonable. 11–17 Scattered t-storms; seasonable coast, hot inland. 18–20 Sunny, seasonable. 21–26 Scattered showers, seasonable. 27–31 Sunny, then showers, cool.

JUNE 2008: Temp. 69° (1° above avg.); precip. 0.1" (avg.). 1–6 Sunny, then t-storms, seasonable. 7–14 Sunny, warm. 15–30 Sunny; cool north, warm south.

JULY 2008: Temp. 72° (1° above avg.); precip. 0" (avg.). 1–4 Sunny, warm. 5–9 Sunny; seasonable coast, hot inland. 10–18 Sunny, seasonable. 19–21 Sunny, hot. 22–31 Sunny, seasonable.

AUG. 2008: Temp. 73.5° (1.5° above avg.); precip. 0.3" (avg. north, 0.4" above south). 1–2 Scattered t-storms. 3–9 Sunny, hot. 10–15 Sunny, seasonable. 16–20 Sunny, warm. 21–27 Sunny, very warm. 28–31 Scattered t-storms, hot.

SEPT. 2008: Temp. 74° (4° above avg.); precip. 0.5" (avg. north, 0.5" above south). 1–5 Sunny, hot. 6–14 Scattered t-storms, cooler. 15–18 Sunny, warm. 19–23 Sunny, hot. 24–30 Scattered t-storms, then sunny, warm.

OCT. 2008: Temp. 67° (2° above avg.); precip. 1" (2" above avg. north, 0.5" below south). 1–5 Showers north, sunny south; warm. 6–8 Sunny, seasonable. 9–15 Showers, then sunny, warm. 16–22 Showers, then sunny north; sunny south; warm. 23–26 Sunny, seasonable. 27–31 Rain, seasonable.

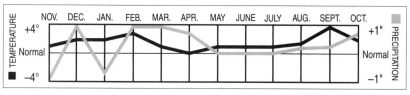

CRAZY 8s

Wild weather events have occurred

in many of the years ending in 8.

Could we be in for more this year?

BY GREGORY A. ZIELINSKI

1748

1888

1898

1908

1918

1928

1938

1948

1958

1978

1988

1998

COINCIDENCES OR CYCLICAL EVENTS?

Big storms and extreme weather events—blizzards, hurricanes, tornadoes, ice storms, heat waves, droughts—occur somewhere in North America just about every year, but in some years they seem to be more abundant and/or extreme. Take years ending in 8, for example: Over the past few centuries, several significant storms have occurred in "8" years. We recount some of them here.

All of this chronological meteorological mayhem got us wondering: Were these predictable cyclical events or random weather phenomena? What conditions spawned these storms? What weather patterns are influencing weather conditions now? In other words, are these past events any indication of what we can expect this year? Read on.

If history repeats itself, and the unexpected always happens, how incapable must Man be of learning from experience.

–George Bernard Shaw, Irish author (1856–1950)

1747–48

This was possibly one of the whitest winters in the U.S. Northeast, with some parts of eastern New England experiencing 25 to 30 snowstorms. Snow depths of 4 to 5 feet were common in some areas of eastern New Hampshire and Massachusetts.

1888

On January 12–13, snow and high-wind conditions swept down from the Dakotas through the Great Plains, resulting in one of the deadliest-ever storms in the prairie states. Winds of 80 mph dropped temperatures by 20 degrees in a few minutes; within a 24-hour period, temperatures went from about 75°F to well below 0°F. About 500 people died, many of them children on their way home from school, causing this event to become known as the Children's Blizzard.

■

On March 12–13, a blizzard blew through the Northeast. Snowfall totals were above 20 inches in most of New England and up to 45 inches in southern Connecticut—rare for that area. Troy, New York, received the greatest accumulation—55 inches. In many New Hampshire towns, March 13 was Town Meeting Day but access to meeting halls was impossible. For this reason, the event has always been known locally as the Town Meeting Day Storm. It is also known as the Great Blizzard or the Great White Hurricane.

A horsecar is abandoned in the streets of New York following a blizzard in March 1888.

-NOAA Photo Library

1898

On July 28, hailstones, some weighing up to 11 ounces, pounded Chicago.

On October 2, a category 4 hurricane roared into Cumberland Island in Florida's Nassau County, killing four people and destroying much of the town. It remains the worst hurricane to have hit that area since record keeping began in 1851.

In November, a storm that developed in the Gulf of Mexico and moved up the East Coast merged with a storm moving eastward from the Great Lakes. The new tempest wreaked havoc in the Northeast on November 26–27, making train tracks impassable, snapping telegraph and telephone poles, and wrecking or stranding more than 200 ships along the coastline. The loss of the steamer *Portland,* with its estimated 191 passengers and crew,

-Chicago History Museum/DN-0069540

During January 1918, 42.5 inches of snow fell the streets of Chicago.

Much devastation occurred in the Northeast as a result of the Portland Gale of 1898.

gave the storm its name: the Portland Gale. (The naming of Atlantic hurricanes after females began in 1953; male names were first used in 1979.)

1908

On April 24–26, as many as 34 tornadoes ripped across southern states from Texas into Georgia and northward from Oklahoma to Tennessee. Some 320 deaths were blamed on the twisters.

1918

A series of blizzards and heavy snowstorms in January brought many U.S. cities to their knees. Snow fell on Chicago on 22 days that month, resulting in a total of 42.5 inches—a record that still stands.

On June 15, one inch of snow was reported in Allentown, Pennsylvania.

1928

On September 16, a category 4 hurricane with a central low pressure of 929 millibars made landfall in southern Florida. Its rain and winds caused Lake Okeechobee to breach dikes on its northern and southern sides, resulting in flooding that led to the deaths of more than 1,800 people. The lake gave the storm its name: the Okeechobee Hurricane.

1938

On April 29, hailstones, some the size of baseballs, fell on Washington, D.C.

(continued)

1938

On September 21, a hurricane swept across Long Island, New York, into Rhode Island, bringing flooding, destruction, and death. Houses on the Rhode Island coast and in downtown Providence were washed away, losses were in the billions (in today's dollars), and over 600 people died. The peak storm surge was 17 feet above normal in the state, and 50-foot-high waves were reported in Gloucester, Massachusetts.

–CelebrateBoston.com

1948

On May 30, devastating floods began in the Pacific Northwest, with the Columbia River at its highest level since 1894. Water crested on June 1 in Portland, Oregon, but remained above flood level for 51 days.

1958

A March storm near Morgantown in southeastern Pennsylvania produced 50 inches of snow.

On April 22, an unusually heavy spring snow dropped 72 inches on Mystic Lake, Montana.

Left: The Great Hurricane of 1938 brought flooding and destruction to many streets along the East Coast, such as this one in Providence, Rhode Island.

Above: In the Pacific Northwest, the Columbia River remained above flood level for 51 days in 1948.

Right: A March 1958, 50-inch snowstorm closed a turnpike in Morgantown, Pennsylvania.

Far right: The blizzard of '78 wreaked havoc in New England, particularly on the streets of Boston, Massachusetts.

1978

On January 26, a storm paralyzed areas around the Great Lakes and in the Ohio River Valley with snow and wind. Thirty inches of snow was reported at Muskegon, Michigan.

On February 6–8, eastern New England experienced a blizzard (unrelated to the January 26 storm) that has been called one of the top weather events of the 20th century. Over 30 inches of snow fell in many areas around Boston, while northeastern Rhode Island reported an unofficial total of 50 inches. Two-story drifts were common, roads were impassable, and some stores and schools closed for up to a week.

On June 24, El Paso, Texas, temperatures reached a record 111°F in the shade.

On December 7, some home owners with swim-ming pools in Los Angeles reported ice on the surface of the water.

1988

A strong high-pressure system entrenched over the central part of North America during most of the summer produced temperatures in excess of 100°F, breaking many long-standing records. The widespread dry conditions contributed to fires that consumed much of Yellowstone National Park. This year saw the peak of the most costly and catastrophic droughts for both the United States and southern Canada since the Dust Bowl of the 1930s. Combined U.S. losses in energy, water, agriculture, and ecosystems were estimated at $39 billion (1987–89). In western Canada, drought-related losses exceeded $1.8 billion in 1988 alone.

◾

In September, Hurricane Gilbert generated the lowest sea-level pressure (26.22 inches, or 888 mb) yet recorded in the Atlantic basin. (In October 2005, Gilbert's mark was eclipsed by Hurricane Wilma's pressure of 882 mb.) Gilbert swept across the Gulf of Mexico, eventually brushing the Brownsville, Texas, area before making landfall in northern Mexico. It later spawned 29 tornadoes.

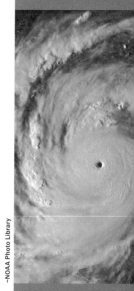

–NOAA Photo Library

1998

On January 5–9, several icing events—precipitation in the form of freezing rain, ice pellets, and snow—completely froze much of northern New England, northern New York,

–Jim Rankin/Toronto Star

southern Quebec and Ontario, and New Brunswick. According to Environment Canada, the storm may have directly affected more people than any other weather event in Canadian history. Total monetary losses were in the hundreds of millions (some say billions) of dollars and millions of people lost power, some for several weeks.

Above: The power of Hurricane Gilbert spawned 29 tornadoes after making landfall in September 1988.

Left: The ice storm of 1998 hit southern Canada hard, causing massive power outages and monetary losses in the hundreds of millions of dollars.

WEATHER OR NOT? Do you have a recollection of a significant weather event in a year ending in 8? Share it with Almanac readers at Almanac.com/weather center. While you're there, get your local forecast and "pastcast"—weather on any day since 1946.

210

CAN THESE HAPPEN AGAIN?

Yes—if conditions are right.

One reason that significant weather events such as those listed could happen again is that some large weather patterns occur in cycles over months, seasons— even years. These patterns are called tele-connections because as they change in one part of the world they influence weather and climate elsewhere. They are "connected" over a great distance, hence the term.

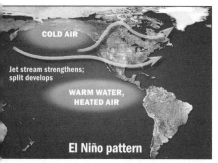

El Niño pattern

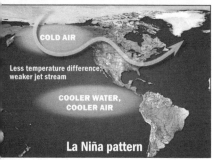

La Niña pattern

One of the patterns, the **El Niño–Southern Oscillation** (ENSO), occurs in the Pacific and changes conditions (or oscillates or flips) every three to seven years. ENSO has two phases, El Niño and La Niña, and each phase portends certain weather conditions based on the movement and temperature of ocean waters.

The snowstorms in 1888 occurred during a weak El Niño, while the Chicago-area snowfalls in 1918 occurred during a La Niña.

For example, during El Niño, when warm waters from the tropical Pacific move eastward toward South America and then northward, we usually experience warm temperatures and increased precipitation in parts of the United States and Canada. On the flip side, when those warm waters move westward toward Australia, we experience a La Niña, which usually results in cool temperatures and much-reduced precipitation.

The key word is "usually"; those conditions are not guaranteed to occur. The very strong El Niño of 1997–98 brought a mild winter to much of the northern United States and southern Canada. However, 1998 was also the year of "the ice storm of the century," which, while not a direct result of the El Niño, occurred under circulation patterns influenced by it. In contrast, the snowstorms in 1888 occurred during a weak El Niño, while both the Chicago-area snowfalls in 1918 and the drought in 1988 occurred during La Niñas.

Other weather patterns dominate the East Coast. One, the **North Atlantic Oscillation** (NAO), is based on a high-pressure system near Bermuda and a low-pressure system near Iceland. The location and strength of these systems can vary throughout the year and influence the course of the jet stream, fast-moving winds

211

North Atlantic Oscillation in a positive phase

North Atlantic Oscillation in a negative phase

in the upper levels of the atmosphere that generally separate cold, dry, polar air from warm, humid, tropical air.

When the pressure difference between the NAO systems is great (a phase that experts call positive, or warm), the jet stream often flows directly across the United States and southern Canada, from west to east, and there is very little major storm activity.

When the pressure difference in the NAO is low (indicating the negative, or cold, phase), the jet stream snakes across the continent, often bringing very cold polar air into the southern United States and very warm air into southern Canada. This extreme contrast leads to the development of major storms, especially during winter in the East—as happened in March 1888, March 1958, and February 1978. An NAO phase can prevail for 10 to 20 years, but during that time, the opposite phase may kick in for a day or a year or two at a time. For example, in 1888, the NAO was mostly positive (or warm) during January, but it was very much in the cold phase for most of the rest of that winter.

A third pattern, the **Atlantic Multi-decadal Oscillation** (AMO), is defined

as fluctuations of about 1°F in northern Atlantic sea-surface temperatures for periods of 20 to 40 years at time. During warm phases of the AMO (the most recent one began in 1995), more tropical storms and weak hurricanes become major hurricanes.

These oscillations have a pronounced impact on our weather, but they are only a few of the patterns that influence it. There are other factors to consider, including sunspots (magnetic storms on the surface of the Sun that occur in 11-year cycles, on average) and episodic events, such as volcanic eruptions that send particles and gases several miles into the atmosphere, blocking the Sun and leading to a very cool year or two. Furthermore, we can not rule out the random year-to-year variability in weather conditions that occurs without the influence of any of these forces. So, keep an eye on the sky for current conditions.

□□

Gregory A. Zielinski is a research professor and the former Maine State Climatologist. He has written a book on New England weather and climate and has taught courses in both meteorology and climate change. He has done extensive research in remote regions of the world on past climate and especially on the effect volcanic eruptions have on climate.

All the Right Reasons to Raise

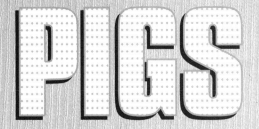

Insights and observations o

the pleasures and peculiarit

of living with swine

BY CHUCK WOOSTER

214

IN A PIG'S STY

- A newborn pig is a piglet.
- A young pig, following weaning, is a shoat.
- An adult domesticated pig, typically heavier than 120 pounds, is a hog.
- A male pig is a boar; a female is a sow.
- The old-fashioned word for a herd of wild pigs is "sounder."
- A herd of domesticated pigs is a drift.

There's something about pigs that doesn't make any sense at all. No barnyard animal has a better nose, yet none produce more odoriferous manure. The pig has cloven hooves—an adaptation shared with flighty prey animals like the sheep, deer, and antelope—yet no barnyard animal displays as much swagger or is less afraid. No animal

is said to be smarter, yet pigs will stay out in the sun so long that they'll repeatedly end up with second-degree sunburns.

The pig is the friendliest animal on the farm by far: always available for a scratch behind the ears, hardly ever moody, and quick with a grunt of delight. Yet the pig would also eat you for supper, if circumstances were right. Pigs are the only meat-eating animals that we humans, in turn, raise for meat.

The pig is said to be the cleanest animal on the farm, yet every child knows that a pig will roll in a mud puddle at the first opportunity. Pigskin (the traditional covering of a football) is one of the toughest and most useful of animal hides, yet a pig's skin is extremely sensitive to temperature and injury. Some breeds of pigs grow ferocious-looking tusks yet dine primarily on roots and vegetables.

As if that's not enough, agriculture itself could scarcely have evolved eons ago without the recycling abilities of the pig, yet fewer and fewer farmers raise even a single pig these days.

ALL IN THE FAMILY. Author Chuck Wooster has the subject of pigs "in the bag." *Opposite, top right:* Cookie, a red and white sow, sniffs at fresh bedding with her piglet; *bottom right:* two Yorkshire crosses enjoy turnip greens atop their daily grain.

At the heart of these conundrums is the relatively straightforward fact that the pig is an omnivore. No other livestock animal has such a wide-ranging and enthusiastic appetite. Pigs will eat anything and everything on the farm, from grain and vegetable scraps to roots, shrubs, meat—even your lawn.

The pig is the original recycler, which is why pigs were the first animals to be domesticated back at the dawn of agriculture. Food items that are no longer fit for consumption by people or other animals (rancid milk, leftovers from the supper table, spoiled hay) are all delicious delights for the accommodating pig, which happily takes everyone else's castoffs and turns them into bacon, sausage, and ham.

Besides recycling, the pig is prized for its earth-moving abilities. Does a new pasture need stumping? Give it over to a drift of pigs, and their rooting and digging for grubs and other insects will have shredded the small stumps by summer's end and made the larger ones easier to dig out. Got too many weeds and weed seeds in the vegetable patch? A season's worth of pig digestion will help solve the problem. Have a daunting pile of winter manure in the barn that needs to be addressed? Poke some holes in it, fill them with grain, and let the pigs at it. You'll have light, well-turned compost in a month or so.

But with most farm energy and fertilizer now being created from fossil fuels, the pig's central role as recycler and earth mover has been eclipsed. This is a shame, because pigs are much easier to raise now than they once were.

The key development has been the invention of the electric fence. Before electricity, the pig's

-photos above: Geoff Hansen/*Living with Pigs*

PIG TALES

- In 1965, more than a million farms in the United States had pigs. Today that number is down to 75,000, even though the number of pigs on U.S. farms has grown from 50 million to 60 million over the same period.

- In Canada, the number of pig farms has decreased from over 220,000 to slightly more than 15,000 since 1965, but the number of pigs has more than doubled.

resemblance to the bulldozer (which, by all rights, should have been named the "hogdozer") made pigs very difficult to

"MIND YOUR SWINE!"

There were often two elected town officials in 18th- and 19th-century America whose positions were directly related to pigs:

- The hog reeve was the equivalent of today's dogcatcher and was responsible for rounding up destructive pigs and keeping them in a town pen until their rightful owner could be summoned to take possession. Some towns required as many as a half-dozen hog reeves at any one time.

- The fence viewer was the neutral third party called in to assign liability after an animal, usually a pig, had broken into a field and laid waste to it. If the property owner's fence met the legal requirements for height and strength, then all damages had to be paid by the pig's owner. If, however, the fence itself was found to be faulty, then the pig's owner was held harmless. Back when most livestock had to be herded to market along town roads, good fences made good neighbors.

contain. To prevent pigs from marauding over the countryside, true two-by-fours, inch-thick (or more) planking, and deeply set posts were required. Pigs are strong enough to unhinge gates and pry boards from posts and are smart enough to figure out the best way to go about it.

But even the smartest pig today has yet to fully understand a "live" wire. Despite their strength and cunning, adult pigs don't jump; so two strands of electric fence, usually strung 6 and 12 inches off the ground, will do the trick. Pigs' wet noses and soft ears guarantee that the wire's message will not be misunderstood.

In the past, strong pigsties were difficult and expensive to build, so they often ended up being smaller than they should have been, causing them to become muddy and stinky—hence the negative connotation associated with "pigsty." But the pig's reputation for filth and stench has more to do with inadequate housing than with the animal itself. A roof is the main requirement to keep off summer sun and the heaviest rains. In regions where cool, wet summers are common, a wall or two to cut down on drafts and a raised floor that stays dry are also in order. Figure on 10 square feet of floor space per pig. This will be excessive when the shoats first arrive home (to contain the shoats in a cozier area, install a partition) but will be quite cramped by the time your hogs reach full size. Cramped isn't necessarily bad. Pigs love social contact; that's why they sleep in pig piles.

Winters are a different story. Boars, sows, and piglets need full shelter to survive cold northern winters because their in bristles provide little insulation. A good layer of fat will keep the main body warm, but those thin, floppy ears are especially prone to frostbite. In the old days, farmers moved their pigs into the dairy barn for the winter to take advantage of the heat thrown off by the cows. These days, with fewer dairy farms, northern pigs usually overwinter in heated buildings.

Given enough space, pigs will quickly define some areas for sleeping, others for eating, and still others for relieving themselves. Ideally, pigs will also have a muddy wallow or two. Pigs don't sweat, so a roll in the mud is good for keeping cool, staving off sunburn, and keeping flies at bay. Pigs don't need to be pampered.

For food, augment whatever supplies are cheaply available (bakery seconds inspire squeals of delight, as do table scraps) with a mixture of grain designed specifically for pigs. The grain ensures a balanced diet. Also be sure to supply clean water in abundance. A pig doesn't lap water like a dog; it inserts its whole mouth into the trough and guzzles with enthusiasm. A few gallons can disappear in a flash.

Most farmers raise pigs just during the summer, buying shoats in the spring; fattening them on grain, greens, and leftovers during the summer; and slaughtering mature hogs in the fall. A few pigs make the cut and go on to live long lives as smart, beloved pets—a development that, from an old farmer's perspective, and like the pig itself, doesn't make any sense at all.

Common Pig Breeds

Most piglets being raised for meat are a mix, either accidental or deliberate, of two (or more!) of the following breeds:

YORKSHIRE: what most people think of when they picture a pig—white bristles, pink skin, upright ears, no spots

CHESTER WHITE: a slightly smaller version of the Yorkshire, with ears that don't stand straight up, but flop forward

LANDRACE: also similar to the Yorkshire except that its big, distinctive, droopy ears flop right in front of its eyes

LACOMBE: a shorter, stockier version of the Landrace that is common in Canada

DUROC: the most common all-red pig

(continued)

THREE LITTLE PIGS. Left to right: the Duroc, Hampshire, and Yorkshire breeds.

BERKSHIRE: a black pig with upright ears whose extremities (nose, tail, feet) appear to have been dipped in white paint

POLAND CHINA: a black pig with white extremities like the Berkshire's yet droopy ears that fall toward the eyes

HAMPSHIRE: a black pig with a white band around the front flank and forelegs

SPOTTED: as the name suggests, a pig with a mixture of black and white spots

ABOUT THE SILK PURSE

- The saying "you can't make a silk purse from a sow's ear" is often used to describe an impossible undertaking. But one time in 1921, the adage was turned on its ear by the consulting firm Arthur D. Little, which turned 100 pounds of pig ears into 10 pounds of gelatin. After much experimentation, the researchers transformed the sticky stew into fine threads, which were woven into a cloth akin to silk and then made into two purses. The extremely expensive "silk" purses, the company admitted, served no purpose other than to create conversation.

–George Homsy

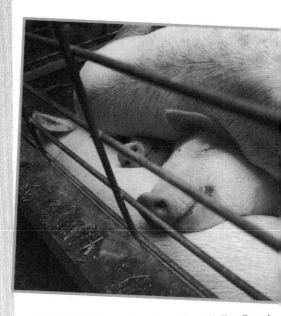

PIG PILE! Piglets nap in a pile at North Hollow Farm in Rochester, Vermont.

PORCINE FACTS AND FIGURES

■ The fastest member of the pig family is th warthog, which can reach speeds of 35 mph.

■ Though "pigging out" is synonymous wi gluttony, the stomach of a pig is proportionate much smaller than that of a cow or sheep.

■ To find out how much a pig weighs, measu its girth (in inches) by wrapping a tape measu around the animal just behind the front legs. The measure the length from the ears to the base of tl tail. The pig's weight (in pounds) will be equal the square of the girth, times the length, divid by 400. If math isn't your thing, buy a hog tape the feed store; the calculations are built into

□

Chuck Wooster, a farmer in Vermont, keeps a drift of th to five pigs each summer. He is the author of *Living with She* (Lyons Press, 2005) and *Living with Pigs* (Lyons Press, 200

–photo: Geoff Hansen/*Living with*

Gestation and Mating Table

	Proper Age for First Mating	Period of Fertility (years)	Number of Females for One Male	Period of Gestation (days)	
				AVERAGE	**RANGE**
Ewe	90 lbs. or 1 yr.	6		147 / 151[1]	142–154
Ram	12–14 mos., well matured	7	50–75[2] / 35–40[3]		
Mare	3 yrs.	10–12		336	310–370
Stallion	3 yrs.	12–15	40–45[4] / Record 252[5]		
Cow	15–18 mos.[6]	10–14		283	279–290[7] 262–300[8]
Bull	1 yr., well matured	10–12	50[4] / Thousands[5]		
Sow	5–6 mos. or 250 lbs.	6		115	110–120
Boar	250–300 lbs.	6	50[2] / 35–40[3]		
Doe goat	10 mos. or 85–90 lbs.	6		150	145–155
Buck goat	Well matured	5	30		
Bitch	16–18 mos.	8		63	58–67
Male dog	12–16 mos.	8	8–10		
Queen cat	12 mos.	6		63	60–68
Tom cat	12 mos.	6	6–8		
Doe rabbit	6 mos.	5–6		31	30–32
Buck rabbit	6 mos.	5–6	30		

[1]For fine wool breeds. [2]Hand-mated. [3]Pasture. [4]Natural. [5]Artificial. [6]Holstein and beef: 750 lbs.; Jersey: 500 lbs. [7]Beef; 8–10 days shorter for Angus. [8]Dairy.

Incubation Period of Poultry (days)
Chicken. 21
Duck 26–32
Goose 30–34
Guinea 26–28

Maximum Life Span of Animals in Captivity (years)
Cat (domestic). 34
Chicken (domestic). 25
Dog (domestic) 29
Duck (domestic) 23
Goat (domestic). 20
Goose (domestic) 20
Horse 62
Rabbit . . . . 18+

	Estral/Estrous Cycle (including heat period)		Length of Estrus (heat)		Usual Time of Ovulation	When Cycle Recurs if Not Bred
	AVERAGE	**RANGE**	**AVERAGE**	**RANGE**		
Mare	21 days	10–37 days	5–6 days	2–11 days	24–48 hours before end of estrus	21 days
Sow	21 days	18–24 days	2–3 days	1–5 days	30–36 hours after start of estrus	21 days
Ewe	16½ days	14–19 days	30 hours	24–32 hours	12–24 hours before end of estrus	16½ days
Goat	21 days	18–24 days	2–3 days	1–4 days	Near end of estrus	21 days
Cow	21 days	18–24 days	18 hours	10–24 hours	10–12 hours after end of estrus	21 days
Bitch	24 days		7 days	5–9 days	1–3 days after first acceptance	Pseudo-pregnancy
Cat		15–21 days	3–4 days, if mated	9–10 days, in absence of male	24–56 hours after coitus	Pseudo-pregnancy

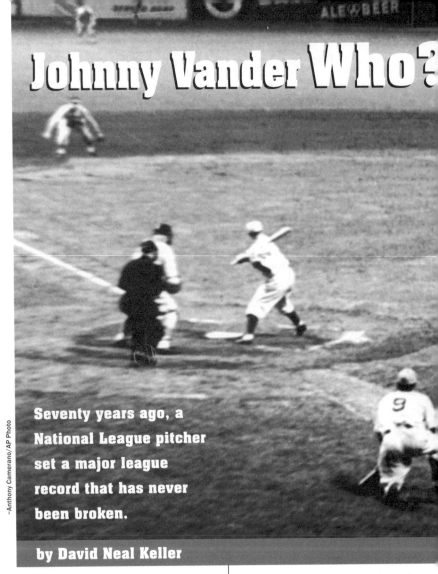

Johnny Vander Who?

Seventy years ago, a National League pitcher set a major league record that has never been broken.

by David Neal Keller

J ohn Vander Meer's love of baseball began when he won a baseball in a first-grade spelling bee. Soon, he found himself playing first base in games with friends in Midland Park, New Jersey. When the older boys discovered that he had an extraordinarily strong arm, they invited

him to pitch. "The opposing player never got a hit off of me that first day o the mound," he recalled later. "The couldn't, because I walked them all.

In August 1928, shortly after com pleting the eighth grade, Johnny be came convinced that contributing to modest family income overshadowe the need for further formal education, s

Johnny Vander Meer
pitches his second
consecutive no-hit,
no-run game against
the Brooklyn Dodgers
on June 15, 1938.

e took a job as an engraver with United Piece
Dye Works in Hawthorne. He satisfied his pas-
ion for baseball by pitching for area semipro
eams in his off-hours.

Fred Pridmore, a fan with major league connec-
ions, was in the stands for more than a few of those
ames, including five in which the 17-year-old hurler al-
owed no hits and no runs. That fall, Pridmore got Johnny
weekend tryout with the New York Giants. Unfortunately,

–National Baseball Hall of Fame Library

A 1938 Cincinnati Reds newsletter *(left)* credits Bill McKechnie *(right)* for Vander Meer's increased control and improvement.

Vander Meer's first no-hitter on June 11, 1938, was featured on a baseball card *(below)*.

Giants manager Bill Terry was not there to watch, so the disappointed young hopeful returned to his job. Within four months, however, a relentless Pridmore convinced the Brooklyn Dodgers to take Vander Meer south for spring training, which began on January 22, 1933.

Johnny's early mound exploits with the Dodgers threatened to shut out any dreams of a career. He would kick his right leg high in the air, twist his 6-foot, 1-inch frame into a corkscrew windup, and throw wildly toward batters who frequently expressed fear for their lives. The young southpaw confessed that he "hardly missed hitting a single spot" on the body of veteran Left O'Doul, one of the few Dodger regulars not afraid to enter the batting cage. Nevertheless, encouragement from the resilient O'Doul, who advised him to "keep firing," helped build Vander Meer's confidence when more than a few baseball men diagnosed him as incurably wild.

When the Dodgers began the regular season, Johnny was assigned to its Dayton, Ohio, farm team. Inconsistency, in the form of alternating strings of strikeouts and walks, persisted at Dayton, then Scranton, Pennsylvania, but his velocity and low earned run averages attracted the attention of major league scouts. In late 1935, the major league Boston Bees claimed him, but reneged when he reported the need to treat a sore arm. Th

-images above courtesy Dick Miller collection

224

Nashville Volunteers, another farm team, felt differently and paid for therapy before he joined that club at the beginning of the 1936 season. Yet, two months later, his wildness prompted a reassignment to Durham, North Carolina.

Vander Meer always credited the Durham manager and coaches for teaching him control. From June 1936 onward, he compiled a 19–6 season record and led all of organized baseball with 295 strikeouts in 214 innings. You can only imagine the buzz in the Boston Bees locker room when *The Sporting News* selected him as the outstanding minor league player of the year.

Signed quickly by the Cincinnati Reds for the 1937 season, Vander Meer appeared in 20 games (he won three and lost five) before being sent down to the team's Syracuse, New York, farm club for more starting opportunities. A disappointing 5–11 record at Syracuse might have been a career-ending skid for some players. But Vander Meer reacted by working harder. "I know I'm a better ball player than the showing I made during the past season," he insisted in a letter he wrote that winter to Reds general manager Warren C. Giles.

The persistence paid off. Vander Meer was invited back to spring training in 1938, and found himself under the patient tutelage of the Reds' new manager, Bill McKechnie. In his first regular-season start against the Pittsburgh Pirates, Vander Meer was taken out in the fourth inning because of wildness. After two relief appearances, he again came up against the Pirates, beating them until the ninth inning when, beset with loss of control, he had to be saved by a relief pitcher. The same thing recurred against the St. Louis Cardinals.

Then came what Johnny Vander Meer often called the greatest day in his career: May 20, 1938. The Reds were playing the defending world champion New York Giants (the team that had once rejected him) at New York City's Polo Grounds, the Giants' home park. McKechnie had not named his starter, but so certain was Vander Meer that he would not be used, he went fishing that morning. Only moments before the game, McKechnie announced his choice: Vander Meer. He did not disappoint, delivering a five-hit, 4–0 shutout, his first complete-game major league victory of the year.

On June 11, Vander Meer was back on the mound, at home, against the Boston Bees for the beginning of what he would consider "miracles beyond my wildest dreams." From the first pitch, he was relaxed and in control. It wasn't until the sixth inning that he realized that the Bees were hitless. Bees manager Casey Stengel and coach George Kelley were chanting steadily in an obvious effort to break his concentration—but their needling didn't sting. In the ninth, considered Vander Meer's "jinx" inning, Stengel sent three top pinch hitters to the plate. Instead of losing his control, the

225

23-year-old hurler retired them all. With that, his 3–0 no-hitter was secure.

While teammates hoisted the new pitching sensation onto their shoulders, fans rushed to greet them. Meanwhile, hundreds of autograph hunters and well-wishers remained long after the game was over to get a glimpse of him leaving the dressing room.

The new hero's next appearance on the rubber was just four days later, against the Dodgers in Brooklyn. Some 40,000 fans crammed into Ebbets Field that evening. Most spectators were enticed by the opportunity to attend the first night game in New York. Vander

"Sign here," they said.

The morning after Vander Meer's record-setting second no-hit, no-run game, agents with offers for radio appearances and endorsements of everything from breakfast foods to clothespins, as well as adoring fans, descended on the New York hotel where the Reds were enjoying a day off. One newsman described "an army of photographers" struggling among autograph seekers in the lobby, until they discovered that the young pitcher had spent the night with his family. The horde then pushed on to Midland Park. No one, however, was able to locate the star. He had risen at 4:30 A.M. to go fishing with his closest boyhood friend, state trooper Orie Yonker.

In Cincinnati, fans and civic organizations rushed to make plans for a homecoming parade. Journalists coined nicknames such as "Dutch Master" and "Vander Miracle." One sportswriter suggested that a statue of "No-Hit Johnny" be erected in Garfield Square, replacing one of former president James Garfield. The Ohio legislature passed a resolution paying tribute "to the newly crowned king of pitching."

In the days that followed, Vander Meer referred the agents to Reds general manager Warren Giles, who had agreed to handle his business affairs and continued to do so—for the total compensation of one dollar. Vander Meer signed so many autographs that a friend observed, "It's a good thing he writes with his right hand, or he would never be able to pitch."

Johnny Vander Meer

226

Meer's appearance seemed almost incidental to most but not all of them. In the stands to watch him for the first time as a big leaguer were his parents. Several busloads of Midland Park rooters were also in attendance. Events that evening might seem ludicrous had they been fiction. Mixing his fastball and sharp-breaking curve, Johnny began retiring batters. When the sixth inning ended without a Brooklyn hit, even Flatbush fans began cheering for him. "Even hard-boiled sportswriters screamed, 'Come on, kid!,'" wrote a *TIME* reporter.

Leading 6–0 going into the bottom of the ninth, Vander Meer retired the first batter on a grounder, amid deafening roars from the stands. Then he walked Babe Phelps, briefly raising the possibility of a game-ending double play. But no chance! Two more consecutive walks filled the bases with only one out. Suddenly, the sympathetic crowd hushed. McKechnie walked to the mound. "You are trying to put too much on the ball, John," he said. "Just get it over. Those hitters are scared to death."

"It wasn't what he said so much, but the way he said it that brought back my waning confidence and control," Vander Meer later explained.

Brooklyn's Ernie Koy hit a roller to third and Lew Riggs made a play to throw him out at the plate. The bases were still loaded, and Leo Durocher, considered a particularly dangerous clutch hitter, was up. After fouling deep into the stands, the peppery shortstop lifted a pop fly to center field. Harry Craft caught it easily and jubilantly raced with other players to swarm their pitcher.

It was a magic moment. At that time, only nine players had pitched two no-hit, no-run games in their careers, but none had achieved the feat in a single season. Johnny Vander Meer had just done it in back-to-back games within one week, in his first full year as a major league pitcher.

In his next appearance, Vander Meer extended his no-hit streak by three and a third innings, in another winning effort against the Bees. When Debs Garms finally broke the string with a single off a fastball, Johnny felt a strange relief from what he described as "the severe tension" that had begun to build. "I think that if I'd had a ten-dollar bill in my baseball pants, I'd have gone over to first base and handed it to Garms," he recalled, laughing. ☐ ☐

EXTRA INNINGS
It's not all over. For more on Johnny Vander Meer's outstanding career, go to **Almanac.com/extras.**

David Neal Keller, who lives near Salem, South Carolina, has spent most of his career combining freelance script-, magazine, and book writing with independent motion picture and videotape production.

Secrets of the Zodiac

The Man of the Signs

Ancient astrologers believed that each astrological sign influenced a specific part of the body. The first sign of the zodiac—Aries—was attributed to the head, with the rest of the signs moving down the body, ending with Pisces at the feet.

♈	Aries, head	**ARI**	*Mar. 21–Apr. 20*
♉	Taurus, neck	**TAU**	*Apr. 21–May 20*
♊	Gemini, arms	**GEM**	*May 21–June 20*
♋	Cancer, breast	**CAN**	*June 21–July 22*
♌	Leo, heart	**LEO**	*July 23–Aug. 22*
♍	Virgo, belly	**VIR**	*Aug. 23–Sept. 22*
♎	Libra, reins	**LIB**	*Sept. 23–Oct. 22*
♏	Scorpio, secrets . . .	**SCO**	*Oct. 23–Nov. 22*
♐	Sagittarius, thighs . .	**SAG**	*Nov. 23–Dec. 21*
♑	Capricorn, knees . .	**CAP**	*Dec. 22–Jan. 19*
♒	Aquarius, legs	**AQU**	*Jan. 20–Feb. 19*
♓	Pisces, feet	**PSC**	*Feb. 20–Mar. 20*

Astrology vs. Astronomy

■ **Astrology** is a tool we use to plan events according to the astrological placements of the Sun, the Moon, and the planets in the 12 signs of the zodiac. The planetary movements do not cause events; rather, they explain the path, or "flow," that events tend to follow. **Astronomy** is the study of the actual placement of the known planets and constellations. *(The placement of the planets in the signs of the zodiac is not the same astrologically and astronomically.)* The Moon's astrological place is given on **page 229**; its astronomical place is given in the **Left-Hand Calendar Pages, 114–140.**

The dates in the **Best Times table, page 230,** are based on the astrological passage of the Moon. However, consider all indicators before making any major decisions.

When Mercury Is Retrograde

■ Sometimes the other planets appear to be traveling backward through the zodiac; this is an illusion. We call this illusion *retrograde motion.*

Mercury's retrograde periods can cause our plans to go awry. However, this is an excellent time to reflect on the past. Intuition is high during these periods and coincidences can be extraordinary.

When Mercury is retrograde, remain flexible, allow extra time for travel, and avoid signing contracts. Review projects and plans at these times, but wait until Mercury is direct again to make any final decisions.

In 2008, Mercury will be retrograde from January 28–February 19, May 26–June 19, and September 24–October 15. *–Celeste Longacre*

Gardening by the Moon's Sign

Use the chart opposite to find the best dates for the following garden tasks:

■ **Plant, transplant, and graft:** Cancer, Scorpio, and Pisces. Taurus, Virgo, and Capricorn are good second choices.

■ **Control insect pests, plow, and weed:** Aries, Gemini, Leo, Sagittarius, or Aquarius.

■ **Prune:** Aries, Leo, or Sagittarius. During a waxing Moon, pruning encourages growth; during a waning Moon, it discourages growth.

■ **Build/fix fences or garden beds:** Capricorn.

■ **Clean out the garden shed:** Virgo.

Setting Eggs by the Moon's Sign

■ Chicks take about 21 days to hatch. Those born under a waxing Moon, in the fruitful signs of Cancer, Scorpio, and Pisces, are healthier and mature faster. To ensure that chicks are born during these times, determine the best days to "set eggs" (to place eggs in an incubator or under a hen). To calculate, find the three fruitful birth signs on the chart below. Use the **Left-Hand Calendar Pages, 114–140,** to find the dates of the new and full Moon. Using only the fruitful dates between the new and full Moon, count back 21 days to find the best days to set eggs.

E X A M P L E :

In June, the Moon is new on the 3rd and full on the 18th. Between these dates, on the 5th and the 6th, the Moon is in the sign of Cancer. To have chicks born on June 5, count back 21 days; set eggs on May 15.

Moon's Astrological Place, 2007–08

	Nov.	Dec.	Jan.	Feb.	Mar.	Apr.	May	June	July	Aug.	Sept.	Oct.	Nov.	Dec.
1	LEO	VIR	LIB	SAG	SAG	AQU	PSC	TAU	GEM	LEO	LIB	SCO	SAG	CAP
2	LEO	VIR	SCO	SAG	CAP	AQU	ARI	TAU	CAN	LEO	LIB	SCO	CAP	AQU
3	VIR	LIB	SCO	CAP	CAP	PSC	ARI	GEM	CAN	VIR	LIB	SAG	CAP	AQU
4	VIR	LIB	SAG	CAP	AQU	PSC	TAU	GEM	LEO	VIR	SCO	SAG	CAP	AQU
5	VIR	LIB	SAG	CAP	AQU	ARI	TAU	CAN	LEO	LIB	SCO	SAG	AQU	PSC
6	LIB	SCO	SAG	AQU	PSC	ARI	GEM	CAN	VIR	LIB	SAG	CAP	AQU	PSC
7	LIB	SCO	CAP	AQU	PSC	TAU	GEM	LEO	VIR	SCO	SAG	CAP	PSC	ARI
8	SCO	SAG	CAP	PSC	ARI	TAU	CAN	LEO	VIR	SCO	SAG	CAP	PSC	ARI
9	SCO	SAG	AQU	PSC	ARI	GEM	CAN	VIR	LIB	SCO	CAP	AQU	PSC	TAU
10	SCO	SAG	AQU	ARI	ARI	GEM	LEO	VIR	LIB	SAG	CAP	AQU	ARI	TAU
11	SAG	CAP	AQU	ARI	TAU	CAN	LEO	LIB	SCO	SAG	AQU	PSC	ARI	GEM
12	SAG	CAP	PSC	TAU	TAU	CAN	LEO	LIB	SCO	CAP	AQU	PSC	TAU	GEM
13	CAP	AQU	PSC	TAU	GEM	LEO	VIR	LIB	SAG	CAP	AQU	ARI	TAU	CAN
14	CAP	AQU	ARI	GEM	GEM	LEO	VIR	SCO	SAG	CAP	PSC	ARI	GEM	CAN
15	CAP	PSC	ARI	GEM	CAN	VIR	LIB	SCO	SAG	AQU	PSC	TAU	GEM	LEO
16	AQU	PSC	TAU	CAN	CAN	VIR	LIB	SAG	CAP	AQU	ARI	TAU	CAN	LEO
17	AQU	PSC	TAU	CAN	LEO	VIR	SCO	SAG	CAP	PSC	ARI	GEM	CAN	VIR
18	PSC	ARI	GEM	CAN	LEO	LIB	SCO	SAG	AQU	PSC	TAU	GEM	LEO	VIR
19	PSC	ARI	GEM	LEO	VIR	LIB	SCO	CAP	AQU	ARI	TAU	CAN	LEO	LIB
20	ARI	TAU	CAN	LEO	VIR	SCO	SAG	CAP	AQU	ARI	GEM	CAN	VIR	LIB
21	ARI	TAU	CAN	VIR	LIB	SCO	SAG	AQU	PSC	ARI	GEM	LEO	VIR	LIB
22	TAU	GEM	LEO	VIR	LIB	SCO	CAP	AQU	PSC	TAU	CAN	LEO	LIB	SCO
23	TAU	GEM	LEO	LIB	LIB	SAG	CAP	AQU	ARI	TAU	CAN	LEO	LIB	SCO
24	GEM	CAN	VIR	LIB	SCO	SAG	CAP	PSC	ARI	GEM	LEO	VIR	LIB	SAG
25	GEM	CAN	VIR	LIB	SCO	CAP	AQU	PSC	TAU	GEM	LEO	VIR	SCO	SAG
26	CAN	LEO	VIR	SCO	SAG	CAP	AQU	ARI	TAU	CAN	VIR	LIB	SCO	SAG
27	CAN	LEO	LIB	SCO	SAG	CAP	PSC	ARI	TAU	CAN	VIR	LIB	SAG	CAP
28	LEO	VIR	LIB	SAG	SAG	AQU	PSC	TAU	GEM	LEO	VIR	SCO	SAG	CAP
29	LEO	VIR	SCO	SAG	CAP	AQU	PSC	TAU	GEM	LEO	LIB	SCO	SAG	AQU
30	LEO	LIB	SCO	—	CAP	PSC	ARI	GEM	CAN	VIR	LIB	SCO	CAP	AQU
31	—	LIB	SCO	—	AQU	—	ARI	—	CAN	VIR	—	SAG	—	AQU

Best Times

The following month-by-month chart is based on the Moon's sign and shows the best days each month for certain activities. *—Celeste Longacre*

	JAN.	FEB.	MAR.	APR.	MAY	JUNE	JULY	AUG.	SEPT.	OCT.	NOV.	DEC.
Quit smoking	1, 24, 28	21, 25	6, 24	3, 22, 30	4, 27	23, 28	2, 21, 25, 29	19, 29	17, 26, 30	15, 23	19, 24	17, 22
Begin diet to lose weight	1, 24, 28	21, 25	6, 24	3, 22, 30	4, 27	23, 28	2, 21, 25, 29	19, 29	17, 26, 30	15, 23	19, 24	17, 22
Begin diet to gain weight	11, 15	8, 12	10, 19	7, 11, 15	12, 17	9, 14	6, 10	2, 6	3, 13	10, 14	7, 11	4, 9
Cut hair to discourage growth	1, 27, 28	23, 24, 25	6, 21, 22, 23	3, 4, 30	1, 28, 29	1, 2, 24, 25	21, 22, 25, 26	17, 18, 22, 23	18, 19, 24, 25	15, 16, 26, 27	18, 19, 22, 23	15, 16, 20, 21
Cut hair to encourage growth	12, 16, 17	12, 13, 19, 20	10, 11, 17, 18	7, 8, 13, 14	10, 11, 15, 16	7, 8, 11, 12, 13	4, 5, 9, 10	2, 5, 6	1, 2, 3, 14	11, 12	7, 8, 12	5, 6, 9, 10
Have dental care	25, 26	21, 22	19, 20	16, 17	13, 14	9, 10	6, 7	3, 4, 30, 31	26, 27, 28	24, 25	20, 21	17, 18
Start projects	9, 10	8, 9	8, 9	7, 8	6, 7	4, 5	4, 5	2, 3	1, 30	29, 30	28, 29	28, 29
End projects	6, 7	5, 6	5, 6	4, 5	3, 4	1, 2	1, 2	28, 29	27, 28	26, 27	25, 26	25, 26
Go camping	5, 6	1, 2, 28, 29	26, 27, 28	23, 24	20, 21	16, 17, 18	13, 14, 15	10, 11	6, 7	3, 4, 31	1, 27, 28	24, 25, 26
Plant aboveground crops	12, 13, 21	8, 9, 16, 17	8, 15, 16	11, 12	17, 18, 19	5, 6, 14, 15	11, 12	7, 8, 9	4, 5, 14	1, 2, 11, 12	7, 8	5, 6
Plant belowground crops	2, 3, 29, 30, 31	26, 27	24, 25	3, 4, 21, 22	1, 27, 28, 29	24, 25	2, 21, 22, 30, 31	17, 18, 26, 27	22, 23	19, 20	16, 17, 25, 26	13, 14, 22, 23
Destroy pests and weeds	14, 15	10, 11	8, 9	5, 6	2, 3, 30, 31	26, 27	23, 24	19, 20	16, 17	13, 14	10, 11	7, 8
Graft or pollinate	19, 20	16, 17	15, 16	11, 12	8, 9	5, 6	2, 3, 30, 31	26, 27	22, 23	19, 20	16, 17	13, 14
Prune to encourage growth	14, 15	10, 11, 19, 20	9, 17, 18	13, 14	10, 11	7, 8, 16, 17	4, 5, 14, 15	2, 10, 11	6, 7	3, 4, 5, 13	1, 10, 11	7, 8
Prune to discourage growth	5, 6, 23	1, 2, 28, 29	1, 27, 28	5, 23, 24	2, 3, 30, 31	26, 27	23, 24	19, 20, 28, 29	16, 17, 24, 25	22, 23	18, 19, 27, 28	15, 16, 24, 25
Harvest aboveground crops	16, 17	12, 13	10, 11, 19, 20	8, 16, 17	13, 14	9, 10	6, 7, 16, 17	3, 4, 13, 14	9, 10	6, 7	2, 3, 12, 30	1, 9, 10
Harvest belowground crops	25, 26	3, 4, 22	2, 3, 29, 30	25, 26, 27	4, 23, 24	19, 20, 28, 29	25, 26	22, 23, 30, 31	18, 19, 26, 27	15, 16, 24, 25	20, 21	17, 18, 27, 28
Make sauerkraut, can, or pickle	2, 3, 30, 31	26, 27	25, 26	3, 4, 21, 22	1, 28, 29	24, 25	21, 22, 30, 31	17, 18, 26, 27	22, 23	19, 20	16, 17, 25, 26	13, 22, 23
Cut hay	14, 15	10, 11	8, 9	5, 6	2, 3, 30, 31	26, 27	23, 24	19, 20	16, 17	13, 14	10, 11	25, 26
Begin logging	7, 8	3, 4	2, 3, 29, 30	25, 26, 27	23, 24	19, 20	16, 17	12, 13, 14	9, 10	6, 7, 8	3, 4, 30	27, 28
Set posts or pour concrete	7, 8	3, 4	2, 3, 29, 30	25, 26, 27	23, 24	19, 20	16, 17	12, 13, 14	9, 10	6, 7, 8	3, 4, 30	27, 28
Breed animals	2, 3, 29, 30, 31	26, 27	24, 25	20, 21, 22	17, 18, 19	14, 15	11, 12	7, 8, 9	4, 5	1, 2, 28, 29, 30	25, 26	22, 23
Wean animals	1, 24, 28	21, 25	6, 24	3, 22, 30	4, 27	23, 28	2, 21, 25, 29	19, 29	17, 26, 30	15, 23	19, 24	17, 22
Castrate animals	9, 10	6, 7	4, 5, 31	1, 2, 28, 29	25, 26	21, 22	19, 20	15, 16	11, 12	9, 10	5, 6	2, 3, 30, 31
Slaughter livestock	2, 3, 29, 30, 31	26, 27	24, 25	20, 21, 22	18, 19	14, 15	11, 12	7, 8, 9	4, 5	1, 2, 28, 29, 30	25, 26	22, 23

Frosts and Growing Seasons

■ Dates given are normal averages for a light freeze; local weather and topography may cause considerable variations. The possibility of frost occurring after the spring dates and before the fall dates is 50 percent. The classification of freeze temperatures is usually based on their effect on plants. **Light freeze:** 29° to 32°F—tender plants killed. **Moderate freeze:** 25° to 28°F—widely destructive effect on most vegetation. **Severe freeze:** 24°F and colder—heavy damage to most plants.

–courtesy of National Climatic Data Center

State	City	Growing Season (days)	Last Spring Frost	First Fall Frost	State	City	Growing Season (days)	Last Spring Frost	First Fall Frost
AK	Juneau	133	May 16	Sept. 26	ND	Bismarck	129	May 14	Sept. 20
AL	Mobile	273	Feb. 27	Nov. 26	NE	Blair	165	Apr. 27	Oct. 10
AR	Pine Bluff	234	Mar. 19	Nov. 8	NE	North Platte	136	May 11	Sept. 24
AZ	Phoenix	309	Feb. 5	Dec. 15	NH	Concord	121	May 23	Sept. 22
AZ	Tucson	274	Feb. 28	Nov. 29	NJ	Newark	219	Apr. 4	Nov. 10
CA	Eureka	325	Jan. 30	Dec. 15	NM	Carlsbad	223	Mar. 29	Nov. 7
CA	Sacramento	290	Feb. 14	Dec. 1	NM	Los Alamos	157	May 8	Oct. 13
CA	San Francisco	*	*	*	NV	Las Vegas	259	Mar. 7	Nov. 21
CO	Denver	157	May 3	Oct. 8	NY	Albany	144	May 7	Sept. 29
CT	Hartford	167	Apr. 25	Oct. 10	NY	Syracuse	170	Apr. 28	Oct. 16
DE	Wilmington	198	Apr. 13	Oct. 29	OH	Akron	168	May 3	Oct. 18
FL	Miami	*	*	*	OH	Cincinnati	195	Apr. 14	Oct. 27
FL	Tampa	339	Jan. 28	Jan. 3	OK	Lawton	217	Apr. 1	Nov. 5
GA	Athens	224	Mar. 28	Nov. 8	OK	Tulsa	218	Mar. 30	Nov. 4
GA	Savannah	250	Mar. 10	Nov. 15	OR	Pendleton	188	Apr. 15	Oct. 21
IA	Atlantic	141	May 9	Sept. 28	OR	Portland	217	Apr. 3	Nov. 7
IA	Cedar Rapids	161	Apr. 29	Oct. 7	PA	Carlisle	182	Apr. 20	Oct. 20
ID	Boise	153	May 8	Oct. 9	PA	Williamsport	168	Apr. 29	Oct. 15
IL	Chicago	187	Apr. 22	Oct. 26	RI	Kingston	144	May 8	Sept. 30
IL	Springfield	185	Apr. 17	Oct. 19	SC	Charleston	253	Mar. 11	Nov. 20
IN	Indianapolis	180	Apr. 22	Oct. 20	SC	Columbia	211	Apr. 4	Nov. 2
IN	South Bend	169	May 1	Oct. 18	SD	Rapid City	145	May 7	Sept. 29
KS	Topeka	175	Apr. 21	Oct. 14	TN	Memphis	228	Mar. 23	Nov. 7
KY	Lexington	190	Apr. 17	Oct. 25	TN	Nashville	207	Apr. 5	Oct. 29
LA	Monroe	242	Mar. 9	Nov. 7	TX	Amarillo	197	Apr. 14	Oct. 29
LA	New Orleans	289	Feb. 20	Dec. 5	TX	Denton	231	Mar. 25	Nov. 12
MA	Worcester	172	Apr. 27	Oct. 17	TX	San Antonio	265	Mar. 3	Nov. 24
MD	Baltimore	231	Mar. 26	Nov. 13	UT	Cedar City	134	May 20	Oct. 2
ME	Portland	143	May 10	Sept. 30	UT	Spanish Fork	156	May 8	Oct. 12
MI	Lansing	140	May 13	Sept. 30	VA	Norfolk	239	Mar. 23	Nov. 17
MI	Marquette	159	May 12	Oct. 19	VA	Richmond	198	Apr. 10	Oct. 26
MN	Duluth	122	May 21	Sept. 21	VT	Burlington	142	May 11	Oct. 1
MN	Willmar	152	May 4	Oct. 4	WA	Seattle	232	Mar. 24	Nov. 11
MO	Jefferson City	173	Apr. 26	Oct. 16	WA	Spokane	153	May 4	Oct. 5
MS	Columbus	215	Mar. 27	Oct. 29	WI	Green Bay	143	May 12	Oct. 2
MS	Vicksburg	250	Mar. 13	Nov. 18	WI	Janesville	164	Apr. 28	Oct. 10
MT	Fort Peck	146	May 5	Sept. 28	WV	Parkersburg	175	Apr. 25	Oct. 18
MT	Helena	122	May 18	Sept. 18	WY	Casper	123	May 22	Sept. 22
NC	Fayetteville	212	Apr. 2	Oct. 31		*Frosts do not occur every year.*			

Outdoor Planting Table

■ The best time to plant flowers and vegetables that bear crops *above ground* is during the *light* of the Moon; that is, from the day the Moon is new to the day it is full. Flowering bulbs and vegetables that bear crops *below ground* should be planted during the *dark* of the Moon; that is, from the day after it is full to the day before it is new again. The Moon Favorable columns at right give these days, which are based on the Moon's phases for 2008 and the safe periods for planting in areas that receive frost. Consult **page 231** for dates of frosts and lengths of growing seasons. See the **Left-Hand Calendar Pages, 114–140**, for the exact days of the new and full Moons.

■ **Aboveground crops are marked *.**

■ **(E) means early; (L) means late.**

■ **Map shades correspond to shades of date columns.**

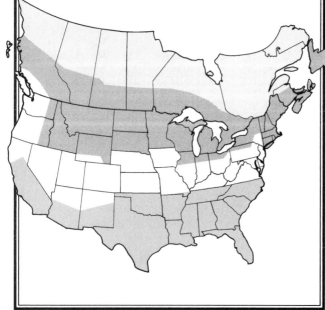

* Barley	
* Beans	(E)
	(L)
Beets	(E)
	(L)
* Broccoli plants	(E)
	(L)
* Brussels sprouts	
* Cabbage plants	
Carrots	(E)
	(L)
* Cauliflower plants	(E)
	(L)
* Celery plants	(E)
	(L)
* Collards	(E)
	(L)
* Corn, sweet	(E)
	(L)
* Cucumbers	
* Eggplant plants	
* Endive	(E)
	(L)
* Kale	(E)
	(L)
Leek plants	
* Lettuce	
* Muskmelons	
* Okra	
Onion sets	
* Parsley	
Parsnips	
* Peas	(E)
	(L)
* Pepper plants	
Potatoes	
* Pumpkins	
Radishes	(E)
	(L)
* Spinach	(E)
	(L)
* Squashes	
Sweet potatoes	
* Swiss chard	
* Tomato plants	
Turnips	(E)
	(L)
* Watermelons	
* Wheat, spring	
* Wheat, winter	

Planting Dates	Moon Favorable	Planting Dates	Moon Favorable	Planting Dates	Moon Favorable	Planting Dates	Moon Favorable
15-3/7	2/15-20, 3/7	3/15-4/7	3/15-21, 4/5-7	5/15-6/21	5/15-19, 6/3-18	6/1-30	6/3-18
15-4/7	3/15-21, 4/5-7	4/15-30	4/15-20	5/7-6/21	5/7-19, 6/3-18	5/30-6/15	6/3-15
1-31	8/7-16, 8/30-31	7/1-21	7/2-18	6/15-7/15	6/15-18, 7/2-15	–	–
1-29	2/21-29	3/15-4/3	3/22-4/3	5/1-15	5/1-4	5/25-6/10	5/25-6/2
1-30	9/16-28	8/15-31	8/17-29	7/15-8/15	7/19-31	6/15-7/8	6/19-7/1
15-3/15	2/15-20, 3/7-15	3/7-31	3/7-21	5/15-31	5/15-19	6/1-25	6/3-18
1-30	9/7-15, 9/29-30	8/1-20	8/1-16	6/15-7/7	6/15-18, 7/2-7	–	–
11-3/20	2/11-20, 3/7-20	3/7-4/15	3/7-21, 4/5-15	5/15-31	5/15-19	6/1-25	6/3-18
11-3/20	2/11-20, 3/7-20	3/7-4/15	3/7-21, 4/5-15	5/15-31	5/15-19	6/1-25	6/3-18
15-3/7	2/21-3/6	3/7-31	3/22-31	5/15-31	5/20-31	5/25-6/10	5/25-6/2
1-9/7	8/17-29	7/7-31	7/19-31	6/15-7/21	6/19-7/1, 7/19-21	6/15-7/8	6/19-7/1
15-3/7	2/15-20, 3/7	3/15-4/7	3/15-21, 4/5-7	5/15-31	5/15-19	6/1-25	6/3-18
1-31	8/7-16, 8/30-31	7/1-8/7	7/2-18, 8/1-7	6/15-7/21	6/15-18, 7/2-18	–	–
15-29	2/15-20	3/7-31	3/7-21	5/15-6/30	5/15-19, 6/3-18	6/1-30	6/3-18
15-30	9/15, 9/29-30	8/15-9/7	8/15-16, 8/30-9/7	7/15-8/15	7/15-18, 8/1-15	–	–
11-3/20	2/11-20, 3/7-20	3/7-4/7	3/7-21, 4/5-7	5/15-31	5/15-19	6/1-25	6/3-18
1-30	9/7-15, 9/29-30	8/15-31	8/15-16, 8/30-31	7/1-8/7	7/2-18, 8/1-7	–	–
15-31	3/15-21	4/1-17	4/5-17	5/10-6/15	5/10-19, 6/3-15	5/30-6/20	6/3-18
1-31	8/7-16, 8/30-31	7/7-21	7/7-18	6/15-30	6/15-18	–	–
1-4/15	3/7-21, 4/5-15	4/7-5/15	4/7-20, 5/5-15	5/7-6/20	5/7-19, 6/3-18	5/30-6/15	6/3-15
1-4/15	3/7-21, 4/5-15	4/7-5/15	4/7-20, 5/5-15	6/1-30	6/3-18	6/15-30	6/15-18
15-3/20	2/15-20, 3/7-20	4/7-5/15	4/7-20, 5/5-15	5/15-31	5/15-19	6/1-25	6/3-18
15-9/7	8/15-16, 8/30-9/7	7/15-8/15	7/15-18, 8/1-15	6/7-30	6/7-18	–	–
11-3/20	2/11-20, 3/7-20	3/7-4/7	3/7-21, 4/5-7	5/15-31	5/15-19	6/1-15	6/3-15
1-30	9/7-15, 9/29-30	8/15-31	8/15-16, 8/30-31	7/1-8/7	7/2-18, 8/1-7	6/25-7/15	7/2-15
15-4/15	2/21-3/6, 3/22-4/4	3/7-4/7	3/22-4/4	5/15-31	5/20-31	6/1-25	6/1-2, 6/19-25
15-3/7	2/15-20, 3/7	3/1-31	3/7-21	5/15-6/30	5/15-19, 6/3-18	6/1-30	6/3-18
15-4/7	3/15-21, 4/5-7	4/15-5/7	4/15-20, 5/5-7	5/15-6/30	5/15-19, 6/3-18	6/1-30	6/3-18
15-6/1	4/15-20, 5/5-19	5/25-6/15	6/3-15	6/15-7/10	6/15-18, 7/2-10	6/25-7/7	7/2-7
1-29	2/1-5, 2/21-29	3/1-31	3/1-6, 3/22-31	5/15-6/7	5/20-6/2	6/1-25	6/1-2, 6/19-25
0-3/15	2/20, 3/7-15	3/1-31	3/7-21	5/15-31	5/15-19	6/1-15	6/3-15
15-2/4	1/23-2/4	3/7-31	3/22-31	4/1-30	4/1-4, 4/21-30	5/10-31	5/20-31
15-2/7	1/15-22, 2/6-7	3/7-31	3/7-21	4/15-5/7	4/15-20, 5/5-7	5/15-31	5/15-19
15-30	9/15, 9/29-30	8/7-31	8/7-16, 8/30-31	7/15-31	7/15-18	7/10-25	7/10-18
1-20	3/7-20	4/1-30	4/5-20	5/15-6/30	5/15-19, 6/3-18	6/1-30	6/3-18
10-29	2/21-29	4/1-30	4/1-4, 4/21-30	5/1-31	5/1-4, 5/20-31	6/1-25	6/1-2, 6/19-25
1-20	3/7-20	4/23-5/15	5/5-15	5/15-31	5/15-19	6/1-30	6/3-18
1-3/1	1/23-2/5, 2/21-3/1	3/7-31	3/22-31	4/15-30	4/21-30	5/15-6/5	5/20-6/2
1-21	10/15-21	9/7-30	9/16-28	8/15-31	8/17-29	7/10-31	7/19-31
3-3/15	2/7-20, 3/7-15	3/15-4/20	3/15-21, 4/5-20	5/15-31	5/15-19	6/1-25	6/3-18
1-21	10/1-14	8/1-9/15	8/1-16, 8/30-9/15	7/17-9/7	7/17-18, 8/1-16, 8/30-9/7	7/20-8/5	8/1-5
5-4/15	3/15-21, 4/5-15	4/15-30	4/15-20	5/15-6/15	5/15-19, 6/3-15	6/1-30	6/3-18
3-4/6	3/23-4/4	4/21-5/9	4/21-5/4	5/15-6/15	5/20-6/2	6/1-30	6/1-2, 6/19-30
3-3/15	2/7-20, 3/7-15	3/15-4/15	3/15-21, 4/5-15	5/1-31	5/5-19	5/15-31	5/15-19
1-20	3/7-20	4/7-30	4/7-20	5/15-31	5/15-19	6/1-15	6/3-15
0-2/15	1/23-2/5	3/15-31	3/22-31	4/7-30	4/21-30	5/10-31	5/20-31
-10/15	9/16-28, 10/15	8/1-20	8/17-20	7/1-8/15	7/1, 7/19-31	–	–
15-4/7	3/15-21, 4/5-7	4/15-5/7	4/15-20, 5/5-7	5/15-6/30	5/15-19, 6/3-18	6/1-30	6/3-18
15-29	2/15-20	3/1-20	3/7-20	4/7-30	4/7-20	5/15-6/10	5/15-19, 6/3-10
15-12/7	10/28-11/13, 11/27-12/7	9/15-10/20	9/15, 9/29-10/14	8/11-9/15	8/11-16, 8/30-9/15	8/5-30	8/5-16, 8/30

Mind-Manglers

Answers appear on page 242.

1. TO MARKET

A farmer goes to market with $100 to buy a total of 100 animals. He has to buy cows, which are $10 each; sheep, which are $3 each; and chickens, which are 50 cents. How many of each animal did he buy for his $100?

–Fred Raby, Fenelon Falls, Ontario

2. NOT JUST ANY OLD JOB

Match these colonial occupations with their modern-day meanings.

1. colporteur	a. female writer
2. amanuensis	b. innkeeper
3. chiffonier	c. one who repairs shoes
4. mantuamaker	d. a minor or worthless author
5. boniface	e. election judge
6. bluestocking	f. wig maker
7. scribler	g. peddler of books
8. scrivener	h. secretary
9. scrutiner	i. notary public
10. scobscat	j. dressmaker or weaver

–Gayle Hedrington, Croydon, New Hampshire

3. VEGETABLE STEW

A potato and a tomato cost 40 cents. A tomato and an onion cost 50 cents. An onion and a potato cost 60 cents. How much does each single vegetable cost?

–Sidney Kravitz, Dover, New Jersey

4. EGGED ON

If a hen-and-a-half lays an egg-and-a-half in a day-and-a-half, how many eggs can six hens lay in six days?

5. CAMP TRAMP

Two men travel by day in the same direction around an island 24 miles in circumference, and camp at night. Mr. A starts 1 mile ahead of Mr. B and goes 1 mile in the first day, 3 miles in the second day, and so on, increasing his rate by 2 miles each day. Mr. B. goes 5 miles every day. When do they camp together?

Time Corrections

■ Times for Sun and Moon rise and set, bright star transits, and planetary observations are given for Boston on **pages 114–140, 100,** and **102–103,** respectively. Use the Key Letter shown to the right of each time on those pages with this table to find the number of minutes (adjusted for location and time zone) that you must add to or subtract from Boston time to get the correct time for your city. (Because of complex calculations for different locales, times may not be precise to the minute.) If your city is not listed, use the figures for the city closest to you in latitude and longitude. Boston's latitude is 42°22' and its longitude is 71°03'. Selected Canadian cities are at the end of the table. For more information on the use of Key Letters and this table, see **How to Use This Almanac, page 110.**

TIME ZONES: Codes represent *standard time.* Atlantic is −1, Eastern is 0, Central is 1, Mountain is 2, Pacific is 3, Alaska is 4, and Hawaii-Aleutian is 5.

State	City	North Latitude °	'	West Longitude °	'	Time Zone Code	A (min.)	B (min.)	C (min.)	D (min.)	E (min.)
AK	Anchorage	61	10	149	59	4	−46	+27	+71	+122	+171
AK	Cordova	60	33	145	45	4	−55	+13	+55	+103	+149
AK	Fairbanks	64	48	147	51	4	−127	+ 2	+61	+131	+205
AK	Juneau	58	18	134	25	4	−76	−23	+10	+49	+86
AK	Ketchikan	55	21	131	39	4	−62	−25	0	+29	+56
AK	Kodiak	57	47	152	24	4	0	+49	+82	+120	+154
AL	Birmingham	33	31	86	49	1	+30	+15	+3	−10	−20
AL	Decatur	34	36	86	59	1	+27	+14	+4	−7	−17
AL	Mobile	30	42	88	3	1	+42	+23	+8	−8	−22
AL	Montgomery	32	23	86	19	1	+31	+14	+1	−13	−25
AR	Fort Smith	35	23	94	25	1	+55	+43	+33	+22	+14
AR	Little Rock	34	45	92	17	1	+48	+35	+25	+13	+4
AR	Texarkana	33	26	94	3	1	+59	+44	+32	+18	+8
AZ	Flagstaff	35	12	111	39	2	+64	+52	+42	+31	+22
AZ	Phoenix	33	27	112	4	2	+71	+56	+44	+30	+20
AZ	Tucson	32	13	110	58	2	+70	+53	+40	+24	+12
AZ	Yuma	32	43	114	37	2	+83	+67	+54	+40	+28
CA	Bakersfield	35	23	119	1	3	+33	+21	+12	+1	−7
CA	Barstow	34	54	117	1	3	+27	+14	+4	−7	−16
CA	Fresno	36	44	119	47	3	+32	+22	+15	+6	0
CA	Los Angeles–Pasadena–Santa Monica	34	3	118	14	3	+34	+20	+9	−3	−13
CA	Palm Springs	33	49	116	32	3	+28	+13	+1	−12	−22
CA	Redding	40	35	122	24	3	+31	+27	+25	+22	+19
CA	Sacramento	38	35	121	30	3	+34	+27	+21	+15	+10
CA	San Diego	32	43	117	9	3	+33	+17	+4	−9	−21
CA	San Francisco–Oakland–San Jose	37	47	122	25	3	+40	+31	+25	+18	+12
CO	Craig	40	31	107	33	2	+32	+28	+25	+22	+20
CO	Denver–Boulder	39	44	104	59	2	+24	+19	+15	+11	+7
CO	Grand Junction	39	4	108	33	2	+40	+34	+29	+24	+20
CO	Pueblo	38	16	104	37	2	+27	+20	+14	+7	+2
CO	Trinidad	37	10	104	31	2	+30	+21	+13	+5	0
CT	Bridgeport	41	11	73	11	0	+12	+10	+8	+6	+4
CT	Hartford–New Britain	41	46	72	41	0	+8	+7	+6	+5	+4
CT	New Haven	41	18	72	56	0	+11	+8	+7	+5	+4
CT	New London	41	22	72	6	0	+7	+5	+4	+2	+1
CT	Norwalk–Stamford	41	7	73	22	0	+13	+10	+9	+7	+5
CT	Waterbury–Meriden	41	33	73	3	0	+10	+9	+7	+6	+5
DC	Washington	38	54	77	1	0	+35	+28	+23	+18	+13
DE	Wilmington	39	45	75	33	0	+26	+21	+18	+13	+10

State	City	North Latitude °	'	West Longitude °	'	Time Zone Code	A (min.)	B (min.)	C (min.)	D (min.)	E (min.)
FL	Fort Myers	26	38	81	52	0	+87	+63	+44	+21	+4
FL	Jacksonville	30	20	81	40	0	+77	+58	+43	+25	+11
FL	Miami	25	47	80	12	0	+88	+57	+37	+14	−3
FL	Orlando	28	32	81	22	0	+80	+59	+42	+22	+6
FL	Pensacola	30	25	87	13	1	+39	+20	+5	−12	−26
FL	St. Petersburg	27	46	82	39	0	+87	+65	+47	+26	+10
FL	Tallahassee	30	27	84	17	0	+87	+68	+53	+35	+22
FL	Tampa	27	57	82	27	0	+86	+64	+46	+25	+9
FL	West Palm Beach	26	43	80	3	0	+79	+55	+36	+14	−2
GA	Atlanta	33	45	84	24	0	+79	+65	+53	+40	+30
GA	Augusta	33	28	81	58	0	+70	+55	+44	+30	+19
GA	Macon	32	50	83	38	0	+79	+63	+50	+36	+24
GA	Savannah	32	5	81	6	0	+70	+54	+40	+25	+13
HI	Hilo	19	44	155	5	5	+94	+62	+37	+7	−15
HI	Honolulu	21	18	157	52	5	+102	+72	+48	+19	−1
HI	Lanai City	20	50	156	55	5	+99	+69	+44	+15	−6
HI	Lihue	21	59	159	23	5	+107	+77	+54	+26	+5
IA	Davenport	41	32	90	35	1	+20	+19	+17	+16	+15
IA	Des Moines	41	35	93	37	1	+32	+31	+30	+28	+27
IA	Dubuque	42	30	90	41	1	+17	+18	+18	+18	+18
IA	Waterloo	42	30	92	20	1	+24	+24	+24	+25	+25
ID	Boise	43	37	116	12	2	+55	+58	+60	+62	+64
ID	Lewiston	46	25	117	1	3	−12	−3	+2	+10	+17
ID	Pocatello	42	52	112	27	2	+43	+44	+45	+46	+46
IL	Cairo	37	0	89	11	1	+29	+20	+12	+4	−2
IL	Chicago–Oak Park	41	52	87	38	1	+7	+6	+6	+5	+4
IL	Danville	40	8	87	37	1	+13	+9	+6	+2	0
IL	Decatur	39	51	88	57	1	+19	+15	+11	+7	+4
IL	Peoria	40	42	89	36	1	+19	+16	+14	+11	+9
IL	Springfield	39	48	89	39	1	+22	+18	+14	+10	+6
IN	Fort Wayne	41	4	85	9	0	+60	+58	+56	+54	+52
IN	Gary	41	36	87	20	1	+7	+6	+4	+3	+2
IN	Indianapolis	39	46	86	10	0	+69	+64	+60	+56	+52
IN	Muncie	40	12	85	23	0	+64	+60	+57	+53	+50
IN	South Bend	41	41	86	15	0	+62	+61	+60	+59	+58
IN	Terre Haute	39	28	87	24	0	+74	+69	+65	+60	+56
KS	Fort Scott	37	50	94	42	1	+49	+41	+34	+27	+21
KS	Liberal	37	3	100	55	1	+76	+66	+59	+51	+44
KS	Oakley	39	8	100	51	1	+69	+63	+59	+53	+49
KS	Salina	38	50	97	37	1	+57	+51	+46	+40	+35
KS	Topeka	39	3	95	40	1	+49	+43	+38	+32	+28
KS	Wichita	37	42	97	20	1	+60	+51	+45	+37	+31
KY	Lexington–Frankfort	38	3	84	30	0	+67	+59	+53	+46	+41
KY	Louisville	38	15	85	46	0	+72	+64	+58	+52	+46
LA	Alexandria	31	18	92	27	1	+58	+40	+26	+9	−3
LA	Baton Rouge	30	27	91	11	1	+55	+36	+21	+3	−10
LA	Lake Charles	30	14	93	13	1	+64	+44	+29	+11	−2
LA	Monroe	32	30	92	7	1	+53	+37	+24	+9	−1
LA	New Orleans	29	57	90	4	1	+52	+32	+16	−1	−15
LA	Shreveport	32	31	93	45	1	+60	+44	+31	+16	+4
MA	Brockton	42	5	71	1	0	0	0	0	0	−1
MA	Fall River–New Bedford	41	42	71	9	0	+2	+1	0	0	−1
MA	Lawrence–Lowell	42	42	71	10	0	0	0	0	0	+1
MA	Pittsfield	42	27	73	15	0	+8	+8	+8	+8	+8
MA	Springfield–Holyoke	42	6	72	36	0	+6	+6	+6	+5	+5
MA	Worcester	42	16	71	48	0	+3	+2	+2	+2	+2
MD	Baltimore	39	17	76	37	0	+32	+26	+22	+17	+13

State	City	North Latitude °	'	West Longitude °	'	Time Zone Code	A (min.)	B (min.)	Key Letters C (min.)	D (min.)	E (min.)
MD	Hagerstown	39	39	77	43	0	+35	+30	+26	+22	+18
MD	Salisbury	38	22	75	36	0	+31	+23	+18	+11	+6
ME	Augusta	44	19	69	46	0	−12	−8	−5	−1	0
ME	Bangor	44	48	68	46	0	−18	−13	−9	−5	−1
ME	Eastport	44	54	67	0	0	−26	−20	−16	−11	−8
ME	Ellsworth	44	33	68	25	0	−18	−14	−10	−6	−3
ME	Portland	43	40	70	15	0	−8	−5	−3	−1	0
ME	Presque Isle	46	41	68	1	0	−29	−19	−12	−4	+2
MI	Cheboygan	45	39	84	29	0	+40	+47	+53	+59	+64
MI	Detroit–Dearborn......	42	20	83	3	0	+47	+47	+47	+47	+47
MI	Flint	43	1	83	41	0	+47	+49	+50	+51	+52
MI	Ironwood	46	27	90	9	1	0	+9	+15	+23	+29
MI	Jackson	42	15	84	24	0	+53	+53	+53	+52	+52
MI	Kalamazoo	42	17	85	35	0	+58	+57	+57	+57	+57
MI	Lansing..............	42	44	84	33	0	+52	+53	+53	+54	+54
MI	St. Joseph	42	5	86	26	0	+61	+61	+60	+60	+59
MI	Traverse City	44	46	85	38	0	+49	+54	+57	+62	+65
MN	Albert Lea	43	39	93	22	1	+24	+26	+28	+31	+33
MN	Bemidji.............	47	28	94	53	1	+14	+26	+34	+44	+52
MN	Duluth...............	46	47	92	6	1	+6	+16	+23	+31	+38
MN	Minneapolis–St. Paul . .	44	59	93	16	1	+18	+24	+28	+33	+37
MN	Ortonville...........	45	19	96	27	1	+30	+36	+40	+46	+51
MO	Jefferson City........	38	34	92	10	1	+36	+29	+24	+18	+13
MO	Joplin	37	6	94	30	1	+50	+41	+33	+25	+18
MO	Kansas City	39	1	94	20	1	+44	+37	+33	+27	+23
MO	Poplar Bluff	36	46	90	24	1	+35	+25	+17	+8	+1
MO	St. Joseph	39	46	94	50	1	+43	+38	+35	+30	+27
MO	St. Louis............	38	37	90	12	1	+28	+21	+16	+10	+5
MO	Springfield..........	37	13	93	18	1	+45	+36	+29	+20	+14
MS	Biloxi	30	24	88	53	1	+46	+27	+11	−5	−19
MS	Jackson..............	32	18	90	11	1	+46	+30	+17	+1	−10
MS	Meridian.............	32	22	88	42	1	+40	+24	+11	−4	−15
MS	Tupelo...............	34	16	88	34	1	+35	+21	+10	−2	−11
MT	Billings..............	45	47	108	30	2	+16	+23	+29	+35	+40
MT	Butte................	46	1	112	32	2	+31	+39	+45	+52	+57
MT	Glasgow	48	12	106	38	2	−1	+11	+21	+32	+42
MT	Great Falls	47	30	111	17	2	+20	+31	+39	+49	+58
MT	Helena	46	36	112	2	2	+27	+36	+43	+51	+57
MT	Miles City............	46	25	105	51	2	+3	+11	+18	+26	+32
NC	Asheville	35	36	82	33	0	+67	+55	+46	+35	+27
NC	Charlotte.............	35	14	80	51	0	+61	+49	+39	+28	+19
NC	Durham..............	36	0	78	55	0	+51	+40	+31	+21	+13
NC	Greensboro...........	36	4	79	47	0	+54	+43	+35	+25	+17
NC	Raleigh	35	47	78	38	0	+51	+39	+30	+20	+12
NC	Wilmington	34	14	77	55	0	+52	+38	+27	+15	+5
ND	Bismarck	46	48	100	47	1	+41	+50	+58	+66	+73
ND	Fargo...............	46	53	96	47	1	+24	+34	+42	+50	+57
ND	Grand Forks	47	55	97	3	1	+21	+33	+43	+53	+62
ND	Minot	48	14	101	18	1	+36	+50	+59	+71	+81
ND	Williston.............	48	9	103	37	1	+46	+59	+69	+80	+90
NE	Grand Island.........	40	55	98	21	1	+53	+51	+49	+46	+44
NE	Lincoln..............	40	49	96	41	1	+47	+44	+42	+39	+37
NE	North Platte	41	8	100	46	1	+62	+60	+58	+56	+54
NE	Omaha	41	16	95	56	1	+43	+40	+39	+37	+36
NH	Berlin	44	28	71	11	0	−7	−3	0	+3	+7
NH	Keene	42	56	72	17	0	+2	+3	+4	+5	+6
NH	Manchester–Concord . .	42	59	71	28	0	0	0	+1	+2	+3

State	City	North Latitude ° '	West Longitude ° '	Time Zone Code	A (min.)	B (min.)	Key Letters C (min.)	D (min.)	E (min.)
NH	Portsmouth............	43 5	70 45	0	−4	−2	−1	0	0
NJ	Atlantic City..........	39 22	74 26	0	+23	+17	+13	+8	+4
NJ	Camden	39 57	75 7	0	+24	+19	+16	+12	+9
NJ	Cape May	38 56	74 56	0	+26	+20	+15	+9	+5
NJ	Newark–East Orange...	40 44	74 10	0	+17	+14	+12	+9	+7
NJ	Paterson	40 55	74 10	0	+17	+14	+12	+9	+7
NJ	Trenton...............	40 13	74 46	0	+21	+17	+14	+11	+8
NM	Albuquerque	35 5	106 39	2	+45	+32	+22	+11	+2
NM	Gallup...............	35 32	108 45	2	+52	+40	+31	+20	+11
NM	Las Cruces	32 19	106 47	2	+53	+36	+23	+8	−3
NM	Roswell..............	33 24	104 32	2	+41	+26	+14	0	−10
NM	Santa Fe	35 41	105 56	2	+40	+28	+19	+9	0
NV	Carson City–Reno	39 10	119 46	3	+25	+19	+14	+9	+5
NV	Elko	40 50	115 46	3	+3	0	−1	−3	−5
NV	Las Vegas	36 10	115 9	3	+16	+4	−3	−13	−20
NY	Albany	42 39	73 45	0	+9	+10	+10	+11	+11
NY	Binghamton	42 6	75 55	0	+20	+19	+19	+18	+18
NY	Buffalo	42 53	78 52	0	+29	+30	+30	+31	+32
NY	New York	40 45	74 0	0	+17	+14	+11	+9	+6
NY	Ogdensburg	44 42	75 30	0	+8	+13	+17	+21	+25
NY	Syracuse.............	43 3	76 9	0	+17	+19	+20	+21	+22
OH	Akron	41 5	81 31	0	+46	+43	+41	+39	+37
OH	Canton	40 48	81 23	0	+46	+43	+41	+38	+36
OH	Cincinnati–Hamilton...	39 6	84 31	0	+64	+58	+53	+48	+44
OH	Cleveland–Lakewood ..	41 30	81 42	0	+45	+43	+42	+40	+39
OH	Columbus.............	39 57	83 1	0	+55	+51	+47	+43	+40
OH	Dayton	39 45	84 10	0	+61	+56	+52	+48	+44
OH	Toledo...............	41 39	83 33	0	+52	+50	+49	+48	+47
OH	Youngstown	41 6	80 39	0	+42	+40	+38	+36	+34
OK	Oklahoma City........	35 28	97 31	1	+67	+55	+46	+35	+26
OK	Tulsa................	36 9	95 60	1	+59	+48	+40	+30	+22
OR	Eugene	44 3	123 6	3	+21	+24	+27	+30	+33
OR	Pendleton	45 40	118 47	3	−1	+4	+10	+16	+21
OR	Portland	45 31	122 41	3	+14	+20	+25	+31	+36
OR	Salem	44 57	123 1	3	+17	+23	+27	+31	+35
PA	Allentown–Bethlehem..	40 36	75 28	0	+23	+20	+17	+14	+12
PA	Erie..................	42 7	80 5	0	+36	+36	+35	+35	+35
PA	Harrisburg	40 16	76 53	0	+30	+26	+23	+19	+16
PA	Lancaster	40 2	76 18	0	+28	+24	+20	+17	+13
PA	Philadelphia–Chester...	39 57	75 9	0	+24	+19	+16	+12	+9
PA	Pittsburgh–McKeesport	40 26	80 0	0	+42	+38	+35	+32	+29
PA	Reading	40 20	75 56	0	+26	+22	+19	+16	+13
PA	Scranton–Wilkes-Barre.	41 25	75 40	0	+21	+19	+18	+16	+15
PA	York	39 58	76 43	0	+30	+26	+22	+18	+15
RI	Providence	41 50	71 25	0	+3	+2	+1	0	0
SC	Charleston	32 47	79 56	0	+64	+48	+36	+21	+10
SC	Columbia	34 0	81 2	0	+65	+51	+40	+27	+17
SC	Spartanburg	34 56	81 57	0	+66	+53	+43	+32	+23
SD	Aberdeen	45 28	98 29	1	+37	+44	+49	+54	+59
SD	Pierre	44 22	100 21	1	+49	+53	+56	+60	+63
SD	Rapid City	44 5	103 14	2	+2	+5	+8	+11	+13
SD	Sioux Falls	43 33	96 44	1	+38	+40	+42	+44	+46
TN	Chattanooga..........	35 3	85 19	0	+79	+67	+57	+45	+36
TN	Knoxville	35 58	83 55	0	+71	+60	+51	+41	+33
TN	Memphis.............	35 9	90 3	1	+38	+26	+16	+5	−3
TN	Nashville	36 10	86 47	1	+22	+11	+3	−6	−14
TX	Amarillo.............	35 12	101 50	1	+85	+73	+63	+52	+43

State/ Province	City	North Latitude °	'	West Longitude °	'	Time Zone Code	A (min.)	B (min.)	Key Letters C (min.)	D (min.)	E (min.)
TX	Austin	30	16	97	45	1	+82	+62	+47	+29	+15
TX	Beaumont	30	5	94	6	1	+67	+48	+32	+14	0
TX	Brownsville	25	54	97	30	1	+91	+66	+46	+23	+5
TX	Corpus Christi	27	48	97	24	1	+86	+64	+46	+25	+9
TX	Dallas–Fort Worth	32	47	96	48	1	+71	+55	+43	+28	+17
TX	El Paso	31	45	106	29	2	+53	+35	+22	6	−6
TX	Galveston	29	18	94	48	1	+72	+52	+35	+16	+1
TX	Houston	29	45	95	22	1	+73	+53	+37	+19	+5
TX	McAllen	26	12	98	14	1	+93	+69	+49	+26	+9
TX	San Antonio	29	25	98	30	1	+87	+66	+50	+31	+16
UT	Kanab	37	3	112	32	2	+62	+53	+46	+37	+30
UT	Moab	38	35	109	33	2	+46	+39	+33	+27	+22
UT	Ogden	41	13	111	58	2	+47	+45	+43	+41	+40
UT	Salt Lake City	40	45	111	53	2	+48	+45	+43	+40	+38
UT	Vernal	40	27	109	32	2	+40	+36	+33	+30	+28
VA	Charlottesville	38	2	78	30	0	+43	+35	+29	+22	+17
VA	Danville	36	36	79	23	0	+51	+41	+33	+24	+17
VA	Norfolk	36	51	76	17	0	+38	+28	+21	+12	+5
VA	Richmond	37	32	77	26	0	+41	+32	+25	+17	+11
VA	Roanoke	37	16	79	57	0	+51	+42	+35	+27	+21
VA	Winchester	39	11	78	10	0	+38	+33	+28	+23	+19
VT	Brattleboro	42	51	72	34	0	+4	+5	+5	+6	+7
VT	Burlington	44	29	73	13	0	0	+4	+8	+12	+15
VT	Rutland	43	37	72	58	0	+2	+5	+7	+9	+11
VT	St. Johnsbury	44	25	72	1	0	−4	0	+3	+7	+10
WA	Bellingham	48	45	122	29	3	0	+13	+24	+37	+47
WA	Seattle–Tacoma– Olympia	47	37	122	20	3	+3	+15	+24	+34	+42
WA	Spokane	47	40	117	24	3	−16	−4	+4	+14	+23
WA	Walla Walla	46	4	118	20	3	−5	+2	+8	+15	+21
WI	Eau Claire	44	49	91	30	1	+12	+17	+21	+25	+29
WI	Green Bay	44	31	88	0	1	0	+3	+7	+11	+14
WI	La Crosse	43	48	91	15	1	+15	+18	+20	+22	+25
WI	Madison	43	4	89	23	1	+10	+11	+12	+14	+15
WI	Milwaukee	43	2	87	54	1	+4	+6	+7	+8	+9
WI	Oshkosh	44	1	88	33	1	+3	+6	+9	+12	+15
WI	Wausau	44	58	89	38	1	+4	+9	+13	+18	+22
WV	Charleston	38	21	81	38	0	+55	+48	+42	+35	+30
WV	Parkersburg	39	16	81	34	0	+52	+46	+42	+36	+32
WY	Casper	42	51	106	19	2	+19	+19	+20	+21	+22
WY	Cheyenne	41	8	104	49	2	+19	+16	+14	+12	+11
WY	Sheridan	44	48	106	58	2	+14	+19	+23	+27	+31
CANADA											
AB	Calgary	51	5	114	5	2	+13	+35	+50	+68	+84
AB	Edmonton	53	34	113	25	2	−3	+26	+47	+72	+93
BC	Vancouver	49	13	123	6	3	0	+15	+26	+40	+52
MB	Winnipeg	49	53	97	10	1	+12	+30	+43	+58	+71
NB	Saint John	45	16	66	3	−1	+28	+34	+39	+44	+49
NS	Halifax	44	38	63	35	−1	+21	+26	+29	+33	+37
NS	Sydney	46	10	60	10	−1	+1	+9	+15	+23	+28
ON	Ottawa	45	25	75	43	0	+6	+13	+18	+23	+28
ON	Peterborough	44	18	78	19	0	+21	+25	+28	+32	+35
ON	Thunder Bay	48	27	89	12	0	+47	+61	+71	+83	+93
ON	Toronto	43	39	79	23	0	+28	+30	+32	+35	+37
QC	Montreal	45	28	73	39	0	−1	+4	+9	+15	+20
SK	Saskatoon	52	10	106	40	1	+37	+63	+80	+101	+119

Tide Corrections

■ Many factors affect the times and heights of the tides: the coastal configuration, the time of the Moon's southing (crossing the meridian), and the Moon's phase. The High Tide column on the **Left-Hand Calendar Pages, 114–140,** lists the times of high tide at Commonwealth Pier in Boston Harbor. The heights of some of these tides, reckoned from Mean Lower Low Water, are given on the **Right-Hand Calendar Pages, 115–141.** Use the table below to calculate the approximate times and heights of high tide at the places shown. Apply the time difference to the times of high tide at Boston and the height difference to the heights at Boston.

E X A M P L E :

■ The conversion of the times and heights of the tides at Boston to those at Cape Fear, North Carolina, is given below:

High tide at Boston	11:45 A.M.
Correction for Cape Fear	– 3 55 hrs.
High tide at Cape Fear	7:50 A.M.
Tide height at Boston	11.6 ft.
Correction for Cape Fear	– 5.0 ft.
Tide height at Cape Fear	6.6 ft.

Estimations derived from this table are *not* meant to be used for navigation. *The Old Farmer's Almanac* accepts no responsibility for errors or any consequences ensuing from the use of this table.

Coastal Site	Difference: Time (h. m.)	Height (ft.)
Canada		
Alberton, PE	*–5 45	–7.5
Charlottetown, PE	*–0 45	–3.5
Halifax, NS.	–3 23	–4.5
North Sydney, NS	–3 15	–6.5
Saint John, NB	+0 30	+15.0
St. John's, NL	–4 00	–6.5
Yarmouth, NS	–0 40	+3.0
Maine		
Bar Harbor	–0 34	+0.9
Belfast	–0 20	+0.4
Boothbay Harbor	–0 18	–0.8
Chebeague Island	–0 16	–0.6
Eastport	–0 28	+8.4
Kennebunkport	+0 04	–1.0
Machias	–0 28	+2.8
Monhegan Island	–0 25	–0.8
Old Orchard	0 00	–0.8
Portland	–0 12	–0.6
Rockland	–0 28	+0.1
Stonington	–0 30	+0.1
York	–0 09	–1.0
New Hampshire		
Hampton	+0 02	–1.3
Portsmouth	+0 11	–1.5
Rye Beach	–0 09	–0.9
Massachusetts		
Annisquam	–0 02	–1.1
Beverly Farms	0 00	–0.5
Boston	0 00	0.0

Coastal Site	Difference: Time (h. m.)	Height (ft.)
Cape Cod Canal		
East Entrance	–0 01	–0.8
West Entrance	–2 16	–5.9
Chatham Outer Coast . .	+0 30	–2.8
Inside	+1 54	**0.4
Cohasset	+0 02	–0.07
Cotuit Highlands	+1 15	**0.3
Dennis Port	+1 01	**0.4
Duxbury–Gurnet Point . .	+0 02	–0.3
Fall River	–3 03	–5.0
Gloucester	–0 03	–0.8
Hingham	+0 07	0.0
Hull	+0 03	–0.2
Hyannis Port	+1 01	**0.3
Magnolia–Manchester . .	–0 02	–0.7
Marblehead	–0 02	–0.4
Marion	–3 22	–5.4
Monument Beach	–3 08	–5.4
Nahant	–0 01	–0.5
Nantasket	+0 04	–0.1
Nantucket	+0 56	**0.3
Nauset Beach	+0 30	**0.6
New Bedford	–3 24	–5.7
Newburyport	+0 19	–1.8
Oak Bluffs	+0 30	**0.2
Onset–R.R. Bridge	–2 16	–5.9
Plymouth	+0 05	0.0
Provincetown	+0 14	–0.4
Revere Beach	–0 01	–0.3
Rockport	–0 08	–1.0
Salem	0 00	–0.5

Coastal Site	Difference:	Time (h. m.)	Height (ft.)
Scituate		−0 05	−0.7
Wareham		−3 09	−5.3
Wellfleet		+0 12	+0.5
West Falmouth		−3 10	−5.4
Westport Harbor		−3 22	−6.4
Woods Hole			
Little Harbor		−2 50	**0.2
Oceanographic Institute		−3 07	**0.2
Rhode Island			
Bristol		−3 24	−5.3
Narragansett Pier		−3 42	−6.2
Newport.		−3 34	−5.9
Point Judith		−3 41	−6.3
Providence		−3 20	−4.8
Sakonnet		−3 44	−5.6
Watch Hill		−2 50	−6.8
Connecticut			
Bridgeport.		+0 01	−2.6
Madison.		−0 22	−2.3
New Haven		−0 11	−3.2
New London		−1 54	−6.7
Norwalk.		+0 01	−2.2
Old Lyme			
Highway Bridge.		−0 30	−6.2
Stamford		+0 01	−2.2
Stonington.		−2 27	−6.6
New York			
Coney Island		−3 33	−4.9
Fire Island Light		−2 43	**0.1
Long Beach.		−3 11	−5.7
Montauk Harbor		−2 19	−7.4
New York City–Battery. .		−2 43	−5.0
Oyster Bay		+0 04	−1.8
Port Chester		−0 09	−2.2
Port Washington		−0 01	−2.1
Sag Harbor		−0 55	−6.8
Southampton			
Shinnecock Inlet		−4 20	**0.2
Willets Point		0 00	−2.3
New Jersey			
Asbury Park		−4 04	−5.3
Atlantic City		−3 56	−5.5
Bay Head–Sea Girt . . .		−4 04	−5.3
Beach Haven.		−1 43	**0.24
Cape May		−3 28	−5.3
Ocean City		−3 06	−5.9
Sandy Hook.		−3 30	−5.0
Seaside Park		−4 03	−5.4
Pennsylvania			
Philadelphia		+2 40	−3.5
Delaware			
Cape Henlopen		−2 48	−5.3

Coastal Site	Difference:	Time (h. m.)	Height (ft.)
Rehoboth Beach		−3 37	−5.7
Wilmington		+1 56	−3.8
Maryland			
Annapolis		+6 23	−8.5
Baltimore		+7 59	−8.3
Cambridge.		+5 05	−7.8
Havre de Grace		+11 21	−7.7
Point No Point.		+2 28	−8.1
Prince Frederick			
Plum Point		+4 25	−8.5
Virginia			
Cape Charles.		−2 20	−7.0
Hampton Roads		−2 02	−6.9
Norfolk		−2 06	−6.6
Virginia Beach		−4 00	−6.0
Yorktown.		−2 13	−7.0
North Carolina			
Cape Fear		−3 55	−5.0
Cape Lookout		−4 28	−5.7
Currituck		−4 10	−5.8
Hatteras			
Inlet.		−4 03	−7.4
Kitty Hawk		−4 14	−6.2
Ocean		−4 26	−6.0
South Carolina			
Charleston.		−3 22	−4.3
Georgetown.		−1 48	**0.36
Hilton Head.		−3 22	−2.9
Myrtle Beach		−3 49	−4.4
St. Helena			
Harbor Entrance.		−3 15	−3.4
Georgia			
Jekyll Island		−3 46	−2.9
St. Simon's Island.		−2 50	−2.9
Savannah Beach			
River Entrance		−3 14	−5.5
Tybee Light		−3 22	−2.7
Florida			
Cape Canaveral.		−3 59	−6.0
Daytona Beach		−3 28	−5.3
Fort Lauderdale		−2 50	−7.2
Fort Pierce Inlet		−3 32	−6.9
Jacksonville			
Railroad Bridge		−6 55	**0.1
Miami Harbor Entrance		−3 18	−7.0
St. Augustine.		−2 55	−4.9

*Varies widely; accurate within only 1½ hours. Consult local tide tables for precise times and heights.

**Where the difference in the Height column is so marked, the height at Boston should be multiplied by this ratio.

Apogean Tide: A monthly tide of decreased range that occurs when the Moon is at apogee (farthest from Earth).

Diurnal Tide: A tide with one high water and one low water in a tidal day of approximately 24 hours.

Mean Lower Low Water: The arithmetic mean of the lesser of a daily pair of low waters, observed over a specific 19-year cycle called the National Tidal Datum Epoch.

Neap Tide: A tide of decreased range that occurs twice a month, when the Moon is in quadrature (during its first and last quarters, when the Sun and the Moon are at right angles to each other relative to Earth).

Perigean Tide: A monthly tide of increased range that occurs when the Moon is at perigee (closest to Earth).

Semidiurnal Tide: A tide with one high water and one low water every half day. East Coast tides, for example, are semi-diurnal, with two highs and two lows during a tidal day of approximately 24 hours.

Spring Tide: A tide of increased range that occurs at times of syzygy each month. Named not for the season of spring but from the German *springen* ("to leap up"), a spring tide also brings a lower low water.

Syzygy: The nearly straight-line configuration that occurs twice a month, when the Sun and the Moon are in conjunction (on the same side of Earth at the new Moon) and when they are in opposition (on opposite sides of Earth at the full Moon). In both cases, the gravitational effects of the Sun and the Moon reinforce each other, and tidal range is increased.

Vanishing Tide: A mixed tide of considerable inequality in the two highs and two lows, so that the lower high (or higher low) may become indistinct or appear to vanish.

Answers to Maddening Mind-Manglers

from page 234

1. To Market: The farmer bought five cows for $50, one sheep for $3, and 94 chickens for $47.

2. Not Just Any Old Job: 1. g; 2. h; 3. f; 4. j; 5. b; 6. a; 7. d; 8. i; 9. e; 10. c

3. Vegetable Stew: A potato costs 25 cents, a tomato costs 15 cents, and an onion costs 35 cents.

4. Egged On: 24. If 1.5 hens lay 1.5 eggs in 1.5 days (1 egg per day), then 1 hen will lay .67 egg ($\frac{2}{3}$ egg) per day. So 6 hens will lay 4 eggs per day, which gives 24 eggs in six days.

5. Camp Tramp: Never.

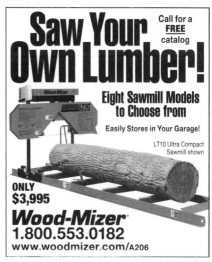

General Store Classifieds

ART

NORMAN ROCKWELL prints, posters, collectibles, calendars. Annual Christmas tree ball and ornament, tc. Rockwell Gallery Collection. 215-969-5619. www.rockwellsite.com

ASTROLOGY/OCCULT

LADY LOVE, Psychic Advisor, Spiritual Healer, helps to find and reunite soulmates. Removes negative nergy. Helps in all situations. 909-636-4891.

FREE READING
Powerful love specialist. Psychic Olivia restores Love, Marriage, Business, Health. Reunites Lovers. Troubled, need answers?
Call 214-902-0045
3618 Walnut Hill, Dallas TX 75229

FREE OCCULT CATALOG! AzureGreen, 48-OFA Chester Rd., Middlefield MA 01243. 413-623-2155. www.azuregreen.com

GIFTED HEALER. Solves all problems, troubles, unusual sickness, bad luck, love, life. Removes evil influences, nature problems, brings back lovers to tay, good luck, money. Uncle Doc Shedrickrack, Hwy. 48, 7905 Bluff Rd., Gadsden SC 29052. Call 803-353-0659.

ASTROLOGY: FREE CATALOG. Books, tapes, oftware, tarot, spirituality. Phone: 800-500-0453 or 805-247-1338. Church of Light, www.Light.org

MASTER PSYCHICS: Love, money. Laura, 1-877-852-8255. Eve, 1-888-237-2263. Crystal, 1-866-571-1111. Fay, 1-900-725-8500 (phone bill). 2.99+ pm, 18+.

MRS. HOPE. 45 years of experience. Reunites Lovers n 24 hours. Removes evil influences. Tells your past, present, and future. Call 1-626-332-1609.

MRS. KING, spiritual reader, advisor, helps in matters of life where others have failed. Call 912-283-0635.

FREE SPIRITUAL CATALOG—Luck, money, and ove can be yours. Huge spiritual catalog with over ',500 items. Church Goods Co., Dept. OFA, PO Box '18, Glenview IL 60025. www.theluckshop.com

LOVE IN YOUR FUTURE? Gifted psychics can guide you to love & happiness. Authentic phone readings 24/7. New member offer: 10 minutes for $10. 1-866-422-9923. Ent. only, 18+. PsychicSource.com

SPIRITUAL ADVICE. Help for all problems: relationships, nature, money, jobs. See results in 3 days. Call Dewberry, 800-989-1059 or 912-264-3259.

OCCULT CATALOG: Hard-to-find Herbs, Oils, Incense, Books, etc. $3.00. Power Products, PO Box 443, Crystal River FL 34423. Web site: www.joanteresapowerproducts.com

ATTENTION: REV. NOAH GIBSON, New Orleans powerful and gifted healer. Miracles performed. Number One Love Doctor. Free spiritual reading. 1-334-450-9906.

SISTER ROGERS, psychic reader and advisor. Can help you with problems, love, business, marriage, and health. 903-454-4406.

FREE MAGIC SPELL! Tell us exactly what you need! 909-473-7470. EKSES, PO Box 9315(B), San Bernardino CA 92427-9315. www.Ekses.com

ANSWERS FOR THE HEART FROM THE HEART
Accurate, gifted, caring psychics.
Increase your awareness. $3.23/minute.
1-800-824-7107
www.voiceofastrology.net

MADAM PEBBLES. She can help all matters in life. Have you been touched by evil hands? She can remove all types of evil. Relationships, lost nature, luck, and love! 706-536-7983.

MRS. STAR, GOD-GIFTED. Can reunite lovers. Guaranteed results with all situations. Free mini-reading. 231-777-2323.

ATTENTION: SISTER LIGHT, Spartanburg, South Carolina. One free reading when you call. I will help in all problems. 864-576-9397.

EUROPEAN PSYCHIC READER and advisor guarantees help with all problems. Call Sylvia for one free reading. 864-583-5776.

PSYCHIC READING BY MIA. Specializing in reuniting loved ones. Guaranteed results in six hours. Call 864-809-2470.

PSYCHIC ANNIE. Specializing in reuniting loved ones. Guaranteed results. Helps in all problems. 864-621-2430.

SUMMER BOWEN does what others claim. Solves all problems. Results in three hours. Call: 423-855-8953. Write: 4919 Brainerd, Chattanooga TN 37411.

FREE ONE QUESTION. Reunites lovers with strong goddess spells, money spells, and removes evil spells. 989-992-3585.

2 QUESTIONS FREE. Sis. Mary, God-Gifted. 1-713-660-9293. Guaranteed, helps in all problems!

$1,000s WEEKLY mailing burglar alarm advertisements! Free supplies/postage! Rush self-addressed, stamped envelope: RBM-FA, PO Box 759, Lake Zurich IL 60047-0759.

WATKINS PRODUCTS. Buy retail or start your own Watkins business. To get information: 800-215-2743 or www.cbbirch.com

CLOTHING

SUSPENDER WEARERS! Frustrated with clips that constantly slip off your pants? Our suspenders feature patented "No-Slip Clip." Brochure/order: 800-700-4515.

CREATE CUSTOM COOKBOOKS

CUSTOM COOKBOOKS are easy and profitable for your fundraising group, church, or family. G&R Publishing. Phone: 1-800-383-1679. Web site: www.gandrpublishing.com

EDUCATION/INSTRUCTION

HIGH SCHOOL BY DISTANCE EDUCATION. American School, a complete, Fully-Accredited High School program. Est. 1897. For more information, call 1-800-531-9268, mention code #348. Or visit: www.americanschoolofcorr.com

FACTORY-DIRECT MATTRESSES

TEMPER-VISCO SWEDISH MEMORY FOAM MATTRESSES; FACTORY-DIRECT PRICES! Twin, $499; full, $599; queen, $699; king, $799; 10"–12" pillowtop or super plush, add $200; cashmere or coolmax, 50% off! Call Arthur, 1-888-229-6720, www.viscodirect.com

FARM & GARDEN

NEPTUNE'S HARVEST ORGANIC FERTILIZERS: Extremely effective. Commercially proven. Outperform chemicals. Wholesale/retail/farm. Catalog. 800-259-4769. www.neptunesharvest.com

FINANCIAL/LOANS BY MAIL

FREE GRANT MONEY! Immediate help. No repayment. Debts, personal needs, business. Rush SASE: Grants-FA, PO Box 458, New Britain CT 06050-0458.

FOOD & RECIPES

TOTALLY NUTS brand peanuts and cashews. Call us at 1-888-489-6887 or visit our Web site at www.totallynuts.biz

FREE INFORMATION

PATENTS: www.charlesk.com

GIFTS

THE BEST ONLINE SUPERSTORE. Unique gifts for home, office, friends, family, and, of course, yourself. www.giftsbytiwa.com

GREENHOUSES

GREENHOUSE KITS & ACCESSORIES. Easy-to-assemble kits. Heaters, fans, grow lights, watering systems, and more! Free shipping! Visit: www.greenhouseoasis.com

EXTEND YOUR GROWING SEASON 3 to 4 Months! Easy-to-assemble Greenhouse Kits starting at $329. Free catalog or see everything online. Hoop House, Mashpee MA. Phone: 1-800-760-5192. www.hoophouse.com

HEALTH & BEAUTY

DETOX FOOT PATCHES. On your feet all day? A must! Sample one! Phone: 888-452-4968. www.mysticwondersinc.com

JESN MASSAGE BALL! Kinetic energy enhanced for aches, pains, and cellulite. Price/Brochure: 888-452-4968. www.mysticwondersinc.com

STEM CELL THERAPY for Dogs and Horses. New product supports the release of Adult Stem Cells. Health for pets today! www.StemCellsHeal.com

ADULT STEM CELLS can help MACULAR DEGENERATION. What your ophthalmologist is not telling you. Natural therapies from an MD can help your eyes regenerate. Phone: 888-838-3937. www.BetterEyeHealth.com

HINTS

GREAT MONEY SAVING. Kitchen, Food Hints, Recipes, Diets, Wine making, etc. Send $3.50 to Hints, PO Box 54, Honey Creek WI 53138.

HOME PRODUCTS

LESS/NO CHEMICALS using Earth-Friendly Wonder Laundry Ball and Dryerballs. Brochure, Info pack, and $10.00 coupon. Phone: 888-452-4968. www.mysticwondersinc.com

INVENTORS/INVENTIONS/PATENTS

PATENTS: www.charlesk.com

AMERICA'S LEADING INVENTION COMPANY helps try to submit ideas/inventions to industry. Patent services. 1-800-INVENTION.

MAINE RESORTS

ATLANTIC EYRIE LODGE, Bar Harbor, Maine. Acadia National Park. 55 Oceanview rooms. Call 800-HabaVue. Online reservations available. E-mail: info@AtlanticEyrieLodge.com. Fax: 207-288-8500. www.AtlanticEyrieLodge.com

MUSIC/RECORDS/TAPES/CDS

ACCORDIONS, CONCERTINAS, Button Boxes, Rolands. Buy, sell, trade, repair, tune. Catalogs, $5. Castiglione, PO Box 40, Warren MI 48090. 586-755-6050. www.castiglioneaccordions.com

NUMEROLOGY

TURN YOUR NAME into multiple Lucky digits. Useful in all activities that require numbers. $15.00. Farrar's, Box 210562, Normandy MO 63121.

NURSERY STOCK

HOME GARDEN FRUIT TREES. Disease-resistant and Heirloom. Berries, grapes, and unusual fruit. Supplies. Free catalog! Phone: 888-276-3187. www.johnsonnursery.com

TREE/SHRUB SEEDLINGS direct from grower. Plants for landscaping, wildlife food and cover, timber, and Christmas tree production. Free color catalog. Carino Nurseries, PO Box 538AL, Indiana PA 15701. Phone: 800-223-7075. Web site: www.carinonurseries.com

OPEN POLLINATED SEED

OPEN-POLLINATED CORN SEED. Silage, Grain, Wildlife. Available Certified Organic, 75-85-87-90-120-Day. Green Haven, Phone: 607-566-9253. www.openpollinated.com

PERSONAL HISTORIAN

PRESERVE PRECIOUS MEMORIES. Professional writer specializing in individual and family histories. Pass on your legacy. Phone: 941-383-2523. gatorisland@comcast.net

PERSONALS

ASIAN BRIDES! Romance, love, marriage! Overseas. Details, Photos: Box 4601-OFA, Thousand Oaks CA 91362. 805-492-8040.

MEET LATIN WOMEN seeking marriage. All ages. Free brochures and Singles Vacations DVD. TLC, 713-896-9993 or www.tlcworldwide.com

POULTRY

GOSLINGS, DUCKLINGS, GUINEAS, chicks, turkeys, bantams, gamebirds. Books and equipment. 1-717-365-3694. Hoffman Hatchery, PO Box 129P, Gratz PA 17030. Visit www.hoffmanhatchery.com

RADIONICS

RADIONICS, THE SCIENCE which can cure where orthodox medicine fails. Help yourself to Health. www.copenlabs.com

REAL ESTATE

LEWIS AND CLARK LAKE, NE, affordable recreational property. Joan Thomson, Realtor, Woods Bros. Realty. Phone: 402-373-4152. Web site: www.JoanThomson.WoodsBros.com

LET GOVERNMENT/FOUNDATION GRANTS pay for your home. 100+ programs. (Web site: www.usgovernmentinformation.com) Free information: 707-448-3210. (8KE1)

CLAIM GOVERNMENT LAND. 320 acres/person now available. (www.usgovernmentinformation.com) Free recorded message: 707-448-1887. (4KE1)

RELIGIOUS

FREE BIBLE STUDY GUIDE. "How to Study the Bible and Have It Make Sense." Associated Bible Students, PO Box 1783AB, Wilmington DE 19899. Telephone: 1-888-946-PRAY(7729). Send e-mail: info@godspromises.org

SEEDS & PLANTS

GROW YOUR OWN tobacco, medicinal plants & herbs, tropicals, heirloom veggies, and more. Free catalog. E.O.N.S., Dept. FA, PO Box 4604, Hallandale FL 33008. 954-455-0229. www.eonseed.com

LIVE HERB PLANTS for Culinary, Medicinal, and Aromatheraphy. Gourmet Vegetables, Plants, Bath Salts, and Bird Houses. 724-735-4700. www.AlwaysSummerHerbs.com

SPIRITUALISTS

MISSISSIPPI'S NUMBER ONE LOVE specialist. Mrs. Harris reunites the separated, Breaks evil spells, restores lost nature. 601-301-0222

MOTHER DOROTHY tells past, present, and future. Gifted Healer. Write or call: 1-702-891-1336. 1214 Ralph David Abernathy Blvd., Atlanta GA 30310.

PSYCHIC READINGS BY ANDREA
Resolves all problems. Specializes in returning lovers. Removes all bad luck. Helps overcome all obstacles. Relieves stress and reveals your true destiny. Will guide you to happiness and success. Immediate results. Free reading.
972-243-0868

MISS LISA, astrology reader and advisor. Extraordinary powers. Call for help with all problems. Waycross, GA. 912-283-3206.

SPIRITUAL HEALER and advisor. Guaranteed help in all problems. Call for your Free reading. Phone: 817-613-0509.

PRINCE OF LIGHT. Spiritual Advisor helps in all matters. Love, relationships, happiness, careers, advises on all court matters. 301-313-0620.

WORLD-RENOWNED READER. Are you unhappy? Unlucky? Health, love, business. Removes bad luck. Free reading. 903-923-8980.

REMOVES EVIL SPELLS, lawsuits, court cases, bad luck. Where others fail, I guarantee results in 24 hours. Mrs. Jackson, 334-281-1116. 35 years of experience.

BROTHER ROY. Spiritual root worker. Healing oils, health, luck. Success guaranteed. 912-262-0427.

SPIRITUAL HEALER. Guaranteed help in all problems. FREE reading. 817-629-1762.

MS. TANYA. Spiritual Reader & Advisor. Helps where others have failed with all problems. Free Reading. 334-370-6828.

SPIRITUAL READER AND ADVISOR. Helps with all problems. Love, marital, business, health. Specializing in spiritual cleansing. Free reading. 662-226-6720.

REV. GEORGIA. God's messenger can help all problems, love, health, money, happiness. Call for your one question. 843-841-0853. 1102 Hwy. 301 North, Dillon SC 29536.

SPIRITUALIST VICTORIA,

Psychic Reader & Advisor. God-gifted and has the power to remove all root work, evil, and block all enemies. Victoria will change your life and will make all your dreams a reality. Results guaranteed! Free blessed reading. Call now! **510-798-0001**

CHEROKEE INDIAN HEALER. Guarantees to help. One Free question. Call 414-461-1573.

READINGS BY NICOLE. Specializing in reuniting lovers, helps in all problems. Guaranteed results! Free reading. 817-461-2683 or 817-350-5443.

SPIRITUAL HEALER SOPHIA helps all problems: love, luck, money, health, marriage, and happiness. Free reading. 662-746-6118.

TIRED OF SUFFERING?

Get guaranteed help now! God-Gifted Spiritualist helps in all problems. **209-200-3679**

DIANA, HEALING SPECIALIST. Think you have been hexed? Removes all evil spells. Call today, 334-365-3499.

REV. JOHN PAUL heals the sick and separated by prayer. Guaranteed results. Call for a Free prayer, 1-800-399-0604. Send $10.00 for a lucky gift. PO Box 41916, Nashville TN 37204.

OTHERS FAILED? Indian healer Rev. Ginger, Louisiana spiritualist, permanently restores stolen lovers immediately! 504-416-0958.

MRS. RUTH, Southern-born spiritualist. Removes evil, bad luck. Helps all problems. Free sample reading. 3938 Hwy. 431 South, Eufaula AL 36027. 334-616-6363.

NINA WELLS. Reunites lovers, solves impossible problems. Gifted miracle powers. For love, luck, happiness. 110% guaranteed results, never fails. 773-641-5877.

MISS TAYLOR. Spiritual psychic and advisor. Reunites lovers in 24 hours. Removes bad luck, helps in all problems. 720-300-7523.

GIFTED SPIRITUALIST. Helps with all problems in life. Will give you solutions that you never thought of or dreamed of. Miss Hart, 2146 Celanese Rd., Rock Hill SC 29732. 803-242-9973.

PARIS FRANCIS helps, heals, and advises on all matters of life. Guaranteed results. Complimentary reading. 662-841-0802.

MRS. ANNIE, SPIRITUALIST, reunites lovers. Removes bad luck. Helps with all problems. One free reading. 219-677-3380.

MOST POWERFUL SPIRITUALIST. Helps in all problems of life. 100% guaranteed immediate results. Call today: 812-218-9843.

STEAM MODEL TOYS

WORKING STEAM ENGINES: Stirling Engines, Limited-Edition Tin Toys, accessories, parts. Catalog $6.95, refundable. Yesteryear Toys, Dept. FA, Box 537, Alexandria Bay NY 13607. 1-800-481-1353. www.yesteryeartoys.com

TREES & SHRUBS

SPRUCE, FIR, PINE SEEDLINGS for reforestation, Christmas trees, landscaping, windbreaks. Wholesale prices. Free catalog. Flickingers' Nursery, Box 245, Sagamore PA 16250. 800-368-7381. Web site: www.flicknursery.com

ANTIQUE APPLE TREES. 100+ varieties! Catalog, $3.00. Urban Homestead, 818-B Cumberland St., Bristol VA 24201. www.OldVaApples.com

WANTED TO BUY

CASH FOR 78-RPM RECORDS! Send $2 (refundable) for illustrated booklet identifying collectible labels, numbers, with actual prices I pay. Docks, Box 780218(FA), San Antonio TX 78278-0218.

The Old Farmer's Almanac classified rates (15-word min.): $23 per word. Payment required with order: MC, Visa, AmEx, and Discover/NOVUS accepted. For ad rates, Web classifieds, or ad information, contact Bernie Gallagher at OFAads@aol.com, phone 203-263-7171, or fax 203-263-7174. Write to: Gallagher Group, PO Box 959, Woodbury CT 06798. *The 2009 Old Farmer's Almanac* closing date is 5/10/08.

Index to Advertisers

101 Liberty Medical Supply, 866-899-2249, libertymedical.com/ADAoffer

44 The Lobster Net, 800-360-9520, thelobsternet.com

44 The Lollipop Tree, 800-842-6691, lollipoptree.com

27 Longlight Candles, 866-583-3400, longlightcandles.com

44, 50 Maine Goodies, 866-385-6238, mainegoodies.com

171 Mantis, 800-366-6268, mantis.com

82 Micron Corp., 800-456-0734, microncorp.com

61 Miller Bros.-Newton, 888-256-1170, mbnmenswear.com

44 Millie's Pierogi, 800-743-7641, milliespierogi.com

243 Monroe Hearing, 800-462-5778

244 Mrs. Hope, 706-548-8598

44 Mrs. Nelson's Candy House, 978-256-4061

243 Murray McMurray Hatchery, 800-456-3280, mcmurrayhatchery.com

73 The Music Barn, 905-513-6998, themusicbarn.com

159 Neutrolox

149 NGC Worldwide, Inc., 800-873-4415, Item #KT, ngcsports.com

33 NogginTops.com, The Outdoor Hatfitters, 877-943-4287, noggintops.com

62 *The Old Farmer's Almanac* Three-Year Subscription, 800-ALMANAC, shop.Almanac.com

55 The Old Farmer's Almanac Products, 800-ALMANAC, shop.Almanac.com

27 The Old Fashioned Milk Paint Co., Inc., 978-448-6336, milkpaint.com

26 Old Village Paint, 800-498-7687, old-village.com

9 OPEI, Outdoor Power Equipment Institute, opei.org

33 Pacific Yurts, 800-944-0240, yurts.com

243 Palmer Industries, 800-847-1304, palmerind.com

244 P.E. Labs, 888-527-0870, ext. OF1, usaveonpills.com

145 Penn Foster Career School, 800-572-1685, ext. 5823, pennfoster.edu, online enter ID# AA2S97T

186 Powerbilt Steel Buildings, Inc., 800-547-8335

11 Premier Bathrooms, Inc., 800-578-2899, code 53097

105 Prime Publishing LLC

243 Psychic Source, 866-446-5963, psychicsource.com

3 Rainhandler, 800-942-3004, rainhandler.com

186 Regency Cap & Gown Co., 800-826-8612, rcgown.com

15 Research Products, 800-527-5551, incinolet.com

61 Rug Factory Store, 401-724-6840, rugfactorystore.com

73 Rush Industries, Inc., 516-741-0346, rushindustries.com/KRE223HA

27 Salt Marsh Pottery, 800-859-5028, saltmarsh.com

26 Sandwich Lantern Works, 888-741-0714, sandwichlantern.com

52 Shaker Workshops, 800-840-9121, shakerworkshops.com/fa

24, 27 Shuttercraft, 203-245-2608, shuttercraft.com

15 Stannah Stairlift, 800-877-8247, stannah.com/us

177 Sun-Mar, 800-461-2461, sun-mar.com

73 Table Top Covers, 603-876-4006, tabletopcovers.com

43 Talnik Publishing, 800-247-6553, preparebook.com

177 Taylor Manufacturing Co., Inc., 800-985-5445, peasheller.com

25 Tempur-Pedic, Inc., 888-702-8557, tempurpedic.com

73 ThyssenKrupp, 800-829-9760, ext. 9584, tkaccess.com

177 TimberKing Inc., 800-942-4406, ext. FA8, timberking.com

27 Timberwolf, 800-340-4386, timberwolfcorp.com

87 Total Research, Inc.

5 Tractor Supply Co., myTSCstore.com

108 T&R Distributing, 800-652-1916, sunheat.info

67 WEBS, 800-367-9327, yarn.com

243 Wood-Mizer, 800-553-0182, woodmizer.com/A206

43 Woodstock Soapstone Co., Inc., 888-664-8188, woodstove.com

52 Yesteryear Toys & Books, Inc., 800-481-1353, yesteryeartoys.com

A sampling from the hundreds of letters, clippings, and e-mails sent to us by Almanac readers from all over the United States and Canada during the past year.

FLASH! Car Color Reveals Personality of Driver

Not only that, but it may indicate the likelihood of having an accident, too!

The scientific research on this was recently done in Great Britain, so although it' possible that it might not be valid in the United States, it's unlikely. Anyway here are the results of a survey of 130,000 insurance claims processed by the Churchill Company—listed, incidentally, in order of the most dangerous (accident wise) colors to the least.

■ Yellow cars signify someone who is idealis tic and novelty loving.

■ Blue cars are chosen by the more intro spective, reflective, and cautious drivers

■ Gray cars represent those who are caln sober, and dedicated to their work.

■ Red cars denote those who are full of zest energy, and drive and who think, move, an talk quickly.

■ Pink cars are chosen by gentle, loving, an affectionate drivers.

■ White cars represent status-seeking extro vert drivers.

■ Cream-color cars denote self-containe and controlled drivers.

■ Black cars denote an aggressive personal-ity or someone who's an outsider or rebel.

■ Silver cars indicate someone who's cool, calm, and slightly aloof.

■ Green cars are often the choice of people with hysterical tendencies.

–courtesy of F. T., Louisville, Kentuck who credits Insurance.co

Clouded Crystal Ball Department

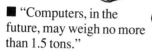

Predicting the future is easy. The hard part is getting it right, as the following predictions clearly show:

■ "Computers, in the future, may weigh no more than 1.5 tons."

–Popular Mechanics, *forecasting "the relentless march of science" in 1949*

■ "There is no reason anyone would want a computer in their home."

–Ken Olson, *president, chairman, and founder of Digital Equipment Corp., in 1977*

■ "This 'telephone' has too many shortcomings to be seriously considered as a means of communication. The device is, inherently, of no value."

–Western Union internal memo, *written in 1876*

■ "The wireless music box has no imaginable commercial value. Who would pay for a message sent to nobody in particular?"

–*one of David Sarnoff's top associates in response to people urging him to invest in the radio, in 1920 (Sarnoff first proposed the concept of broadcast radio in 1915.)*

■ "Who wants to hear actors talk?"

–H. M. Warner *of Warner Brothers, in 1927*

■ "I'm just glad it'll be Clark Gable who's falling on his face and not Gary Cooper."

–Gary Cooper, *commenting on his decision to turn down the leading role in* Gone With the Wind

■ "Stocks have reached what looks like a permanently high plateau."

–Irving Fishe, *a professor of economics at Yale University, in 1929*

■ "Airplanes are interesting toys but of no military value."

–Maréchal Ferdinand Foch, *a professor of strategy at l'École Supérieure de Guerre in France, in 1911*

■ "A guitar's all right, John, but you'll never earn your living by it."

–John Lennon's Aunt Mimi

–*courtesy of R. S., St. Louis, Missouri*

Exciting News About Chickens

It's recently been discovered that chickens can talk! (Well, sort of.)

It used to be thought that when a chicken goes "tck, tck, tck" as it pecks at newly found food, said clucks merely triggered an automatic reflex in other chickens nearby to search for the food. Now, thanks to extensive research by scientists at Macquarie University in Sydney, Australia, we know that it seems that these clucks affect the other chickens differently, depending on whether or not they happen to be hungry. So the original clucks are, like words, a true communication.

Mmmm. Looks like science is discovering that there's more to chickens than we all thought. (But maybe not a lot more.)

–*courtesy of B.R.T., Chicago, Illinois, who credits* Science News

(c o n t i n u e d)

A Brand-New Way to Make an Omelet

All you need are the ingredients— and a bag?

Set out bowls of cubed ham, bacon bits, cheese cubes, sliced mushrooms, cubed onion or sliced green onions, frozen hash browns, salsa, etc. Have a quart-size zipper-close freezer bag for each person. Have each one write his or her name on a bag with a permanent magic marker. Then . . .

Crack two large or extra-large eggs into each bag and agitate it to scramble the eggs.

Add ham, onions, etc.

Squeeze the air out of the bags and then zip them up.

Place the bags in rolling boiling water for exactly 15 minutes.

Open the bags and the omelets will roll out easily and amaze everyone.

–courtesy of D. M., Cannon Beach, Oregon

One Secret of a Long Marriage

You'll never guess it . . .

At a meeting of the church men's group in a small New England town, the upcoming 50th anniversary of Brother Ralph came up. The minister asked Ralph to take a few minutes and share some insight into how he had managed to stay married to the same woman all those years.

Brother Ralph replied, "Basically, I treated her with respect and spent money on her, but mostly I took her traveling on special occasions."

"Like to where?" asked the minister.

"Well, for our 25th anniversary," said Ralph, "I took her to Beijing, China."

"Wow! What a terrific example you are to all the members of our group," said the minister. "Can you tell us what you're doing for your 50th?"

Brother Ralph: "I'm going to go get her."

–courtesy of C.W.F., Regina, Saskatchewan

Guess What's Going to Happen in August 2008

We're not sure if it's good or bad. (But it's probably bad.)

According to the United Nations Population Division, the number of people in the world's cities will surpass that of those in rural areas during the latter part of August 2008. At midmonth, the urban and rural populations are forecast to be equally split, each having about 3.35 billion people.

–courtesy of S.L.W., Bangor, Maine

Ideal Corporate Mergers in 2008

Eight possibilities we just hope and pray will actually come to pass . . .

■ Polygram Records, Warner Bros., and Zesta Crackers will join forces and become **Poly, Warner, Cracker.**

■ 3M will merge with Goodyear and issue forth as **MMMGood.**

■ Zippo Manufacturing, Audi Motors, Mountain Dew, and Dakota Mining will merge and become **ZipAudiDewDa.**

■ FedEx is expected to join its major competitor, UPS, and become **FedUp.**

■ Grey Poupon and Docker Pants are expected to become **Poupon Pants.**

■ Fairchild Electronics and Honeywell Computers will become **Fairwell, Honeychild.**

■ Knott's Berry Farm and the National Organization for Women will become **Knott NOW!**

–courtesy of F. P., West Caldwell, New Jersey

Ten Easy Questions We Answered Incorrectly

Bet you will, too! (Hint: The answers are not the obvious.)

1. How long did the Hundred Years War last?

2. What country makes genuine Panama hats?

3. From what animal do we get catgut?

4. In which month do Russians celebrate the October Revolution?

5. What is a camel hair brush made of?

6. The Canary Islands in the Pacific are named after what animal?

7. What was King George VI's first name?

8. What color is the male purple finch?

9. Where are Chinese gooseberries from?

10. What color is the black box in a commercial airplane?

–courtesy of J. C. and W. G., Andover, Massachusetts

ANSWERS: *1. 116 years. 2. Ecuador. 3. Sheep and horses. 4. November. 5. Squirrel, ox, goat, or pony fur. 6. Dogs (and by the way, the islands are in the Atlantic). 7. Albert. 8. Crimson. 9. New Zealand. 10. Orange.*

☐☐

SHARE YOUR ANECDOTES & PLEASANTRIES

Send your contributions for the 2009 edition of *The Old Farmer's Almanac* by January 25, 2008, to "A & P," The Old Farmer's Almanac, P.O. Box 520, Dublin, NH 03444; or e-mail them to almanac@yankeepub.com (subject: A & P).

Vinegar Can Be Used For WHAT?

CANTON (Special)- Research from the U.S. to Asia reports that VINEGAR-- *Mother Nature's Liquid Gold*-- is one of the most powerful aids for a healthier, longer life.

Each golden drop is a natural storehouse of vitamins and minerals to help fight ailments and extend life. In fact:

- Studies show it helps boost the immune system to help prevent cancer, ease arthritic pain, and fight cholesterol build-up in arteries.

And that's not all!

Want to control Your weight?

Since ancient times a teaspoon of apple cider vinegar in water at meals has been the answer. Try it.

Worried about age spots ? Troubled by headaches? Aches and pain?

You'll find a vinegar home remedy for your problem among the 308 researched and available for the first time in the exclusive *"The Vinegar Book,"* by natural health author Emily Thacker.

As *The Wall Street Journal* wrote in a vinegar article: "Have a Problem? Chances are Vinegar can help solve it."

This fascinating book shows you step by step how to mix *inexpensive* vinegar with kitchen staples to help:

- Lower blood pressure
- Speed up your metabolism
- Fight pesky coughs, colds
- Relieve painful leg cramps
- Soothe aching muscles
- Fade away headaches
- Gain soft, radiant skin
- Help lower cholesterol
- Boost immune system in its prevention of cancer
- Fight liver spots
- Natural arthritis reliever
- Use for eye and ear problems
- Destroy bacteria in foods
- Relieve itches, insect bites

- Skin rashes, athlete's foot
- Heart and circulatory care, and so much more

You'll learn it's easy to combine vinegar and herbs to create tenderizers, mild laxatives, tension relievers.

Enjoy bottling your own original and delicious vinegars. And tasty pickles and pickling treats that win raves!

You'll discover vinegar's amazing history through the ages *PLUS easy-to-make cleaning formulas that save you hundreds of dollars every year.*

"The Vinegar Book" is so amazing that you're invited to use and enjoy its wisdom on a **90 day No-Risk Trial basis. If not delighted simply tear off and return** *the cover only* **for a prompt refund.** To order right from the publisher at the introductory low price of $12.95 plus $3.98 postage & handling (total of $16.93) do this now:

Write "Vinegar Preview" on a piece of paper and mail it along with your check or money order payable to: James Direct Inc., Dept. V1255, 1459 South Main Street, Box 3093, North Canton, Ohio 44720.

You can charge to your VISA, MasterCard, Discover or American Express by mail. Be sure to include your card number, expiration date and signature.

Want to save even more? Do a favor for a relative or friend and order 2 books for only $20 postpaid. It's such a thoughtful gift.

Remember: It's not available in book stores at this time. And you're protected by the publisher's 90-Day Money Back Guarantee.

SPECIAL BONUS - Act promptly and you'll also receive Brain & Health Power Foods booklet absolutely FREE. It's yours to keep just for previewing *"The Vinegar Book."* Supplies are limited. Order today.   ©2007 JDI V0116S05

http://www.jamesdirect.com

A Reference Compendium

compiled by Mare-Anne Jarvela

R
E
F
E
R
E
N
C
E

A Table Foretelling the Weather Through All the Lunations of Each Year, or Forever

This table is the result of many years of actual observation and shows what sort of weather will probably follow the Moon's entrance into any of its quarters. For example, the table shows that the week following January 15, 2008, will be fair and mild, because the Moon enters the first quarter that day at 2:46 P.M. EST. (See the **Left-Hand Calendar Pages, 114–140,** for 2008 Moon phases.)

Editor's note: Although the data in this table is taken into consideration in the yearlong process of compiling the annual long-range weather forecasts for *The Old Farmer's Almanac*, we rely far more on our projections of solar activity.

Time of Change	Summer	Winter
Midnight to 2 A.M.	Fair	Hard frost, unless wind is south or west
2 A.M. to 4 A.M.	Cold, with frequent showers	Snow and stormy
4 A.M. to 6 A.M.	Rain	Rain
6 A.M. to 8 A.M.	Wind and rain	Stormy
8 A.M. to 10 A.M.	Changeable	Cold rain if wind is west; snow, if east
10 A.M. to noon	Frequent showers	Cold with high winds
Noon to 2 P.M.	Very rainy	Snow or rain
2 P.M. to 4 P.M.	Changeable	Fair and mild
4 P.M. to 6 P.M.	Fair	Fair
6 P.M. to 10 P.M.	Fair if wind is northwest; rain if wind is south or southwest	Fair and frosty if wind is north or northeast; rain or snow if wind is south or southwest
10 P.M. to midnight	Fair	Fair and frosty

This table was created about 175 years ago by Dr. Herschell for the Boston Courier; *it first appeared in* The Old Farmer's Almanac *in 1834.*

Safe Ice Thickness*

Ice Thickness	Permissible Load
3 inches	Single person on foot
4 inches	Group in single file
7½ inches	Passenger car (2-ton gross)
8 inches	Light truck (2½-ton gross)
10 inches	Medium truck (3½-ton gross)

Ice Thickness	Permissible Load
12 inches	Heavy truck (8-ton gross)
15 inches	10 tons
20 inches	25 tons
30 inches	70 tons
36 inches	110 tons

*Solid, clear, blue/black pond and lake ice

Slush ice has only half the strength of blue ice. The strength value of river ice is 15 percent less.

The UV Index for Measuring Ultraviolet Radiation Risk

The U.S. National Weather Service daily forecasts of ultraviolet levels use these numbers for various exposure levels:

UV Index Number	Exposure Level	Time to Burn	Actions to Take
0, 1, 2	Minimal	60 minutes	Apply SPF 15 sunscreen
3, 4	Low	45 minutes	Apply SPF 15 sunscreen; wear a hat
5, 6	Moderate	30 minutes	Apply SPF 15 sunscreen; wear a hat
7, 8, 9	High	15–25 minutes	Apply SPF 15 to 30 sunscreen; wear a hat and sunglasses
10 or higher	Very high	10 minutes	Apply SPF 30 sunscreen; wear a hat, sunglasses, and protective clothing

"Time to Burn" and "Actions to Take" apply to people with fair skin that sometimes tans but usually burns. People with lighter skin need to be more cautious. People with darker skin may be able to tolerate more exposure.

What Are Cooling/ Heating Degree Days?

■ Each degree of a day's average temperature above 65°F is considered one cooling degree day, an attempt to measure the need for air-conditioning. If the average of the day's high and low temperatures is 75°, that's ten cooling degree days.

Similarly, each degree of a day's average temperature below 65°F is considered one heating degree and is an attempt to measure the need for fuel consumption. For example, a day with temperatures ranging from 60°F to 40°F results in an average of 50°, or 15 degrees less than 65°. Hence, that day would be credited as 15 heating degree days.

Richter Scale for Measuring Earthquakes

Magnitude	Possible Effects
1	Detectable only by instruments
2	Barely detectable, even near the epicenter
3	Felt indoors
4	Felt by most people; slight damage
5	Felt by all; minor to moderate damage
6	Moderate destruction
7	Major damage
8	Total and major damage

–devised by American geologist Charles W. Richter in 1935 to measure the magnitude of an earthquake

Heat Index °F (°C)

	RELATIVE HUMIDITY (%)								
TEMPERATURE °F (°C)	40	45	50	55	60	65	70	75	80
100 (38)	109 (43)	114 (46)	118 (48)	124 (51)	129 (54)	136 (58)			
98 (37)	105 (41)	109 (43)	113 (45)	117 (47)	123 (51)	128 (53)	134 (57)		
96 (36)	101 (38)	104 (40)	108 (42)	112 (44)	116 (47)	121 (49)	126 (52)	132 (56)	
94 (34)	97 (36)	100 (38)	103 (39)	106 (41)	110 (43)	114 (46)	119 (48)	124 (51)	129 (54)
92 (33)	94 (34)	96 (36)	99 (37)	101 (38)	105 (41)	108 (42)	112 (44)	116 (47)	121 (49)
90 (32)	91 (33)	93 (34)	95 (35)	97 (36)	100 (38)	103 (39)	106 (41)	109 (43)	113 (45)
88 (31)	88 (31)	89 (32)	91 (33)	93 (34)	95 (35)	98 (37)	100 (38)	103 (39)	106 (41)
86 (30)	85 (29)	87 (31)	88 (31)	89 (32)	91 (33)	93 (34)	95 (35)	97 (36)	100 (38)
84 (29)	83 (28)	84 (29)	85 (29)	86 (30)	88 (31)	89 (32)	90 (32)	92 (33)	94 (34)
82 (28)	81 (27)	82 (28)	83 (28)	84 (29)	84 (29)	85 (29)	86 (30)	88 (31)	89 (32)
80 (27)	80 (27)	80 (27)	81 (27)	81 (27)	82 (28)	82 (28)	83 (28)	84 (29)	84 (29)

EXAMPLE: *When the temperature is 88°F (31°C) and the relative humidity is 60 percent, the heat index,*

CLOUDS have many characteristics and are classified by altitude and type:

HIGH CLOUDS
(bases start above 20,000 feet, on average)

Cirrus: Thin, featherlike, crystal clouds.

Cirrocumulus: Thin clouds that appear as small "cotton patches."

Cirrostratus: Thin white clouds that resemble veils.

MIDDLE CLOUDS
(bases start at between 6,500 and 20,000 feet)

Altocumulus: Gray or white layer or patches of solid clouds with rounded shapes.

Altostratus: Grayish or bluish layer of clouds that can obscure the Sun.

LOW CLOUDS
(bases start below 6,500 feet)

Stratus: Thin, gray, sheet-like clouds with low bases; may bring drizzle or snow.

Stratocumulus: Rounded cloud masses that form in a layer.

Nimbostratus: Dark, gray, shapeless cloud layers containing rain, snow, or ice pellets.

85	90	95	100
135 (57)			
126 (52)	131 (55)		
117 (47)	122 (50)	127 (53)	132 (56)
110 (43)	113 (45)	117 (47)	121 (49)
102 (39)	105 (41)	108 (42)	112 (44)
96 (36)	98 (37)	100 (38)	103 (39)
90 (32)	91 (33)	93 (34)	95 (35)
85 (29)	86 (30)	86 (30)	87 (31)

how hot it feels, is 95°F (35°C).

CLOUDS WITH VERTICAL DEVELOPMENT

(form at almost any altitude and can reach to more than 39,000 feet)

Cumulus: Fair-weather clouds with flat bases and dome-shape tops.

Cumulonimbus: Large, dark, vertical clouds with bulging tops that bring showers, thunder, and lightning.

How to Measure Hail

The **Torro Hailstorm Intensity Scale** was introduced by Jonathan Webb of Oxford, England, in 1986 as a means of categorizing hailstorms. The name derives from the private and mostly British research body named the TORnado and storm Research Organisation.

INTENSITY/DESCRIPTION OF HAIL DAMAGE

H0 True hail of pea size causes no damage

H1 Leaves and flower petals are punctured and torn

H2 Leaves are stripped from trees and plants

H3 Panes of glass are broken; auto bodies are dented

H4 Some house windows are broken; small tree branches are broken off; birds are killed

H5 Many windows are smashed; small animals are injured; large tree branches are broken off

H6 Shingle roofs are breached; metal roofs are scored; wooden window frames are broken away

H7 Roofs are shattered to expose rafters; cars are seriously damaged

H8 Shingle and tile roofs are destroyed; small tree trunks are split; people are seriously injured

H9 Concrete roofs are broken; large tree trunks are split and knocked down; people are at risk of fatal injuries

H10 Brick houses are damaged; people are at risk of fatal injuries

How to Measure Wind Speed

The **Beaufort Wind Force Scale** is a common way of estimating wind speed. It was developed in 1805 by Admiral Sir Francis Beaufort of the British Navy to measure wind at sea. We can also use it to measure wind on land.

Admiral Beaufort arranged the numbers 0 to 12 to indicate the strength of the wind from calm, force 0, to hurricane, force 12. Here's a scale adapted to land.

"Used Mostly at Sea but of Help to All Who Are Interested in the Weather"

Beaufort Force	Description	When You See or Feel This Effect	Wind Speed (mph)	(km/h)
0	Calm	Smoke goes straight up	less than 1	less than 2
1	Light air	Wind direction is shown by smoke drift but not by wind vane	1–3	2–5
2	Light breeze	Wind is felt on the face; leaves rustle; wind vanes move	4–7	6–11
3	Gentle breeze	Leaves and small twigs move steadily; wind extends small flags straight out	8–12	12–19
4	Moderate breeze	Wind raises dust and loose paper; small branches move	13–18	20–29
5	Fresh breeze	Small trees sway; waves form on lakes	19–24	30–39
6	Strong breeze	Large branches move; wires whistle; umbrellas are difficult to use	25–31	40–50
7	Moderate gale	Whole trees are in motion; walking against the wind is difficult	32–38	51–61
8	Fresh gale	Twigs break from trees; walking against the wind is very difficult	39–46	62–74
9	Strong gale	Buildings suffer minimal damage; roof shingles are removed	47–54	75–87
10	Whole gale	Trees are uprooted	55–63	88–101
11	Violent storm	Widespread damage	64–72	102–116
12	Hurricane	Widespread destruction	73+	117+

Atlantic Tropical (and Subtropical) Storm Names for 2008

Arthur	Gustav	Marco	Teddy
Bertha	Hanna	Nana	Vicky
Cristobal	Ike	Omar	Wilfred
Dolly	Josephine	Paloma	
Edouard	Kyle	Rene	
Fay	Laura	Sally	

Eastern North-Pacific Tropical (and Subtropical) Storm Names for 2008

Alma	Genevieve	Marie	Trudy
Boris	Hernan	Norbert	Vance
Cristina	Iselle	Odile	Winnie
Douglas	Julio	Polo	Xavier
Elida	Karina	Rachel	Yolanda
Fausto	Lowell	Simon	Zeke

R
E
F
E
R
E
N
C
E

Retired Atlantic Hurricane Names

These storms have been some of the most destructive and costly; as a result, their names have been retired from the six-year rotating list of names.

NAME	YEAR	NAME	YEAR	NAME	YEAR
Allen	1980	Andrew	1992	Juan	2003
Alicia	1983	Opal	1995	Charley	2004
Elena	1985	Roxanne	1995	Frances	2004
Gloria	1985	Fran	1996	Ivan	2004
Gilbert	1988	Mitch	1998	Jeanne	2004
Joan	1988	Floyd	1999	Dennis	2005
Hugo	1989	Keith	2000	Katrina	2005
Diana	1990	Lili	2002	Rita	2005
Klaus	1990	Fabian	2003	Stan	2005
Bob	1991	Isabel	2003	Wilma	2005

How to Measure Hurricane Strength

The **Saffir-Simpson Hurricane Scale** assigns a rating from 1 to 5 based on a hurricane's intensity. It is used to give an estimate of the potential property damage and flooding expected along the coast from a hurricane landfall. Wind speed is the determining factor in the scale, as storm surge values are highly dependent on the slope of the continental shelf in the landfall region. Wind speeds are measured using a 1-minute average.

CATEGORY ONE. Average wind: 74–95 mph. No real damage to building structures. Damage primarily to unanchored mobile homes, shrubbery, and trees. Also, some coastal road flooding and minor pier damage.

CATEGORY TWO. Average wind: 96–110 mph. Some roofing material, door, and window damage to buildings. Considerable damage to vegetation, mobile homes, and piers. Coastal and low-lying escape routes flood 2 to 4 hours before arrival of center. Small craft in unprotected anchorages break moorings.

CATEGORY THREE. Average wind: 111–130 mph. Some structural damage to small residences and utility buildings; minor amount of curtainwall failures. Mobile homes destroyed. Flooding near coast destroys smaller structures; larger structures damaged by floating debris.

CATEGORY FOUR. Average wind: 131–155 mph. More extensive curtainwall failures with

some complete roof failures on small residences. Major beach erosion. Major damage to lower floors near the shore.

CATEGORY FIVE. Average wind: 156+ mph. Complete roof failures on many residences and industrial buildings. Some complete building failures; small buildings blown over or away. Major damage to lower floors located less than 15 feet above sea level (ASL) and within 500 yards of the shoreline.

How to Measure a Tornado

The **Fujita Scale** (or F Scale) is a system developed by Dr. Theodore Fujita to classify tornadoes based on wind damage. All tornadoes, and most other severe local windstorms, are assigned a single number from this scale according to the most intense damage caused by the storm.

F0 (weak)	40–72 mph, light damage
F1 (weak)	73–112 mph, moderate damage
F2 (strong)	113–157 mph, considerable damage
F3 (strong)	158–206 mph, severe damage
F4 (violent)	207–260 mph, devastating damage
F5 (violent)	261–318 mph (rare), incredible damage

Wind/Barometer Table

Barometer (Reduced to Sea Level)	Wind Direction	Character of Weather Indicated
30.00 to 30.20, and steady	westerly	Fair, with slight changes in temperature, for one to two days.
30.00 to 30.20, and rising rapidly	westerly	Fair, followed within two days by warmer and rain.
30.00 to 30.20, and falling rapidly	south to east	Warmer, and rain within 24 hours.
30.20 or above, and falling rapidly	south to east	Warmer, and rain within 36 hours.
30.20 or above, and falling rapidly	west to north	Cold and clear, quickly followed by warmer and rain.
30.20 or above, and steady	variable	No early change.
30.00 or below, and falling slowly	south to east	Rain within 18 hours that will continue a day or two.
30.00 or below, and falling rapidly	southeast to northeast	Rain, with high wind, followed within two days by clearing, colder.
30.00 or below, and rising	south to west	Clearing and colder within 12 hours.
29.80 or below, and falling rapidly	south to east	Severe storm of wind and rain imminent. In winter, snow or cold wave within 24 hours.
29.80 or below, and falling rapidly	east to north	Severe northeast gales and heavy rain or snow, followed in winter by cold wave.
29.80 or below, and rising rapidly	going to west	Clearing and colder.

Note: A barometer should be adjusted to show equivalent sea-level pressure for the altitude at which it is to be used. A change of 100 feet in elevation will cause a decrease of ⅒ inch in the reading.

Wind Chill Table

A s wind speed increases, the air temperature against your body falls. The combination of cold temperature and high wind can create a cooling effect so severe that exposed flesh can freeze. (Inanimate objects, such as cars, do not experience windchill.)

WIND SPEED (mph) \ Calm	TEMPERATURE (°F)														
	35	30	25	20	15	10	5	0	−5	−10	−15	−20	−25	−30	−35
5	31	25	19	13	7	1	−5	−11	−16	−22	−28	−34	−40	−46	−52
10	27	21	15	9	3	−4	−10	−16	−22	−28	−35	−41	−47	−53	−59
15	25	19	13	6	0	−7	−13	−19	−26	−32	−39	−45	−51	−58	−64
20	24	17	11	4	−2	−9	−15	−22	−29	−35	−42	−48	−55	−61	−68
25	23	16	9	3	−4	−11	−17	−24	−31	−37	−44	−51	−58	−64	−71
30	22	15	8	1	−5	−12	−19	−26	−33	−39	−46	−53	−60	−67	−73
35	21	14	7	0	−7	−14	−21	−27	−34	−41	−48	−55	−62	−69	−76
40	20	13	6	−1	−8	−15	−22	−29	−36	−43	−50	−57	−64	−71	−78
45	19	12	5	−2	−9	−16	−23	−30	−37	−44	−51	−58	−65	−72	−79
50	19	12	4	−3	−10	−17	−24	−31	−38	−45	−52	−60	−67	−74	−81
55	18	11	4	−3	−11	−18	−25	−32	−39	−46	−54	−61	−68	−75	−82
60	17	10	3	−4	−11	−19	−26	−33	−40	−48	−55	−62	−69	−76	−84

Frostbite occurs in ▢ 30 minutes ▢ 10 minutes ▢ 5 minutes

EXAMPLE: When the temperature is 15°F and the wind speed is 30 miles per hour, the windchill, or how cold it feels, is −5°F. For a Celsius version of this table, visit Almanac.com/weathercenter/wind chill.php. —*courtesy National Weather Service*

The Volcanic Explosivity Index (VEI) for Measuring Volcanic Eruptions

VEI/Description	Plume	Volume Height	Classification	Frequency
0 Nonexplosive	<100 m	1,000 m³	Hawaiian	Daily
1 Gentle	100–1,000 m	10,000 m³	Hawaiian/Strombolian	Daily
2 Explosive	1–5 km	1,000,000 m³	Strombolian/Vulcanian	Weekly
3 Severe	3–15 km	10,000,000 m³	Vulcanian	Yearly
4 Cataclysmic	10–25 km	100,000,000 m³	Vulcanian/Plinian	10 years
5 Paroxysmal	>25 km	1 km³	Plinian	100 years
6 Colossal	>25 km	10 km³	Plinian/Ultra-Plinian	100 years
7 Supercolossal	>25 km	100 km³	Ultra-Plinian	1,000 years
8 Megacolossal	>25 km	1,000 km³	Ultra-Plinian	10,000 years

REFERENCE

Weather Lore Calendar

For centuries, farmers and sailors—people whose livelihoods depended on the weather—relied on lore to forecast the weather. They quickly connected changes in nature with rhythms or patterns of the weather. Here is a collection of proverbs relating to months, weeks, and days.

January

Fog in January brings a wet spring.

[13th] St. Hilary, the coldest day of the year.

[22nd] If the Sun shine on St. Vincent, there shall be much wind.

February

There is always one fine week in February.

If bees get out in February, the next day will be windy and rainy.

Fogs in February mean frosts in May.

Winter's back breaks about the middle of February.

March

When March has April weather, April will have March weather.

Thunder in March betokens a fruitful year.

Dust in March brings grass and foliage.

A March Sun sticks like a lock of wool.

April

If it thunders on All Fools' Day, it brings good crops of corn and hay.

Moist April, clear June.

Cloudy April, dewy May.

Snow in April is manure.

May

Hoar frost on May 1st indicates a good harvest.

A swarm of bees in May is worth a load of hay.

In the middle of May comes the tail of winter.

June

A good leak in June, sets all in tune.

When it is hottest in June, it will be coldest in the corresponding days of the next February.

[24th] Rain on St. John's Day, and we may expect a wet harvest.

July

If the 1st of July be rainy weather, it will rain more or less for three weeks together.

Ne'er trust a July sky.

[3rd] Dog days bright and clear, indicate a happy year.

August

If the first week in August is unusually warm, the winter will be white and long.

[24th] Thunderstorms after St. Bartholomew are mostly violent.

When it rains in August, it rains honey and wine.

September

Fair on September 1st, fair for the month.

Heavy September rains bring drought.

If on September 19th there is a storm from the south, a mild winter may be expected.

[29th] If St. Michael's brings many acorns, Christmas will cover the fields with snow.

October

Much rain in October, much wind in December.

For every fog in October, a snow in the winter.

Full Moon in October without frost, no frost till full Moon in November.

November

A heavy November snow will last till April.

Thunder in November, a fertile year to come.

Flowers in bloom late in autumn indicate a bad winter.

December

Thunder in December presages fine weather.

A green Christmas, a white Easter.

As the days lengthen, so the cold strengthens.

If it rains much during the twelve days after Christmas, it will be a wet year.

Animal Signs of the Chinese Zodiac

The animal designations of the Chinese zodiac follow a 12-year cycle and are always used in the same sequence. The Chinese year of 354 days begins three to seven weeks into the western 365-day year, so the animal designation changes at that time, rather than on January 1. See **page 113** for the exact date of the start of the Chinese New Year.

Rat

Ambitious and sincere, you can be generous with your money. Compatible with the dragon and the monkey. Your opposite is the horse.

1900	1936	1984
1912	1948	1996
1924	1960	2008
	1972	

Ox or Buffalo

A leader, you are bright, patient, and cheerful. Compatible with the snake and the rooster. Your opposite is the sheep.

1901	1937	1985
1913	1949	1997
1925	1961	2009
	1973	

Tiger

Forthright and sensitive, you possess great courage. Compatible with the horse and the dog. Your opposite is the monkey.

1902	1938	1986
1914	1950	1998
1926	1962	2010
	1974	

Rabbit or Hare

Talented and affectionate, you are a seeker of tranquility. Compatible with the sheep and the pig. Your opposite is the rooster.

1903	1939	1987
1915	1951	1999
1927	1963	2011
	1975	

Dragon

Robust and passionate, your life is filled with complexity. Compatible with the monkey and the rat. Your opposite is the dog.

1904	1940	1988
1916	1952	2000
1928	1964	2012
	1976	

Snake

Strong-willed and intense, you display great wisdom. Compatible with the rooster and the ox. Your opposite is the pig.

1905	1941	1989
1917	1953	2001
1929	1965	2013
	1977	

Horse

Physically attractive and popular, you like the company of others. Compatible with the tiger and the dog. Your opposite is the rat.

1906	1942	1990
1918	1954	2002
1930	1966	2014
	1978	

Sheep or Goat

Aesthetic and stylish, you enjoy being a private person. Compatible with the pig and the rabbit. Your opposite is the ox.

1907	1943	1991
1919	1955	2003
1931	1967	2015
	1979	

Monkey

Persuasive, skillful, and intelligent, you strive to excel. Compatible with the dragon and the rat. Your opposite is the tiger.

1908	1944	1992
1920	1956	2004
1932	1968	2016
	1980	

Rooster or Cock

Seeking wisdom and truth, you have a pioneering spirit. Compatible with the snake and the ox. Your opposite is the rabbit.

1909	1945	1993
1921	1957	2005
1933	1969	2017
	1981	

Dog

Generous and loyal, you have the ability to work well with others. Compatible with the horse and the tiger. Your opposite is the dragon.

1910	1946	1994
1922	1958	2006
1934	1970	2018
	1982	

Pig or Boar

Gallant and noble, your friends will remain at your side. Compatible with the rabbit and the sheep. Your opposite is the snake.

1911	1947	1995
1923	1959	2007
1935	1971	2019
	1983	

REFERENCE

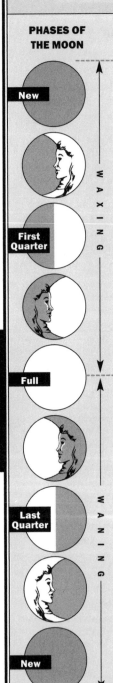

PHASES OF THE MOON

New

WAXING

First Quarter

Full

Last Quarter

WANING

New

Origin of Full-Moon Names

Historically, the Native Americans who lived in the area that is now the northern and eastern United States kept track of the seasons by giving a distinctive name to each recurring full Moon. This name was applied to the entire month in which it occurred. These names, and some variations, were used by the Algonquin tribes from New England to Lake Superior.

Name	Month	Variations
Full Wolf Moon	**January**	Full Old Moon
Full Snow Moon	**February**	Full Hunger Moon
Full Worm Moon	**March**	Full Crow Moon Full Crust Moon Full Sugar Moon Full Sap Moon
Full Pink Moon	**April**	Full Sprouting Grass Moon Full Egg Moon Full Fish Moon
Full Flower Moon	**May**	Full Corn Planting Moon Full Milk Moon
Full Strawberry Moon	**June**	Full Rose Moon Full Hot Moon
Full Buck Moon	**July**	Full Thunder Moon Full Hay Moon
Full Sturgeon Moon	**August**	Full Red Moon Full Green Corn Moon
Full Harvest Moon*	**September**	Full Corn Moon Full Barley Moon
Full Hunter's Moon	**October**	Full Travel Moon Full Dying Grass Moon
Full Beaver Moon	**November**	Full Frost Moon
Full Cold Moon	**December**	Full Long Nights Moon

The Harvest Moon is always the full Moon closest to the autumnal equinox. If the Harvest Moon occurs in October, the September full Moon is usually called the Corn Moon.

Love calendar lore? Find more at Almanac.com.

R E F E R E N C E

When Will the Moon Rise Today?

A lunar puzzle involves the timing of moonrise. If you enjoy the out-of-doors and the wonders of nature, you may wish to commit to memory the following gem:

 The new Moon always rises at sunrise

 And the first quarter at noon.

 The full Moon always rises at sunset

 And the last quarter at midnight.

■ Moonrise occurs about 50 minutes later each day.

■ The new Moon is invisible because its illuminated side faces away from Earth, which occurs when the Moon lines up between Earth and the Sun.

■ One or two days after the date of the new Moon, you can see a thin crescent setting just after sunset in the western sky as the lunar cycle continues. (See **pages 114–140** for exact **rise and set times.**)

Origin of Month Names

JANUARY
■ Named for the Roman god Janus, protector of gates and doorways. Janus is depicted with two faces, one looking into the past, the other into the future.

FEBRUARY
■ From the Latin word *februa,* "to cleanse." The Roman Februalia was a month of purification and atonement.

MARCH
■ Named for the Roman god of war, Mars. This was the time of year to resume military campaigns that had been interrupted by winter.

APRIL
■ From the Latin word *aperio,* "to open (bud)," because plants begin to grow in this month.

MAY
■ Named for the Roman goddess Maia, who oversaw the growth of plants. Also from the Latin word *maiores,* "elders," who were celebrated during this month.

JUNE
■ Named for the Roman goddess Juno, patroness of marriage and the well-being of women. Also from the Latin word *juvenis,* "young people."

JULY
■ Named to honor Roman dictator Julius Caesar (100 B.C.–44 B.C.). In 46 B.C., Julius Caesar made one of his greatest contributions to history: With the help of Sosigenes, he developed the Julian calendar, the precursor to the Gregorian calendar we use today.

AUGUST
■ Named to honor the first Roman emperor (and grandnephew of Julius Caesar), Augustus Caesar (63 B.C.–A.D. 14).

SEPTEMBER
■ From the Latin word *septem,* "seven," because this had been the seventh month of the early Roman calendar.

OCTOBER
■ From the Latin word *octo,* "eight," because this had been the eighth month of the early Roman calendar.

NOVEMBER
■ From the Latin word *novem,* "nine," because this had been the ninth month of the early Roman calendar.

DECEMBER
■ From the Latin word *decem,* "ten," because this had been the tenth month of the early Roman calendar.

R
E
F
E
R
E
N
C
E

Origin of Day Names

The days of the week were named by the Romans with the Latin words for the Sun, the Moon, and the five known planets. These names have survived in European languages, but English names also reflect an Anglo-Saxon influence.

English	Latin	French	Italian	Spanish	Saxon
SUNDAY	Solis (Sun)	dimanche	domenica	domingo	Sun
MONDAY	Lunae (Moon)	lundi	lunedì	lunes	Moon
TUESDAY	Martis (Mars)	mardi	martedì	martes	Tiw (the Anglo-Saxon god of war, the equivalent of the Norse Tyr or the Roman Mars)
WEDNESDAY	Mercurii (Mercury)	mercredi	mercoledì	miércoles	Woden (the Anglo-Saxon equivalent of the Norse Odin or the Roman Mercury)
THURSDAY	Jovis (Jupiter)	jeudi	giovedì	jueves	Thor (the Norse god of thunder, the equivalent of the Roman Jupiter)
FRIDAY	Veneris (Venus)	vendredi	venerdì	viernes	Frigg (the Norse god of love and fertility, the equivalent of the Roman Venus)
SATURDAY	Saturni (Saturn)	samedi	sabato	sábado	Saterne (Saturn, the Roman god of agriculture)

Best Planetary Encounters of the 21st Century

Me = Mercury   V = Venus   Mn = Moon   Ma = Mars   J = Jupiter   S = Saturn

In all of these cases, face west between twilight and 10 P.M. to see the conjunction.

DATE	OBJECTS	DATE	OBJECTS	DATE	OBJECTS
December 1, 2008	V, Mn, J	May 13, 2066	V, Ma	November 15, 2080	Ma, J, S
February 20, 2015	V, Mn, Ma	July 1, 2066	V, S	November 17, 2080	Mn, Ma, J, S
June 30–July 1, 2015	V, J	March 14, 2071	V, J	December 24, 2080	V, J
July 18, 2015	V, Mn, J	June 21, 2074	V, J	March 6, 2082	V, J
December 20, 2020	J, S	June 27, 2074	V, Mn, J	April 28, 2085	Mn, Ma, J
March 1, 2023	V, J	June 28, 2076	Ma, J	June 13, 2085	Me, V, J
December 1–2, 2033	Ma, J	October 31, 2076	Mn, Ma, S	May 15, 2098	V, Ma
February 23, 2047	V, Ma	February 27, 2079	V, Ma	June 29, 2098	V, J
March 7, 2047	V, J	November 7, 2080	Ma, J, S		

R
E
F
E
R
E
N
C
E

How to Find the Day of the Week for Any Given Date

To compute the day of the week for any given date as far back as the mid–18th century, proceed as follows:

■ Add the last two digits of the year to one-quarter of the last two digits (discard any remainder), the day of the month, and the month key from the key box below. Divide the sum by 7; the remainder is the day of the week (1 is Sunday, 2 is Monday, and so on). If there is no remainder, the day is Saturday. If you're searching for a weekday prior to 1900, add 2 to the sum before dividing; prior to 1800, add 4. The formula doesn't work for days prior to 1753. From 2000 to 2099, subtract 1 from the sum before dividing.

Example:
The Dayton Flood was on March 25, 1913.

Last two digits of year:	13
One-quarter of these two digits:	3
Given day of month:	25
Key number for March:	4
Sum:	45

45 ÷ 7 = 6, with a remainder of 3. The flood took place on Tuesday, the third day of the week.

KEY	
January	1
leap year	0
February	4
leap year	3
March	4
April	0
May	2
June	5
July	0
August	3
September.	6
October.	1
November	4
December	6

Easter Dates (2008–12)

■ Christian churches that follow the Gregorian calendar celebrate Easter on the first Sunday after the full Moon that occurs on or just after the vernal equinox.

YEAR	EASTER
2008.	March 23
2009.	April 12
2010.	April 4
2011.	April 24
2012.	April 8

■ Eastern Orthodox churches follow the Julian calendar.

YEAR	EASTER
2008.	April 27
2009.	April 19
2010.	April 4
2011.	April 24
2012.	April 15

Friggatriskaidekaphobia Trivia

Here are a few facts about Friday the 13th:

■ In the 14 possible configurations for the annual calendar (see any perpetual calendar), the occurrence of Friday the 13th is this:

6 of 14 years have one Friday the 13th.
6 of 14 years have two Fridays the 13th.
2 of 14 years have three Fridays the 13th.

■ There is no year without one Friday the 13th, and no year with more than three.

■ There is one Friday the 13th in 2008. The next year to have three Fridays the 13th is 2009.

■ We say "Fridays the 13th" because it is hard to say "Friday the 13ths."

R
E
F
E
R
E
N
C
E

Sowing Vegetable Seeds

Sow or plant in cool weather	Beets, broccoli, brussels sprouts, cabbage, lettuce, onions, parsley, peas, radishes, spinach, Swiss chard, turnips
Sow or plant in warm weather	Beans, carrots, corn, cucumbers, eggplant, melons, okra, peppers, squash, tomatoes
Sow or plant for one crop per season	Corn, eggplant, leeks, melons, peppers, potatoes, spinach (New Zealand), squash, tomatoes
Resow for additional crops	Beans, beets, cabbage, carrots, kohlrabi, lettuce, radishes, rutabagas, spinach, turnips

A Beginner's Vegetable Garden

A good size for a beginner's vegetable garden is 10x16 feet. It should have crops that are easy to grow. A plot this size, planted as suggested below, can feed a family of four for one summer, with a little extra for canning and freezing (or giving away).

Make 11 rows, 10 feet long, with 6 inches between them. Ideally, the rows should run north and south to take full advantage of the sunlight. Plant the following:

ROW
1 Zucchini (4 plants)
2 Tomatoes (5 plants, staked)
3 Peppers (6 plants)
4 Cabbage

ROW
5 Bush beans
6 Lettuce
7 Beets
8 Carrots
9 Chard
10 Radishes
11 Marigolds (to discourage rabbits!)

Traditional Planting Times

■ Plant **corn** when elm leaves are the size of a squirrel's ear, when oak leaves are the size of a mouse's ear, when apple blossoms begin to fall, or when the dogwoods are in full bloom.

■ Plant **lettuce, spinach, peas,** and other cool-weather vegetables when the lilacs show their first leaves or when daffodils begin to bloom.

■ Plant **tomatoes, early corn,** and **peppers** when dogwoods are in peak bloom or when daylilies start to bloom.

■ Plant **cucumbers** and **squashes** when lilac flowers fade.

■ Plant **perennials** when maple leaves begin to unfurl.

■ Plant **morning glories** when maple trees have full-size leaves.

■ Plant **pansies, snapdragons,** and other hardy annuals after the aspen and chokecherry trees leaf out.

■ Plant **beets** and **carrots** when dandelions are blooming.

Fertilizer Formulas

Fertilizers are labeled to show the percentages by weight of nitrogen (N), phosphorus (P), and potassium (K). Nitrogen is needed for leaf growth. Phosphorus is associated with root growth and fruit production. Potassium helps the plant fight off diseases. A 100-pound bag of 10-5-10 contains 10 pounds of nitrogen, 5 pounds of phosphorus, and 10 pounds of potassium. The rest is filler.

Manure Guide

		PRIMARY NUTRIENTS (pounds per ton)		
Type of Manure	**Water Content**	**Nitrogen**	**Phosphorus**	**Potassium**
Cow, horse	60%–80%	12–14	5–9	9–12
Sheep, pig, goat	65%–75%	10–21	7	13–19
Chicken:				
Wet, sticky, and caked	75%	30	20	10
Moist, crumbly to sticky	50%	40	40	20
Crumbly	30%	60	55	30
Dry	15%	90	70	40
Ashed	None	None	135	100

TYPE OF GARDEN	BEST TYPE OF MANURE	BEST TIME TO APPLY
Flowers	Cow, horse	Early spring
Vegetables	Chicken, cow, horse	Fall, spring
Potatoes or root crops	Cow, horse	Fall
Acid-loving plants (blueberries, azaleas, mountain laurels, rhododendrons)	Cow, horse	Early fall or not at all

Soil Fixes

If you have . . .

CLAY SOIL: Add coarse sand (not beach sand) and compost.

SILT SOIL: Add coarse sand (not beach sand) or gravel and compost, or well-rotted horse manure mixed with fresh straw.

SANDY SOIL: Add humus or aged manure, or sawdust with some extra nitrogen. Heavy, clay-rich soil can also be added.

Soil Amendments

To improve soil, add . . .

BARK, GROUND: Made from various tree barks; improves soil structure.

COMPOST: Excellent conditioner.

LEAF MOLD: Decomposed leaves; adds nutrients and structure to soil.

LIME: Raises the pH of acidic soil; helps loosen clay soil.

MANURE: Best if composted; a good conditioner.

SAND: Improves drainage in clay soil.

TOPSOIL: Usually used with another amendment; replaces existing soil.

How to Grow Vegetables

VEGETABLE	START SEEDS INDOORS (weeks before last spring frost)	START SEEDS OUTDOORS (weeks before or after last spring frost)	MINIMUM SOIL TEMPERATURE TO TO GERMINATE (°F)	COLD HARDINESS
Beans		Anytime after	48–50	Tender
Beets		4 before to 4 after	39–41	Half-hardy
Broccoli	6–8	4 before	55–75	Hardy
Brussels sprouts	6–8		55–75	Hardy
Cabbage	6–8	Anytime after	38–40	Hardy
Carrots		4–6 before	39–41	Half-hardy
Cauliflower	6–8	4 before	65–75	Half-hardy
Celery	6–8		60–70	Tender
Corn		2 after	46–50	Tender
Cucumbers	3–4	1–2 after	65–70	Very tender
Lettuce	4–6	2–3 after	40–75	Half-hardy
Melons	3–4	2 after	55–60	Very tender
Onion sets		4 before	34–36	Hardy
Parsnips		2–4 before	55–70	Hardy
Peas		4–6 before	34–36	Hardy
Peppers	8–10		70–80	Very tender
Potato tubers		2–4 before	55–70	Half-hardy
Pumpkins	3–4	1 after	55–60	Tender
Radishes		4–6 before	39–41	Hardy
Spinach		4–6 before	55–65	Hardy
Squash, summer	3–4	1 after	55–60	Very tender
Squash, winter	3–4	1 after	55–60	Tender
Tomatoes	6–8		50–55	Tender

R E F E R E N C E

WHEN TO FERTILIZE	WHEN TO WATER
After heavy bloom and set of pods	Regularly, from start of pod to set
At time of planting	Only during drought conditions
Three weeks after transplanting	Only during drought conditions
Three weeks after transplanting	At transplanting
Three weeks after transplanting	Two to three weeks before harvest
Preferably in the fall for the following spring	Only during drought conditions
Three weeks after transplanting	Once, three weeks before harvest
At time of transplanting	Once a week
When eight to ten inches tall, and again when first silk appears	When tassels appear and cobs start to swell
One week after bloom, and again three weeks later	Frequently, especially when fruits form
Two to three weeks after transplanting	Once a week
One week after bloom, and again three weeks later	Once a week
When bulbs begin to swell, and again when plants are one foot tall	Only during drought conditions
One year before planting	Only during drought conditions
After heavy bloom and set of pods	Regularly, from start of pod to set
After first fruit-set	Once a week
At bloom time or time of second hilling	Regularly, when tubers start to form
Just before vines start to run, when plants are about one foot tall	Only during drought conditions
Before spring planting	Once a week
When plants are one-third grown	Once a week
Just before vines start to run, when plants are about one foot tall	Only during drought conditions
Just before vines start to run, when plants are about one foot tall	Only during drought conditions
Two weeks before, and after first picking	Twice a week

R
E
F
E
R
E
N
C
E

pH Preferences of Trees, Shrubs, Vegetables, and Flowers

An accurate soil test will tell you where your pH currently stands and will specify the amount of lime or sulfur that is needed to bring it up or down to the appropriate level. A pH of 6.5 is just about right for most home gardens, since most plants thrive in the 6.0 to 7.0 (slightly acidic to neutral) range. Some plants (blueberries, azaleas) prefer more strongly acidic soil, while a few (ferns, asparagus) do best in soil that is neutral to slightly alkaline. Acidic (sour) soil is counteracted by applying finely ground limestone, and alkaline (sweet) soil is treated with gypsum (calcium sulfate) or ground sulfur.

Common Name	Optimum pH Range	Common Name	Optimum pH Range	Common Name	Optimum pH Range
TREES AND SHRUBS		Spruce	5.0–6.0	Canna	6.0–8.0
Apple	5.0–6.5	Walnut, black	6.0–8.0	Carnation	6.0–7.0
Ash	6.0–7.5	Willow	6.0–8.0	Chrysanthemum	6.0–7.5
Azalea	4.5–6.0			Clematis	5.5–7.0
Basswood	6.0–7.5	**VEGETABLES**		Coleus	6.0–7.0
Beautybush	6.0–7.5	Asparagus	6.0–8.0	Coneflower, purple	5.0–7.5
Birch	5.0–6.5	Bean, pole	6.0–7.5	Cosmos	5.0–8.0
Blackberry	5.0–6.0	Beet	6.0–7.5	Crocus	6.0–8.0
Blueberry	4.0–6.0	Broccoli	6.0–7.0	Daffodil	6.0–6.5
Boxwood	6.0–7.5	Brussels sprout	6.0–7.5	Dahlia	6.0–7.5
Cherry, sour	6.0–7.0	Carrot	5.5–7.0	Daisy, Shasta	6.0–8.0
Chestnut	5.0–6.5	Cauliflower	5.5–7.5	Daylily	6.0–8.0
Crab apple	6.0–7.5	Celery	5.8–7.0	Delphinium	6.0–7.5
Dogwood	5.0–7.0	Chive	6.0–7.0	Foxglove	6.0–7.5
Elder, box	6.0–8.0	Cucumber	5.5–7.0	Geranium	6.0–8.0
Fir, balsam	5.0–6.0	Garlic	5.5–8.0	Gladiolus	5.0–7.0
Fir, Douglas	6.0–7.0	Kale	6.0–7.5	Hibiscus	6.0–8.0
Hemlock	5.0–6.0	Lettuce	6.0–7.0	Hollyhock	6.0–8.0
Hydrangea, blue-flowered	4.0–5.0	Pea, sweet	6.0–7.5	Hyacinth	6.5–7.5
Hydrangea, pink-flowered	6.0–7.0	Pepper, sweet	5.5–7.0	Iris, blue flag	5.0–7.5
		Potato	4.8–6.5	Lily-of-the-valley	4.5–6.0
Juniper	5.0–6.0	Pumpkin	5.5–7.5	Lupine	5.0–6.5
Laurel, mountain	4.5–6.0	Radish	6.0–7.0	Marigold	5.5–7.5
Lemon	6.0–7.5	Spinach	6.0–7.5	Morning glory	6.0–7.5
Lilac	6.0–7.5	Squash, crookneck	6.0–7.5	Narcissus, trumpet	5.5–6.5
Maple, sugar	6.0–7.5	Squash, Hubbard	5.5–7.0	Nasturtium	5.5–7.5
Oak, white	5.0–6.5	Tomato	5.5–7.5	Pansy	5.5–6.5
Orange	6.0–7.5			Peony	6.0–7.5
Peach	6.0–7.0	**FLOWERS**		Petunia	6.0–7.5
Pear	6.0–7.5	Alyssum	6.0–7.5	Phlox, summer	6.0–8.0
Pecan	6.4–8.0	Aster, New England	6.0–8.0	Poppy, oriental	6.0–7.5
Pine, red	5.0–6.0	Baby's breath	6.0–7.0	Rose, hybrid tea	5.5–7.0
Pine, white	4.5–6.0	Bachelor's button	6.0–7.5	Rose, rugosa	6.0–7.0
Plum	6.0–8.0	Bee balm	6.0–7.5	Snapdragon	5.5–7.0
Raspberry, red	5.5–7.0	Begonia	5.5–7.0	Sunflower	6.0–7.5
Rhododendron	4.5–6.0	Black-eyed Susan	5.5–7.0	Tulip	6.0–7.0
		Bleeding heart	6.0–7.5	Zinnia	5.5–7.0

Lawn-Growing Tips

■ Test your soil: The pH balance should be 7.0 or more; 6.2 to 6.7 puts your lawn at risk for fungal diseases. If the pH is too low, correct it with liming, best done in the fall.

■ The best time to apply fertilizer is just before it rains.

■ If you put lime and fertilizer on your lawn, spread half of it as you walk north to south, the other half as you walk east to west to cut down on missed areas.

■ Any feeding of lawns in the fall should be done with a low-nitrogen, slow-acting fertilizer.

■ In areas of your lawn where tree roots compete with the grass, apply some extra fertilizer to benefit both.

■ Moss and sorrel in lawns usually means poor soil, poor aeration or drainage, or excessive acidity.

■ Control weeds by promoting healthy lawn growth with natural fertilizers in spring and early fall.

■ Raise the level of your lawn-mower blades during the hot summer days. Taller grass resists drought better than short.

■ You can reduce mowing time by redesigning your lawn, reducing sharp corners and adding sweeping curves.

■ During a drought, let the grass grow longer between mowings, and reduce fertilizer.

■ Water your lawn early in the morning or in the evening.

Herbs to Plant in Lawns

Choose plants that suit your soil and your climate. All these can withstand mowing and considerable foot traffic.

Ajuga or bugleweed *(Ajuga reptans)*

Corsican mint *(Mentha requienii)*

Dwarf cinquefoil *(Potentilla tabernaemontani)*

English pennyroyal *(Mentha pulegium)*

Green Irish moss *(Sagina subulata)*

Pearly everlasting *(Anaphalis margaritacea)*

Roman chamomile *(Chamaemelum nobile)*

Rupturewort *(Herniaria glabra)*

Speedwell *(Veronica officinalis)*

Stonecrop *(Sedum ternatum)*

Sweet violets *(Viola odorata* or *V. tricolor)*

Thyme *(Thymus serpyllum)*

White clover *(Trifolium repens)*

Wild strawberries *(Fragaria virginiana)*

Wintergreen or partridgeberry *(Mitchella repens)*

A Gardener's Worst Phobias

Name of Fear	Object Feared
Alliumphobia	Garlic
Anthophobia	Flowers
Apiphobia	Bees
Arachnophobia	Spiders
Batonophobia	Plants
Bufonophobia	Toads
Dendrophobia	Trees
Entomophobia	Insects
Lachanophobia	Vegetables
Melissophobia	Bees
Mottephobia	Moths
Myrmecophobia	Ants
Ornithophobia	Birds
Ranidaphobia	Frogs
Rupophobia	Dirt
Scoleciphobia	Worms
Spheksophobia	Wasps

R
E
F
E
R
E
N
C
E

How to Grow Herbs

HERB	PROPAGATION METHOD	START SEEDS INDOORS (weeks before last spring frost)	START SEEDS OUTDOORS (weeks before or after last spring frost)	MINIMUM SOIL TEMPERATURE TO GERMINATE (°F)	HEIGHT (inches)
Basil	Seeds, transplants	6–8	Anytime after	70	12–24
Borage	Seeds, division, cuttings	Not recommended	Anytime after	70	12–36
Chervil	Seeds	Not recommended	3–4 before	55	12–24
Chives	Seeds, division	8–10	3–4 before	60–70	12–18
Cilantro/ coriander	Seeds	Not recommended	Anytime after	60	12–36
Dill	Seeds	Not recommended	4–5 before	60–70	36–48
Fennel	Seeds	4–6	Anytime after	60–70	48–80
Lavender, English	Seeds, cuttings	8–12	1–2 before	70–75	18–36
Lavender, French	Transplants	Not recommended	Not recommended	—	18–36
Lemon balm	Seeds, division, cuttings	6–10	2–3 before	70	12–24
Lovage	Seeds, division	6–8	2–3 before	70	36–72
Oregano	Seeds, division, cuttings	6–10	Anytime after	70	12–24
Parsley	Seeds	10–12	3–4 before	70	18–24
Rosemary	Seeds, division, cuttings	8–10	Anytime after	70	48–72
Sage	Seeds, division, cuttings	6–10	1–2 before	60–70	12–48
Sorrel	Seeds, division	6–10	2–3 after	60–70	20–48
Spearmint	Division, cuttings	Not recommended	Not recommended	—	12–24
Summer savory	Seeds	4–6	Anytime after	60–70	4–15
Sweet cicely	Seeds, division	6–8	2–3 after	60–70	36–72
Tarragon, French	Cuttings, transplants	Not recommended	Not recommended	—	24–36
Thyme, common	Seeds, division, cuttings	6–10	2–3 before	70	2–12

R
E
F
E
R
E
N
C
E

SPREAD (inches)	BLOOMING SEASON	USES	SOIL	LIGHT*	GROWTH TYPE
12	Midsummer	Culinary	Rich, moist	○	Annual
12	Early to midsummer	Culinary	Rich, well-drained, dry	○	Annual, biennial
8	Early to midsummer	Culinary	Rich, moist	◑	Annual, biennial
18	Early summer	Culinary	Rich, moist	○	Perennial
4	Midsummer	Culinary	Light	○◑	Annual
12	Early summer	Culinary	Rich	○	Annual
18	Mid- to late summer	Culinary	Rich	○	Annual
24	Early to late summer	Ornamental, medicinal	Moderately fertile, well-drained	○	Perennial
24	Early to late summer	Ornamental, medicinal	Moderately fertile, well-drained	○	Tender perennial
18	Midsummer to early fall	Culinary, ornamental	Rich, well-drained	○◑	Perennial
36	Early to late summer	Culinary	Fertile, sandy	○◑	Perennial
18	Mid- to late summer	Culinary	Poor	○	Tender perennial
6–8	Mid- to late summer	Culinary	Medium-rich	◑	Biennial
48	Early summer	Culinary	Not too acid	○	Tender perennial
30	Early to late summer	Culinary, ornamental	Well-drained	○	Perennial
12–14	Late spring to early summer	Culinary, medicinal	Rich, organic	○	Perennial
18	Early to midsummer	Culinary, medicinal, ornamental	Rich, moist	◑	Perennial
6	Early summer	Culinary	Medium rich	○	Annual
36	Late spring	Culinary	Moderately fertile, well-drained	○◑	Perennial
12	Late summer	Culinary, medicinal	Well-drained	○◑	Perennial
7–12	Early to midsummer	Culinary	Fertile, well-drained	○◑	Perennial

R
E
F
E
R
E
N
C
E

Two Seasons of Bulb Basics

	COMMON NAME	LATIN NAME	HARDINESS ZONE	SOIL	SUN/SHADE*	SPACING (inches)
SPRING-PLANTED BULBS	Allium	*Allium*	3–10	Well-drained/moist	○	12
	Begonia, tuberous	*Begonia*	10–11	Well-drained/moist	◐●	12–15
	Blazing star/gayfeather	*Liatris*	7–10	Well-drained	○	6
	Caladium	*Caladium*	10–11	Well-drained/moist	◐●	8–12
	Calla lily	*Zantedeschia*	8–10	Well-drained/moist	○◐	8–24
	Canna	*Canna*	8–11	Well-drained/moist	○	12–24
	Cyclamen	*Cyclamen*	7–9	Well-drained/moist	◐	4
	Dahlia	*Dahlia*	9–11	Well-drained/fertile	○	12–36
	Daylily	*Hemerocallis*	3–10	Adaptable to most soils	○◐	12–24
	Freesia	*Freesia*	9–11	Well-drained/moist/sandy	○◐	2–4
	Garden gloxinia	*Incarvillea*	4–8	Well-drained/moist	○	12
	Gladiolus	*Gladiolus*	4–11	Well-drained/fertile	○◐	4–9
	Iris	*Iris*	3–10	Well-drained/sandy	○	3–6
	Lily, Asiatic/Oriental	*Lilium*	3–8	Well-drained	○◐	8–12
	Peacock flower	*Tigridia*	8–10	Well-drained	○	5–6
	Shamrock/sorrel	*Oxalis*	5–9	Well-drained	○◐	4–6
	Windflower	*Anemone*	3–9	Well-drained/moist	○◐	3–6
FALL-PLANTED BULBS	Bluebell	*Hyacinthoides*	4–9	Well-drained/fertile	○◐	4
	Christmas rose/hellebore	*Helleborus*	4–8	Neutral–alkaline	○◐	18
	Crocus	*Crocus*	3–8	Well-drained/moist/fertile	○◐	4
	Daffodil	*Narcissus*	3–10	Well-drained/moist/fertile	○◐	6
	Fritillary	*Fritillaria*	3–9	Well-drained/sandy	○◐	3
	Glory of the snow	*Chionodoxa*	3–9	Well-drained/moist	○◐	3
	Grape hyacinth	*Muscari*	4–10	Well-drained/moist/fertile	○◐	3–4
	"Iris, bearded"	*Iris*	3–9	Well-drained	○◐	4
	"Iris, Siberian"	*Iris*	4–9	Well-drained	○◐	4
	Ornamental onion	*Allium*	3–10	Well-drained/moist/fertile	○	12
	Snowdrop	*Galanthus*	3–9	Well-drained/moist/fertile	○◐	3
	Snowflake	*Leucojum*	5–9	Well-drained/moist/sandy	○◐	4
	Spring starflower	*Ipheion uniflorum*	6–9	Well-drained loam	○◐	3–6
	Star of Bethlehem	*Ornithogalum*	5–10	Well-drained/moist	○◐	2–5
	Striped squill	*Puschkinia scilloides*	3–9	Well-drained	○◐	6
	Tulip	*Tulipa*	4–8	Well-drained/fertile	○◐	3–6
	Winter aconite	*Eranthis*	4–9	Well-drained/moist/fertile	○◐	3

REFERENCE

DEPTH (inches)	BLOOMING SEASON	HEIGHT (inches)	NOTES
3–4	Spring to summer	6–60	Usually pest-free; a great cut flower
1–2	Summer to fall	8–18	North of Zone 10, lift in fall
4	Summer to fall	8–20	An excellent flower for drying; north of Zone 7, plant in spring, lift in fall
2	Summer	8–24	North of Zone 10, plant in spring, lift in fall
1–4	Summer	24–36	Fragrant; north of Zone 8, plant in spring, lift in fall
Level	Summer	18–60	North of Zone 8, plant in spring, lift in fall
1–2	Spring to fall	3–12	Naturalizes well in warm areas; north of Zone 7, lift in fall
4–6	Late summer	12–60	North of Zone 9, lift in fall
2	Summer	12–36	Mulch in winter in Zones 3 to 6
2	Summer	12–24	Fragrant; can be grown outdoors in warm climates
3–4	Summer	6–20	Does well in woodland settings
3–6	Early summer to early fall	12–80	North of Zone 10, lift in fall
4	Spring to late summer	3–72	Divide and replant rhizomes every two to five years
4–6	Early summer	36	Fragrant; self-sows; requires excellent drainage
4	Summer	18–24	North of Zone 8, lift in fall
2	Summer	2–12	Plant in confined area to control
2	Early summer	3–18	North of Zone 6, lift in fall
3–4	Spring	8–20	Excellent for borders, rock gardens and naturalizing
1–2	Spring	12	Hardy, but requires shelter from strong, cold winds
3	Early spring	5	Naturalizes well in grass
6	Early spring	14–24	Plant under shrubs or in a border
3	Midspring	6–30	Different species can be planted in rock gardens, woodland gardens, or borders
3	Spring	4–10	Self-sows easily; plant in rock gardens, raised beds, or under shrubs
2–3	Late winter to spring	6–12	Use as a border plant or in wildflower and rock gardens; self-sows easily
4	Early spring to early summer	3–48	Naturalizes well; good cut flower
4	Early spring to midsummer	18–48	An excellent cut flower
3–4	Late spring to early summer	6–60	Usually pest-free; a great cut flower
3	Spring	6–12	Best when clustered and planted in an area that will not dry out in summer
4	Spring	6–18	Naturalizes well
3	Spring	4–6	Fragrant; naturalizes easily
4	Spring to summer	6–24	North of Zone 5, plant in spring, lift in fall
3	Spring	4–6	Naturalizes easily; makes an attractive edging
4–6	Early to late spring	8–30	Excellent for borders, rock gardens, and naturalizing
2–3	Late winter to spring	2–4	Self-sows and naturalizes easily

REFERENCE

Plant Resources

Bulbs

American Daffodil Society
4126 Winfield Rd., Columbus, OH 43220
www.daffodilusa.org

American Dahlia Society
1 Rock Falls Ct., Rockville, MD 20854
www.dahlia.org

American Iris Society
P.O. Box 28, Cedar Hill, MO 63016
www.irises.org

International Bulb Society
P.O. Box 336, Sanger, CA 93657
www.bulbsociety.org

Netherlands Flower Bulb Information Center
www.bulb.com

Ferns

American Fern Society
Missouri Botanical Garden
P.O. Box 299, St. Louis, MO 63166
http://amerfernsoc.org

The Hardy Fern Foundation
P.O. Box 166, Medina, WA 98036
www.hardyferns.org

Flowers

American Peony Society
www.americanpeonysociety.org

American Rhododendron Society
P.O. Box 525, Niagra Falls, NY 14304
416-424-1942 • www.rhododendron.org

American Rose Society
P.O. Box 30,000, Shreveport, LA 71119
318-938-5402 • www.ars.org

Hardy Plant Society/Mid-Atlantic Group
1549 Clayton Rd., West Chester, PA 19382
www.hardyplant.org

International Waterlily and Water Gardening Society
6828 26th St. W., Bradenton, FL 34207
www.iwgs.org

Lady Bird Johnson Wildflower Center
4801 La Crosse Ave., Austin, TX 78739
512-292-4100 • www.wildflower.org

Perennial Plant Association
3383 Schirtzinger Rd., Hilliard, OH 43026
614-771-8431 • www.perennialplant.org

Fruits

California Rare Fruit Growers
The Fullerton Arboretum-CSUF
P.O. Box 6850, Fullerton, CA 92834
www.crfg.org

Home Orchard Society
P.O. Box 230192, Tigard, OR 97281
www.homeorchardsociety.org

North American Fruit Explorers
1716 Apples Rd., Chapin, IL 62628
www.nafex.org

Herbs

American Herb Association
P.O. Box 1673, Nevada City, CA 95959
530-265-9552 • www.ahaherb.com

The Flower and Herb Exchange
3094 North Winn Rd., Decorah, IA 52101
563-382-5990 • www.seedsavers.org

Herb Research Foundation
4140 15th St., Boulder, CO 80304
303-449-2265 • www.herbs.org

The Herb Society of America
9019 Kirtland Chardon Rd.,
Kirtland, OH 44094
440-256-0514 • www.herbsociety.org

Cooperative Extension Services

Contact your local state cooperative extension Web site to get help with tricky insect problems, best varieties to plant in your area, or general maintenance of your garden.

Alabama
www.aces.edu

Alaska
www.uaf.edu/coop-ext

Arizona
www.ag.arizona.edu/
extension

Arkansas
www.uaex.edu

California
www.ucanr.org

Colorado
www.ext.colostate.edu

Connecticut
www.extension.uconn.edu

Delaware
ag.udel.edu/extension

Florida
www.solutionsforyourlife
.ufl.edu

Georgia
www.caes.uga.edu/extension

Hawaii
www2.ctahr.hawaii.edu/
extout/extout.asp

Idaho
www.extension.uidaho.edu

Illinois
web.extension.uiuc.edu/
state/index.html

Indiana
www.ces.purdue.edu

Iowa
www.extension.iastate.edu

Kansas
www.oznet.ksu.edu

Kentucky
www.ca.uky.edu/ces

Louisiana
www.lsuagcenter.com

Maine
www.umext.maine.edu

Maryland
extension.umd.edu

Massachusetts
www.umassextension.org

Michigan
www.msue.msu.edu

Minnesota
www.extension.umn.edu

Mississippi
www.msucares.com

Missouri
www.extension.missouri.edu

Montana
www.extn.msu.montana.edu

Nebraska
www.extension.unl.edu

Nevada
www.unce.unr.edu

New Hampshire
www.ceinfo.unh.edu

New Jersey
www.rce.rutgers.edu

New Mexico
www.cahe.nmsu.edu/ces

New York
www.cce.cornell.edu

North Carolina
www.ces.ncsu.edu

North Dakota
www.ext.nodak.edu

Ohio
extension.osu.edu

Oklahoma
www.dasnr.okstate.edu/oces

Oregon
www.osu.orst.edu/extension

Pennsylvania
www.extension.psu.edu

Rhode Island
www.uri.edu/ce

South Carolina
www.clemson.edu/
extension

South Dakota
sdces.sdstate.edu

Tennessee
www.utextension.utk.edu

Texas
texasextension.tamu.edu

Utah
www.extension.usu.edu

Vermont
www.uvm.edu/~uvmext

Virginia
www.ext.vt.edu

Washington
ext.wsu.edu

West Virginia
www.wvu.edu/~exten

Wisconsin
www.uwex.edu/ces

Wyoming
ces.uwyo.edu

REFERENCE

Body Mass Index (BMI) Formula

Here's an easy formula to figure your Body Mass Index (BMI), thought to be a fairly accurate indicator of relative body size. **W** is your weight in pounds and **H** is your height in inches.

$$BMI = \left(\frac{W}{H^2}\right) \times 703$$

■ If the result is 18.5 to 24.9, you are within a healthy weight range.

■ If it's below 18.5, you are too thin.

■ From 25 to 29.9, you are overweight and at increased risk for health problems.

■ At 30 and above, you are considered obese and at a dramatically increased risk for serious health problems.

There are exceptions to the above, including children, expectant mothers, and the elderly. Very muscular people with a high BMI generally have nothing to worry about, and extreme skinniness is generally a symptom of some other health problem, not the cause.

Tape-Measure Method

■ Here's another way to see if you are dangerously overweight. Measure your waistline. A waist measurement of more than 35 inches in women and more than 40 inches in men, regardless of height, suggests a serious risk of weight-related health problems.

Calorie-Burning Comparisons

If you hustle through your chores to get to the fitness center, relax. You're getting a great workout already. The left-hand column lists "chore" exercises, the middle column shows the number of calories burned per minute per pound of body weight, and the right-hand column lists comparable "recreational" exercises. For example, a 150-pound person forking straw bales burns 9.45 calories per minute, the same workout he or she would get playing basketball.

Chore	Cal	Recreational
Chopping with an ax, fast	**0.135**	Skiing, cross-country, uphill
Climbing hills, with 44-pound load	**0.066**	Swimming, crawl, fast
Digging trenches	**0.065**	Skiing, cross-country, steady walk
Forking straw bales	**0.063**	Basketball
Chopping down trees	**0.060**	Football
Climbing hills, with 9-pound load	**0.058**	Swimming, crawl, slow
Sawing by hand	**0.055**	Skiing, cross-country, moderate
Mowing lawns	**0.051**	Horseback riding, trotting
Scrubbing floors	**0.049**	Tennis
Shoveling coal	**0.049**	Aerobic dance, medium
Hoeing	**0.041**	Weight training, circuit training
Stacking firewood	**0.040**	Weight lifting, free weights
Shoveling grain	**0.038**	Golf
Painting houses	**0.035**	Walking, normal pace, asphalt road
Weeding	**0.033**	Table tennis
Shopping for food	**0.028**	Cycling, 5.5 mph
Mopping floors	**0.028**	Fishing
Washing windows	**0.026**	Croquet
Raking	**0.025**	Dancing, ballroom
Driving a tractor	**0.016**	Drawing, standing position

R
E
F
E
R
E
N
C
E

Tile and Vinyl Flooring

Make a scale drawing of your room with all measurements clearly marked, and take it with you when you shop for tile flooring. Ask the salespeople to help you calculate your needs if you have rooms that feature bay windows, unusual jogs or turns, or if you plan to use special floor patterns or tiles with designs.

Ceramic Tile

■ Ceramic tiles for floors and walls come in a range of sizes, from 1x1-inch mosaics up to 12x12-inch (or larger) squares. The most popular size is the 4¼-inch-square tile, but there is a trend toward larger tiles (8x8s, 10x10s, 12x12s). Installing these larger tiles can be a challenge because the underlayment must be absolutely even and level.

■ Small, one-inch mosaic tiles are usually joined together in 12x12-inch or 12x24-inch sheets to make them easier to install. You can have a custom pattern made, or you can mix different-color tiles to create your own mosaic borders, patterns, and pictures.

Sheet Vinyl

■ Sheet vinyl typically comes in 6- and 12-foot widths. If your floor requires two or more pieces, your estimate must include enough overlap to allow you to match the pattern.

Vinyl Tile

■ Vinyl tiles generally come in 9- and 12-inch squares. To find the number of 12-inch tiles you need, just multiply the length of the room (in feet) by the width (rounding fractions up to the next foot) to get the number of tiles you need. Add 5 percent extra for cutting and waste. Measure any obstructions on the floor that you will be tiling around (such as appliances and cabinets), and subtract that square footage from the total. To calculate the number of 9-inch tiles, divide the room's length (in inches) by 9, then divide the room's width by 9. Multiply those two numbers together to get the number of tiles you need, and then add 5 percent extra for cutting and waste.

Wallpaper

Before choosing your wallpaper, keep in mind that wallpaper with little or no pattern to match at the seams and the ceiling will be the easiest to apply, thus resulting in the least amount of wasted wallpaper. If you choose a patterned wallpaper, a small repeating pattern will result in less waste than a large repeating pattern. And a pattern that is aligned horizontally (matching on each column of paper) will waste less than one that drops or alternates its pattern (matching on every other column).

To determine the amount of wall space you're covering:

■ Measure the length of each wall, add these figures together, and multiply by the height of the walls to get the area (square foot-age) of the room's walls.

■ Calculate the square footage of each door, window, and other opening in the room. Add these figures together and subtract the total from the area of the room's walls.

■ Take that figure and multiply by 1.15, to account for a waste rate of about 15 percent in your wallpaper project. You'll end up with a target amount to purchase when you shop.

■ Wallpaper is sold in single, double, and triple rolls. Coverage can vary, so be sure to refer to the roll's label for the proper square footage. (The average coverage for a double roll, for example, is 56 square feet.) After choosing a paper, divide the coverage figure (from the label) into the total square footage of the walls of the room you're papering. Round the answer up to the nearest whole number. This is the number of rolls you need to buy.

■ Save leftover wallpaper rolls, carefully wrapped to keep clean.

HOW MUCH DO YOU NEED?
Interior Paint

Estimate your room size and paint needs before you go to the store. Running out of a custom color halfway through the job could mean disaster. For the sake of the following exercise, assume that you have a 10x15-foot room with an 8-foot ceiling. The room has two doors and two windows.

For Walls
■ Measure the total distance (perimeter) around the room:
(10 ft. + 15 ft.) x 2 = 50 ft.

■ Multiply the perimeter by the ceiling height to get the total wall area:
50 ft. x 8 ft. = 400 sq. ft.

■ Doors are usually 21 square feet (there are two in this exercise):
21 sq. ft. x 2 = 42 sq. ft.

■ Windows average 15 square feet (there are two in this exercise):
15 sq. ft. x 2 = 30 sq. ft.

■ Take the total wall area and subtract the area for the doors and windows to get the wall surface to be painted:

```
  400 sq. ft. (wall area)
 – 42 sq. ft. (doors)
 – 30 sq. ft. (windows)
  328 sq. ft.
```

■ As a rule of thumb, one gallon of quality paint will usually cover 400 square feet. One quart will cover 100 square feet. Because you need to cover 328 square feet in this example, one gallon will be adequate to give one coat of paint to the walls. (Coverage will be affected by the porosity and texture of the surface. In addition, bright colors may require a minimum of two coats.)

For Ceilings
■ Using the rule of thumb for coverage above, you can calculate the quantity of paint needed for the ceiling by multiplying the width by the length:
10 ft. x 15 ft. = 150 sq. ft.
This ceiling will require approximately two quarts of paint. (A flat finish is recommended to minimize surface imperfections.)

For Doors, Windows, and Trim
■ The area for the doors and windows has been calculated above. (The windowpane area that does not get painted should allow for enough paint for any trim around doors and windows.) Determine the baseboard trim by taking the perimeter of the room, less 3 feet per door (3 ft. x 2 = 6 ft.), and multiplying this by the average trim width of your baseboard, which in this example is 6 inches (or 0.5 feet).
50 ft. (perimeter) – 6 ft. = 44 ft.
44 ft. x 0.5 ft. = 22 sq. ft.

■ Add the area for doors, windows, and baseboard trim.

```
   42 sq. ft. (doors)
 +30 sq. ft. (windows)
 +22 sq. ft. (baseboard trim)
   94 sq. ft.
```

One quart will be sufficient to cover the doors, windows, and trim in this example.

–courtesy M.A.B. Paints

Lumber and Nails

The amount of lumber and nails you need will depend on your project, but these guidelines will help you determine quantities of each.

Lumber Width and Thickness (in inches)

Nominal Size	Actual Size DRY OR SEASONED	Nominal Size	Actual Size DRY OR SEASONED
1 x 3	¾ x 2½	2 x 3	1½ x 2½
1 x 4	¾ x 3½	2 x 4	1½ x 3½
1 x 6	¾ x 5½	2 x 6	1½ x 5½
1 x 8	¾ x 7¼	2 x 8	1½ x 7¼
1 x 10	¾ x 9¼	2 x 10	1½ x 9¼
1 x 12	¾ x 11¼	2 x 12	1½ x 11¼

Nail Sizes

The nail on the left is a 5d (five-penny) finish nail; on the right, 20d common. The numbers below the nail sizes indicate the approximate number of nails per pound.

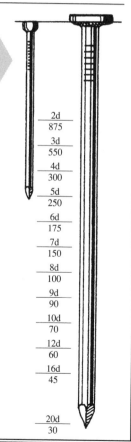

Size	2d	875
	3d	550
	4d	300
	5d	250
	6d	175
	7d	150
	8d	100
	9d	90
	10d	70
	12d	60
	16d	45
	20d	30

Lumber Measure in Board Feet

Size in inches	LENGTH				
	12 ft.	14 ft.	16 ft.	18 ft.	20 ft.
1 x 4	4	4⅔	5⅓	6	6⅔
1 x 6	6	7	8	9	10
1 x 8	8	9⅓	10⅔	12	13⅓
1 x 10	10	11⅔	13⅓	15	16⅔
1 x 12	12	14	16	18	20
2 x 3	6	7	8	9	10
2 x 4	8	9⅓	10⅔	12	13⅓
2 x 6	12	14	16	18	20
2 x 8	16	18⅔	21⅓	24	26⅔
2 x 10	20	23⅓	26⅔	30	33⅓
2 x 12	24	28	32	36	40
4 x 4	16	18⅔	21⅓	24	26⅔
6 x 6	36	42	48	54	60
8 x 8	64	74⅔	85⅓	96	106⅔
10 x 10	100	116⅔	133⅓	150	166⅔
12 x 12	144	168	192	216	240

The Golden Rule

(It's true in all faiths.)

Brahmanism:
This is the sum of duty: Do naught unto others which would cause you pain if done to you.
Mahabharata 5:1517

Buddhism:
Hurt not others in ways that you yourself would find hurtful.
Udana-Varga 5:18

Christianity:
All things whatsoever ye would that men should do to you, do ye even so to them; for this is the law and the prophets.
Matthew 7:12

Confucianism:
Surely it is the maxim of loving-kindness: Do not unto others what you would not have them do unto you. *Analects 15:23*

Islam:
No one of you is a believer until he desires for his brother that which he desires for himself.
Sunnah

Judaism:
What is hateful to you, do not to your fellowman. That is the entire Law; all the rest is commentary. *Talmud, Shabbat 31a*

Taoism:
Regard your neighbor's gain as your own gain and your neighbor's loss as your own loss.
T'ai Shang Kan Ying P'ien

Zoroastrianism:
That nature alone is good which refrains from doing unto another whatsoever is not good for itself.
Dadistan-i-dinik 94:5

—courtesy Elizabeth Pool

Famous Last Words

■ **Waiting, are they? Waiting, are they? Well—let 'em wait.**
(To an attending doctor who attempted to comfort him by saying, "General, I fear the angels are waiting for you.")
—Ethan Allen, American Revolutionary general, d. February 12, 1789

■ **A dying man can do nothing easy.**
—Benjamin Franklin, American statesman, d. April 17, 1790

■ **Now I shall go to sleep. Good night.**
—Lord George Byron, English writer, d. April 19, 1824

■ **Is it the Fourth?**
—Thomas Jefferson, 3rd U.S. president, d. July 4, 1826

■ **Thomas Jefferson—still survives . . .**
(Actually, Jefferson had died earlier that same day.)
—John Adams, 2nd U.S. president, d. July 4, 1826

■ **Friends, applaud. The comedy is finished.**
—Ludwig van Beethoven, German-Austrian composer, d. March 26, 1827

■ **Moose . . . Indian . . .**
—Henry David Thoreau, American writer, d. May 6, 1862

■ **Go on, get out—last words are for fools who haven't said enough.**
(To his housekeeper, who urged him to tell her his last words so she could write them down for posterity.)
—Karl Marx, German political philosopher, d. March 14, 1883

■ **Is it not meningitis?**
—Louisa M. Alcott, American writer, d. March 6, 1888

■ **How were the receipts today at Madison Square Garden?**
—P. T. Barnum, American entrepreneur, d. April 7, 1891

■ **Turn up the lights, I don't want to go home in the dark.**
—O. Henry (William Sidney Porter), American writer, d. June 4, 1910

■ **Get my swan costume ready.**
—Anna Pavlova, Russian ballerina, d. January 23, 1931

■ **I should never have switched from Scotch to martinis.**
—Humphrey Bogart, American actor, d. January 14, 1957

■ **Is everybody happy? I want everybody to be happy. I know I'm happy.**
—Ethel Barrymore, American actress, d. June 18, 1959

■ **I'm bored with it all.**
(Before slipping into a coma. He died nine days later.)
—Winston Churchill, English statesman, d. January 24, 1965